AS
OU PLAY

The True Price of Success in the Premier League Era

Paul Tomkins, Graeme Riley
& Gary Fulcher

Introducing the
Trans£er
Price Index

www.transferpriceindex.com

For all the children at Post Pals who sadly passed away during the writing of this book: Hannah E, Sophie A, Holly C, Madison P, Kian B, Jamie W, Rhianna J, Nicole D, Chintzia M, Amelia-Grace C, Ben H, Lewis R, and Ashley H.

Authors' royalties will be donated to the charity.

www.postpals.co.uk

ISBN 978-0-9559253-3-7

Published By GPRF Publishing

© **Paul Tomkins, Gary Fulcher and Graeme Riley**

All rights reserved. The moral right of the authors has been asserted.

First edition published 2010.

Printed by Anchor Print Group Limited.
All design, typesetting and graphics by Paul Tomkins.

Transfer Price Index
© Paul Tomkins and Graeme Riley

www.transferpriceindex.com

Contents

Introduction   **6**

Part One: The Price of Success   **13**

    Chapter One: The Rising Cost   14
    Chapter Two: Over- and Underachievement   18
    Chapter Three: The 'Newcastle Effect'   27
    Chapter One Four: Competitive Balance   37
    Chapter Five: Squad Analysis   47
    Chapter Six: Transfer Fee by Age, Position and Nationality   55
    Chapter Seven: The Premier League Age   60
    Chapter Eight: Dead Dreams: Was It Worth It?   66
    Chapter Nine: Getting a Start   69

Part Two: The Clubs   **71**

Arsenal, Aston Villa, Barnsley, Birmingham, Blackburn, Bolton, Bradford, Burnley, Charlton, Chelsea, Coventry, Crystal Palace, Derby, Everton, Fulham, Hull, Ipswich, Leeds, Leicester, Liverpool, Man City, Man Utd, Middlesbrough, Newcastle, Norwich, Nottm Forest, Oldham, Portsmouth, QPR, Reading, Sheff Utd, Sheff Wed, Southampton, Spurs, Stoke, Sunderland, Swindon, Watford, West Brom, West Ham, Wigan, Wimbledon, Wolves,

Part Three: The 18 Seasons, 1992-2010   **234**

Part Four: The Main Managers   **278**

Conclusions   **301**
2010/11 Inflation Projections   302
Conclusions   304

Appendix   **309**
    Season-by-season Tables   310
    Top 200-Ranking Transfers   328
    Managerial Statistics by Club   331

Acknowledgements

It is fair to say that 'Pay As You Play' is a very modern collaboration. As well as myriad loons, goons and buffoons, the internet has introduced me to countless talented people in the past decade, and it was many of these who helped out with this project. Although the concept of the Transfer Price Index dates back to 2009, the idea for the book only came to us in the spring of 2010; and yet it was produced in just six months, thanks to a quite remarkable team effort.

I'd obviously like to thank Graeme Riley, whose incredible database underpins the entire concept, and who focused on the *Seasons* section. And of course, the third key player, Gary Fulcher, whose organisational skills were vital, and who worked on the *Clubs* section.

Further gratitude:

To Gordon Fawcett, who helped with the research into transfer prices, and also helped track down so many esteemed writers and bloggers for the *Clubs* section. To Dan Kennett, whose expertise in commercial data analysis was invaluable in terms of the look at competitive balance. To Damien Parsonage, for help with the examination of the role played by youth graduates. To Daniel Geey (@footballlaw on Twitter), for his expertise on UEFA's new financial rules. To Andrew Fanko (@afanko) and Chris Hadley, for their proofreading and editing skills. To Anu Gupta (@anu), for his logistical assistance, and the background team members: Fady Ibrahim, Andrew Beasley, Chris Rowland and Erin McCloskey.

And finally, a special thanks to the writers, journalists and bloggers who gave their time to tell the story of 'their' club, based on our research findings; adding a fantastic extra dimension to the project in the process.

Paul Tomkins (@paul_tomkins)
October 2010

Introduction

One of the more interesting theories associated with football is that success can be 'bought'; that it's almost off-the-peg, waiting to be snapped up by any willing buyer who'll meet the asking price. Often intended to be dismissive – and disregarding the success of others is what football fans do best – the claim was made of Blackburn Rovers in the '90s, and, more recently, has been directed at Chelsea. The latest club apparently intent on 'buying' success is Manchester City. But is there really a price that can be put on certain levels of achievement, be it avoiding relegation, qualifying for the Champions League or landing the Premier League title? Just what role does money play in the modern English game? And which clubs of the past 18 years have punched above or below their weight?

Competitive balance is essential in sport in order to keep results unpredictable – and therefore the audience engaged. But has the way the game has been structured since 1992 – both in the English league and with the changes to the old European Cup – caused too much disparity? Is there now a lack of competitive balance in the Premier League? And is the problem growing worse?

It was from a curiosity about converting old transfer fees into present-day money that this project was devised. That curiosity led to questions about what kind of value for money clubs were getting for their transfer outlay. Did the big spenders really have it all their own way?

Much has been made of the correlation between wages and success in football, but what about the role played by transfer spending? While some clubs have excelled with a policy of picking up out-of-contract, highly-rated players on Bosman 'free' transfers – in the process handing them relatively big wages – most transfers do not involve this kind of discount.

One of the problems with analysing success in relation to wages is that a pay packet can radically alter further down the line, upon signing a new contract, whereas a transfer fee remains constant; even potential add-ons are known in advance. As author and journalist Gabriele Marcotti told us: "What tends to happen is that, because successful teams tend to be successful (and cash-rich), year-on-year their wages tend to be higher, creating a chicken and egg situation. In other words, wages are as much a reflection of past performance as they are an estimate of future performance."

Neither method is perfect – some clubs will always perform better or worse than expected, for a whole host of unpredictable reasons – but as we will outline in this book, we feel that we've found the strongest-ever link between transfer spending and success.

So, what makes one player cost £23.7m and another 25 worn tracksuits and a half-eaten packet of chocolate digestives? Many factors go into deciding a transfer fee. But ultimately, any player is only worth what the buying club are willing to pay, and what the selling club are happy to accept. Precedents are often used for comparison – Ade Akinbiyi cost £5m, therefore *my* player, even with two broken legs and acute blindness, is worth more – but it seems there's always someone brave (or stupid) enough to go against the generally perceived market value and offer a king's ransom for a right royal turnip.

One of the enduring problems with comparing managers (and clubs) across the eras is how inflation distorts their dealings in the transfer market. After all, when Nottingham Forest's Brian Clough paid £1m for Trevor Francis in 1979, he was doing much the same as Manchester City did 29 years later when purchasing Brazilian star Robinho from Real Madrid: agreeing to pay more money for one player than any English club had ever done. Only now, that figure had risen to £32.5m.

There is almost infinitely more money in the game now. Decidedly different from standard inflation, where the price of everything tends to rise at a steady rate, there is 'football inflation', which reflects the driving financial forces of increased TV revenue and, more recently, the influx of billionaire owners who don't have a need to balance the books. (Of course, this may change with the introduction of UEFA's Financial Fair Play Rules in 2012, after which clubs will be expected to stick to spending only the money they earn, but to date, their outlay has gone largely unchecked.)

This project came about when Graeme Riley contacted me after reading my own method of comparing players across the eras: the Relative Transfer System (RTS). RTS was devised for my book *Dynasty: 50 Years of Shankly's Liverpool*, as a way of comparing the signings of Bill Shankly with those of his seven successors as Liverpool manager up until 2009. For this, I set every record-breaking English transfer at 100%; Francis and Robinho were therefore both '100%' transfers. Anyone who cost half of that current-day record would have a 50% value, and so on. So, in 1979, £500,000 was 50%, whereas in 2009, £16.25m was 50%.

But I made it clear that it wasn't without its flaws; not least how a big anomalous transfer can occur, raising the bar, at a time when the mid-range transfers might be of a lower average value. It was with this flaw in mind that Graeme, Head of Tax, Treasury and Risk at a large corporation by day and author of several mind-bendingly replete statistical books on European football by night, suggested looking at another way to solve the problem.

And with this he came up with the idea of the Transfer Price Index. He ran his idea by me, I made a few suggestions, and with the help of fellow football fanatic Gordon Fawcett, we researched and double-checked every single transfer fee in the new satellite TV era, in order to create a database with thousands of entries, each with its own list of figures, relating to things such as age, nationality, position, number of appearances and any eventual sell-on fee.

(Quick note: a pet peeve of mine is when people treat football history as commencing in 1992. However, for this project, we needed to make the data manageable. And the aim had to be to see how – if at all – the Premier League has changed clubs' ability to challenge for the title, for European places and to avoid relegation. To do this, it is acceptable to look at those first years – when the money had yet to really kick in – and compare them to the later seasons.)

Of course, it's important to stress that determining a definitive transfer fee for any given player is often far from straightforward. Some clubs do their best to cloud the information, and 'undisclosed' can start a thousand arguments raging; and that's before getting onto part-exchanges and the increasingly common additional bonus clauses (£100,000 upon making 50 appearances, £50,000 for winning an international cap, £10,000 with every radical change of hairstyle), not to mention people using different exchange rates for deals originally listed in euros.

But even though we searched only trusted sources (often the *Rothmans/Sky Football Yearbook*), it is impossible to be 100% accurate – and as such, at times we had to rely on other people's educated guesses. However, we feel that the majority of fees will be between 97-100% correct, with most bang on the money. (Fans and/ or associated 'experts' of all 43 clubs were invited to look at the data we had, in order to point out anything they saw as inaccurate, as well as contributing their thoughts to the chapter on their respective club.)

Once we had every transfer between 1992 and the end of the 2009/10 season on record, the Transfer Price Index could be created, to monitor inflation throughout the Premier League era. And once we had the season-on-season rises (and at times, falls) of the TPI, all sorts of interesting comparisons could be made, because now, all transfers – be they from 1992, 1999 or 2007 – could be converted to present-day prices: the Current Transfer Purchase Price (CTPP). Therefore, in current terms,

Chris Sutton cost Blackburn £18.9m in 1994 (£5m at the time), while Stan Collymore cost Liverpool £22.2m (£8.5m) in 1995. To add insult to injury, Ade Akinbiyi's £5m transfer to Leicester City in 2000/01 now equates to £8.9m.

With this in mind, squads of any Premier League season could be compared not just against those of the same year, but against those of *any* year. If the playing field wasn't levelled in this way, then of course teams would now be far more expensive than they were 10 or fifteen years ago. By applying TPI, we can see that some of the squads from the '90s actually rank as more expensive than those of fairly big-spending clubs of more recent years. On top of converting the fees to modern-day money, we also looked at the overall price of each squad, to see who had amassed the most costly collections, as well as the price of every starting XI fielded in the past 18 years, to see how much of each club's 'investments' made it onto the pitch during a campaign (it's one thing paying lots of money for players, but what if all your big buys were out injured?).

We could see which teams spent the largest percentages of the overall Premier League outlay over the course of each 12-month period, in both gross and net terms, along with who had the costliest average side over the 38 (or 42) games, and examine how that affected their league position. The spending of individual managers could also be studied, to see who paid their way to success, and who punched well above their financial weight. Some of the results are as expected; others are very surprising.

It's fair to say that when managers buy players they often sell others at the same time. Gross spends are usually misleading, but even a net figure doesn't explain the all-important *starting point*; after all, Carlo Ancelotti hasn't yet spent that much at Chelsea in comparison with José Mourinho because he inherited a side that was already a well-oiled machine, with a deep squad behind it; whereas other managers have taken over at clubs and been unable to see the dead wood for the dying trees.

A new method of comparing players' values

In everyday life, most people are familiar with the concept of the Retail Price Index (RPI) as a measure of inflation. A basket of goods is identified and every month the same items are checked to see what the value would be if these were to be purchased. The difference between the current value and that from the previous month is calculated and termed the RPI. By comparing the value this month with the corresponding value for the same month last year, we obtain the annual RPI.

The same methodology applies to the TPI, except that the "basket" contains every single footballer bought and sold each season, rather than grocery produce (although a few rotten eggs remain.)

Inflation, 1992–2010

Before getting on to who spent what, and the success or failure to which this expenditure led thereafter, it's important to establish the overall spending pattern of the past 18 years, and to understand how that determines the Transfer Price Index.

On the whole, transfer prices have risen dramatically during the 18 full Premier League seasons to date. Twelve seasons have seen an increase, six a decrease.

Overall, since 1992, the average cost of a player has risen 565%, although at one point (2009) that figure was as high as 751%.

Year	Average Transfer Fee	Rise/Fall
1992/93	£594,309	+8.5%
1993/94	£662,543	+11.5%
1994/95	£1,044,144	+57.6%
1995/96	£1,504,397	+44.1%
1996/97	£1,495,288	−0.6%
1997/98	£1,171,726	−21.6%
1998/99	£1,614,904	+37.8%
1999/00	£1,685,725	+4.4%
2000/01	£2,222,537	+31.8%
2001/02	£3,018,200	+35.8%
2002/03	£2,451,510	−18.8%
2003/04	£1,957,464	−20.2%
2004/05	£2,174,455	+11.1%
2005/06	£2,167,877	−0.3%
2006/07	£2,276,322	+5.0%
2007/08	£3,504,886	+54.0%
2008/09	£5,059,310	+44.4%
2009/10	£3,955,840	−21.8%

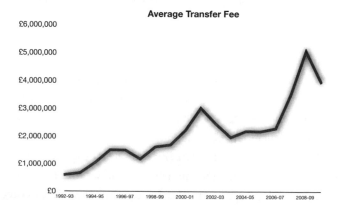

Average Transfer Fee

Important Notes and Small Print

Current Transfer Purchase Price (CTPP)

One of the benefits of looking at the cost of a team by converting all fees to the current price (CTPP) is that it reduces the artificial benefit of clubs that include expensive buys made many years earlier. For example, if a club purchased a whole XI of £3m players in the 20-25 age range in 1992, then five years down the line the team, if successful and still together, will retrospectively seem relatively cheap; after all, a side that cost £33m suddenly doesn't look expensive considering that, in 1996, Alan Shearer alone moved for £15m. But in 1992, when this fictional team was (astutely) assembled, £3m *was a lot of money*. By 1997, that £33m XI equated to closer to £100m, given that the average price of a transfer trebled in the intervening five years. It's not a case of punishing that side or its manager for the foresight, simply pointing out that, at the time of the deals, the club would have been spending serious amounts of money; and of course, once a big club signs a player for a fee approaching or breaking the transfer record of the day, it removes him from the market and keeps other clubs from buying him.

Terminology

For the purposes of this project, two key values were calculated for each club in any given season: the cost of the squad as a whole (excluding any youngsters who never featured, unless they cost more than nominal fees), and the average cost of the starting XI. This latter figure is hereby referred to as the '**£XI**'. All prices for the £XIs are converted to CTPP. The £XI figure is the club's 'utilisation' over the course of a season.

'**Sq£**' is the cost of a club's squad, adjusted to current-day prices.

When the term 'genuine profit' is used, it refers to a sale where the amount received is in excess of the fee originally paid *when inflation is taken into account*. So if a club buys a player for £1m, and sells him for £1.1m five years later, that would not represent a *genuine* profit if there was significant inflation.

Cost per game and appearances all relate only to the Premier League. While cup success is discussed at various points, this is primarily a league-based study.

Transfers and Trainees

The first time a player appears for a club, his status is assessed. Generally, this is classed as a transfer (for a value or on a "Bosman"), a loan, a trialist or a youth player from the academy (trainee).

Transfers can be for cash, (part-) exchange or undisclosed. In this last case, unless a very reliable estimate can be found, the existence of the transfer is acknowledged, but is not used in calculating the TPI – as this would give a false value. We are effectively removing them from the numerator (value) and the denominator (number of transfers) for the calculation. In cases where several players were acquired as part of the same transfer, the fee is divided equally amongst the players, unless otherwise stated.

Transfer values are taken from a number of sources – these will be made available on the Transfer Price Index website. For players purchased when the team was playing in a lower division, the transfer value is noted with the letter 'd' preceding the fee, but is not used in calculating TPI. (Players signed before the Premier League was formed are marked with a capital 'D'; their inclusion is purely in the analysis of £XIs and does not contribute to the inflation calculation.)

Example of Calculation

To refer back to an earlier example, Stan Collymore cost Liverpool £8.5m in July 1995. The average transfer price in 1995/96 was £1.59m and by 2008/09 it was £5.35m, giving a price inflation of 236%. This suggests that the equivalent transfer in 2008/09 would have cost £28.5m. A year later, however, Collymore's 'current-day price' had dropped to £22.2m, due to a decrease in the average value of transfers as the credit crunch struck. As such, players' current-day values will rise or fall each year depending on that season's rate of inflation.

One interesting quirk is that, due to a drop of approximately 22% in the value of transfers between 1995 and 1997 (i.e. deflation), Collymore actually cost Villa *more* at £7m than he had cost Liverpool two years earlier at £8.5m. (Taking the average transfer fee at three points in time may make this easier to follow. In the season he was signed by Liverpool, the average fee was £1.5m. In the season he was sold to Aston Villa, the average fee was down to £1.17m. And in 2009/10 the average was £3.96m.)

Small Print

None of the work within this book is intended to *definitively* prove anything, especially when findings are taken in isolation or removed from their context. It is simply intended to be *a very good indication* of what has been spent, courtesy of our attempts to analyse the data. It may help settle a few arguments, but in all likelihood, it may well start a few too.

While some of this book involves in-depth, technical explanations of the concepts – especially early on, to set the scene – the aim has been to make it as readable and enjoyable as possible, without 'dumbing down'. We trust your intelligence.

Should you know for a *fact* that a particular transfer fee is incorrect, please email **Transfers@transferpriceindex.com**. Corrections can then be made to the database, and for further editions of this book.

Very Small Print

Your optician must be proud.

Part One

The Price of Success

Chapter One:
The Rising Cost

One way of judging a club and its manager's performance is by looking at how many pounds had to be spent for each Premier League point won.

Excluding wages, there are two key valuations that can be studied: first, how much (on average) the XI cost over the course of the season (£XI); and second, the overall cost of the squad.

However, while the ability to choose from a large, expensive squad is a luxury (which we will come to later), it's harder to determine what role that plays than it is to understand the effect of the £XI. The increasing importance of substitutes also plays a role, but for the purposes of 'utilisation' in this book, the starting XI is the prime consideration. (Including substitutes opens up a whole new area of confusion. How long did they play? How do you differentiate between a half-time introduction and one used to wind down the clock in the 93rd minute?)

On average, over the course of the Premier League's 18-year history, it has cost £854,323 to win each point. In other words, if the average cost of an £XI over 38 games is £854,323, it will, in theory, win just a single point. If that average cost is £8.5m, it will win 10 points. And to get 50 points, it would need an £XI of £42.7m.

However, this does not take into account the difference between the early and later days of the league, nor does it factor in the different expense needed at opposing ends of the table in order to meet specific goals.

From the data, it is clear that points are harder (and therefore costlier) to win the further up the table you go. Even the worst Premier League side – Derby County in 2007/08 – managed 11 points. Teams costing as much as £68m (Roy Hodgson/Brian Kidd's Blackburn Rovers in 1999) have been relegated; but teams averaging as little as £8m – or in other words, a team that should have won just 10 points – racked up 52 (Ipswich Town, albeit in the first year of the new league, before the financial impact of the expanding riches had been felt). In 2002, both Southampton and Bolton reached the hallowed 40-point mark with XIs costing £14m and £11.7m respectively. It seems that you can be relatively expensive and fall into the relegation zone – as did Newcastle's £63m £XI in 2009 – but you cannot be relatively cheap and succeed at the sharp end of the table. At least, not any more.

An average 'price of attainment' can be calculated by grouping the points tallies of each team into distinct categories, and working out the mean cost of those teams. The categories used here are as follows: 11-39 points; 40-49 points; 50-59 points; 60-69 points; 70-79 points; 80-89 points; and 90+ points. (All 42-game seasons taken as pro rata to 38-games.)

Obviously more clubs have had 50-59 point seasons than 95-point ones; for that reason, at the top end of the scale the sample data is limited. There's only been one 95-point season since 1992, and that team – José Mourinho's Chelsea – won points at an average cost of £2,054,349. In other words, the £XI was £195.1m (dividing that by the 95 points won reveals the cost per point). On only five other occasions has a team racked up 90 points or more, and the overall average of those six figures is £1,591,665.

So from this limited data, we could take £1,591,665 as the average cost per point to break the 90-point barrier between 1992 and 2010.

However, then there's the change in spending patterns over the course of the league to take into account, and the difference in pre- and post-millennial figures. This is clearly visible in the 80-89 point range. Prior to 2000/01, five teams had registered a total in that bracket – Manchester United three times and Blackburn twice, racking up 85.4 points on average – and the average cost per point was £902,743. However, since then, 16 teams have registered a total in the 80-89 point range (Manchester United six times, Chelsea four times, and Arsenal and Liverpool three times each), and the average cost per point has almost doubled, at £1,621,812 – even though the average points worked out slightly lower, at 84, than the mean.

The same pattern can be seen in the other points ranges. As mentioned, in the '90s the average cost per point between 80 and 89 was £902,743; come down to the 70-79 point range and it falls to £887,988 – not a steep drop, but a drop all the same. Nineteen teams registered a total in this range – including Norwich City and Nottingham Forest – at an overall average of 74.5 points. Come forward to the new millennium, and to date, the tallies of just eleven teams have fallen between 70 and 79 (again, the overall average is 74.5 points). However, the cost per point for the same level of achievement has now risen from £887,988 10 years earlier to £1,341,221.

So the same pattern is clearly visible in both sets of points ranges: it costs a lot of money to get 80+ points, and not quite as much to get 70+, with the figures in both cases rising sharply since the end of the 1990s.

The cheapest cost per point in the 70+ range dates back to the Premier League's inaugural season: a mere £211,998, courtesy of Mike Walker's Norwich City (72 points); a true shoestring budget. The cheapest between 2001 and 2010 in the same point range is the £797,545 for Arsenal's 72 points in 2008/09. And of the eleven totals in this range, only one other is below £1m per point: also Arsenal, a year later, at £864,868. Spurs finally broke into the top four in the same season (2009/10), although their 70 points worked out at £1,119,580 each; even so, it's still more than £200,000 a point below the 2001-2010 average (but equally, at 'just' 70 points, almost five points below the mean of 74.5; more on this later).

The same pattern continues in the 60-69 point range. Up until the end of 1999/2000, 22 teams fell between these two totals (at an average of 63.8 points). Incredibly – at least when looking back from a present-day perspective – three times Queens Park Rangers found themselves in this bracket. And from 2001 to 2010, a further 26 teams, at an average of 64.2 points, qualify; including Ipswich Town, possibly the last 'unfashionable' (/tractor-related) club to gain such an impressive tally (66 points in 2001). The average cost per point in the old millennium was £878,718 – again, a minimal decrease from the higher points bracket that decade – compared with the new millennium figure of £1,101,117; another significant and fairly evenly spaced reduction from the higher points bracket.

This confirms that, on the whole, money was needed in the '90s to reach the higher levels, but not serious amounts. To some degree, a meritocracy still existed. In contrast to the current landscape, in the first few years of the league there was a lot more 'cross pollination', with a mixture of wealthy and spendthrift clubs side by side throughout the league, all the way up to 3rd place. (The top two was still reserved for the wealthy elite: from 1993 to 2000, it consisted of two from Manchester United, Blackburn, Newcastle and Arsenal.)

Come forward a few years, and 90+ points 'cost' in excess of £2m per point; to get 80 points averaged £1.6m per point; to get 70 points averaged £1.3m per point; and to get 60 points averaged £1.1m per point.

In this past decade, only four of the 26 teams to register 60+ points have an average 'point cost' below £700,000: Ipswich (£331,339) in 2001, Everton (£446,392 in 2005) and on two occasions Blackburn Rovers: £571,592 in 2003 under the much-maligned (and at Liverpool and Newcastle, financially disastrous) Graeme Souness, and £423,764 three years later, under Mark Hughes. No fewer than 16 of the 26 teams 'paid' in excess of £1m per point.

And so it continues, down into the 50+ point range. In total, 52 teams from the '90s rank in this bracket, and 42 from the 2000s. The '90s cost per point works out at £687,047 (54.2 points won on average); the new decade's cost per point weighs in at £730,654 (53.4 points).

So, does the pattern continue in the 40-49 point range? In a word, no. It actually reverses between the two decades. In the first nine Premier League seasons, 44 teams posted such a tally; 55 from 2001 onwards. But in the earlier decade the average cost of a point in this range was £866,905 (43.85); compared with £753,084 (44.5) in more recent times.

So in the '90s, to get between 40 and 90 points cost an average of between £866,905 and £902,743 – an incredibly narrow range of expense (with the bizarre exception the 50-59 point grouping, which, at £687,047, was actually significantly less expensive than the teams who only registered 40-49).

The 40-49 point reveals a more expensive cost per point in the '90s than in the '00s. Clearly, you could spend more money in the previous decade and still find yourself caught in the mire; with less of a spread of resources, even the cheaper sides were not financially adrift. The same applies with what is traditionally the relegation zone: below 40 points. Between 1992 and the end of 1999/00, the average cost per point was £761,397. Come forward to 2000/01 onwards, and it drops to £654,734.

The trends in cost per point can be clearly seen in the graphs below. The first graph shows the overall cost per point, which on the whole has risen since 1992/93.

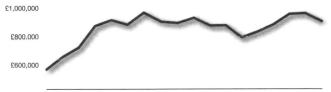

However, the next graph clearly shows how the average cost per point has grown markedly more expensive in the higher echelons of the league in more recent years.

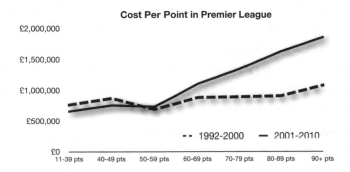

The most expensive cost per point in the past 18 years belongs to Chelsea in 2006/07: £3,075,503, upon finishing as runners-up to Manchester United. Only one other club has a cost in excess of £2.5m – again, Chelsea, a year earlier. But of the top nine ranking figures, only two clubs feature. Chelsea and Manchester United? Actually, no. It's a northern United all right, but not the one you'd expect. It's Newcastle.

The 2010/11 season will be revealing – Manchester City will certainly close the gap for this unwanted honour (although if they win the league, they won't care what people think; they could probably afford to pay £4m or £5m per point if it would guarantee them success). Last year, City's total of over £1.8m per point ranks as the Premier League's 19th-highest to date; but as they were the summer of 2010's big spenders, that figure will more than likely increase.

The cheapest cost per point in a single season – and the second-cheapest – belongs to Sam Allardyce's Bolton. He remains the only manager to go below the £100,000 mark; between 2003 and 2005, Wanderers' figures were £82,256 and £81,710. His style may not have pleased the purists, but in terms of getting results on a shoestring budget, it was a real achievement. His assistant at the time, Phil Brown, either contributed significant ideas toward that success, learned from Allardyce, or it was a bit of both: his Hull City also make the top 10 for cheapest cost per point.

Chapter Two:
Over– and Underachievement

There's an accepted notion in football that points are easier to win in some seasons than others. This is possibly true, although on the whole, there won't be massive deviation. (There's more on standard deviation later; briefly, it shows a steady overall increase, but no great fluctuations between consecutive seasons.)

Since the league moved to 20 teams in 1995/96, the overall average points per season has been between 50.9 and 52.5. Given that for every team that gains points another will drop them, it cannot vary much from such an average. But obviously, some years the teams near the bottom will be stronger, and in other years there will be some real strugglers down there; reaching the 'magical 40-point mark' will save you most years, but not every year. And in the past 18 seasons, the number of points racked up by the champions has dipped as low as 78 and risen as high as 95.

The totals *actually needed* to win the league, however – i.e. gaining a single point more than the runners-up – are as follows: 75, 85, 89, 79, 69, 78, 79, 74, 71, 81, 79, 80, 84, 84, 84, 86, 87 and 86. The first three totals are from 42-game seasons, the rest from 38. In 38-game seasons during the '90s, on average, 76 points were required to win the league; in the 2000s, that figure stands at 82. In 1997, 69 points would have won the title; these days, that won't even necessarily guarantee Champions League football. Since 2003/04, the total needed to win the title has not dipped below 84 points.

Judgement

As outlined in the previous chapter, the fairest way to judge how a manager has performed over the course of his career appears to be to work out his average points tally, along with the average cost of every one of his team selections, and calculate an average cost per point. This figure can then be compared against the averages from various points ranges within the table; so that all those whose average is/was in the 60-69 point range can be compared only against *that* overall average, and not the average of higher or lower points scorers (where different aims require different resources). His team's levels of achievement can be weighted against the expected cost based on where it finished in the league: if it outperformed against the norm, the result would be a positive figure; if it fell short of the norm, the result would be a negative one.

Take the example of the three Premier League managers whose average ranks in the 70-79 point bracket. It's a particularly valid example, because there are also three date ranges used in the assessments, and in this case, each of the managers fits into his own distinct category. These are as follows: one whose Premier League career did not extend beyond the 1990s; one who joined the league after 1999/2000; and one whose tenure spanned both decades.

Excluding his time before the Premier League was formed, Kenny Dalglish managed only in the 1990s, spending time at two clubs: Blackburn and Newcastle. He averaged 71.2 points (66 when adjusted to a pro rata 38-game season), although it's fair to say that he had wildly differing fortunes at the Parks of Ewood and St James.

Rafael Benítez managed only in the 2000s. His average is 72.2 points. He too had some mixed fortunes during his time at Liverpool, not least a poor final season that saw the Reds finish 7th, a year after finishing 2nd with their highest points total for 21 years.

Finally, Arsène Wenger has been at Arsenal since 1996, and therefore started out in the more meritocratic era, but has also been part of the increasingly plutocratic modern period. His average is 76.4 points. He has tasted the highs of three titles in that time, but also seen his increasingly cheap side fail to mount a significant challenge since 2004.

Each of the three men has his major achievements as a manager: Dalglish has four league titles, with two different clubs; Benítez, after two league titles with unfancied Valencia in Spain, won the Champions League with Liverpool and took the club to its highest points tally since 1988 (when, coincidentally, Dalglish was manager); and Wenger revolutionised English football, turning Arsenal from 'boring, boring' to passing, passing – and winning countless trophies along the way. As such, they are ripe for comparison.

Of the three, Arsène Wenger has the lowest cost per point: £1.1m. Kenny Dalglish has the next-lowest, at £1.21m, fractionally ahead of Rafa Benítez, with £1.24m per point. Given that the manager with the lowest overall cost per point in the study has a figure of £0.4m, and the highest a whopping £2.5m, these three men are closely matched in the middle of the spectrum.

However, as Dalglish managed only in the '90s, he must therefore be measured only against the general resources of that decade. As the average cost per point for 70-79 points between 1992 and 2000 was £887,998, his £XI was actually significantly more expensive than the norm. Had he not taken the job at Newcastle in 1997, and quit football instead, his previously unblemished record would still shine today; however, that failure with an expensive £XI clearly tarnishes his record. (If there's one moral of this book for highly regarded managers, it is this: do not, under any circumstances, manage Newcastle United. Run away, run far, far away.)

Wenger's average cost per point is also more expensive than the average – in his case, for the full '90s-'00s gamut. His £1.132m is higher than the mean figure of £1.081m.

However, Rafa Benítez – the one of the trio considered by many to be something of a flop in the league (and the only one without an English league title to his name) – actually has a more impressive average than other two in the 70-79 point range.

But with these figures, Dalglish, Wenger and Benítez are being compared against the *mean average* in terms of points won, which was 74.5 points. The points averages of Dalglish and Benítez are below this mean; meaning that their final cost per point figures are artificially inflated. By contrast, Wenger's average is above the mean, and therefore his is artificially deflated. So the cost per point for the mean figure needs to be adjusted to what it would be for 71.2 points, 72.2 points and 76.4 points, not just the 'average' 74.5 points.

Once this adjustment is applied, Dalglish and Benítez see their figures suffer as a result. The Spaniard remains in 'credit', with a cost per point some £60,942 better than the average for the point range in the time period; a fall of around £50,000 from the unadjusted figure of £110,000. Dalglish, however, sees his figure increase to £356,000 per point worse than the norm. Meanwhile, Wenger's differential improves, but he still ends up with a negative figure; for every point he has won, he has fielded a team costing £50,518 above the norm.

But there is an additional caveat with the Frenchman. In recent years – since the expensive side of 2005/06 – he has been winning points with a far lower £XI. Excluding his 1990s figures, and comparing him only against managers who worked in the new millennium (or others who have worked in both but who have also had their '90s tallies removed) he moves from a rank of 34th out of 61 up to 5th out of 41. Instead of a negative cost per point figure in excess of £50,000, he now has a score of + £242,517. Of course, it also means that during the '90s, Wenger won points at a worse than average rate with regard to the £XI; while he revolutionised the game, it's often overlooked that he did so with a fairly costly side.

The Big Overachievers

'Big' Sam Allardyce certainly lives up to his nickname in this category. Only Ipswich's John Lyall, whose Premier League career never lasted beyond the first three seasons (he was sacked in his third), won points at an average lower cost over the course of his career. And of all the figures, Allardyce's towards the end of his time at Bolton are by far the best in the study.

There are, of course, different ways of measuring achievement. One is to see where each team ranks in terms of its average £XI in a season, and compare this against its league position. If the team's £XI rank is below its league position, then the team has overachieved; and vice versa. However, there is less scope to overachieve higher up the league, since a club that wins the title with the third-most expensive £XI has only 'overachieved' by two places. So by using this measure, managers of top-end clubs cannot score highly. However, dividing a team's average £XI with every point won that season, and then weighting the figure, provides a more telling picture.

It's largely a list of 'unfashionable' names that feature; men who have got their teams to punch above their weight, but whose reputations are not generally stellar – possibly due to a total lack of trophies (excluding winning lower league division titles) from the entire top 15. They can boast a few cup finals, but no silverware whatsoever. Sam Allardyce, Joe Kinnear, Jim Smith and Alan Curbishley are joined in the top 10 by some additional oft-maligned figures, such as Iain Dowie, Dave Jones, Dave Bassett and Alan Ball. Steve Coppell, Alan Pardew, Gary Megson, Paul Jewell, George Burley and Glenn Hoddle follow, all ahead of the first trophy winner, Harry Redknapp, in 16th place. Martin O'Neill, in 28th place, is the last of the managers 'in credit' in terms of £XI-related performance across their entire Premier League careers. Of the really big names, only Alex Ferguson and Rafa Benítez feature in the top half of the table.

As previously mentioned, the two lowest cost per point tallies in a single season over the past 18 years belong to Sam Allardyce. Only one other side has got close: Steve Coppell's Reading in 2006/07, at a rate of £111,640 per point. Coppell's Reading (2007/08) appear again in the top five seasons of overachievement, one place behind Lyall's Ipswich.

In the following table the final column, *Differential +/-* is the key figure.

Overachievers: cost per point less expensive than the average

#	Manager	Average Cost of XI	Manager's Av Points	Av no. of Points in Range	Manager's Av Cost Per Point	Years active	Av Cost Per Point for Point-range during Years Active	Manager's Cost Per point WEIGHTED	DIFFERENTIAL + / -
1	John Lyall	£12,855,256	40.7	43.9	£363,153	1990s Only	£866,905	£804,630	£441,477
2	Sam Allardyce	£18,895,339	49.0	44.5	£410,781	2000s Only	£753,084	£830,171	£419,390
3	Steve Coppell	£16,673,805	43.3	44.2	£415,620	1990s & 2000s	£804,415	£788,392	£372,772
4	Dave Jones	£15,961,335	41.5	44.2	£390,102	1990s & 2000s	£804,415	£755,618	£365,516
5	Alan Curbishley	£24,468,242	46.8	44.2	£515,675	1990s & 2000s	£804,415	£852,119	£336,444
6	Iain Dowie	£13,651,942	32.3	32.4	£417,526	2000s Only	£753,084	£750,528	£333,002
7	Dave Bassett	£20,007,386	38.0	32.7	£608,316	1990s & 2000s	£804,415	£935,080	£326,764
8	Joe Kinnear	£25,550,009	49.0	44.2	£593,264	1990s & 2000s	£804,415	£892,176	£298,912
9	Jim Smith	£21,286,157	43.8	44.2	£508,560	1990s & 2000s	£804,415	£797,496	£288,936
10	Alan Ball	£25,648,617	45.0	43.9	£615,335	1990s Only	£866,905	£889,640	£274,305
11	Paul Jewell	£15,978,791	34.0	32.7	£602,039	1990s & 2000s	£804,415	£836,651	£234,612
12	Alan Pardew	£20,530,640	43.3	44.5	£503,885	2000s Only	£753,084	£733,600	£229,715
13	Gary Megson	£21,225,585	35.4	32.4	£597,626	2000s Only	£753,084	£822,560	£224,934
14	George Burley	£22,234,221	43.0	44.2	£575,927	1990s & 2000s	£804,415	£782,930	£207,003
15	Glenn Hoddle	£34,496,852	49.5	44.2	£696,015	1990s & 2000s	£804,415	£901,280	£205,265
16	Harry Redknapp	£34,493,000	48.8	44.2	£690,555	1990s & 2000s	£804,415	£888,534	£197,979
17	Chris Coleman	£28,298,806	46.2	44.5	£604,423	2000s Only	£753,084	£782,733	£178,310
18	Gordon Strachan	£30,808,990	44.6	44.2	£713,433	1990s & 2000s	£804,415	£812,062	£98,629
19	Alex Ferguson	£111,271,453	83.0	84.4	£1,335,270	1990s & 2000s	£1,450,605	£1,426,881	£91,611
20	Rafael Benítez	£89,351,302	72.2	74.6	£1,238,000	2000s Only	£1,341,221	£1,298,942	£60,942
21	Stuart Pearce	£30,213,454	42.8	44.2	£719,003	1990s & 2000s	£804,415	£779,288	£60,285

#	Manager	Average Cost of XI	Manager's Av Points	Av no. of Points in Range	Manager's Av Cost Per Point	Years active	Av Cost Per Point for Point-range during Years Active	Manager's Cost Per point WEIGHTED	DIFFERENTIAL + / -
22	Frank Clark	£34,246,553	56.3	54.2	£660,350	1990s Only	£687,047	£713,799	£53,449
23	Mike Walker	£31,906,165	54.8	54.2	£645,907	1990s Only	£687,047	£694,781	£48,874
24	Peter Reid	£30,610,059	43.9	44.2	£756,182	1990s & 2000s	£804,415	£799,317	£43,135
25	Ron Atkinson	£42,738,179	47.8	43.9	£902,104	1990s Only	£866,905	£944,996	£42,892
26	Steve Bruce	£28,701,638	42.6	44.5	£686,680	2000s Only	£753,084	£721,741	£35,061
27	Gerry Francis	£37,225,966	56.6	54.2	£694,854	1990s Only	£687,047	£717,602	£22,748
28	Martin O'Neill	£40,080,583	55.0	53.8	£705,471	1990s & 2000s	£706,785	£722,147	£16,676

Involvement in at least 3 Premier League seasons required to qualify, excluding caretaker roles.

Special mention should go to the managers of two teams promoted to the top flight in recent years. If this part of the study were to be widened to include those bosses who took charge for a minimum of only two full seasons instead of three, a new top two would emerge: Tony Pulis of Stoke and Phil Brown of Hull (although he parted company with the Tigers just before the end of his second season). These two men punched significantly above their weight, with a lower average cost per point than any of the 61 longest-serving Premier League managers.

#	Manager	Average Cost of XI	Manager's Av Points	Av no. of Points in Range	Manager's Av Cost Per Point	Years active	Av Cost Per Point for Point-range during Years Active	Manager's Cost Per point WEIGHTED	DIFFERENTIAL + / -
1	Tony Pulis	£13,733,915	46.0	44.5	£298,563	2000s Only	£753,084	£779,345	£480,781
2	Phil Brown	£9,188,310	32.5	32.4	£282,717	2000s Only	£753,084	£755,408	£472,691

Underachievers?

A lot of the more celebrated Premier League managers feature at the wrong end of the cost per point table. Indeed, José Mourinho weighs in at 59th, just two places from the bottom. Was he anything but an excellent manager? Surely not. The same applies to Carlo Ancelotti, who, as a league title winner, was included in this particular category as an exception. His one season to date ended with the league title and a record number of goals scored, but sees him ranked 58th. Both men achieved notable things. But they did so with what many consider an unfair advantage.

Perhaps the problem in judging such men is that they drove the Formula One Ferrari while their rivals had commercial BMWs at best, and clapped-out Skodas at worst. They won the race; but they were expected to.

Could Mourinho and Ancelotti have done as much without such expensive teams? Who knows. But of course, that's not Chelsea's concern. They had the money, they spent the money, and as a result, they had to build a new trophy cabinet. So while these managers had an unfair advantage in terms of judging everyone on a level playing field, their advantage was not illegal or unsporting. Also, it has to be remembered that managing expensive teams brings its own pressures and pitfalls. It's not easy keeping everyone happy, but at the same time, it provides a greater avenue to success than a smaller, cheaper collection of players.

Ancelotti, for example, wasn't going to omit stars he inherited, such as Didier Drogba and Michael Essien, simply because they had cost the club a lot of money – and instead attempt to win the league with relatively inexpensive rookies such as Gaël Kakuta and Daniel Sturridge, just to show he could work on a tighter budget. That would be counter-productive at best, professional suicide at worst.

Interestingly, in the case of Mourinho, the greater his £XI grew, the worse he started to fare. His team was bolstered with signings up to the start of his fourth season, but by then results were on a downward spiral. Maybe this was also a case of 'after the Lord Mayor's show', where a team fresh from back-to-back league titles became sated, and instead, as the primary target switched to Europe, put more of its focus on the elusive Holy Grail of Champions League success. There was also the deteriorating relationship between manager and owner to consider.

The average cost of Chelsea's £XI rose from £195m in Mourinho's initial title-winning campaign, through £229m for the successful defence in 2006, to a staggering £255m a year later, at its peak. In Mourinho's fourth season it fell sharply to £189m, although early in the campaign he was replaced by Avram Grant, whose signings in the winter transfer window account for some of that average. For Phil Scolari's ill-fated campaign (brought back to some life by Guus Hiddink) it dropped further, to £168m, but rose again to £187m by the time Ancelotti brought the title back to Stamford Bridge in 2010. The six seasons between 2004 and 2010 all rank in the overall top eight highest cost per point tallies in the study.

The only way you could say Chelsea underachieved (aside from in the Champions League) was in failing to win the title in three of the past six seasons, having had the most expensive £XI each time. But being the costliest – and even being the best (which is not to say that Chelsea were) – does not mean success is inevitable. Even the most dominant footballing dynasties around the world have seasons when it just isn't their year.

Underachievers: cost per point more expensive than the average

#	Manager	Average Cost of XI	Manager's Av Points	Av no. of Points in Range	Manager's Av Cost Per Point	Years active	Av Cost Per Point for Point-range during Years Active	Manager's Cost Per point WEIGHTED	DIFFERENTIAL + / −
29	Steve McClaren	£39,365,016	48.4	44.5	£821,140	2000s Only	£753,084	£820,006	−£1,134
30	Joe Royle	£37,565,306	45.2	44.2	£825,605	1990s & 2000s	£804,415	£822,987	−£2,618
31	Micky Adams	£22,180,734	30.3	32.7	£749,303	1990s & 2000s	£804,415	£745,603	−£3,700
32	Trevor Francis	£44,653,904	58.0	54.2	£780,792	1990s Only	£687,047	£735,352	−£45,440
33	Arsène Wenger	£86,224,243	76.4	74.5	£1,131,987	1990s & 2000s	£1,054,573	£1,081,468	−£50,519
34	David Moyes	£44,970,353	55.4	53.4	£820,589	2000s Only	£730,654	£758,019	−£62,570
35	David O'Leary	£51,175,301	59.3	53.8	£848,950	1990s & 2000s	£706,785	£778,606	−£70,344
36	Kevin Keegan	£60,240,677	60.3	64.0	£1,017,615	1990s & 2000s	£999,184	£940,831	−£76,784
37	Bryan Robson	£35,440,039	41.6	44.2	£842,682	1990s & 2000s	£804,415	£757,439	−£85,243
38	Gérard Houllier	£72,382,430	65.7	64.0	£1,111,701	1990s & 2000s	£999,184	£1,025,084	−£86,617
39	Danny Wilson	£40,132,617	37.3	33.3	£1,083,211	1990s Only	£866,905	£971,038	−£112,173
40	Graeme Souness	£47,353,630	49.0	44.5	£1,006,258	1990s & 2000s	£804,415	£885,760	−£120,498
41	Mark Hughes	£51,287,345	55.3	53.4	£908,403	2000s Only	£730,654	£756,651	−£151,752
42	Walter Smith	£42,821,620	44.5	44.2	£966,084	1990s & 2000s	£804,415	£810,241	−£155,843
43	Roy Hodgson	£36,855,498	45.6	44.2	£1,020,670	1990s & 2000s	£804,415	£830,270	−£190,400
44	Gareth Southgate	£34,650,769	40.0	44.5	£868,827	2000s Only	£753,084	£677,691	−£191,136
45	Roy Evans	£71,817,352	65.3	63.8	£1,095,854	1990s Only	£878,718	£899,096	−£196,758
46	Brian Little	£45,621,210	51.6	54.2	£860,655	1990s Only	£687,047	£654,210	−£206,445
47	David Pleat	£52,686,396	47.0	43.9	£1,150,298	1990s Only	£866,905	£929,180	−£221,118
48	Glenn Roeder	£52,541,580	49.0	44.5	£1,070,890	2000s Only	£753,084	£830,171	−£240,719
49	Mick McCarthy	£16,925,269	24.0	32.4	£801,027	2000s Only	£753,084	£557,668	−£243,359
50	Gianluca Vialli	£76,211,181	66.0	63.8	£1,160,738	1990s Only	£878,718	£908,734	−£252,004
51	George Graham	£53,085,647	55.4	53.8	£991,807	1990s & 2000s	£706,785	£727,399	−£264,408
52	Howard Kendall	£53,253,216	45.7	43.9	£1,192,517	1990s Only	£866,905	£903,479	−£289,038
53	John Gregory	£51,037,846	50.7	53.8	£977,977	1990s & 2000s	£706,785	£665,688	−£312,289
54	Kenny Dalglish	£79,830,792	71.2	74.5	£1,205,378	1990s Only	£887,988	£848,996	−£356,382
55	Howard Wilkinson	£49,299,885	50.3	53.8	£1,058,180	1990s & 2000s	£706,785	£660,436	−£397,744
56	Claudio Ranieri	£109,023,133	67.8	64.3	£1,589,434	2000s Only	£1,101,117	£1,161,595	−£427,839
57	Martin Jol	£69,505,567	57.0	53.4	£1,284,778	2000s Only	£730,654	£779,912	−£504,866
58	Carlo Ancelotti	£187,436,346	86.0	84.1	£2,179,492	2000s Only	£1,621,812	£1,659,241	−£520,251
59	José Mourinho	£220,439,758	88.5	84.1	£2,506,549	2000s Only	£1,621,812	£1,707,475	−£799,074
60	Ruud Gullit	£79,163,849	55.0	54.2	£1,506,837	1990s Only	£687,047	£697,317	−£809,520
61	Bobby Robson	£105,244,347	59.8	53.8	£1,794,548	1990s & 2000s	£706,785	£785,171	−£1,009,377

Involvement in at least three Premier League seasons required to qualify, excluding caretaker roles. Carlo Ancelotti included as an exception due to league title.

One surprising result to emerge from the study is David Moyes' relatively poor figure. Overall the Everton manager, who is perceived to work wonders on a tighter budget, ranks 35th, with an average of −£62,569. On the whole, Everton aren't a 'cheap' side by any stretch of the imagination; equally, they are nowhere near up there with the rich elite who block their path to honours. But, as is the case for many managers, a couple of really poor seasons skew Moyes' figures. Remove those two campaigns, and the remaining seven leave an average that improves to

£31,302 better than the average per point cost, which would move him up to 27th, into the 'in credit' list.

His one truly great season – finishing 4th, above local rivals Liverpool – was a massive overachievement. The average £XI was just £27.2m, and the 61 points were amassed at a cost per point of just £446,392. But almost immediately, Everton's £XI more or less doubled, and in the five seasons since that 4th-place finish the cost per point averages close to the £900,000 mark. The investment in personnel hasn't led to massive improvements on the pitch – although seasons of 63 and 65 points are indicative of slow but steady progress. But what this increased investment has done is enable Everton to stay up towards the Europa League places, and avoid the yo-yoing up and down the table in the manner of the manager's early years. Moyes has clearly done a very good job – especially as he inherited a poor set-up, – but perhaps not quite as 'on the cheap' as is widely perceived.

It's fair to say that most medium-term managers would benefit from the removal of their first year's figures, when they have had to get to grips with what they inherited; and also their final year's figures, when, presumably, the wheels were coming off. To go back to an earlier example, in the four seasons from 2006 to 2009, Rafa Benítez averaged 78 points, and had a cost per point a sizeable £212,995 lower than the norm for the points range. But of course, the bad years are all part of any overall picture.

In Kenny Dalglish's case, to look only at his Premier League seasons at Blackburn would see his figure rise significantly to £31,679 better than the norm, from £356,381 below it; meaning that in building up to, and winning the title, Dalglish – in contrast to Chelsea's managers – won points at a cost below what was reasonably expected given the outlay. While Blackburn are generally believed to have 'bought' the title from a position as paupers a few years earlier – and financial strength certainly played a major part – their spending was more a case of buying the right to challenge. (Though in the new millennium, it's unlikely even this would be possible for a club that was a 'newcomer'.)

However, at Newcastle, it was a different story for the Scot. It seems that some clubs are just harder to win points at, no matter how much money is spent. Some clubs – but mostly Newcastle – leave you scratching your head.

Chapter Three:
The 'Newcastle Effect'

As we've just established, Kenny Dalglish's record took a nosedive at St James' Park. But he's not the only manager to find his copybook not so much blotted as obliterated on Tyneside.

One of the strangest results to emerge from this analysis is the one that sees Bobby Robson marooned in 61st place out of the 61 eligible managers in the cost per point table, with an average *a full £1m* worse than the expected norm. In this case, it was the late manager's only Premier League job, some 17 years after leaving Ipswich for the England national team. Following his scandalous treatment by the tabloids in the lead up to Italia '90, he packed his bags for Holland, Portugal and Spain, winning the Dutch Championship twice with PSV Eindhoven, the Portuguese Championship twice and the Cup of Portugal with Benfica, and both the *Copa del Rey* and European Cup Winners' Cup with Barcelona.

Although that success across the continent didn't always appease the locals at his various clubs, Robson is rightly regarded as one of the game's better managers, and certainly one of its true gentlemen. But by the time he arrived at his hometown club in 1999, Newcastle had been throwing money at the team for the best part of a decade. In his first season – which involved taking over from Ruud Gullit early in the campaign – the average cost per point was a staggering £2,273,715; the third highest in Premier League history.

Remove that, and Robson's average drops from in excess of a million pounds above the expected figure to £707,917 over the odds; still not great, but it would all the same lift him off the bottom of the table. (Although only above two managers, one of whom is Gullit.)

Some managers inherit expensive, badly assembled or poorly balanced squads. This seems to be even more the case when there's a rapid turnover of managers; and at Newcastle, in just the previous two years, Kevin Keegan, Dalglish and Gullit had all been in charge, and free to buy players who fitted their ideas. Between Robson's dismissal in 2004 and their relegation five years later, Graeme Souness, Glenn Roeder, Sam Allardyce, Keegan again, Joe Kinnear, Chris Hughton and Alan Shearer all had spells in charge of the side.

At Chelsea, Gullit appeared to be a top-class manager in the making. He averaged 61 points in his two seasons, and won points at a respectable cost per point of £846,354. However, the two seasons on his Newcastle record yielded an average of just 49 points won at a cost of £2,167,320 each. His overall record shows he was 'paying' more than £800,000 over the odds for each point in four seasons of Premier League management, but at Chelsea, he was just £12,379 in the red. The damage was done at St James'.

And so, following Keegan's 'nearly' great side of the mid-'90s, which entertained and won the hearts of the neutrals but just failed to win the title, two managers with near-faultless reputations (Dalglish and Gullit) had moved in to replace him, and both left with seriously blemished records.

Next came Robson, who took the Geordies back into the Champions League, and between 2001 and 2003, averaged 70 points per season, won at a cost of one for every £1,492,876 spent: still £232,000 over the odds, but far better than the going rate at Newcastle in the years before and since. Then, as so often happens at St James' Park, Robson hit a rough spot at the start of a campaign, and was unceremoniously dismissed just a couple of games into the 2004/05 season.

At this point it's worth considering how Newcastle became so expensive in the first place. It began with their arrival in the Premier League in 1993, after spending their way out of the old Second Division. They finished with 77 points in 1993/94, with an £XI that cost 'only' £44m (much of it spent when in the division below). In this great opening to life back in the top flight, Keegan's points cost a mere £580,190 each; more than £300,000 better than the average for the 70-79 point range in that decade. This was an inspirational manager in touch with the people of the city. This was boom time in Toon town.

Just one season later, the £XI had shot up to £63.6m, but the points fell to 72: £883,266 each. On the whole, though, they were adjusting well to life in the top flight, once a little of the euphoria had ebbed away; and investment was almost certainly necessary to avoid becoming a one-season wonder.

By 1995/96, the £XI was £80.9m, and the 78 points came at a rate of one every £1,037,230. So far so good, although it was the season when Newcastle 'blew' the title from a leading position, and the manager had an apparent meltdown live on TV in response to Alex Ferguson's jibes.

One year further on, and the £XI was now up to £107.8m – but the total points amassed had dropped to 68 (which was nonetheless still enough to finish in 2nd place, seven points behind United and level on points with Arsenal and Liverpool). In the space of four seasons, the £XI had more than doubled, and Newcastle's cost per point had virtually trebled, from £580,190 to £1,585,523. This final season is the point when Keegan made his exit, and Dalglish arrived (at the beginning of January). By the time Dalglish ended his first full season in charge – 1997/98 – the

Geordies had made it to an FA Cup Final, but a disappointing 44 points in the Premier League cost £1,961,106 each; close to the £2m-per-point range.

So in came Ruud Gullit – replete with promises of 'sexy football' – and Newcastle registered just 46 and 52 points in the two seasons in which he was associated with the club. The cost per point continued to rise: £2,060,925, and then £2,273,715.

While this was the peak of their poor return, even now Newcastle have yet to really escape the £1.5m-per-point range; hovering just below or above it, and racing back up towards the £2m mark in the season of relegation in 2009.

Enter Souness

Following Robson's dismissal in 2004, the next to damage his standing in the game while at Newcastle was Graeme Souness. After an awful time at Anfield between 1991 and 1994, he'd gone some way towards rehabilitating his reputation in the following decade, enjoying periods at Southampton and Blackburn when he punched above his weight in terms of points achieved, not least when guiding the Ewood Park club to 60 points in 2002/03, at a cost of just £571,592 each – almost half a million pounds better than the expected figure for such a points total.

But again, the move to Newcastle proved disastrous. Spending £8.?m (£14.9m Current Transfer Purchase Price, or CTPP) on Jean-Alain Boumsong was not a good omen; a player with a fine pedigree, but who had an horrendous time in the Newcastle back line, alongside £5m Titus Bramble (£8.1m, signed by Robson in 2002). Finding good centre-backs – and overspending on those who subsequently fail – seems to be the recurring theme; no sooner had £9m Jonathan Woodgate (£14.5m CTPP) settled into the side and started to look the real deal than he was sold to Real Madrid, albeit for a nice profit (£13.4m/£24.4m CTPP).

Signing overpriced, injury-prone stars has been a recurring theme for much of the past decade and beyond. Worst of these was Michael Owen, a player whose signing by Souness was greeted like a trophy, but whose £31m CTPP fee (and stellar wages) dwindled down to zero and a free transfer, as he failed to start six out of every 10 league games between 2005 and 2009.

Using only CTPP fees, Hugo Viana cost £13.7m in 2002 and left for a genuine loss in excess of £10m. Laurent Robert cost £13.8m, but left for nothing. Spanish centre-back Marcelino cost £13.6m, and was later released. Duncan Ferguson cost £17.1m, left for £6.7m. Kieron Dyer cost £14m, and was eventually sold for a £7.3m genuine loss. Albert Luque set the club back £17.5m, but only £2.3m was recouped. Obefemi Martins cost £17.4m, and was sold for £9m. Carl Cort's CTPP works out at £12.5m, yet the value of the money recouped translates to less than a third of that figure. So much money, so badly invested.

Glenn Roeder had a brief spell in charge following Souness' sacking, before Sam Allardyce – the ultimate Premier League overachiever – was appointed. Surely he would break the pattern of failure? In six seasons at Bolton, Allardyce had averaged 51.2 points at a cost of just £213,138 each. More recently, at Blackburn he has averaged 45.5 at a cost of £495,587 per point; not as good, but still better than the norm. But at Newcastle, in his one season (of which he was in charge for eight months, including the full pre-season), the club won just 43 points at a cost of £1,427,028 each – almost seven times as costly as his Reebok average, and almost 18 times as expensive as his best two seasons there.

Lurching

Allardyce's style was unpopular with Geordie fans, who wanted more attractive football. The Newcastle fans we spoke to were deeply unimpressed. The modern scientific approach was forward-thinking; the tactics were not. But his appointment, and subsequent dismissal, epitomises Newcastle's 'lurching' policy: from one extreme to the other. Kenny Dalglish succeeding Kevin Keegan made sense, although neither the free-flowing football seen at Anfield nor the more basic but equally exciting attacking football seen at Ewood Park were on display, as Dalglish tried to shore up the defence first and foremost. So the cry went up for the aforementioned sexy football, and out went a 'dour Scot' (who, incidentally, had bought well with players like Dietmar Hamann, Gary Speed, Shay Given, and Nolberto Solano) and in came a young, up-and-coming Continental Cosmopolitan with dreadlocks (a fashion that Dalglish was thankfully never tempted to adopt).

When that approach 'inevitably' failed (and I say inevitably purely because it's Newcastle), they switched to the likeable, local and experienced Bobby Robson; as diametrically opposed to Gullit as you could get. He did well for a few years, but then he too suffered the chop after a bad start to the season (the usual procedure). Apparently he was too 'nice'; a tough bastard was needed. Step up Graeme Souness, for whom that epithet could well have been invented.

But Souness wasn't a top-class manager. He applied an erratic buying policy and failed to connect with the Newcastle public. When he was sacked in February 2006, Glenn Roeder – a former captain, and at the club as the head of their academy – became caretaker manager; a good end to the season saw him appointed on a full-time basis, but he left before the last game of 2006/07. He understood Newcastle; but perhaps he was just too nice.

That's not an accusation that's ever been levelled at Sam Allardyce, or his teams. He'd toughen them up. Except, within a few months, fans were chanting

"You don't know what you're doing". He knew what he was doing; they just didn't like it, and it wasn't quite working.

And then, when all else had failed, Newcastle went with the sentimental. Bring back the Messiah! First time around, Kevin Keegan had averaged 73.8 points, at a cost of just over £1m each. Upon his return, the points dropped to just 38.5 – more or less half his previous average – and the cost rose to £1.65m each. The reunion didn't last long.

If Keegan was the sentimental choice, selecting Joe Kinnear was simply bizarre. This is no slight on the manager's record in the '90s, simply an acknowledgement that he'd been out of work for so long, and was known to have heart problems. Also, his association with Wimbledon didn't exactly promise the aesthetic delights the Geordies craved; but maybe, just maybe, he'd be able to dig them out of a hole. In seven seasons with the London 'crazy gang' he had averaged 51.1 points, at a cost of £411,062 each, £236,688 better than the norm: he was another manager adept at punching above his weight at a smaller club. But at the North East's crazy club, in a season for which he was only partly responsible, the Magpies registered just 34 points, at a whopping cost of £1,868,676 each. Even the ultimate fan-appeasing appointment – local hero Alan Shearer – couldn't save the club from relegation. Thankfully, for those long-suffering supporters (a description they could almost copyright), and for those who like to see the biggest clubs in the land play each other twice a season, they were back in the top flight 12 months later. With any luck, lessons will have been learned along the way.

Beyond the 'Barcodes'

The Newcastle Effect, while it clearly affects many managers on Tyneside, isn't confined solely to St James' Park. There are a whole host of other examples of managers whose fortunes reversed as soon as they went to a bigger club.

Indeed, it's hard to find too many successful managers at the top end of the Premier League table who first built over-arching empires at one of the minnows; most have either come from abroad, having already proven themselves at the top end (although they obviously had to work their way up first) or were already proven commodities when the league was formed (such as Dalglish). In the case of Alex Ferguson, it was a bit of both: success achieved at Aberdeen in the early '80s, before being given time at United to overcome four largely shaky years at the start of his tenure that would not be tolerated today. To date, no manager promoted from an unfashionable club to a bigger one has finished within the top two since 1993. In that time, those positions have been attained by Ferguson, Dalglish with two clubs, Keegan (first job), Wenger (non-UK), Houllier (non-UK),

Ranieri (non-UK), Mourinho (non-UK), Mourinho/Grant (non-UK), Benítez (non-UK) and Ancelotti (non-UK). Of course, much of the time these prime jobs went to continental coaches. However, on the occasions when clubs with the potential resources to break into the top two have appointed someone from a smaller English outfit, the tactic has failed. More than that, too often they've failed to even meet more modest expectations at clubs with realistic aims of the top four or top six.

We've mentioned Allardyce, Kinnear and Souness, who all had at least one season of really punching above their weight at a less fashionable club, only to falter when given the chance at a bigger one (twice, in Souness' case, although his first job in English football was with reigning champions Liverpool). But there are plenty of others. Why is this?

Is it purely down to the pressure involved at the top end? Or is it the greater patience shown by clubs outside the elite, where an empire can be slowly constructed – providing relegation doesn't befall them (although even then, this can see a club that retains its manager coming back stronger the next time; see Alan Curbishley and Charlton).

Time certainly seems to be a factor. Take Mark Hughes, whose reputation seemed cemented after several impressive seasons at Blackburn. However, his tenure at Manchester City was brief; and in fairness, he was sacked while possessing far from the worst record around – it just wasn't anything special, and too many games were being drawn. At Blackburn, Hughes averaged 53.8 points, at a per point cost of £584,081. In 18 months at City, he averaged 58.5 points (with Roberto Mancini collecting some of those with Hughes' team) – better than at Blackburn – but only marginally, and coming at a cost of £1,557,045 each.

Martin O'Neill is perhaps regarded as the ultimate overachiever, but even he hit a brick wall at Aston Villa. A decade earlier, at Leicester, the Ulsterman had averaged 51 points in four top-flight seasons, at a cost of £453,849 each, and, rather impressively, had won two League Cups for the Midlanders. By contrast, his 59-point average at Villa came at almost £1m each; and the 64 points of what turned out to be his final season came at one for every £1,133,892 of the £XI – higher than the average (albeit only fractionally). On the whole, he pretty much punched his weight at Villa Park, and it has to be noted that he took over a club that was struggling at the time and got them to the level where they 'should' have been. However, even his purportedly great powers of motivation could not get Villa to *overstretch* themselves; at times they broke into the top three, only for his team to hit a wall in the spring almost every season (perhaps because he was not rotating his XI anywhere near as much as his rivals). He did a good job, but no more, as the side became increasingly expensive.

At both Birmingham and Wigan, Steve Bruce's £XI averaged £25m, and he won points at a virtually identical rate: £617,985 and £613,370 respectively. Historically, Sunderland are bigger than both (based on honours, points won in the top flight and average attendance), and Bruce's current employers have provided the funds for him to field an £XI (£52m) more than double that of his previous clubs. The result? In his one full season to date he won points at a rate of £1,176,778; a very poor performance for a team towards the bottom of the table.

Roy Hodgson is another example, although his is a back-to-front story: bigger job first, smaller job a decade later. In some ways he also qualifies as 'continental', as that's where he made his name, although he did so with the very British approach of the FA's 1970s coaching guru, Allen Wade. (Hodgson changed his European teams from their continental sweeper and man-marking centre-backs to a method of zonal marking in open play; i.e., defenders not following strikers around the pitch as a libero acts as a spare man, but two centre-backs picking up whoever comes into the zone.) Recently installed as the Liverpool manager, it is Hodgson's previous two jobs in English football that provide one of the starker contrasts available. At Fulham he averaged 45 points, at a cost of £602,702: very respectable stuff, with a great run to the Europa League Final thrown in to boot. But despite a promising first season at Blackburn in the late '90s, his time there ended up proving somewhat disastrous. He took over just two years after they won the league title; and although the wheels had come off somewhat since the high of 1995, he spent almost £75m in today's terms in just 16 months, with only one success: Stéphane Henchoz.

Hodgson's average points haul at Rovers was almost identical to that of his later sojourn by the Thames: 46.5. But the per point cost at Blackburn was a whopping £1.65m; splitting the difference between £1.35m in his first season, and £1.95m upon the Lancashire club's eventual relegation. In fairness, Hodgson only managed the club for the first 14 games of his final season, but they were rooted to the bottom of the table at the time of his dismissal; indeed, one place below their eventual position. And of course, his sacking was, in part, a consequence of some of his bad signings, not least the £17m CTPP spent on Kevin Davies (subsequently a success at Bolton, it has to be noted). Hodgson now has the chance to prove he really can handle a club with higher expectations, and that he has learned from his previous failure. (At the time of going to press, his Liverpool team are in the relegation zone, with just six points from eight games; the pro rata cost per point so far is currently an horrific £2.84m ... but it's early days.)

Alan Curbishley, himself heavily tipped for a job at Liverpool (replacing Gérard

Houllier in 2004), gained kudos for his excellent record at Charlton. In seven top-flight seasons he averaged 46.7 points, attained at a per point cost of just £436,007. And while West Ham was no longer one of the very biggest clubs in England, a move there was still seen as a fairly significant step up. And yet in the three seasons he worked at Upton Park he averaged 47 points – virtually identical to his time at The Valley. Only this time it was achieved at an average cost of £701,568 per point. While this is one of the less extreme examples, Curbishley's ultimate failure to reinvigorate West Ham sufficiently still follows the general pattern.

To end this analysis, two examples from the early years of the Premier League. First, Mike Walker, father of Spurs' goalkeeper Ian, who was a revelation at Norwich, taking them into the UEFA Cup with a 3rd-place finish. This earned him a shot at the big time: Everton Football Club, champions of England just seven years earlier. But again, the transition was painful; at Norwich he'd averaged 62.5 points in the Premier League's first two years; in the next two seasons, following his move, Everton's average was just 47. In Norfolk, points came at a measly cost of one every £219,451 fielded in the £XI, but at Everton, the average – at £1,072,364 – was almost five times this amount.

Finally, Gerry Francis. In three seasons between 1992 and 1995, Francis' QPR averaged 61 points, won at a rate almost comparable with Walker's at Norwich: £274,538. Spurs, at the time still seen as one of the traditional 'big five' (with Manchester United, Liverpool, Arsenal and Everton), would enable him to field a side with more than three times the average £XI. The result? In the four seasons in which he managed at White Hart Lane, Spurs couldn't even get close to matching the manager's average points haul at his previous club: at just 53.3, it was almost eight points worse. Given that the team was more than three times as expensive, the cost per point rocketed up to £1,010,091.

Tactical Translations

How could all these miracle workers at smaller clubs fail to translate their skills into success at more fashionable footballing institutions?

Of course, luck plays a part in any manager's reign – injuries and blows to confidence can be hard to overcome, and can result in a downward spiral – but why, with the possible exception of Harry Redknapp, have all of the plucky little Davids turned into vulnerable Goliaths when their opportunities came along?

Bad owners/chairmen also play a part. Alan Curbishley was eventually compensated for constructive dismissal after key players were sold from under him – forcing him to resign – but this came at the end of his tenure; these were new men in control of the club, and therefore it doesn't explain the relative failure up to that point.

Restless supporters don't help, either. This is almost certainly one of Newcastle's problems: so much passion and desire for success that, at times, it clouds judgement on the Tyne.

And could it be that increased expectations mean that tactics which often involve not getting beaten (good for mid-table sides) fall apart when a win is demanded almost every single week? Is the problem that both style and substance are demanded at the elite clubs?

Whatever the reasons, it does seem abundantly clear that managing at the top of the Premier League is a very different task to the one faced by those lower down. "You can be a very good manager of a corner shop," former Manchester City player and director Dennis Tueart famously said, "but that doesn't mean you can run a multinational. It's a different skill set."

Modest to a fault, Sam Allardyce clearly thinks he has what it takes to not just take on the biggest jobs in world football, but also succeed. His bizarre statement when Newcastle sacked him was the first of several to suggest he feels he can translate his approach to any club in the world. "Newcastle was not big enough for me," he said. "It didn't live up to my ambitions in the short time that I was there." (And yet no-one bigger than Blackburn has come calling since.)

When, in 2008, England appointed Fabio Capello – with his glittering CV of silverware (including seven *Serie A* titles won with three different clubs, and two *La Liga* titles with Real Madrid) – 'Big Sam' was not impressed. "At the time I should have got the job and I really don't know why I didn't. It had to be political for me, rather than my credentials."

Which, of course, leads back to the question of just what his credentials are. While research shows that Allardyce can do a brilliant job managing a corner shop, there is no evidence that he could cope with the demands of a multinational. It's true that he didn't get a lot of time at Newcastle, but he did not seem to be tailoring his approach to suit his new surroundings.

Undeterred, in the autumn of 2010, Allardyce went further. "I'm not suited to Bolton or Blackburn; I would be more suited to Inter Milan or Real Madrid. It wouldn't be a problem to me to go and manage those clubs because I would win the double or the league every time. Give me Manchester United or Chelsea and I would do the same, it wouldn't be a problem. It's not where I'm suited to, it's just where I've been for most of the time. It's not a problem to take me into the higher reaches of the Champions League or Premier League and would make my job a lot easier in winning it."

Despite his ability to punch above his weight with a rank outsider, and the fact that richer clubs are more likely to win the major trophies, that smacks of delusion. Even the richest and best-managed clubs fail sometimes. Even Alex Ferguson and José Mourinho don't win the major trophies *every* season.

Allardyce also felt Mark Hughes was harshly treated during his time at a big club. "His Manchester City reign obviously was not long enough. A little bit like me at Newcastle, but I didn't last quite as long as 'Sparky' though. He was given the chance and unfortunately at that stage of his career they decided to have a change. You look back on it and he'll be very disappointed because they only lost two games I think [although they had dropped lots of points with draws]. But that is the way it is sometimes, there's a perception that other people can do better than you, but often the reality is not the case."

Perhaps Allardyce would adapt his approach at a club like Real Madrid, Manchester United or Inter Milan, but on the limited evidence seen at Newcastle, it's still unlikely to prove sophisticated enough. While the long-ball approach works for smaller clubs, it's impossible to recall a major Premier League side employing such tactics more than intermittently. The long ball can of course be the *right* ball, but there's a difference between mixing it up with a technically gifted targetman (Didier Drogba, Peter Crouch), and a systematic loading of the team with giants in order to play a 'set-piece' game based on winning free-kicks and delivering towering long throws into the box. 'Route one' is a tactic that clearly works up to a point – or up to about 60 points – given that it's the style of football preferred by many of the managers with the lowest cost per point values. It simply appears to hit a glass ceiling in terms of effectiveness. Allardyce wasn't *all* about the long ball, but it has been a key weapon in his armoury.

Speaking in August 2010, Arsène Wenger – the ultimate purist – gave his take on managers like Tony Pulis (whose team he was referring to) and Sam Allardyce (whose team he was about to face): "When a team plays long ball, and head the ball, and become physical, I accept that completely and I respect that – but it has to be in respect of the rules. I believe everybody looks at his squad and tries to find a way where the game is most efficient and we [at Arsenal] developed one way. It is not the only way; I respect every other way as long as the referees get the rules respected. I saw some pictures last Sunday – you cannot say anymore it is football; it is rugby on the goalkeepers more than football."

Most likely, a failure to transfer success to bigger clubs is a combination of some, or all, of the factors mentioned in this section. But next time a manager has great success at getting a smaller club to punch above its weight, don't think that it will automatically translate to the top of the table. He may well be the right man for the job – after all, each case should be judged on its individual merits. But the vast majority of footballing history suggests that one should proceed with caution.

Chapter Four:
Competitive Balance

So, without large amounts of money to lavish on players, what are the chances of a club winning the Premier League title? Or indeed, simply challenging for the top four? Is there a decreasing amount of competitive balance in England's flagship league?

Jonathan Wilson, writing for *Sports Illustrated* in August 2010, said "Watch the television coverage of any English Premier League game between a side near the top of the table and a side near the bottom and you can guarantee that before kickoff one of the pundits will say something along these lines: 'The great thing about this league is that on any given day anybody can beat anybody.' Except it's not true, not anymore.

"This isn't U.S. sports with a franchise system, salary caps, drafts and collective negotiating for TV rights that help to ensure general equality and thus competitiveness. This is the dog-eat-dog, every-man-for-himself European model, in which the big boys beat up the little kids on a regular basis."

Gone are the days of newly-promoted clubs, such as Nottingham Forest, winning the title. In 1977, Forest finished 3rd in the old Second Division; a year later, they were English champions, and a year after that, the conquerors of Europe. Leeds United took a season longer from gaining promotion in 1990 to winning the title in 1992; the final First Division title before the name changed. Indeed, it's inconceivable to imagine a promoted side even finishing in the top four, unless seriously bankrolled. Blackburn (1993), Newcastle (1994) and Nottingham Forest (1995) remain the last newly or recently promoted clubs to break into the elite. Since then the top four has been the preserve of the biggest names: Manchester United, Liverpool, Arsenal and Chelsea (until recently known as the 'big four'), with occasional appearances from Leeds, Everton, Newcastle and Spurs.

Writing in *The Guardian* on the issue of competitive balance in February 2006,

Gavyn Davies noted: "Surprisingly, football in this country is much more competitive than any sport in the USA, where the rules are specifically intended to level the playing field between teams. A statistical study led by Eli Ben-Naim at Los Alamos National Laboratory shows that in the whole of league history, the underdog has won 45% of the time in British football, compared with only 36-44% of the time in American football, baseball, hockey and basketball. The more often the underdog wins, the more competitive (and attractive) the sport.

"However, the Los Alamos figures suggest that the performance of underdogs in football has been on a clear downtrend since about 1960, when the maximum wage was abolished. This, along with the arrival of massive television revenue for the biggest clubs in the 1990s, and then the huge rewards for Champions League qualification, has left the Premier League tilted heavily in favour of the biggest clubs."

Davies also spoke about standard deviation. "One way of measuring the competitiveness of the Premier League is to estimate the standard deviation (or variation) of points earned by each of the clubs every season. The higher the standard deviation, the greater the variation between teams' strength, and the less competitive the league. The Premier League has existed in its current 20-team format for 10 seasons. In the first five seasons, the standard deviation of points was 13.6, while in the last five seasons, this has risen to 15.3 points. Therefore, the league has become less competitive, though not massively so."

Standard deviation shows how much variation there is from the "average" (mean). A low standard deviation indicates that the data points tend to be very close to the mean – tightly grouped – whereas high standard deviation indicates that the data is spread out over a large range of values.

In the five seasons since Davies' piece, the standard deviation has risen yet again, to an average of 17.9; and in 2007/08, it peaked at 19.7. By comparison, 1992/93 was just 10.37, the lowest in Premier League history. This means that the top places and bottom places are becoming further away from the average points; the league is effectively becoming stretched.

Jonathan Michie and Christine Oughton, in their study "Competitive Balance In Football: Trends and Effects" (2004), state that: "Using a number of new indicators of competitive balance for the period 1947-2004 we find that competitive balance in top-flight English football remained roughly constant between 1947 and 1987. However, since then all three indicators – the Herfindahl Index of Competitive Balance (HICB), the C5 Index of Competitive Balance (C5CIB) and the Lorenz Seasonal Balance Curve – show a significant decline in competitive balance.

... The analysis of both the C5 ratio and the H-index shows that there has been a significant decline in competitive balance between 1947 and 2004 with the H-index and C5 ratio showing increases of 13 per cent and 21 per cent respectively. Further analysis of the evolution of this trend reveals that there was no real change in competitive balance between 1947 and 1987 and that virtually all of the increase has occurred since 1989 ... Over the past decade Premier League clubs have experienced unprecedented growth in revenue. Between 1992 and 2003 turnover of the Premier League increased by around 650 per cent, that is a 6.5 fold increase in revenue. By far the largest source of growth in turnover came from increased income from broadcasting rights, which rose by over 3500 per cent (or more than 35 times) from just £15m in 1992 to £543m in 2003."

Michie and Oughton conclude that: "In a standard industry it would be normal to see such rapid growth in revenue translated into increased profitability. However, this is not the case in football where the objective of attaining sporting success provides an incentive for clubs to spend increased revenue on player transfers and wages ... As a result, only five clubs recorded a pre-tax profit in 2003 and Premier League clubs as a whole recorded a pre-tax loss of £153m."

Transfer Price Index and Competitive Balance

So, how does the Transfer Price Index – and specifically, £XI – help in understanding competitive balance? Does it provide its own accurate methods of analysis?

The following 'heat map' (overleaf) graphs the £XIs of each Premier League season, and lists teams in terms of finishing position. The shades in each rectangle represent the cost of the £XI. The darkest shade refers to the most expensive £XI that season, and the remaining shades are shown as a percentage of that costliest side.

What's revealing is how the picture changes from the first nine seasons (left) to the second nine seasons (right). Even if you can't read the name of the teams, you can see the pattern; and that pattern is clearly visible (although squinting helps draw it into greater focus). The first nine years show a clear mix-and-match effect, whereas since 2001/02, the expensive teams, with only one or two notable exceptions, have gravitated to the top.

The top two positions in the table are universally dark: none of the 36 top-two teams in the 18 league tables had a cost below 50% of the most expensive £XI. The four lightest-shaded top-two sides are Manchester United in 1997, Arsenal in 2004 and 2005, and Liverpool in 2009. The 'lightest' top five side to date belongs to David Moyes' Everton, in 2005: just 14.3% of the season's most expensive £XI; though visually it doesn't stand out of the image quite as much as Ipswich Town,

League Champions: % of Most Expensive £XI

League Position

Season

League Position	1992-3	1993-4	1994-5	1995-6	1996-7	1997-98	1998-9	1999-0	2000-1	2001-2	2002-3	2003-4	2004-5	2005-6	2006-7	2007-8	2008-9	2009-10
1	Manchester United	Manchester United	Blackburn Rovers	Manchester United	Manchester United	Arsenal	Manchester United	Manchester United	Manchester United	Arsenal	Manchester United	Arsenal	Chelsea	Chelsea	Manchester United	Manchester United	Manchester United	Chelsea
2	Aston Villa	Blackburn Rovers	Manchester United	Newcastle United	Newcastle United	Manchester United	Arsenal	Arsenal	Arsenal	Liverpool	Arsenal	Chelsea	Arsenal	Manchester United	Chelsea	Chelsea	Liverpool	Manchester United
3	Norwich City	Newcastle United	Nottingham Forest	Liverpool	Arsenal	Liverpool	Chelsea	Leeds United	Liverpool	Manchester United	Newcastle United	Manchester United	Manchester United	Liverpool	Liverpool	Arsenal	Chelsea	Arsenal
4	Blackburn Rovers	Arsenal	Liverpool	Aston Villa	Liverpool	Chelsea	Leeds United	Liverpool	Leeds United	Newcastle United	Chelsea	Liverpool	Everton	Arsenal	Arsenal	Liverpool	Arsenal	Tottenham Hotspur
5	QPR	Leeds United	Leeds United	Arsenal	Aston Villa	Leeds United	West Ham United	Chelsea	Ipswich Town	Leeds United	Liverpool	Newcastle United	Liverpool	Tottenham Hotspur	Tottenham Hotspur	Everton	Everton	Manchester City
6	Liverpool	Wimbledon	Newcastle United	Everton	Chelsea	Blackburn Rovers	Aston Villa	Aston Villa	Chelsea	Chelsea	Blackburn Rovers	Aston Villa	Bolton Wanderers	Blackburn Rovers	Everton	Aston Villa	Aston Villa	Aston Villa
7	Sheffield Wednesday	Sheffield Wednesday	Tottenham Hotspur	Blackburn Rovers	Sheffield Wednesday	Aston Villa	Liverpool	Sunderland	Sunderland	West Ham United	Everton	Charlton Athletic	Middlesbrough	Newcastle United	Bolton Wanderers	Blackburn Rovers	Fulham	Liverpool
8	Tottenham Hotspur	Liverpool	QPR	Tottenham Hotspur	Wimbledon	West Ham United	Derby County	Leicester City	Aston Villa	Aston Villa	Southampton	Bolton Wanderers	Manchester City	Bolton Wanderers	Reading	Portsmouth	Tottenham Hotspur	Everton
9	Manchester City	QPR	Wimbledon	Nottingham Forest	Leicester City	Derby County	Middlesbrough	West Ham United	Charlton Athletic	Tottenham Hotspur	Manchester City	Fulham	Tottenham Hotspur	West Ham United	Portsmouth	Manchester City	West Ham United	Birmingham City
10	Arsenal	Aston Villa	Southampton	West Ham United	Tottenham Hotspur	Leicester City	Leicester City	Tottenham Hotspur	Southampton	Blackburn Rovers	Tottenham Hotspur	Birmingham City	Aston Villa	Wigan Athletic	Blackburn Rovers	West Ham United	Manchester City	Blackburn Rovers
11	Chelsea	Coventry City	Chelsea	Chelsea	Leeds United	Coventry City	Tottenham Hotspur	Newcastle United	Newcastle United	Southampton	Middlesbrough	Middlesbrough	Charlton Athletic	Everton	Aston Villa	Tottenham Hotspur	Wigan Athletic	Stoke City
12	Wimbledon	Norwich City	Arsenal	Middlesbrough	Derby County	Southampton	Sheffield Wednesday	Middlesbrough	Tottenham Hotspur	Middlesbrough	Charlton Athletic	Southampton	Birmingham City	Fulham	Middlesbrough	Newcastle United	Stoke City	Fulham
13	Everton	West Ham United	Sheffield Wednesday	Leeds United	Blackburn Rovers	Newcastle United	Newcastle United	Everton	Leicester City	Fulham	Birmingham City	Portsmouth	Fulham	Charlton Athletic	Newcastle United	Middlesbrough	Bolton Wanderers	Sunderland
14	Sheffield United	Chelsea	West Ham United	Wimbledon	West Ham United	Tottenham Hotspur	Everton	Coventry City	Middlesbrough	Charlton Athletic	Fulham	Tottenham Hotspur	Newcastle United	Middlesbrough	Manchester City	Wigan Athletic	Portsmouth	Bolton Wanderers
15	Coventry City	Tottenham Hotspur	Everton	Sheffield Wednesday	Everton	Wimbledon	Coventry City	Southampton	West Ham United	Everton	Leeds United	Blackburn Rovers	Blackburn Rovers	Manchester City	West Ham United	Sunderland	Blackburn Rovers	Wolverhampton Wanderers
16	Ipswich Town	Manchester City	Coventry City	Coventry City	Southampton	Sheffield Wednesday	Wimbledon	Derby County	Everton	Bolton Wanderers	Aston Villa	Manchester City	Portsmouth	Aston Villa	Fulham	Bolton Wanderers	Sunderland	Wigan Athletic
17	Leeds United	Everton	Manchester City	Southampton	Coventry City	Everton	Southampton	Bradford City	Derby County	Sunderland	Bolton Wanderers	Everton	West Bromwich Albion	Portsmouth	Wigan Athletic	Fulham	Hull City	West Ham United
18	Southampton	Southampton	Aston Villa	Manchester City	Sunderland	Bolton Wanderers	Charlton Athletic	Wimbledon	Manchester City	Ipswich Town	West Ham United	Leicester City	Crystal Palace	Birmingham City	Sheffield United	Reading	Newcastle United	Burnley
19	Oldham Athletic	Ipswich Town	Crystal Palace	QPR	Middlesbrough	Barnsley	Blackburn Rovers	Sheffield Wednesday	Coventry City	Derby County	West Bromwich Albion	Leeds United	Norwich City	West Bromwich Albion	Charlton Athletic	Birmingham City	Middlesbrough	Hull City
20	Crystal Palace	Sheffield United	Norwich City	Bolton Wanderers	Nottingham Forest	Crystal Palace	Nottingham Forest	Watford	Bradford City	Leicester City	Sunderland	Wolverhampton Wanderers	Southampton	Sunderland	Watford	Derby County	West Bromwich Albion	Portsmouth*
21	Middlesbrough	Oldham Athletic	Leicester City															
22	Nottingham Forest	Swindon Town	Ipswich Town															

who finished 5th in 2001 with an £XI that cost just 22.3% of Arsenal's, but who appear in a more densely shaded section of the map. While Everton had the lowest percentage, Ipswich remain the cheapest top-four team: an £XI of just £21.8m, almost £6m below Everton's (the difference being that Chelsea's wealth raised the high-water mark after 2003).

Table: Cost In Relation To League Position: Top five Only

1992-3	1993-4	1994-5	1995-6	1996-7	1997-98	1998-9	1999-0	2000-1	2001-2	2002-3	2003-4	2004-5	2005-6	2006-7	2007-8	2008-9	2009-10

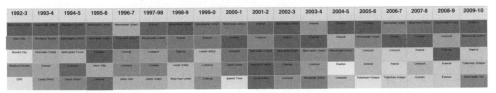

Beyond 2001/02, there are only a few examples of significant over- or underachievement in the entire map. Manchester City in 2008/09 leap out as a dark shade amid lighter rectangles, while Newcastle's position in the bottom three that same season is clearly a case of massive mis-management. Spurs were in the bottom two when Harry Redknapp took over early in 2007/08, and even though they eventually finished 11th they were still seven places below their expected placing.

Fulham, Bolton and Blackburn each have a season or two in which they appear significantly higher than expected, and Reading finishing 8th in 2006/07 was a minor miracle. Otherwise, the dispersal is minimal.

Trend Analysis

The following section uses various indicators employed in industrial studies to measure the competitiveness of industries.

Four-Firm Concentration Ratio (CR4)

CR4 is a common indicator used to show the extent of market control of the four largest firms in an industry and to illustrate the degree to which an industry is trending towards monopoly (or at least oligopoly).

Medium concentration starts at 50% and this indicates oligopoly. High concentration starts at 80%.

In Premier League terms the CR4 is useful as there are four Champions League spots up for grabs every season while the term 'big four' is commonplace. The chart (overleaf) shows the £XI CR4 of the teams who finished in the top four positions in each Premier League season. The chart also shows the amount of Champions League spots open to Premier League clubs and overlays key events.

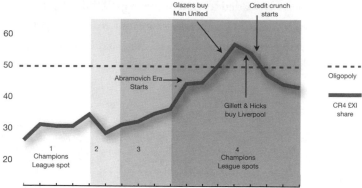

£XI concentration of top 4 clubs

The period from 1998/99 to 2002/03 sees a sharp rise in the £XI CR4 of 13.4%. This coincided with the increase to three and then four Champions League qualifying positions. The first three years of what could be called the Abramovich Era then sees another surge through the 50% barrier to a peak of 56.8% in 2005/06.

The rise in the CR4 can be explained by the fact that in the 2002/03 to 2006/07 period, the four teams with the greatest £XI finished in either the top four positions (2003, 2006) or the top three positions and 5th (2004, 2005, 2007). Every year before and since has seen at least one of the most expensive £XIs underperform and finish down the table. This was when the 'big four' were not only investing in their squads but, crucially, were also managed by Alex Ferguson, José Mourinho, Arsène Wenger and Rafa Benítez – four internationally renowned bosses. In this period, Benítez, twice, and Wenger, once, took their sides to Champions League finals, while Chelsea were perennial semi-finalists. With Manchester United reaching two finals shortly after, this was arguably the strongest the top four has been in English football history. Unfortunately, it meant that they were head and shoulders above everyone else in the Premier League.

Herfindahl-Hirschman Index

The CR4 is useful in illustrating such inequalities between the top four and the rest. However, to look at the inequalities between all the firms in an industry (or all the clubs in a league), you need to consider the market share of each. The Herfindahl-Hirschman Index (or HH Index) allows us to do this. The HH Index is widely used as any rise signifies an increase in inequality.

(The United States uses the HH Index to determine whether mergers are equitable to society; increases of over 0.0100 points generally provoke scrutiny, although this varies from case to case. The Department of Justice considers HH indices between

0.1000 and 0.1800 to be moderately concentrated and indices above 0.1800 to be concentrated. As the market concentration increases, competition and efficiency decrease and the chances of collusion and monopoly increase.)

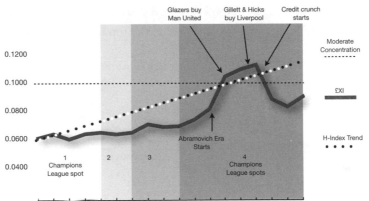

HH Index of Competitiveness

The HHI has a similar line to the CR4. Both graphs show the Premier League going beyond a key threshold and into the realms of oligopoly for the same three seasons, 2005-2007. This aligns with Mourinho's reign at Chelsea. In the first year of the Abramovich Era under Claudio Ranieri, the HHI showed an above-average 10% increase. However in the first year under Mourinho, the HHI saw its biggest year-on-year rise, a massive 29%. In the year Mourinho left Chelsea (also the year the credit crunch started), the HHI shows its biggest year-on-year fall: 22%.

As the CR4 and HHI show a similar pattern, we need to look at another measure to get a holistic view of competitive balance in the Premier League era. The Lorenz Curve is a traditional measure used for income distribution and social inequality. For £XI in the Premier League era, the Lorenz Curve gives us our most conclusive results yet.

Lorenz Curve

The purpose of the Lorenz Curve is to show the concentration of ownership of economic quantities such as wealth and income; it is formed by plotting the cumulative distribution of the amount of the variable concerned against the cumulative frequency distribution of the individuals possessing the amount. The closer the data lines are to the diagonal 'equality' line, the fairer the distribution of wealth.

In terms of Premier League equality, 1998/99 generally tracks closest on the Lorenz Curve. This was the last time that the league as a whole saw a fair

	Season	
	1998-9	**2006-7**
1	Manchester United	Manchester United
2	Arsenal	Chelsea
3	Chelsea	Liverpool
4	Leeds United	Arsenal
5	West Ham United	Tottenham Hotspur
6	Aston Villa	Everton
7	Liverpool	Bolton Wanderers
8	Derby County	Reading
9	Middlesbrough	Portsmouth
10	Leicester City	Blackburn Rovers
11	Tottenham Hotspur	Aston Villa
12	Sheffield Wednesday	Middlesbrough
13	Newcastle United	Newcastle United
14	Everton	Manchester City
15	Coventry City	West Ham United
16	Wimbledon	Fulham
17	Southampton	Wigan Athletic
18	Charlton Athletic	Sheffield United
19	Blackburn Rovers	Charlton Athletic
20	Nottingham Forest	Watford

The heatmap above shows the Premier League's two most contrasting seasons in terms of wealth distribution; far less predictability in terms of finishing position in 1999 than eight years later.

distribution of wealth. The first season of the Abramovich Era – 2003/04 – shows a sharp rise in the cumulative £XI of the top five clubs (56%) before the curve flattens out somewhat.

We have already established that the plutocratic peak of the Premier League was 2005-2007. The 2006/07 season is one of five shown in the graph below, and you can see 40% of the cumulative £XI in the top two and 61% in the top five (up from 33% in 97/98).

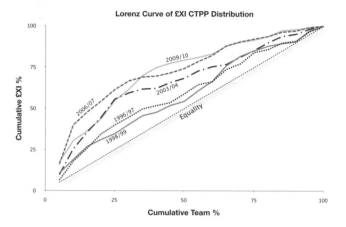

Lorenz Curve of £XI CTPP Distribution

By 2009/10 there was a new popular concept of a "top eight". This was the traditional 'big four' plus Man City, Spurs, Everton and Aston Villa. Most fans and pundits seemed to think the top eight were in a league of their own and a significant cut above the rest of the Premier League. The Lorenz Curve confirms this. In 2009/10, 75% of the cumulative £XI is in the top eight clubs. Ten years earlier the figure was only 45%.

The 2009/10 line outperforms all others from 8th to 12th positions, suggesting that another level of inequality may have been built into the league. This compression of £XI into the top 8/top 12 has to come at the expense of somewhere else. There's a slight narrowing between the top four and the rest but, unsurprisingly, the impact is mainly felt at the bottom of the league. The bottom seven clubs in 2009/10 represented a mere 10% of the cumulative £XI. In the 1990s this figure was as much as 23%. The bottom three clubs had a measly 2% of the cumulative £XI. Frankly, it's a miracle if any promoted club manages to hold onto its Premier League status for even a single season.

Conclusions

Both the CR4 and HHI show how inequality in the Premier League has increased steadily since its inception. The rate of increase quickened at the turn of the century but accelerated sharply in the Abramovich Era to the extent that the league officially became an oligopoly for three seasons. Only the credit crunch halted the upward trend. The Lorenz Curve demonstrates that while the Premier League has become more unequal, there are other noticeable trends. A greater percentage of the clubs at the top are increasing their £XI at the expense of the sides at the bottom. The clubs at the bottom of the Premier League have never had it so bad. Not only is competing with the top clubs an impossible dream but it's even becoming more difficult to compete with the middle-tier clubs as well. With the current season already under way, uncompetitiveness remains historically high, and the Premier League is once again on the verge of becoming an oligopoly.

The Price of Ultimate Success

In the 18 Premier League seasons to date, the team with the highest £XI has won the title on 10 occasions: 55% of the time. In the first nine years this happened just four times; meaning that more often than not, the most expensive side did not end up as champions. However, in the most recent nine seasons, the costliest £XI has landed the title on six occasions. So, the likelihood has increased from 44% of the time between 1992 and 2001 to 66% of the time between 2002 and 2010.

Of the other eight Premier League crowns, four went to the second-most expensive side: two in the '90s, two in the '00s. Since the end of 2000/01, only once has a club that didn't have the most or second-most expensive £XI won the title: Arsenal's incredible 2003/2004 Invincibles, with a fourth-place ranking.

Prior to this date, the three 'cheapest' £XIs to win the title all belong to Manchester United: the fifth-highest £XI in both 1995/96 and 2000/01, and the six-highest in 1996/97. Expressed as a percentage of the most expensive £XI, the most impressive figure for a title winner comes from 1997, when Manchester United were champions with an £XI that worked out at only 51.4% of Newcastle United's. (Largely down to the number of home-grown players in Alex Ferguson's team.) The next lowest percentage belongs to Arsenal's unbeaten side, at just 63.7% of Chelsea's first Abramovich-era £XI.

On average, during the 18 Premier League seasons, the title-winners had a ranking of 89% of the cost of the most expensive £XI; as previously stated, ten times the champions contributed the full 100% figure. Between 1992 and 2001, the champions averaged 87%, and since 2001, the figure has risen to 91%; not a great increase, but an increase all the same. So in other words, on average, if your £XI is not the costliest, it needs to cost at least 89% of the costliest to win the title. The heat map below shows each year's champions, with the relative shades representing the cost of the £XI in relation to the most expensive that season.

£XI Rank For season	Season	Champions	% of season's most expensive £XI	£XI	Cost Per Point	Points
1	1992-3	Manchester United	100.00%	£73,379,127	£873,561	84
1	1993-4	Manchester United	100.00%	£92,208,897	£1,002,271	92
1	1994-5	Blackburn Rovers	100.00%	£87,541,696	£983,615	89
5	1995-6	Manchester United	79.20%	£70,776,892	£863,133	82
6	1996-7	Manchester United	51.40%	£59,611,462	£794,819	75
2	1997-8	Arsenal	93.90%	£85,245,901	£1,092,896	78
1	1998-9	Manchester United	100.00%	£106,197,289	£1,344,269	79
2	1999-0	Manchester United	82.00%	£104,323,670	£1,146,414	91
5	2000-1	Manchester United	78.60%	£78,358,412	£979,480	80
1	2000-2	Arsenal	100.00%	£104,115,888	£1,196,734	87
1	2002-3	Manchester United	100.00%	£113,757,434	£1,370,571	83
4	2003-4	Arsenal	63.70%	£95,692,961	£1,063,255	90
1	2004-5	Chelsea	100.00%	£195,163,150	£2,054,349	95
1	2005-6	Chelsea	100.00%	£229,619,425	£2,523,290	91
1	2006-7	Manchester United	69.20%	£171,702,282	£1,929,239	89
2	2007-8	Manchester United	88.50%	£167,770,664	£1,928,398	87
2	2008-9	Manchester United	95.50%	£158,436,770	£1,760,409	90
1	2009-10	Chelsea	100.00%	£187,436,346.00	£2,179,492	86
2.1			89.00%	£121,185,459	£1,393,678	86

The average £XI of the title winners in the first half of the Premier League era is clearly dwarfed by the more recent figure: £84.2m up to 2001, compared with £158.2m thereafter. Year seven was the first time an £XI went above £100m (Manchester United), and within a further seven years it had surpassed the £200m mark (Chelsea). Remember, all these values are converted to today's prices.

Only once during the first five seasons did the cost per point of the champions rise above the £1m mark: Manchester United in 1993/94; and even then, the figure was only just beyond £1m, at £1,002,271. However, in the most recent 13 seasons, it's only once fallen below £1m – and again, it was Manchester United, and again, it was marginal (£979,480).

In the first nine seasons, the champions' average cost per point was £1,008,940; in the next nine seasons, £1,778,415 – a rise of 76%.

Four clubs have won the Premier League title: United on 11 occasions, Arsenal and Chelsea three times each, and Blackburn once. But to win the title for the 'first' time – meaning after a significant break (and on average it was approximately 40 years since the pre-Premier League titles of these clubs) – three of those four 'first timers' had the most expensive £XI (Man United, Blackburn and Chelsea), and the other, Arsenal, wasn't far behind at 94%. So over those four seasons, the average was 98.5%. While this is a small sample size, it seems to support the accepted wisdom that to win a title for the first time is the hardest; not least, in psychological terms, when the pressure really starts to mount. It seems that to overcome this hurdle an even more expensive team is required; more or less the most expensive in the land.

Chapter Five:
Squad Analysis

As we've already seen, the cost per point for the £XI is very revealing, showing that fielding the most expensive side leads to the title more often than not. But what about the overall squad cost (Sq£)? After all, even if players aren't utilised, they are still on hand (unless injured), just in case. A bigger squad means increased competition amongst the players, and more choice for the manager. Above all else, it provides *insurance*.

In current money, the most expensive squad ever seen in the Premier League is Chelsea's from 2006/07, at a mind-boggling £439m. The next six places in the top 10 are also taken up by Abramovich-years Chelsea, with Manchester United also occupying seven positions in a row, from 8th to 14th. These two clubs therefore inhabit the top 14 places, before the duopoly is broken by Manchester City's 2009/10 squad. Perhaps surprisingly, Spurs appear next on the list, with their collection of players in 2008/09. Newcastle and Arsenal each appear twice between 17th and 20th. All of the top 20 have a CTPP cost in excess of £200m.

It's clear that some of those sides enjoyed success: Chelsea won the league (although not in 2007 with their costliest squad); Manchester United won the league with their two costliest squads (but came 2nd, 2nd and 3rd with their third-, fourth- and fifth-most expensive ones); Arsenal won the league with their second-most expensive collection of players (yet not with their most expensive); but Manchester City, Spurs and Newcastle all fell short of expectations during their 'top 20' seasons.

Most Expensive Premier League Squads (CTPP)

#	Team	League Position	Year	Sq£	£XI	Unused Squad (£)
1	Chelsea	2	2006/07	£438,985,943	£255,266,748	£183,719,195
2	Chelsea	2	2007/08	£432,360,309	£201,709,707	£230,650,602
3	Chelsea	1	2005/06	£415,553,023	£229,619,425	£185,933,598
4	Chelsea	1	2009/10	£401,297,570	£187,436,346	£213,861,224
5	Chelsea	1	2004/05	£391,093,809	£195,163,150	£195,930,659
6	Chelsea	3	2008/09	£376,624,798	£168,193,359	£208,431,439
7	Chelsea	2	2003/04	£337,922,626	£153,144,833	£184,777,793
8	Man United	1	2008/09	£297,526,757	£158,436,770	£139,089,987
9	Man United	1	2007/08	£288,560,616	£171,806,255	£116,754,361
10	Man United	2	2009/10	£281,728,812	£141,384,155	£140,344,657
11	Man United	2	2005/06	£273,760,465	£161,688,549	£112,071,916
12	Man United	3	2004/05	£270,622,126	£149,992,332	£120,629,794
13	Man United	1	2006/07	£259,498,185	£171,702,282	£87,795,903
14	Man United	3	2001/02	£225,870,100	£95,175,852	£130,694,248
15	Man City	5	2009/10	£223,413,108	£121,147,357	£102,265,751
16	Spurs	8	2008/09	£215,429,965	£93,623,149	£121,806,816
17	Newcastle	13	1998/99	£210,471,784	£94,802,568	£115,669,216
18	Arsenal	2	2002/03	£204,149,376	£111,559,544	£92,589,832
19	Arsenal	1	2001/02	£201,515,504	£104,115,888	£97,399,616
20	Newcastle	11	1999/00	£201,433,953	£118,233,197	£83,200,756

What about the cost per point in relation to squad value (rather than in relation to £XI, as discussed earlier)? What's most interesting here is that three seasons of failure rank within the top 10; including both positions in the top two. Kenny Dalglish's Newcastle won points at a cost of almost £6m each in relation to their Sq£; part of the problem was that Alan Shearer, who accounted for £39m of their playing staff, missed a lot of that season. Even so, it was a bitterly disappointing campaign, as was the case with Blackburn a year later, when the side managed first by Roy Hodgson and then by Brian Kidd suffered relegation. In both cases, the Sq£ was fairly high, and the points return insufficient.

As with the £XI analysis, Chelsea (2006/07) rank highly, rising from £3.1m to £5.3m when taking the whole set-up into account. Basically, over the course of the season, £184m of talent didn't make the starting XI. Some of this would have been down to injury, some of it down to resting big-name players, and some of it providing the luxury of a bench worth its weight in gold.

One particular surprise is Sunderland's presence — with their 2002/03 squad — in the top 10. Although that particular squad was nowhere near as expensive as the others at the top of the list — it's the only one that cost less than £100m — the winning of a paltry 19 points makes for a hefty cost of £4.2m each.

Most Expensive Cost Per Point (Squad)

#	Club	Year	Sq£	Points	Cost Per Point	Manager
1	Newcastle United	1997/98	£259,498,185	44	£5,897,686	Kenny Dalglish
2	Blackburn	1998/99	£185,216,234	35	£5,291,892	Roy Hodgson/Brian Kidd
3	Chelsea	2006/07	£438,985,943	83	£5,288,987	José Mourinho
4	Chelsea	2003/04	£401,297,570	79	£5,079,716	Claudio Raniero
5	Man United	2004/05	£376,624,798	77	£4,891,231	Alex Ferguson
6	Chelsea	2005/06	£432,360,309	91	£4,751,212	José Mourinho
7	Chelsea	2007/08	£391,093,809	85	£4,601,104	Mourinho/Avram Grant
8	Newcastle United	1998/99	£204,149,376	46	£4,438,030	Ruud Gullit
9	Chelsea	2004/05	£415,553,023	95	£4,374,242	José Mourinho
10	Sunderland	2002/03	£80,496,911	19	£4,236,680	3 Managers
11	Man City	2009/10	£281,728,812	67	£4,204,908	Hughes/Mancini
12	Man United	2005/06	£337,922,626	83	£4,071,357	Alex Ferguson
13	Tottenham	2007/08	£178,944,744	46	£3,890,103	Martin Jol
14	Newcastle United	2006/07	£165,304,917	43	£3,844,300	Glenn Roeder
15	Newcastle United	1999/00	£199,276,660	52	£3,832,243	Gullit/Bobby Robson
16	Everton	1997/98	£146,782,278	40	£3,669,557	Howard Kendall
17	Man United	2003/04	£273,760,465	75	£3,650,140	Alex Ferguson
18	Tottenham	2008/09	£185,287,281	51	£3,633,084	Harry Redknapp
19	Liverpool	2004/05	£201,433,953	58	£3,472,999	Rafael Benítez
20	Chelsea	2009/10	£297,526,757	86	£3,459,613	Carlo Ancelotti

Points pro rata for 42-game seasons.

Remarkably, at the other end of the cost effectiveness rankings, Bolton take up four of the top seven places; the figures again confirming Sam Allardyce's mastery of the plucky underdog role at the Reebok. As well as Bolton, Ipswich, Wimbledon, Reading and Norwich all feature more than once in the top 20. What's particularly interesting is that Norwich were relegated in 2005 with a similar cost per point to when they finished 3rd just over a decade earlier — when they gained 72 points, and qualified for Europe.

Top 20 - Best Value Cost Per Point (Squad)

#	Club	Year	Sq£	PTS	Cost Per Point	Manager
1	Bolton	2004/05	£6,113,683	58	£105,408	Sam Allardyce
2	Bolton	2003/04	£7,949,068	53	£149,982	Sam Allardyce
3	Ipswich Town	1992/93	£12,480,387	52	£240,007	John Lyall
4	QPR	1994/95	£20,151,983	60	£335,866	Francis/Ray Wilkins
5	Reading	2006/07	£19,244,845	55	£349,906	Steve Coppell
6	Bolton	2005/06	£20,451,194	56	£365,200	Sam Allardyce
7	Bolton	2001/02	£15,322,496	40	£383,062	Sam Allardyce
8	Southampton	2000/01	£20,090,507	52	£386,356	Hoddle/Stuart Gray
9	Wimbledon	1993/94	£27,790,344	65	£427,544	Joe Kinnear
10	Reading	2007/08	£15,687,338	36	£435,759	Steve Coppell
11	Wimbledon	1996/97	£25,192,853	56	£449,872	Joe Kinnear
12	Bolton	2002/03	£19,926,303	44	£452,871	Sam Allardyce
13	Burnley	2009/10	£13,712,798	30	£457,093	Owen Coyle/Brian Laws
14	Norwich City	2004/05	£15,230,198	33	£461,521	Nigel Worthington
15	Watford	1999/00	£11,196,496	24	£466,521	Graham Taylor
16	Ipswich Town	2000/01	£30,962,486	66	£469,129	George Burley
17	Norwich City	1992/93	£34,609,588	72	£480,689	Mike Walker
18	Sheffield United	1992/93	£25,232,612	52	£485,243	Dave Bassett
19	Norwich City	1993/94	£26,323,781	53	£496,675	Walker/Deehan
20	Coventry City	1993/94	£27,865,551	56	£497,599	Bobby Gould/Phil Neal

Points pro rata for 42-game seasons.

Squad Expense in Relation to Winning the Title

While Manchester United won three of their first five titles (all between 1993 and 1997) with the league's costliest £XIs, it wasn't until 2002 that they topped the 'most expensive squad' chart (although ironically, when they finally did, they finished as runners-up to Arsenal in the title race). In 2002/03 they retained top spot in the costliest Sq£, and also landed the Premier League crown. These were their only two seasons at the top of the Sq£ rankings; by 2003/04, Chelsea had begun their dominance of the category. For the next six years, as they shared titles with the Londoners, United ranked in second place.

What's interesting is that not once in the first 10 seasons of the Premier League did a club with the most expensive squad win the title. However, in the past eight seasons it has happened on four occasions: three times with Chelsea, once with United.

Liverpool, for the first three seasons, followed by Blackburn for one year in 1995/96, and Newcastle, for the next four seasons, possessed the costliest squads in the first eight Premier League seasons. The title eluded the most expensive squad on all of those occasions, proving that money didn't guarantee success. Blackburn finished 7th, just a year after winning the league. Newcastle flitted between 2nd and 13th. And Liverpool finished 6th, 8th and 4th.

Top Four

Although the number of entrants into the Champions League began with just one, and has been limited to just two or three clubs on other occasions, the top four has come to represent what it takes to qualify for the competition. Therefore, it is worth looking at the change in the wherewithal needed to finish in the first four positions.

Average Sq£ of Top Four

Season	Sq£ of Top Four	Squad cost as % of champions
1992/93	£77,972,464	63.9%
1993/94	£103,481,203	81.8%
1994/95	£122,322,185	86.4%
1995/96	£122,864,316	111.4%
1996/97	£134,118,926	119.5%
1997/98	£126,879,481	90.5%
1998/99	£128,457,843	74.1%
1999/00	£143,152,150	78.2%
2000/01	£165,146,423	90.2%
(1992–2001 Average)	(£124,932,777)	(84.4%)
2001/02	£183,327,960	91.0%
2002/03	£183,397,001	99.0%
2003/04	£226,755,206	114.5%
2004/05	£226,755,206	57.8%
2005/06	£264,209,967	63.6%
2006/07	£252,129,775	97.2%
2007/08	£264,738,345	91.8%
2008/09	£241,186,193	81.1%
2009/10	£247,685,860	61.7%
(2001–2010 Average)	(£232,169,917)	(84.2%)
1992–2010 Average	**£178,551,347**	**86.3%**

As mentioned in the previous chapter, only 12 clubs have featured in the top four since the Premier League was formed; Manchester United, Aston Villa, Norwich, Blackburn, Newcastle, Liverpool, Arsenal, Nottingham Forest, Chelsea and Leeds were the 10 to do so between 1992 and 2001. Since the end of 2000/01, only two 'new' clubs have broken into that group – Everton and Spurs – with the overall number of top four clubs across those nine seasons reduced to seven; not least because neither Manchester United nor Arsenal have finished outside the top four since 1996.

The Great Unused

So what percentage of talent on a club's books goes unused (in terms of the starting XI) throughout a season? And how does that figure correlate with success and failure?

First of all it's important to note that it's impossible to say, by looking purely at the numbers, whether exclusions were down to tactics, form or injury. Managers may have bought unwisely, and ended up with a surplus of talent (in some cases they may have bought too many good players and, with no injuries, simply not have had enough chances to play them all; in other cases, if the player turned out to be as good as useless, the word *talent* may simply be a misnomer). Or they could have had wretched luck, with their costliest signings sitting out much of the campaign with knee ligament injuries and broken legs.

What's fascinating – and unexpected, in the age of mega-squads and rotation – is that, on the whole, successful clubs utilise (in the £XI) a greater percentage of their resources than unsuccessful ones. On average, the top four between 1992 and 2010 used 55% of their overall squad expenditure in their starting XIs. Further down, teams that finished between 5th and 17th (or between 5th and 19th in 1993-1995) used 51.7% of their squad. And surprisingly, relegated sides utilised only 47.4% of the cost of the players at their disposal; the only group to omit more of their resources (in CTPP terms) than they deployed from the start of games.

Now, did the failure of those clubs occur because of badly managed resources, or were they forced to get by without those players? Unfortunately, without investigating each on a case-by-case basis, there's no way of knowing.

Of the 50 'worst' cases of non-utilised squad excess – expressed as a percentage of the unused players' CTPP – only three were top four sides: Liverpool in 1997/98 (62.5% unused); Everton in 2004/05 (60.6% unused); and Manchester United in 2001/02 (57.9% unused). None of these sides finished higher than 3rd. By contrast, no fewer than 19 of the 50 were relegated. On the whole, the average league position for these sides was 15th.

At the other end of the scale, the fortunes of those clubs who used the highest percentage of their available resources was more mixed: nine finished in the top four, five were relegated, and the remaining 36 were somewhere in between.

Of course, for teams lower down the table, 30% of their entire squad expenditure can easily be accounted for with just one or two players; injuries, or bad buys, can be especially hard to cope with. When Sheffield United were relegated in 2007, 70.3% of their Sq£ went unused. But as that 70.3% equated to just £18m (CTPP, as with all the figures in this section), then even if this represented their best players, this was clearly not a selection of world-class talent. Contrast that with Chelsea, who occupy the top seven places when it comes to the cost of the talent that didn't make the starting XI. In that same season, 53.3% of their squad expense was not utilised from the start of matches: a staggering £230.7m.

To complete the top 10, Manchester United rank 8th, 9th and 10th. But the first major surprise is Blackburn's appearance at 11th: in 1998/99, when they suffered relegation. While £68.2m featured in the £XI – the highest amount for any side that suffered demotion – an incredible £122.8m was accounted for by a combination of substitutes, unfortunately injured stars and peripheral characters (such as £17m Kevin Davies). You have to go down the list to number 73 to find the next relegated side: Newcastle United from 2009, with £64.8m of unused talent; almost exactly half of the overall squad cost.

At the other end of this particular table – those who fielded most of the money they had spent on players – only three of those ranked in the lowest 125 (out of 366 teams) finished in the top four of the Premier League: Aston Villa from 1996, ranked 280th, with £21.5m of unused talent; Norwich from 1993, ranked 318th, with just £15.5m of unused talent; and Aston Villa again, also from 1993, with only £11.5m (of a £67.3m squad) of unused talent. You have to go as high as 146th place – Everton, 2005 – to find a top four side from this millennium. In that bottom 125, no fewer than 36 teams were relegated – more than 10 times the amount that finished 4th or above. Even though they were able to utilise the vast majority of their resources, it often ended in failure.

Competitive Balance and Squad Costs

In 1992/93, there were just five places separating the average Sq£ of the top four, the 'rest of table' and those doomed to Division One.

(Note: these three averages are listed as being part of each season's league table; so that instead of 20 teams, there are 23, with 25 between 1993 and 1995. Therefore, if one of these three averages was higher than that of the team that finished 3rd, then that team would be pushed down into 4th, and so on.)

In that first season, the average squad value of the top four teams ranked 7th (because some expensive squads underperformed); the average of the 'rest of table' ranked 12th; and the average of the relegated teams ranked 14th. Only once since then – 1998/99 – has the grouping been so close together: 7th, 12th and 13th, although by then there were two fewer teams. Otherwise the general trend, bar the occasional surprise, has been one of a widening gap between the bands.

While the gap between the averages has expanded and contracted to varying degrees over the past 18 years, it has never once changed order: the 'top four' average is always higher than the 'rest of table' average, which in turn is higher than the 'relegated' average [see graph overleaf].

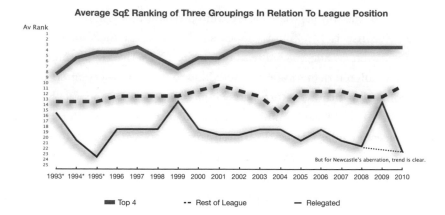

Average Sq£ Ranking of Three Groupings In Relation To League Position

Av Rank

But for Newcastle's aberration, trend is clear.

1993* 1994* 1995* 1996 1997 1998 1999 2000 2001 2002 2003 2004 2005 2006 2007 2008 2009 2010

■ Top 4   - - Rest of League   — Relegated

On two of the three occasions when the average Sq£ of relegated teams rose to become almost equal with the 'rest of league', this was due to an expensively assembled collection of players failing their club: Blackburn in 1999, and Newcastle a decade later. The other occasion – 1993 – was the one time when all three relegated teams ranked fairly highly in the table; on paper, based on the money spent on their players, they should have remained top-flight clubs, with at least six others ranked below them. This was also the same season that clubs ranked 10th and 18th in Sq£ cost finished in the top four. This – the inaugural Premier League campaign – was the picture of a relative meritocracy.

Come forward to the four most recent seasons, and the picture changes.

Each time, the average Sq£ of the top four ranked 3rd (two of the sides above it, two below it; just as has been the case for eight of the past nine years). The average for the 'rest of table' sides ranked between 10th and 12th (pretty much in keeping with the entire 18 seasons). And the relegated teams were ranked 20th or below in three of the four years (Newcastle's aforementioned 2009 squad explaining the one anomaly). Between 1999 and 2006, the average Sq£ of the relegated sides was six places from the bottom of the table; in 2007 it was five places; in 2008 it was four places; and in 2010 it was down to just two places from the foot of the table.

All of this effectively means that the seven-place gap between the 'top', the 'rest' and the 'relegated' in 1993 had expanded to 19 places by 2010. What began as a meritocracy has become an imbalanced league, courtesy of a very unequal distribution of money. While the cash has helped bring some of the world's best footballers to these shores, it has also seen cases of stockpiling (Yuri Zhirkov, Ryan Babel, David Bentley, Jo and Anderson being the equivalent of the EU butter mountain), and a reduction of competitive balance.

Chapter Six:
Transfer Fee by Age, Position and Nationality

The talent of an individual is not the only factor taken into account when a transfer fee is determined. The position he plays is one consideration, his age another. There's also his nationality; while overseas players seem to possess greater technical ability, they are often at a disadvantage when it comes to the language and the style of football in England, and will be more prone to homesickness.

Position

The notion that the goalkeeper – the one truly specialist football position, not to mention the vital last line of defence – is the most undervalued in the transfer market is backed up by statistics. On average, it is the cheapest position so far as transfers are concerned; with prices rising in increments as you move further up the pitch. (In this section, actual transfer fees take preference over CTPP.)

In actual, uninflated terms, the average cost of a striker over the course of the entire Premier League is £2.9m – as it happens, the exact same figure as the British transfer record when the old First Division changed name, paid for Dean Saunders, who of course was himself a forward. However, the goalkeeper's average is just £1m, with defenders (£1.7m) and midfielders (£2.1m) rising up the scale. Even now, a goalkeeper has yet to cost in excess of £10m in British football (although Arsenal were reported to have bid £21m for Liverpool's Pepe Reina in the summer of 2010, and before his head injury, Petr Čech was worth at least that amount). In 2008/09, Premier League clubs spent £305.7m on strikers, and just £26m on goalkeepers. Of course, only one goalkeeper can start a game, whereas two or three strikers can be in the XI (even more if some are played in midfield, something a goalkeeper can't do). Even so, a club needs a minimum of two senior goalkeepers in the squad, and perhaps only four strikers. On average, four times as many forwards are transferred in a season as those whose job it is to deny them. Perhaps this is because once a club finds a good keeper it tends to stick with him for a number of years; and even though they may take a buffeting, injuries are less common and careers last longer (another reason to invest heavily in a top-class custodian; plenty still look the part at 40).

	92-93	93-94	94-95	95-96	96-97	97-98	98-99	99-00	00-01	01-02	02-03	03-04	04-05	05-06	06-07	07-08	08-09	09-10	AV.
Total cost by position																			
Goalkeeper	£1.8	£3.4	£1.2	£4.0	£7.8	£10.7	£4.4	£12.6	£10.4	£36.9	£12.0	£19.4	£4.3	£13.7	£14.3	£12.0	£26.2	£3.6	**£11.0**
Defender	£14.5	£22.7	£32.6	£41.7	£30.9	£72.3	£77.7	£62.2	£101.5	£63.5	£82.7	£31.4	£57.3	£66.2	£117.0	£152.9	£184.1	£166.2	**£76.5**
Midfielder	£10.2	£22.4	£22.5	£43.3	£37.3	£55.0	£56.3	£69.5	£92.2	£124.9	£48.5	£94.3	£93.8	£103.9	£92.9	£227.8	£194.6	£162.6	**£86.2**
Forward	£31.3	£30.1	£60.3	£82.7	£55.4	£83.3	£124.7	£93.6	£115.0	£142.5	£84.5	£145.5	£138.1	£154.5	£158.2	£231.7	£305.7	£158.1	**£122.0**
Number of transfers by position																			
Goalkeeper	6	5	8	9	13	14	9	14	12	12	15	18	10	18	12	6	12	5	**11.0**
Defender	30	37	37	36	33	49	57	42	52	37	28	41	41	38	58	62	42	49	**42.7**
Midfielder	19	30	24	24	23	43	35	38	41	36	30	38	55	43	47	56	46	42	**37.2**
Forward	43	45	42	43	36	62	56	44	42	40	23	43	39	47	48	53	45	30	**43.4**
Average cost by position																			
Goalkeeper	£0.3	£0.7	£0.1	£0.4	£0.6	£0.8	£0.5	£0.9	£0.9	£3.1	£0.8	£1.1	£0.4	£0.8	£1.2	£2.0	£2.2	£0.7	**£1.0**
Defender	£0.5	£0.6	£0.9	£1.2	£0.9	£1.5	£1.4	£1.5	£2.0	£1.7	£3.0	£0.8	£1.4	£1.7	£2.0	£2.5	£4.4	£3.4	**£1.7**
Midfielder	£0.5	£0.7	£0.9	£1.8	£1.6	£1.3	£1.6	£1.8	£2.2	£3.5	£1.6	£2.5	£1.7	£2.4	£2.0	£4.1	£4.2	£3.9	**£2.1**
Forward	£0.7	£0.7	£1.4	£1.9	£1.5	£1.3	£2.2	£2.1	£2.7	£3.6	£3.7	£3.4	£3.5	£3.3	£3.3	£4.4	£6.8	£5.3	**£2.9**

Age

On average, over the past 18 years, the most expensive players have been aged between 21 and 25. The age ranges either side – 16-20 and 26-30 – share the same average fee: £1.8m; but in the middle the figure stands at £2.1m.

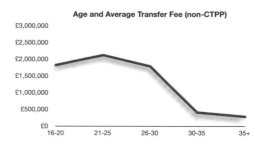

Age and Average Transfer Fee (non-CTPP)

The 21-25 age group is more costly for a reason. While players aged under 21 may have glittering careers ahead of them (such as Wayne Rooney, in 2004 – a sure-fire thing when purchased at the age of 18), and those in their late 20s are generally regarded as being at the peak of their powers, these two age groups also offer drawbacks: inexperience and shorter careers (and a lower – or zero – sell-on value) respectively. At the age of 22/23, a player may have full international experience – and therefore be proven as 'the real deal' – and comes with the chance of either a decade's service, or a fairly high sell-on fee in four or five years' time. Teenagers can be too unpredictable (most youth development coaches see 21/22 as the age when a player is fully matured – by which time you know what you're going to get), and older players are closer to winding down their careers.

Wingers and strikers tend to peak earlier – when raw pace will get them by – while defenders and goalkeepers, who rely more on positional sense borne of experience, mature later in their careers.

	92-93	93-94	94-95	95-96	96-97	97-98	98-99	99-00	00-01	01-02	02-03	03-04	04-05	05-06	06-07	07-08	08-09	09-10	AV.
Average cost by age group																			
16-20	£0.2	£0.2	£0.9	£0.3	£0.6	£0.9	£0.6	£2.3	£1.0	£4.1	£1.8	£2.6	£4.6	£2.1	£1.2	£4.2	£3.1	£2.0	**£1.8**
21-25	£0.5	£0.5	£1.1	£1.4	£1.3	£0.9	£1.7	£1.7	£2.3	£2.5	£2.5	£2.3	£1.8	£3.0	£2.0	£3.5	£4.3	£4.8	**£2.1**
26-30	£0.6	£0.8	£0.9	£1.5	£1.2	£1.5	£1.7	£1.7	£1.9	£2.5	£1.4	£1.2	£1.7	£1.2	£2.1	£2.6	£4.6	£3.0	**£1.8**
30-35	£0.2	£0.2	£0.3	£0.4	£0.3	£0.5	£0.9	£0.4	£0.3	£0.2	£0.0	£0.3	£0.1	£0.3	£0.3	£0.3	£1.4	£0.9	**£0.4**
35+	£0.0	£0.0	£0.0	£0.0	£0.1	£0.5	£0.0	£0.1	£0.1	£0.1	£0.1	£0.3	£0.0	£0.0	£0.4	£0.0	£2.5	£0.8	**£0.3**

Nationality

Perhaps surprisingly, given the premium apparently placed on them due to various 'home-grown' rulings over the years, British players are actually cheaper on average than those from overseas. European Union and non-EU European countries rank highest, at £2.3m each, with Rest of the World at £2.1m, and British players at £2m; not a huge difference, admittedly.

	92-93	93-94	94-95	95-96	96-97	97-98	98-99	99-00	00-01	01-02	02-03	03-04	04-05	05-06	06-07	07-08	08-09	00-10	AV.
Total cost by nationality																			
UK	£44.8	£66.3	£77.6	£100.3	£72.3	£91.4	£123.9	£86.8	£91.6	£123.7	£91.8	£79.1	£93.3	£134.7	£149.4	£223.8	£217.9	£180.4	**£113.8**
EU	£8.9	£9.5	£27.6	£30.9	£41.4	£83.3	£80.1	£92.4	£107.6	£167.4	£79.8	£131.5	£133.6	£90.0	£106.0	£184.6	£250.8	£115.3	**£97.3**
E	£2.1	£2.2	£1.0	£22.6	£13.8	£34.6	£11.2	£25.4	£62.2	£10.5	£8.8	£8.6	£8.5	£26.8	£36.2	£43.2	£81.6	£55.1	**£24.7**
ROW	£2.0	£1.5	£10.0	£17.9	£3.9	£12.1	£47.9	£33.4	£67.7	£66.2	£47.3	£71.5	£58.1	£86.7	£91.0	£162.9	£160.3	£139.7	**£60.0**
Number of transfers by nationality																			
UK	77	97	77	73	55	69	62	60	57	47	36	61	54	56	64	63	47	42	**62.1**
EU	12	12	20	16	30	36	49	40	47	54	34	44	52	47	43	48	51	39	**38.7**
E	5	5	2	11	13	26	5	19	16	5	8	9	6	10	9	16	8	13	**10.3**
ROW	4	3	12	12	7	15	21	19	27	10	18	26	33	33	49	50	39	32	**23.3**
Average cost by nationality																			
UK	£0.6	£0.7	£1.0	£1.4	£1.3	£1.3	£1.5	£1.4	£1.6	£2.6	£2.6	£1.3	£1.7	£2.4	£2.3	£3.6	£4.6	£4.3	**£2.0**
EU	£0.7	£0.8	£1.4	£1.9	£1.4	£1.4	£1.6	£2.3	£2.3	£3.1	£2.3	£3.0	£2.6	£1.9	£2.5	£4.1	£4.9	£3.0	**£2.3**
E	£0.4	£0.4	£0.5	£2.1	£1.1	£1.3	£2.2	£1.3	£3.3	£2.1	£1.1	£1.0	£1.4	£2.7	£4.0	£2.7	£10.2	£4.2	**£2.3**
ROW	£0.5	£0.5	£0.9	£1.5	£0.6	£0.8	£2.3	£1.8	£2.5	£3.5	£2.6	£2.8	£1.8	£2.6	£1.9	£3.3	£4.1	£4.4	**£2.1**

Roughly half as many British players were bought by Premier League clubs in 2009/10 compared with the first few seasons of the Premier League. With the introduction of UEFA's new quota ruling for the 20010/11 season – with only English and Welsh qualifying as home-grown – this ratio looks set to increase fairly rapidly.

The number of European players signed each season rose from 16 in 1995/96 to 58 two years later. While this remains the peak, numbers haven't slipped below 34 since then, and the majority of the past 13 seasons have seen tallies in the 40s or 50s. The influx of non-EU Europeans also peaked in 1997/98, at 26; a sharp rise from the 12 in total between 1992 and 1995. But it's the Rest of World category that sees the steepest increase, from just seven in the first two seasons to an average of 32 per season since the turn of the millennium.

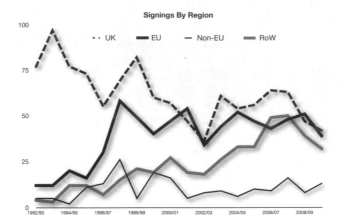

Signings By Region

Spurs have signed the greatest number of players in total – 117 – with West Ham just one signing behind in 2nd. Chelsea rank 3rd, with 112, Newcastle 4th, with 109, and Blackburn 5th, with 106. What's interesting is that these are the clubs with very high manager turnover. It validates the theory that changing manager can be an expensive business, because he will then want to reshape the squad.

Of the big clubs, Liverpool employed only four managers between 1992 and 2010 (infamously, two at the same time for a while in 1998). So for quite a big spending club, 96 signings does not look too excessive a total. Arsenal, with only one manager since 1996 (and just two more since the start of the Premier League) have signed even fewer players: 80. And Manchester United, who have spent approximately £420m (£700m CTPP) in the Premier League era have done so on just 63 players. People don't need reminding of how many managers they have had in that time.

The only two other clubs with over 100 signings are Everton (103) and Manchester City (101). Between them, the seven clubs with 100+ signings average almost nine full-time managerial appointments each. Coincidence, or correlation?

Surprisingly, Bolton – who haven't even been in the Premier League for seven of the 18 seasons – top the list for the greatest number of 'Rest of World' signings, with 24, while Blackburn and Chelsea, with a total of 14, have signed the most non-EU Europeans. In terms of Europeans from within the EU, Chelsea again rank 1st, with 50 signings, just ahead of Arsenal and Liverpool, on 47 each. West Ham, with 61, and Southampton, with 60, have proven the keenest to buy British.

Signings by Region of Birth

Club	Rest of Europe	EU	Rest of World	UK	Grand Total
Arsenal	6	47	12	15	80
Aston Villa	8	25	10	49	92
Barnsley	2	3	1	2	8
Birmingham	1	14	13	31	59
Blackburn	14	29	15	48	106
Bolton	9	19	24	41	93
Bradford	1	3	–	16	20
Burnley	–	–	2	4	6
Charlton	2	11	12	23	48
Chelsea	14	50	17	31	112
Coventry	4	14	12	39	69
Crystal Palace	3	10	3	25	41
Derby	5	17	16	28	66
Everton	6	27	13	57	103
Fulham	5	24	22	26	77
Hull	8	6	6	–	20
Ipswich	1	7	3	18	29
Leeds	4	10	7	33	54
Leicester	2	6	4	46	58
Liverpool	10	47	18	21	96
Man City	8	32	20	41	101
Manchester United	6	25	18	14	63
Middlesbrough	2	23	19	30	74
Newcastle	5	33	23	48	109
Norwich	–	4	2	17	23
Nottm Forest	1	5	1	18	25
Oldham	1	1	–	6	8
Portsmouth	8	25	20	22	75
QPR	1	3	9	–	13
Reading	1	2	6	5	14
Sheff United	3	4	3	15	25
Sheff Wed	3	14	3	29	49
Southampton	7	20	7	60	94
Spurs	13	36	18	50	117
Stoke	1	3	6	10	20
Sunderland	4	30	9	39	82
Swindon	1	1	–	9	11
Watford	2	7	4	11	24
West Brom	2	12	5	22	41
West Ham	9	24	22	61	116
Wigan	1	16	15	18	50
Wimbledon	8	3	1	20	32
Wolves	3	4	4	4	15
Grand Total	**186**	**696**	**419**	**1117**	**2418**

Financial Fair Play Rules – The End of the 'Mega Transfer'?

In a move that is perhaps long overdue, UEFA are seeking to make football clubs live within their means; über-rich super benefactors will no longer be able to pump money indiscriminately into their clubs.

Daniel Geey is a solicitor for Field Fisher Waterhouse LLP, and advises entities wishing to invest in the football industry (specifically in relation to the 'fit and proper person' test, conflicts of interest, multiple club ownership and third-party player ownership). According to Geey, "UEFA's overall aim for the Financial Fair Play Rules (FFPR) is for its affiliated football clubs to balance their books, not spend more than they earn, and to promote investment in their stadia and training facility infrastructure, and in youth development. This idea of self-sustainability relates to UEFA's underlying belief that transfer fee and wage inflation continues unabated because each set of new club owners injects more money into the European football club market. This 'keeping up with the Joneses' effect spirals further because a new owner then has to outbid other high-spending clubs.

"It should be noted that the new FFPR relate only to Champions League and Europa League, and not to domestic league participation. Each club that believes it can qualify for that season's European competitions must, prior to the beginning of that season, apply for a UEFA Club Licence."

The conventional reward for big-spending is entry into European competition, which, if it's the Champions League, earns clubs vast sums (as much as £30m for a successful run). So it's unlikely that clubs will invest excessive amounts of money on transfers and jeopardise this traditional reward.

Geey continues: "From the 2013/14 season, the licence stipulations will include adherence to the FFPR. Until the 2013/14 season, there are no sanctions for breaching the FFPR. However, the rules need to be borne in mind from the 2011/12 season onwards because the 2011/12 and 2012/13 season accounts are used to determine a club's licence application in the 2013/14 season.

"Therefore, the FFPR may signal the end of the mega transfer because a club may simply not be able to afford a £50m fee and then break even. This is of course unless a club makes big commercial profits, which very few clubs (bar Arsenal) have done recently."

Chapter Seven:
The Premier League Age

How much money a manager needs to spend on transfers depends to some degree on the quality of his academy's production line. Most clubs give debuts to the occasional outstanding youth graduate, and some clubs even manage to blood a handful of youngsters over the course of a 10-year period. This of course lowers both the £XI and the Sq£, although it's rare for successful clubs to use more than a couple of trainees on a regular basis. In some cases, academy players give cash-starved clubs a chance to avoid expensive transfer fees; in others, they simply free up more money to lavish on marquee signings. Either way, the talented youth graduate represents the ideal player: connected to the club at a deeper level than the average fly-by-night, and the only cost involved (beyond the wider expense of maintaining an academy) is his wages.

Kids

"You don't win anything with kids," Alan Hansen famously remarked in 1995 when assessing Manchester United's new-look side. They had just lost their opening day fixture against Aston Villa 3-1. Well it turns out Hansen was both right *and* wrong.

However, he wasn't wrong because United went on to win the League by four points from Newcastle United that season. He was wrong because, on the whole, they weren't really kids.

They were a young side, certainly, but one also bolstered by plenty of experience. The Manchester United starting team that day (with their ages in brackets) was: Schmeichel (31), Parker (31), Irwin (29), Pallister (30), Neville G (20), Sharpe (24), Butt (20), Keane (24), Scholes (20), Neville P (18) and McClair (31). Hardly a team made up of babies, with only one teenager.

In fact, it's almost like a good conjuring trick, the way journalists and pundits can be fooled through simple misdirection. Throw in a few young players to grab the headlines and suddenly you're fielding a team full of kids. Everyone focuses on the three or four youngsters (in United's case, Butt, G Neville and Scholes at 20 and P Neville at 18) and forgets about the rest of your team.

The average age of United's XI that day was 25.27 years – and they won the title that season with an average team age of 25.46. That is indeed relatively young; in fact, the second-lowest average age for a Premier League-winning side. But it's a long way from being the lowest *ever* average age for a Premier League side (which really was a team full of kids, at just 20 years. More on that later).

So in that sense, Hansen was right. Teams do not win the Premier League with kids. The conventional wisdom is that a player reaches his peak at around 27 years old (although defenders and goalkeepers peak later than forwards). And the evidence from the Premier League certainly seems to bear that out; the average age of Premier League Champions is 26.69 years. And it's hovered around there for the whole 18 years, with little significant movement either way.

As for youthfulness, only five times has a team won the title with an average playing age under 26: United in 1995/96; Blackburn the season before (25.53); United again in 1996/97 (25.69); and Chelsea in 2004-5 (25.21) and 2005/06 (25.86). Going the other way, seven times teams have won the title with an average age of over 27. United have done it three times; 1994/95 (27.07), 2006/07 (27.19) and 2008/09 (27.05).

Perhaps somewhat surprisingly given his own reputation for playing kids, Arsène Wenger's Arsenal have also won the Premier League three times with an average age of over 27: 1997/98 – Wenger's first title (28.09), 2001/02 (27.09) and 2003/04 (27.28). That first season's average team age of 28.09 is the second-highest in Premier League history. Only Carlo Ancelotti's Chelsea in 2009/10 had a higher average age, at 28.73. Funnily enough, that title win for Chelsea gives them both the youngest and oldest title-winning teams in the Premier League era, with key elements of their first success proving instrumental when five years older in 2010 (showing the importance of buying players who are not yet at their peak, as opposed to overpriced 28-year-olds).

Overall, there's no real trend in terms of average age of Premier League winners; teams are not getting older or younger in any discernible pattern. (Although since Mourinho's Chelsea won the title in 2005/06 with a side that averaged 25.86 years of age, the average has crept up to 27.42 years. Perhaps we're starting to see an upward shift; only time will tell.)

In terms of the Premier League as a whole, the average age of a team has been 26.83 years. The youngest club – based on the average age of all XIs they have fielded in the Premier League – is Crystal Palace, at 25.48. But they have only been in the Premier League for four of the 18 seasons, and have been relegated in each of those seasons. Similarly, the second-youngest club, Watford (with an average team age of 25.64) has only played in two Premier League seasons and went down each time.

The youngest club with some Premiership longevity (in fact, an ever-present) is Liverpool, with an average team age of just 25.73 years over the 18 seasons, the third lowest ever. Oldham also boast an average team age of just 25.73 years, but again, they were only in the Premier League for the first two seasons. However, they did manage to stay up with a side that averaged just 25.41 under Joe Royle. Leeds United are next with an average age of 25.81 years. But even they have been absent for six of the 18 seasons, going down in 2003/04 with a young side (average age just 25.12, although the club was in crisis).

Three other ever-presents come in below the average club age of 26.83: Spurs (26.13), Aston Villa (26.34) and Manchester United (26.59). Chelsea comes in just above the all-club average (26.90), while Arsenal (27.02) and Everton (27.16) complete the older end of the Premiership perennials. The 'oldest' Premier League club is Bradford City, who in their two seasons in the Premier League had an average team age of almost 30 years (29.98).

Managers: who's really down with the kids?
And what of individual managers? Who puts his faith in youngsters?

The youngest team ever to play a Premier League season had an incredibly low average age of just 23.97 years: Leeds United in 1999/00 under David O'Leary. Indeed O'Leary, over his seven seasons in the Premier League with Leeds United and Aston Villa, managed teams that averaged an age of just 25.07 years. To put that into context, only 17 times has a manager played a Premier League season with an average team age of under 25 years – just 5% of the total.

Arsène Wenger has an average playing age of 26.84, almost exactly the Premier League average. As mentioned earlier, his reputation seems somewhat undeserved – in the league, at least. Much of the notion of his implicit faith in youth comes from the League Cup, where some great performances by collections of teenagers have caught the eye. However, until recently, many of these starlets have failed to force their way into the XI for Premier League games. This does appear to be changing, with Jack Wilshere, Kieran Gibbs, Nicklas Bendtner, Gaël Clichy, Aaron Ramsey and Theo Walcott all having made the breakthrough at a tender age, although some of these were bought rather than home-grown.

As well as O'Leary, plenty of managers have lower average ages than Wenger's (and most of them get little or no praise for playing 'the kids'). Benítez's Liverpool averaged an age of 26.22; Ferguson's United have an average playing age of 26.59; and Martin O'Neill in his time at Leicester and Aston Villa fielded teams with an average age of 26.74. Gérard Houllier is well below Wenger, with the average age of his Liverpool teams standing at 25.21 years – a good year and a half younger than the average Arsenal side under Arsène.

Of course, many of these players will have been purchases, rather than home-grown talent. But if a manager has bought four or five outstanding 22/23-year-olds, the chances are he won't want to fill the rest of the side with teenagers.

Trainees: are they a dying breed?
And how about players who emerge through the youth teams? Are fewer trainees coming through the academies now that the Premier League attracts the world's greatest players?

In the past 18 years, 535 players have made their way through the youth ranks of their clubs and played a Premier League game. On average, 30 new youth players have been blooded each season across the Premier League era. There's really no suggestion that there has been a great tapering off of opportunities for young players as the mega-money has rolled into the game, although the early Premier League seasons did see a greater consistency in the number of young players coming through. The highest number in a single season came in 1993/94 when 44 youngsters took their bows. The inaugural season (1992/93) saw the second-highest number, 43.

There was an alarming dip towards the turn of the millennium, which might have suggested a serious downward trend. The lowest-ever total came in 2001/02 when just 17 youth players made their debuts. (1999/00 saw 24 and 2000/01 saw

22.) But 2002/03 saw a jump to 32 and in 2005/06 36 trainee players made their debuts – the fourth-highest number from the 18 seasons.

Since then, though, the numbers have been falling steadily – mirroring the rise in average playing age since 2005/06. The most recent season, 2009/10, saw just 18 youth players debut for their clubs – the second-lowest total ever. We could well be seeing the emergence of an older Premier League, with fewer chances for the youngsters to come through the ranks.

Young blood: who gives youngsters their Premier League break?

So which clubs like to develop home-grown talent and which managers give their youngsters a chance?

There do seem to be clubs who produce more high-quality young players than others. And there are managers who give those youngsters a break. Of course, some managers get lucky and inherit a golden generation who just happen to come of age as they take over. Others radically change the youth setup, only to leave before the fruits of their labours have fully ripened, and then see other managers reap all the rewards. But the basic point is, you have to have the guts to throw a young player into the mix; and yet, equally true is the fact that they have to be good enough – clubs just cannot afford to gamble on 'maybe' players. (It can be a bit of a catch-22: youngsters need games to improve, but if they are not yet good enough to play, it becomes a risk; hence loans to lower divisions becoming more popular.)

The club that has given Premier League debuts to the most youth team players is Manchester United with an impressive 40 since 1992. A good few of those were part of the golden generation of the early-to-mid 90s: Beckham, Scholes, the Nevilles and Butt. To average more than two trainee debuts per season in Premier League games is no mean feat. However, like Liverpool, having had a stream of talent in the '90s, they have not unearthed any *great* players in the past decade. And it's not really been a case of the kids being good enough but just not getting a chance; neither club has released youngsters who have subsequently looked first-team material for a top four club. (And where are all the great Geordie footballers? The '80s saw the emergence of Peter Beardsley, Chris Waddle, Paul Gascoigne and Alan Shearer, but in recent years there's been nothing like that quality emerging.)

Next is Middlesbrough, with a very healthy 32 debuts for youngsters – even better when you consider they have been out of the top flight for four of the 18 seasons. Of course, their owner Steve Gibson famously wanted to create a team of locals. And indeed, Steve McClaren handed debuts to an impressive 18 youngsters during his reign – including a team made up almost entirely of local academy players for his final game against Fulham in the 2005/06 season. The average age of the starting XI at Fulham that day was just 20 years, making it the youngest ever Premier League side. Fifteen of the 16-man squad were locals, with Malcolm Christie (who was born just 25 miles away) the only non Teessider. Of course, this was not a fixture with anything at stake.

Arsenal rank 3rd, with a total of 28 youth team players coming through the ranks. Arsène Wenger has been responsible for 18 of those debuts – again perhaps not as many as you might think; after all, it's the same number as Steve McClaren, who was in the Middlesbrough job for just five seasons compared with Wenger's 14 so far. Next are Manchester City with 26 youth team debuts, and a host of other clubs fairly well renowned for their academies: Spurs (25), Aston Villa (22), West Ham (22), Newcastle (22), Leeds United (21) and Everton (21). Perhaps surprisingly, given their status and the number of well-known players who have come through the ranks, Liverpool have given debuts to just 15 players since the Premier League kicked off. Chelsea have also managed only 15 youth debuts. Watford managed an incredible 17 youth team debutants in just two seasons of Premier League football. (Although you might argue that's why they went straight back down each time.)

When it comes to managers, no one can live with Ferguson, who can lay claim to giving all 40 of Manchester United's youths their Premier League debuts. Wenger and McClaren are next with their 18 apiece – over 14 seasons in Wenger's case and just five seasons in McClaren's. Next are Peter Reid and George Graham with a laudable 17 youth player debuts each in respective spells at Man City and Sunderland, and Arsenal, Leeds and Spurs. Perhaps surprisingly Bryan Robson is next alongside Kevin Keegan. They both gave debuts to 14 youngsters. Alan Curbishley has 13 at Charlton and West Ham, along with Graham Taylor who gave 13 trainee debuts at Watford and Aston Villa. Gerry Francis, Howard Wilkinson and Graeme Souness have 12 each. Trevor Francis handed out 11 youth debuts, while Harry Redknapp, Joe Royle and Brain Little each gave 10.

At the low end, José Mourinho gave debuts to just two trainees in his three seasons at Chelsea. Ruud Gullit managed six in his two seasons at Chelsea, and Ossie Ardiles gave four youngsters their debuts in his single season at Spurs. Martin O'Neill – often praised for playing a team full of English youngsters at Villa – only gave debuts to two players in his four seasons there. Glenn Hoddle was not a prolific giver of debuts either. In his six-and-a-half seasons in the Premier League at Chelsea, Southampton and Spurs, he introduced just two trainees to Premier League football: Michael Duberry and Jody Morris.

Kenny Dalglish fares even worse. He gave a Premier League debut to Jason Wilcox at Blackburn, but no other trainees either in his three seasons in the top flight at Blackburn or in his six-month spell with Newcastle. (He did, however, bring through Steve McManaman while at Liverpool, and was heavily involved in persuading a young Robbie Fowler to join the Academy.)

Foreign imports: stopping English youngsters from making it?

So, since the globalisation of the Premier League, are English lads getting squeezed out as many would have us believe? Are the academies filling up with foreigners scouted from around the world, curtailing the chances of home-grown talent?

In a word, no.

Of the 535 trainees to have made their debuts during the Premier League era, 73% have been English. Add Scotland, Wales and Northern Ireland, and the UK proportion becomes 91%.

Furthermore, that English proportion has remained fairly constant across all 18 seasons. In 1992/93, 74% of the youth players who made their debuts were English. In 2009/10, it was 72%. The lowest ever percentage of English debutants was 59% in 2000/01. But add the rest of the UK nationalities for that season and the figure increases to 91%.

The lowest overall percentage of UK debutants was 70% in 2007/08 (with 60% Englishmen). But the following season it was back up to 70% from England and 80% from the UK.

Of course, more foreign youngsters are coming into the academies and perhaps their impact has not yet been felt. Also, there are those young players recruited from overseas who bypass the academy system, and who are listed as transfers rather than trainees.

So it could be that in seasons to come, fewer youngsters – and fewer English youngsters – will get their chances. But there is no real evidence to suggest that is the case up until now – whatever the media might claim.

Chapter Eight:
Dead Dreams: Was It Worth It?

As with stocks and shares, the fortunes of football clubs can fall as well as rise. The aim is to always strive for more; but with it comes the risk of overstretching one's financial means. So far, two clubs stand out for having flown too close to the sun and, as a result, have seen their wings melt like a cheese slice seared by a blowtorch.

In recent years, both Leeds United and Portsmouth found themselves in better positions than they'd occupied for decades. Leeds had won the league in 1992, but had not made the semi-final of the European Cup since 1975; in 2001, they were back in the big time. Within three years they were bankrupt and relegated, following a swift fire sale of all their key players. In 2007/08 Portsmouth finished in the top eight for the first time in over 50 years, and also won the FA Cup. Could it get any better? And yet by 2010 they were in administration, relegated to the Championship and close to being wound up by a court order.

Who was to blame? Well, entire books could be written on the issue, covering all manner of financial mismanagements. But fans don't help; it's the natural inclination of us all to want better and better. Satisfaction in sport is often dangerous, with the satiation of desire. But too much desire is equally insidious.

Indeed, merely maintaining equilibrium is rarely enough: fans always want to see improvement; we just can't help ourselves. Standing still is like a painful regression. Promoted clubs who finish 17th may appease their fans, but if they're still 17th the following season, unrest will ensue; even though being relegated could be the more realistic outcome for their team.

In the cases of these two clubs, delight turned to despair in almost record time. In 1997/98, when Leeds finished 5th, they had the 14th-costliest squad in the Premier League, at £64m. A year later, when they finished 4th, their Sq£ (£79.6m) was still ranked nine places below their actual league position; a fine achievement. By 1999/00, the rank (£97m) was up to 8th; but again they climbed the league table, by a single place: they were now up to 3rd. This meant Champions League qualification, and the start of the glorious dream. Their Sq£ rank continued to climb; in 2000/01 it was 7th. Although Leeds dropped to 4th in the league (perhaps with all the extra European games taking their toll), the squad cost was now at £141.3m. One further year later, 2001/02, and their league position had again slipped by a single place – down to 5th – but the Sq£ rank was now in the top five: £157.6m.

So, for the first time, the Elland Road club were performing on a par with their resources, having over-performed for the previous four seasons.

This was to prove the peak of Leeds' Sq£. The finances were starting to pinch, and a further one-place drop down the league table ensued: finishing 6th, but now with the fifth-highest squad cost, in 2003. Relegation a year later, upon a finish in 19th place, was the swift payback for all the flights of fancy. Even then, the Sq£ was ranked as high as 9th, at £82.5m, but players were being sold all the time, and the team itself was getting radically cheaper: in 2002 the £XI was £95.3m; by 2004, it was less than a third of that amount, at £31.7m. In the same period, the Sq£ had roughly halved. This was a club haemorrhaging money and personnel.

Just 37% of the players on Leeds' books during that fateful season were utilised, possibly because many of them had left during the campaign as part of an ongoing fire sale. On paper, the team was costly enough to stay in the top flight, but once a negative energy surrounds a club it becomes easy to slip into a downward spiral. Relegation was inevitable. Their problems would continue down into the third tier of English football where, in 2007, they were hit with a 15-point deduction upon entering administration. Now back in the Championship, things are at last looking up again for the Yorkshiremen. But the lessons from Peter Ridsdale's time as Chairman cannot be forgotten.

As *The Guardian* reported at the time, the club "forked out £5.7m in compensation to their sacked former managers David O'Leary and Terry Venables while still spending £600,000 a year on a fleet of over 70 company cars – £70,000 on one vehicle alone ... The club spent £70,000 in one year on private jets for directors and senior management, handed out £300,000 a year to charity despite announcing losses of £33m in the last financial year, and still contribute £500,000 a year to Robbie Fowler's wages despite selling him to Manchester City in January. Amid those staggering figures, the £20 a month spent looking after Ridsdale's goldfish, resplendent in his plush office in the directors' suite, pales into insignificance. The fish, like the £450,000-a-year chairman, have since moved on."

At the other end of the country, Portsmouth became the next Premier League club to find the dream turn sour more quickly than milk left out in the Sahara. When they finished 16th and 17th in 2005 and 2006 respectively, their squad was ranked at a similar level. In 2007, when they ended the campaign in 9th place, the Sq£ rank was still 15th, at £44.2m. However, manager Harry Redknapp was now investing fairly heavily in the team. The next year, 2008, the rank was up to 11th; the Sq£ £73.6m. This was the side that won the FA Cup. But for a club with an ancient stadium that held only 20,688 fans, and no kind of global brand to cash in on, this was a business with limited revenue streams. A year later, 2008/09, the Sq£ ranked 14th, and with Redknapp having moved on to Spurs, a 12th-placed finish wasn't too bad. The squad still 'cost' £68.2m, with the £XI roughly half that amount, at £33.8m.

But then came the season of their relegation. Entering administration meant that they were ushered on their way to the second tier by a deduction of nine points. The Sq£ had halved; as it had at Leeds. Also mirroring Leeds was the fact that the £XI fell to a third the value of the previous season: in Portsmouth's case, the £XI was £33.8m in 2008/09 but just £10.8m a year later. Only Burnley had a less expensive team over the course of 2009/10. Whereas Leeds failed to utilise 63% of the players that were on their books at some stage of their final Premier League season, for Portsmouth this figure was even higher: 70%.

In 2009/10 Portsmouth had no fewer than four different owners: Alexandre 'Sacha' Gaydamak (January 2006 to August 26th, 2009); Sulaiman Al-Fahim (August 26th, 2009 to October 5th, 2009); Ali Al-Faraj (October 5th, 2009 to February 4th, 2010); and Balram Chainrai (from February 4th, 2010). It was chaos; farcical. Manager

Avram Grant was desperately trying to steer a sinking ship, and reaching another FA Cup Final, while admirable in the circumstances, was of little consolation.

Even the biggest clubs in the land are not exempt. Both Manchester United and Liverpool have been forced into monumental debt on the back of leveraged buyouts. At the time of going to print, there is an outside chance that Liverpool could be forced into administration because of a possible inability to pay off debt imposed on the club by the very men the fans thought were supposed to be their saviours. (News of a possible rescue by the owners of the Boston Red Sox comes just as this book heads to the presses.)

Living the dream in football is often just a prelude to a much greater nightmare. Yes, winning FA Cups and reaching Champions League semi-finals is what football is all about. But as with a fraudster whose hedonistic lifestyle leads to five years in jail, the fans of those clubs, as the dream crumbled, were left asking themselves "Was it really worth it?"

Chapter Nine:
Getting a Start

One of the common abuses of a transfer fee in debates is how it is used to conclusively encapsulate a player's time at a club: "each of the striker's goals cost £1.1m" or "each appearance set the club back £800,000". On its own, such a claim can miss a lot of the details – maybe the striker also set up 50 goals, or maybe the player then left for considerably more than he cost. And of course, on the debit side, there is the loss due to cost of wages to take into account, too.

But in terms of analysing a large database of transfers in pure numbers, to find trends and patterns, such an approach definitely has some merit. When combined, the 2,418 Premier League transfers weigh in at £5.135 billion. Apply inflation, and it makes for a staggering total of £9.365 billion; almost 10 billion pounds in today's money for players who were bought by Premier League clubs.

Those 2,418 players racked up 94,150 appearances between August 1992 and May 2010. The remainder of the appearances – 41,414, from a total of 135,564 spaces on team sheets – were accounted for by the clubs' home-grown players.

(Basically, the equation is *38 [games] x 11 [starting players] x 20 [teams] x 18 [seasons]*, with adjustments for the extra teams in the first three seasons of the

Premier League.)

On average, for *every game* a player starts (and not including wages), Premier League clubs have had to pay £54,541 in transfer fees. However, this is before applying TPI; in current terms this equates to £99,467. So, pay £5m for someone, and on average you will get 50 starts out of them. Add wages onto the transfer cost, and the average cost per player is well above £100,000 per game.

Of course, there's also the money recouped to be taken into account. Players aren't just bought; they're sold, too. In today's money, the total raised by Premier League sales works out at £5.989bn, almost £4bn less than the total amount spent. Of course, many of the deals were inter-Premier League transfers, and so appear in both totals.

Plenty were also purchases from lower-league clubs, for a higher fee than that recouped when the player was eventually sold back out of the Premier League (either because he was a flop, or because he returned to the lower leagues when past his prime; top-division clubs may over-pay for talent from lower down the food chain, but rarely does it work the other way around).

The remainder were overseas deals. Indeed, the most lucrative sales by Premier League clubs have been to Spain. Cristiano Ronaldo and Xabi Alonso, at £80m and £30m respectively, are the two most expensive in standard terms, while in current-day prices, Nicolas Anelka's sale for £22.5m in 1999 now equates to £54m, and David Beckham's £25m fee effectively doubles to £50.5m. All four of these players were bought by Real Madrid, while their arch rivals, Barcelona, were responsible for the fourth-costliest Premier League export to date, Marc Overmars, at £44.5m CTPP.

Part Two

The Clubs

Arsenal

Total Spend (Actual): £284.9m
Total Spend (CTPP): £533.3m
Average League Position: 3.4
Number of Managers: 3
Most Expensive Signing: Andrei Arshavin £15m (CTPP £11.7m)
Best Value Signing: Nicolas Anelka
Worst Value Signing: Francis Jeffers

Player Signings Breakdown (data correct up to end of January transfer window 2010)

• UK: 15   EU: 47   Rest of Europe: 6   Rest of World: 12

Major Trophies Won Since Premier League Began

Premier League Champions: 3 (1997/98, 2001/02, 2003/04)
FA Cup: 5 (1993, 1998, 2002, 2003, 2005)
League Cup: 1 (1993)
European Cup Winners Cup: 1 (1994)

Premier League Statistics (correct to the end of the 2009/10 season)

Seasons: 18   Played: 696
Won: 375   Drawn: 186   Lost:135
Goals Scored: 1,199 Goals Conceded: 625   Goal Difference: +574
Total Points: 1,311

Overview

With three league titles to their name, Arsenal are behind only Manchester United and Chelsea when it comes to success during the Premier League era. Although they've amassed more points than Chelsea, and more top-two finishes after being runners–up five times, their London rivals have won more trophies.

Life in the Premier League didn't start off too well for the Gunners. Under manager George Graham, and in a sharp fall from winning the league title at the end of the 1990/91 season, they finished the first three Premier League seasons in 10th, 4th and 12th place respectively. Some solace was gained in that first 1992/93 season however, when they won both the League Cup and FA Cup. A similar decline during the early years of the Premier League was shared by two other clubs who were crowned champions during the three seasons preceding the formation of the new league: Liverpool (1989/90) and Leeds United (1991/92). Graham was sacked in February 1995 after it was revealed that he had taken illegal payments from Norwegian football agent Rune Hauge. This followed the 1992 signings of two of Hauge's clients – John Jensen and Pål Lydersen. Bruce Rioch left Bolton to take over at Arsenal in 1995, but he left after just one season (1995/96) and a 5th-place finish. It would take the arrival of Frenchman Arsène Wenger in September 1996 to turn Arsenal's fortunes around.

Wenger's first season in charge brought a 3rd-place finish for the Gunners, before they were crowned champions at the end of 1997/98. They finished with 78 points, a low total by recent standards, and one point ahead of runners-up Manchester United. The roles were reversed in the following season, with Arsenal finishing one point behind Alex Ferguson's side, who racked up 79 points. Under Arsène Wenger, Arsenal continued to fight it out with United for the top honours in English football between 1997/98 and 2004/05, before the emergence of Chelsea broke the duopoly. During this period Arsenal finished no lower than 2nd, winning the league title three times and completing the Premier League and FA Cup double on two occasions (1998 and 2002).

The 2003/04 season saw Arsenal win the Premier League title without losing a single game, becoming only the second team to go the entire league season in the top flight unbeaten. This feat earned them the tagline 'The Invincibles', a term that was originally used to describe Preston North End's team after their undefeated record in winning the 1888/89 league title.

Arsenal hold a number of Premier League records including the most consecutive wins (14: shared with three other teams) and the fewest defeats in a season (0: 2003/04), and they are also the only team to have scored in every league game during a Premier League season (2001/02).

Most Utilised Players

Thirteen of Arsenal's Most Utilised Players in the Premier League era are Arsène Wenger signings; perhaps not surprising considering he has been in charge for 14 of the 18 years. Despite Wenger's dominance as a Premier League manager, a number of George Graham's signings figure high in the top 20. Two of the top five, and four of the top 10, were brought to the club by Graham. Signed for the start of the 2009/10 season, Thomas Vermaelen currently ranks as number one, having started 33 out of a possible 38 League games, giving him an 87% starting ratio. This figure may decrease the longer he stays at Arsenal. However, it is still a sound return from a player who cost £10m and also scored seven league goals, especially considering that overseas players can take up to 18 months to find their feet in English football.

Bacary Sagna, signed for £6m (£6.8m) from Auxerre in 2007, is in second place having started 94 out of a possible 114 games, meaning he has an 82% starting ratio for Arsenal since he joined. Another left-back, Nigel Winterburn, also has an 82% starting ratio, starting 260 out of 316 games. This makes Winterburn, a £400k (£2.4m) signing from Wimbledon in 1987, George Graham's finest value for money acquisition, ahead of right-back Lee Dixon who also cost £400k (£2.4m) from Stoke City in 1988. Incredibly for two players so intrinsically linked to both golden eras at Arsenal since the 1970s, the pair share almost identical starting ratios. Dixon's is a fraction behind his fellow full-back, having started 311 out of 392 Premier League games, to give an 81% ratio.

Least Utilised Players

Three of the top four are Wenger's signings; the exception being Perry Groves who was George Graham's first signing as Arsenal manager for £75k (£435k) from Colchester in 1986, and was still on the books when the new league was formed. All four failed to start a match for Arsenal in the Premier League era. None of the four can be labelled as expensive failures; the most costly is Tomas Danilevičius, who cost £1m (£1.7m).

Possibly Arsène Wenger's most disappointing signing is Francis Jeffers. Signed from Everton for £10m (£13.1m) in 2001, he started just two out of a possible 114 matches – although plenty of those 112 failures to feature were because he was out on loan from 2002 onwards – before he was eventually sold to Charlton in 2004; giving him a starting ratio of just 1.5%.

Managers

Year	£XI	£XI Rank	Points	Cost Per Point	Position League	Manager
1992/93	£45,350,952	7	56.0	£809,838	10	George Graham
1993/94	£52,243,495	7	71.0	£735,824	4	George Graham
1994/95	£54,681,810	7	51.0	£1,072,192	12	George Graham
Average	£50,758,752	7	59.3	£872,618	8.67	George Graham
1995/96	£79,580,015	4	63	£1,263,175	5	Bruce Rioch
Average	£79,580,015	4	63	£1,263,175	5	Bruce Rioch
1996/97	£75,225,361	3	68.0	£1,106,255	3	Arsène Wenger
1997/98	£85,245,901	2	78.0	£1,092,896	1	Arsène Wenger
1998/99	£81,681,147	4	78.0	£1,047,194	2	Arsène Wenger
1999/00	£96,609,330	3	73.0	£1,323,415	2	Arsène Wenger
2000/01	£99,650,688	1	70.0	£1,423,581	2	Arsène Wenger
2001/02	£104,115,888	1	87.0	£1,196,734	1	Arsène Wenger
2002/03	£109,175,613	3	78.0	£1,399,687	2	Arsène Wenger
2003/04	£95,692,961	4	90.0	£1,063,255	1	Arsène Wenger
2004/05	£101,747,999	3	83.0	£1,225,880	2	Arsène Wenger
2005/06	£96,270,276	3	67.0	£1,436,870	4	Arsène Wenger
2006/07	£71,372,631	5	68.0	£1,049,598	4	Arsène Wenger
2007/08	£68,063,312	5	83.0	£820,040	3	Arsène Wenger
2008/09	£57,423,207	9	72.0	£797,545	4	Arsène Wenger
2009/10	£64,865,090	7	75.0	£864,868	3	Arsène Wenger
Average	£86,224,243	4	76.4	£1,131,987	2.43	Arsène Wenger

Top 5 Players Sold for a Profit

- Anelka - Bought for: £500k (£1.5m), Sold for: £23m (£54m), Profit of: £22.5m (£52.5m)
- Overmars - Bought for: £5m (£17m), Sold for: £25m (£44.5m), Profit of: £20m (£27.5m)
- Adebayor - Bought for: £7m (£12.8m), Sold for: £25m (£25m), Profit of: £18m (£12.4m)
- Cole - Bought for: £0, Sold for: £16m (£28m), Profit of: £16m (£28m)
- Touré - Bought for: £150k (£197k), Sold for: £16m (£16m), Profit of: £15.85m (£15.83)

Top 20 CTPP Purchases

#	Player	CTPP	Original fee	Year	% of poss starts
1	Henry T	£24,640,038	£10,500,000	1999/00	77%
2	Overmars M	£23,632,552	£7,000,000	1997/98	80%
3	Wiltord S	£23,138,382	£13,000,000	2000/01	51%
4	Walcott T	£21,897,039	£12,000,000	2005/06	29%
5	Reyes J *	£21,219,452	£10,500,000	2003/04	47%
6	Hleb A	£20,437,236	£11,200,000	2005/06	64%
7	Bergkamp D	£19,721,386	£7,500,000	1995/96	61%
8	Wright I	£16,640,516	D2500000	1992/93	76%
9	Keown M	£13,312,412	£2,000,000	1992/93	60%
10	Jeffers F	£13,106,620	£10,000,000	2001/02	5%
12	Platt D	£12,490,211	£4,750,000	1995/96	57%
13	Lauren	£12,459,129	£7,000,000	2000/01	67%
14	Rosický T	£11,817,182	£6,800,000	2006/07	45%
15	Petit E	£11,816,276	£3,500,000	1997/98	72%
16	Vieira P	£11,816,276	£3,500,000	1997/98	80%
17	Arshavin A	£11,728,397	£15,000,000	2008/09	49%
18	Van Bronckhorst	£11,140,627	£8,500,000	2001/02	29%
19	Kanu N	£11,023,117	£4,500,000	1998/99	28%
20	Edu	£10,679,253	£6,000,000	2000/01	22%

* Fee could have potentially risen to £17.6m, but £10.5m was final total paid.

Expert View
Kieron O'Connor (@SwissRamble)

Arsenal fan & Editor of The Swiss Ramble, a blog about the business of football: www.swissramble.blogspot.com

Arsène Wenger is arguably the best manager that Arsenal have ever had. He's certainly the most successful in terms of trophies and is also the club's longest-serving manager. However, his reign has been a little like the proverbial "game of two halves", winning three Premier League titles and four FA Cups in his first nine years, followed by no silverware at all in the last five years.

It's probably over-simplistic to say that this is due to changes in the club's finances, but that has certainly played a part. For example, many fans might be surprised to hear that Arsenal's first league win under Wenger was achieved with pretty much the league's most expensive XI in current-day prices. Having said that, the legendary Invincibles, featuring the glorious talents of Thierry Henry, Patrick Vieira, Robert Pires and Dennis Bergkamp, should also be called the Incredibles, as they won the 2004 title with a team worth only 64% of that season's most expensive £XI.

Since then, austerity has been the order of the day with Arsenal spending far less than other major clubs, having been hit with a double whammy. Externally, the transfer market was artificially inflated by the presence of extremely wealthy benefactors like Roman Abramovich and Sheikh Mansour, leading to the "financial doping" so despised by Wenger. This relative financial weakness was then compounded by the self-imposed constraints arising from the construction of the Emirates stadium.

Arsenal's response has been to focus on younger players. In fact, there are two elements to the youth policy. The one that everyone understands is utilising the worldwide scouting network to buy young players from other clubs, develop them for a few years, hoping that they will ultimately become a fixture in the first team, but selling them for good money if they do not – the best examples being Cesc Fàbregas (whose value, in current terms, is £36m higher than the fee paid in 2003) and Nicolas Anelka (an amazing £53m CTPP profit).

The second strand is what might be described as the extreme youth policy, based on the successful approach that Barcelona, and Ajax in days gone by, have adopted. This is a long-term project, whereby the academy recruits young English talent and brings it through to the first team, Jack Wilshere being the obvious success story.

For Arsenal to spend so little in this period and yet still remain competitive, epitomised by qualifying for the Champions League a record 13 years in a row, all the time playing a dazzling brand of football unrecognisable from the days of "boring, boring" Arsenal, is a tremendous feat, which is why the vast majority of fans idolise Wenger: "In Arsène we trust".

There is no doubt that he is an outstanding manager, though there is a feeling that he might need to modify his transfer policy and loosen the purse strings to ensure that his legacy is not tarnished. Either that, or UEFA's Financial Fair Play Regulations will bring the other clubs' way of thinking round to "The Professor's".

Expert View
Michael Cox (@zonal_marking)
Editor, Zonal Marking www.zonalmarking.net

Arsène Wenger has embraced – or has been forced to embrace – a different way of assembling a squad to his title rivals. The Frenchman's commitment to developing young players and moulding them into a cohesive group has so far yielded little success in terms of trophies. A recent Arsenal Supporters' Trust survey showed that 75% are optimistic for the future, but more intriguingly, 53% said Wenger's football philosophy took too much precedence over the objective of winning trophies.

Openly admitting "what is difficult for me is not that clubs have more money", his plan was to "get young players in early so I do not find myself exposed on the transfer market". This has had mixed results. When Arsenal's attacking players combine well, they are the most beautiful side in the country – but with the main three centre-backs all having been recruited in the past two summer transfer windows, Arsenal still lack cohesion in the one area of the pitch where working as a unit is the most important.

In a model most similar to Barcelona's belief in bringing through as many players as possible from their *La Masia* academy, Wenger's idea is "to compensate by creating a style of play, by creating a culture at the club". Many of Arsenal's key players this season joined the club as teenagers, and their close relationship will, in Wenger's words, "give us strength that other clubs will not have."

"I agreed on a structure to the club four or five years ago, I believed it could work and we are at the period now when we will see whether I was right or not." If he is, the man with the Master's degree in economics might change the way other clubs go about their transfer business.

Aston Villa

Total Spend (Actual): £256.9m
Total Spend (CTPP): £448.7m
Average League Position: 8.39
Number of Managers: 6
Most Expensive Signing: Stan Collymore £7m (CTPP £23.7m)
Best Value Signing: Brad Friedel
Worst Value Signing: Boško Balaban

Player Signings Breakdown (data correct up to end of January transfer window 2010)

• UK: 49   EU: 25   Rest of Europe: 8   Rest of the World: 10

Major Trophies Won Since Premier League Began

League Cup: 2 (1994 & 1996)

Premier League Statistics (correct to the end of the 2009/10 season)

Seasons: 18	Played: 696	
Won: 264	Drawn: 211	Lost:221
Goals Scored: 888	Goals Conceded: 811	Goal Difference: +77
Total Points: 1,003		

Overview

Despite being the fifth-most successful club in English football with 23 trophies won to date, Aston Villa have found it difficult to assert themselves as strong contenders in the Premier League. The last time they won the title was in 1980/81, which was followed the next season by their only European Cup success, when they defeated Bayern Munich 1-0. Villa have found success harder to come by since then, with two League Cup wins and two runners-up spots in the league, as well as twice ending up as beaten cup finalists – in the FA Cup (2000) and League Cup (2010).

Villa finished runners-up to Manchester United at the end of the first Premier League season. However, since then the highest they have finished is 4th in 1995/96, under Brian Little. Villa's 14 top-10 finishes in the Premier League gives them an average league placing of 8th.

Villa are one of seven clubs to have featured in all 18 seasons of the Premier League, the other six being Arsenal, Chelsea, Everton, Liverpool, Manchester United and Spurs. They are also one of only seven clubs to have finished as runners-up in the Premier League along with Arsenal, Blackburn, Chelsea, Liverpool, Manchester United and Newcastle United. They are currently fifth in the all-time Premier League table of total points amassed.

Other Aston Villa records of interest in the Premier League include most draws to date (211) and most draws during an individual season (17 in 2006/07; a record shared with Newcastle United in 2003/04).

Most Utilised Players

Brad Friedel tops the list of Most Utilised Players at Villa, with a start ratio of 100%, having started all 76 league games for the club since arriving from Blackburn in July 2008 for a fee of £2.5m (£2m). Friedel holds the record for most consecutive appearances in the Premier League with over 200 games spanning six seasons. (He is also one of only three goalkeepers who have scored a goal in the Premier League, netting for Blackburn in their 3-2 defeat to Charlton in February 2004.)

One of Ron Atkinson's most successful signings in terms of starts was Dean Saunders, who became Villa's record purchase when he arrived from Liverpool in September 1992 for a fee of £2.3m (£15.4m). Saunders scored 12 league goals in his debut season for Villa, and 10 the following season – a campaign in which he also scored a brace in the League Cup Final victory over Manchester United. In his final season at Villa he netted 15 times in the league before he was sold to Galatasaray in July 1995 for £1m (£2.7m). He left Villa having started 111 out of 126 league games (88%).

Least Utilised Players

Boško Balaban tops the list of the Least Utilised Players for Aston Villa in the Premier League. Signed for £6m (£7.9m) from Dinamo Zagreb in 2001, Balaban failed to make a single start in the league during his time in the West Midlands. He was sent back to Dinamo Zagreb on loan for 2002/03 and was released from his Villa contract in December 2003. Marlon Harewood is another signing that failed to pay off for Aston Villa. Signed by Martin O'Neill for £4.5m (£5.1m) in July 2007, Harewood was used mainly as a substitute and started just one Premier League game in his debut season – although he did come off the bench to score five league goals. The 2008/09 campaign proved to be even more disappointing for Harewood, as he failed to start a single league game and was limited to just six substitute appearances in the league (without scoring a single goal). After loan spells with Wolves and Newcastle, he was released from his contract at the end of the 2009/10 season – leaving Villa with a start ratio of just 1%.

Managers

Year	£XI	£XI Rank	Points	Cost Per Point	Position League	Manager
1992/93	£55,828,533	3	74	£754,439	2	Ron Atkinson
1993/94	£59,937,492	4	57	£1,051,534	10	Ron Atkinson
1994/95	£55,740,913	6	48	£1,161,269	18	Atkinson/Little
Average	£57,168,979	4.3	59.7	£989,081	10	**Ron Atkinson**
1994/95	£55,740,913	6	48	£1,161,269	18	Atkinson/Little
1995/96	£50,321,269	9	63	£798,750	4	Brian Little
1996/97	£52,180,765	9	61	£855,422	5	Brian Little
1997/98	£54,385,867	8	57	£954,138	7	Little/Gregory
Average	£53,157,204	8	57.3	£942,394	8.5	**Brian Little**
1997/98	£54,385,867	8	57	£954,138	7	Little/Gregory
1998/99	£55,399,823	9	55	£1,007,269	6	John Gregory
1999/00	£51,054,060	8	58	£880,242	6	John Gregory
2000/01	£75,705,900	6	54	£1,401,961	8	John Gregory
2001/02	£52,384,939	8	50	£1,047,698	8	Gregory/Taylor
Average	£57,786,118	7.8	54.8	£1,058,261	7	**John Gregory**
2001/02	£52,384,939	8	50	£1,047,698	8	Gregory/Taylor
2002/03	£24,995,357	15	45	£555,452	16	Graham Taylor
Average	£38,690,148	11.5	47.5	£801,575	12	**Graham Taylor**
2003/04	£37,067,183	11	56	£661,913	6	David O'Leary
2004/05	£32,768,410	9	47	£697,200	10	David O'Leary
2005/06	£33,026,043	9	42	£786,334	16	David O'Leary
Average	£34,287,212	9.7	48.3	£715,149	10.7	**David O'Leary**
2006/07	£45,328,516	8	50	£906,570	11	Martin O'Neill
2007/08	£52,872,104	8	60	£881,201	6	Martin O'Neill
2008/09	£61,519,261	7	62	£992,246	6	Martin O'Neill
2009/10	£72,569,119	6	64	£1,133,892	6	Martin O'Neill
Average	£58,072,250	7.3	59.0	£978,477	7.3	**Martin O'Neill**

Top 5 Players Sold for a Profit

- Yorke – Bought for: £0, Sold for: £12.6m (£30.9m), Profit of: £12.6m (£30.9m)
- Barry – Bought for: £0 (trainee), Sold for: £12m (£12m), Profit of: £12m (£12m)
- Ehiogu – Bought for: £40k (£270k), Sold for: £8m (£6.3m), Profit of: £7.96m (£6m)
- Southgate – Bought for: £2.5m (£6.6m), Sold for: £6.5m (£8.6m), Profit of: £4m (£2m)
- Cahill – Bought for: £0 (trainee), Sold for: £4.5m (£5.1m), Profit of: £4.5m (£5.1m)

(James Milner's £26m move to Manchester City will be counted as part of 2010/11's dealings.)

Top 20 CTPP Purchases

#	Player	CTPP	Original fee	Year transferred	% of poss starts
1	Collymore S	£23,632,552	£7,000,000	1997/98	45%
2	Angel JP	£16,908,818	£9,500,000	2000/01	50%
3	Young A	£16,769,972	£9,650,000	2006/07	80%
4	Merson P	£16,534,675	£6,750,000	1998/99	66%
5	Saunders D	£15,309,274	£2,300,000	1992/93	88%
6	Stone S	£13,472,698	£5,500,000	1998/99	43%
7	Dublin D	£12,247,907	£5,000,000	1998/99	53%
8	Downing S	£12,000,000	£12,000,000	2009/10	61%
9	Townsend A	£11,941,388	£2,000,000	1993/94	67%
10	Baroš M	£11,860,896	£6,500,000	2005/06	45%
11	Barrett E	£11,315,551	D1700000	1992/93	83%
12	Petrov S	£11,295,836	£6,500,000	2006/07	82%
13	Atkinson D	£10,649,930	D1600000	1992/93	54%
14	Curčić S	£10,582,145	£4,000,000	1996/97	26%
15	Boateng G	£10,560,017	£4,500,000	1999/00	84%
16	Alpay	£9,967,303	£5,600,000	2000/01	37%
17	Watson S	£9,798,326	£4,000,000	1998/99	51%
18	Reo–Coker N	£9,593,646	£8,500,000	2007/08	54%
19	Milošević S	£9,203,313	£3,500,000	1995/96	74%
20	Draper M	£8,545,934	£3,250,000	1995/96	57%

Expert View

Eliot Pollak (@epollak)

Writer for TV, print and online media

Everyone likes to think they support a big club. But Villa really *are* a big club. Only the second club to win the double, the unparalleled potential UK support base, Peter Withe in '82 and all that. Hell, we even invented the football league.

But no additions to the trophy cabinet in the past 15 years tells its own story; perhaps we're not quite as big as we think anymore. The most eye-boggling fact emerging from the data is that on 63 different occasions since 1992 a Premier League club has had a more valuable squad than us. In other words, over close to 20 seasons, on sheer finance at least, we have had no right to finish in the top three. Conveniently enough, we haven't been higher than 4th since 1993.

So is it purely lack of cash that has produced 15 years of the footballing equivalent of the *Truman Show* down at Villa Park? Clearly not – if football were purely about money, we would actually have done slightly better than we often did. The David O'Leary years for example, would have been a figment of my imagination. So what often went wrong, leading to underperformance even when we did spend?

The mediocrity since those early Premier League years, when examined through the prism of transfers, produce two clear patterns. First of all, the Villa's propensity to pay too much for second-rate English players. With the club lacking either the budget or the geographical glamour (with all due disrespect to the Bullring) to attract big foreign stars, managers such as John Gregory and Martin O'Neill have been forced to shop at home and consequently, pay the silly prices that entails. Stone, Watson, Downing – all English, all overpriced, and all spotted trudging down a Villa Park wing at one time or another. The other, less-explainable phenomenon is the atrocious centre-forward. Ever since Peter Withe, the Villa have been searching high and wide (or Peter Crouch and Dalian Atkinson if you please) for the next great no.9. Collymore, Balaban, Whittingham, Fashanu and Heskey were all signed as the final piece of the jigsaw – but ended up simply going to pieces in the box. None started more than 50% of games while at the club.

Will we ever get back to where we were? Can we still dream? Well in 2009/10, our squad was worth the same as Blackburn's in 1993/94. They challenged for the title that season, and ended 2nd. Sadly in those days, a little went a lot, lot further.

Barnsley

Total Spend (Actual): £6m
Total Spend (CTPP): £20.3m
Average League Position: 19
Number of Managers: 1
Most Expensive Signing: Ǵorǵi Hrstov: £1.5m (£5.1m)
Best Value Signing: Darren Barnard
Worst Value Signing: Ǵorǵi Hrstov

Player Signings Breakdown (data correct up to end of January transfer window 2010)

• UK: 2   EU: 3   Rest of Europe: 2   Rest of the World: 1

Major Trophies Won Since Premier League Began: 0

Premier League Statistics (correct to the end of the 2009/10 season)

Seasons: 1   Played: 38

Won: 10   Drawn: 5   Lost:23

Goals Scored: 37   Goals Conceded: 82   Goal Difference: −45

Total Points: 35

Overview

After finishing 2nd in Division One at the end of 1996/97, Barnsley were promoted to the Premier League for the first and only time in their history. Life in the top flight didn't go according to plan for the Tykes however, and they were relegated at the end of 1997/98 with 35 points, five points adrift from safety. For the first time in Premier League history, all three teams that were promoted at the end of one campaign were relegated the following season. Under the guidance of former player Danny Wilson Barnsley did manage to have a good FA Cup run, reaching the quarter-finals and beating Manchester United along the way.

Barnsley have spent 69 seasons in the second tier of English football, more than any other club.

Managers:

Year	£XI	£XI Rank	Points	Cost Per Point	Position League	Manager
1997/98	£11,674,175	20	35	£333,547	19	Danny Wilson

Top 10 CTPP Purchases

#	Player	CTPP	Original fee	Year transferred	% of poss starts
1	Hristov Ǵ	£5,064,118	£1,500,000	1997/98	29%
2	Ward A	£4,388,902	£1,300,000	1997/98	74%
3	Fjørtoft J	£2,700,863	£800,000	1997/98	32%
4	Barnard D	£2,532,059	£750,000	1997/98	87%
5	Tinkler E	£2,194,451	£650,000	1997/98	55%
6	Križan A	£1,688,039	£500,000	1997/98	32%
7	Redfearn N	£998,431	d150000	1991/92	97%
8	Leese L	£844,020	£250,000	1997/98	21%
9	Markstedt P	£844,020	£250,000	1997/98	16%
10	Hendrie J	£661,384	d250000	1996/97	18%

Expert View

Alan Swift

Barnsley fan

We came, we saw, we left. One-season wonders, the Tykes. We had the cheapest team and so, in that sense, did well to finish above Crystal Palace. Small consolation, though – we both went down.

Gorǵi Hristov – currently Macedonia's second-top goalscorer of all time – was just 21 when he arrived for what today equates to £5m. The next two names on the list of most expensive transfers – Ashley Ward and Jan Åge Fjørtoft – were also strikers who helped the Tykes at least have a chance of staying up. Ward scored 20 goals in 46 games – making him a firm favourite at Oakwell, and scored the winner at Anfield. (He also scored, missed a penalty and got sent off in the space of five minutes in a game against Sunderland.) Fjørtoft – brought in during the second half of the campaign – scored six goals in 11 Premier League games, but it wasn't enough to stave off relegation.

As fans we left richer for the experience. As a club? – not so much.

Birmingham City

Total Spend (Actual): £99.8m
Total Spend (CTPP): £140.3m
Average League Position: 13.5
Number of Managers: 2
Most Expensive Signing: David Dunn – £5.5m (CTPP £11.1m)
Best Value Signing: Roger Johnson
Worst Value Signing: Luciano Figueroa

Player Signings Breakdown (data correct up to end of January transfer window 2010)

• UK: 31   EU: 14   Rest of Europe: 1   Rest of the World: 13

Major Trophies Won Since Premier League Began: 0

Premier League Statistics (correct to the end of the 2009/10 season)

Seasons: 6	Played: 228	
Won: 65	Drawn: 67	Lost:96
Goals Scored: 236	Goals Conceded: 302	Goal Difference: –66
Total Points: 262		

Overview
Birmingham City won promotion to the Premier League at the end of 2001/02 when they beat Norwich City on penalties in the play–off final. Under Steve Bruce they spent the next four seasons in the Premier League, three of them in mid–table positions (13th,

10th and 12th), before being relegated at the end of 2005/06. The Blues spent the next three seasons switching between the Championship and Premier League, before Alex McLeish broke the annual yo-yo cycle by leading Birmingham to 9th place at the end of the 2009/10 Premier League campaign.

Although Birmingham have failed to win a major trophy since their 1963 League Cup triumph over local rivals Aston Villa, they do have the distinction of being the first English side to enter European competition, back in May 1956. They took part in the inaugural Inter-Cities Fairs Cup (later to become the UEFA Cup, and now known as the Europa League), in which they made it as far as the semi-finals, only to lose to Barcelona. They also became the first English club side to reach a European final when, in 1960, they reached the final of the same competition, only to come up short once more against Barcelona.

Most Utilised Players
Roger Johnson proved to be an inspired signing by Alex McLeish in the summer of 2009. Signed from Cardiff City for £5m, a club-record fee for a defender, Johnson started in all 38 Premier League games. Steve Bruce signed Stephen Kelly from Tottenham in June 2006 for £750,000 (£1.4m), and he was the only outfield player to play every minute of every Premier League game during 2006/07.

Least Utilised Players
Steve Bruce had a mixed record in the transfer market while in charge at Birmingham. Luciano Figueroa, signed from Argentine side Rosario Central in 2003 for a fee of £2.5m (£5.1m), is among Bruce's most disappointing purchases. Figueroa failed to make a single start for Birmingham during 2003/04 and made only one substitute appearance before his contract was cancelled at the end of the season.

Managers

Year	£XI	£XI Rank	Points	Cost Per Point	Position League	Manager
2002/03	£20,869,206	17	48	£434,775	13	Steve Bruce
2003/04	£25,206,260	14	50	£504,125	10	Steve Bruce
2004/05	£24,809,786	13	45	£551,328	12	Steve Bruce
2005/06	£23,759,497	12	34	£698,808	18	Steve Bruce
2007/08	£31,530,984	14	35	£900,885	19	Bruce/McLeish
Average	**£25,235,147**	**14**	**42.4**	**£617,984**	**14.4**	**Steve Bruce**
2007/08	£31,530,984	14	35	£900,885	19	Bruce/McLeish
2009/10	£28,467,758	11	50	£569,355	9	Alex McLeish
Average	**£29,999,371**	**12.5**	**42.5**	**£735,120**	**14**	**Alex McLeish**

Top 5 Players Sold for a Profit

- Upson – Bought for: £1m (£1.6m), Sold for: £7.5m (£13.1m), Profit of: £6.5m (£11.5m)
- Pennant – Bought for: £3m (£5.5m), Sold for: £6.7m (£11.7m), Profit of: £3.7m (£6.2m)
- Heskey – Bought for: £3.5m (£6.4m), Sold for: £5.5m (£9.6m), Profit of: £2m (£3.2m)
- Carter – Bought for: £0 (trainee), Sold for: £1.5m (£2.8m), Profit of: £1.5m (£2.8m)
- Muamba – Bought for: £4m (£4.5), Sold for: £5.5m (£4.3), Profit of: £1.5m (£-200k)

Top 20 CTPP Purchases

#	Player	CTPP	Original fee	Year transferred	% of poss starts
1	Dunn D	£11,114,951	£5,500,000	2003/04	32%
2	Cissé A	£7,261,352	£4,500,000	2002/03	34%
3	McSheffrey G	£6,951,284	£4,000,000	2006/07	33%
4	Morrison C	£6,857,944	£4,250,000	2002/03	37%
5	McFadden J	£6,489,820	£5,750,000	2007/08	55%
6	Heskey E	£6,367,315	£3,500,000	2004/05	89%
7	Pennant J	£5,457,698	£3,000,000	2004/05	62%
8	Jerome C	£5,213,463	£3,000,000	2006/07	70%
9	Figueroa L	£5,052,251	£2,500,000	2003/04	0%
10	Johnson R	£5,000,000	£5,000,000	2009/10	100%
11	Muamba F	£4,514,657	£4,000,000	2007/08	97%
12	Savage R	£4,034,084	£2,500,000	2002/03	72%
13	Grønkjær J	£4,002,312	£2,200,000	2004/05	34%
14	Horsfield G	£3,559,751	d2000000	2000/01	22%
15	Lazaridis S	£3,520,006	£1,500,000	1999/00	45%
16	Dann S	£3,500,000	£3,500,000	2009/10	79%
17	Jaïdi R	£3,475,642	£2,000,000	2006/07	47%
18	Kapo O	£3,385,993	£3,000,000	2007/08	58%
19	Nafti M	£3,183,657	£1,750,000	2004/05	24%
20	Taylor M (VI)	£3,031,350	£1,500,000	2003/04	75%

Note: On 3 June 2009, Birmingham City announced the signing of Cristian 'Chucho' Benítez on a three-year contract for an undisclosed club-record transfer fee, which press reports speculated to be in the region of £6 million rising to £9m. The move was subject to the striker receiving a work permit and passing a medical. The medical revealed unforeseen knee problems, which prompted the deal to be renegotiated on a "protected purchase" basis. The club would pay an initial $2m (£1.2m) with an option to abort the deal on medical grounds after the first year; thereafter the fee could potentially rise, depending on appearances and success, to a club record $12.5m (£7.7m). The player eventually signed on July 7. However, the club later clarified that it was in fact a loan.

Expert View

Nicole Carroll (@_NicoleCarroll_)

Fromthepressbox.co.uk

A team such as Birmingham seems to have had a mixed bag of fortune in terms of where they have been positioned in the league, and it seems that this has almost been mirrored in terms of our signings. Without the money that surrounds the modern-day top four, Birmingham have tended to put together teams of grafters, who typically cost a minimal amount, with the occasional flourish of genuine skill and talent.

In particular, during our Premier League years under the stewardship of Steve Bruce, Birmingham seemed to strike it lucky in terms of loan deals. Christophe Dugarry was one such deal during the 2002/03 January transfer window, and is hailed by some Blues fans as the reason we managed to stay up during our first Premier League campaign. Lightning obviously struck twice for Bruce, for the very next season he managed to bring Mikael Forssell on loan from high-flying Chelsea. The flying Finn scored 17 goals for Birmingham in this season and arguably had the finest year in his professional career so far.

Bruce's marquee signing could arguably be seen as David Dunn, whose fee was a record £5.5m at the time (£11.1m in today's market). The potential of the player from Blackburn was exciting – but that potential never entirely materialised. With injuries limiting Dunn's Birmingham appearances, we saw only quick flashes of the player's talent, and our relegation saw Dunn return to his home-town club and, quite disappointingly for Blues fans, saw him return to form somewhat and left us wondering "what if?".

On a limited budget during the 2009/2010 season, Alex McLeish seemingly took a calculated risk on bringing Championship centre-backs Roger Johnson (£5.5m) and Scott Dann (£3.5m) to the club. However, it seems his risk was justified with Birmingham finishing in 9th position and some whispers emerging in the media about the England potential of these players. Other bargain-basement signings for McLeish have included ex-Rangers captain Barry Ferguson and his midfield partner Lee Bowyer, continuing Birmingham's reputation for being a team built on hard-working players. McLeish himself also dabbled in the loan market, bringing in Joe Hart, whose fantastic exploits during the season led to him becoming the current England no. 1.

More recently, McLeish bringing in ex-Arsenal and Barcelona midfielder Hleb shocked some teams in the Premier League, and possibly heralded a new standard of signings for the team of the second city.

Blackburn Rovers

Total Spend (Actual): £182.9m
Total Spend (CTPP): £437.9m
Average League Position: 9.13
Number of Managers: 8
Most Expensive Signing: Alan Shearer – £3.3m (CTPP £22m)
Best Value Signing: Brad Friedel
Worst Value Signing: Paul Warhurst

Player Signings Breakdown (data correct up to end of January transfer window 2010)

• UK: 48   EU: 29   Rest of Europe: 14   Rest of the World: 15

Major Trophies Won Since Premier League Began

Premier League Champions: 1 (1994/95)
League Cup Winners: 1 (2002)

Premier League Statistics (correct to the end of the 2009/10 season)

Seasons: 16	Played: 620	
Won: 243	Drawn: 167	Lost:210
Goals Scored: 833	Goals Conceded: 770	Goal Difference: +63
Total Points: 896		

Overview

Blackburn Rovers are one of only four teams – along with Manchester United, Arsenal and Chelsea – to have been crowned Premier League champions in the competition's 18-year history. Along with Aston Villa and Everton, they are also one of only three teams who are founding members of both the Football League (1888) and the Premier League (1992).

After winning promotion from the football league the previous season, Blackburn finished the inaugural Premier League campaign in 4th place. Backed heavily by Jack Walker's millions, Kenny Dalglish assembled an impressive squad leading Blackburn to the runners-up spot behind Manchester United at the end of 1993/94. They won the Premier League title at the end of 1994/95, the first time they had been champions of England's top division since 1914. However, a 7th-place finish in 1995/96 proved a big disappointment for Rovers, earning the lowest follow-up placing to date by a team defending their Premier League title.

Blackburn's fortunes continued to decline as they finished 1996/97 in 13th, before a 6th-place finish in 1997/98 gave supporters hope that Rovers could challenge once again. This optimism proved to be short lived; Blackburn were relegated at the end of 1998/99, finishing 2nd-bottom with 35 points, just four seasons after winning the Premier League title. This is the most expensive Sq£ and £XI to be relegated in the Premier League era. It would be two years before they returned to the top flight.

In 2001/02 Rovers were able to consolidate their position in the top division, ending the season in 10th place. Indeed, all three promoted clubs stayed up that season – the only time this has happened since the Premier League began. 2001/02 also saw Blackburn win their first ever League Cup, beating Tottenham 2-1 in the final. Rovers finished 2002/03 in 6th place, earning them a spot in the following season's UEFA Cup for the second season in a row. However, Blackburn were unable to continue this momentum and another downturn beset them: finishing 16th (2003/04) and 15th (2004/05). Again, they bounced back: ending up 6th in 2005/06, which earned them a spot in the UEFA

Cup for the third time in five seasons.

Rovers finished three of the next four seasons in the top half of the table (10th in 2006/07, 7th in 2007/08 and 10th in 2009/10), with a 15th-place finish in 2008/09 the only truly disappointing season in recent times.

Most Utilised Players

There are two players who have start ratios of over 90% for Blackburn and both are goalkeepers. Brad Friedel was signed from Liverpool on a free transfer in 2000, and went on to start 261 out of a possible 266 Premier League games for Rovers (98% start ratio) before he was sold to Aston Villa in 2008. Friedel's replacement, Paul Robinson, has started 70 out of a possible 76 games for Blackburn, giving him a 92% start ratio.

Out of all of Blackburn's big-money signings it is Alan Shearer who provided the best return with a start ratio of 80%, having started 132 out of 164 Premier League games. Apparently he scored one or two goals as well.

Least Utilised Players

Blackburn have a number of high-profile and big-money signings with low start ratios. Paul Warhurst was a £2.65m (£15.8m) signing from Sheffield Wednesday in the summer of 1993, but started only 30 out of a possible 160 Premier League games. His start ratio of just 19% is one of the lowest in the Premier League for such an expensive signing. Warhurst is one of four Blackburn players who are valued at CTPP £10m or higher to have a start ratio below 25%.

Managers

Year	£XI	£XI Rank	Points	Cost Per Point	Position League	Manager
1992/93	£44,840,643	8	71	£631,558	4	Kenny Dalglish
1993/94	£72,667,419	3	84	£865,088	2	Kenny Dalglish
1994/95	£87,541,696	1	89	£983,615	1	Kenny Dalglish
Average	**£68,349,919**	**4**	**81**	**£826,754**	**2**	**Kenny Dalglish**
1995/96	£88,456,548	2	61	£1,450,107	7	Ray Harford
1996/97	£70,796,265	4	42	£1,685,625	13	Ray Harford/Tony Parkes
Average	**£79,626,406**	**3**	**52**	**£1,567,866**	**10**	**Ray Harford**
1997/98	£78,122,446	3	58	£1,346,939	6	Roy Hodgson
1998/99	£68,190,692	5	35	£1,948,305	19	Roy Hodgson/Brian Kidd
Average	**£73,156,569**	**4**	**47**	**£1,647,622**	**13**	**Roy Hodgson**
2001/02	£38,909,807	12	46	£845,865	10	Graeme Souness
2002/03	£34,295,509	12	60	£571,592	6	Graeme Souness
2003/04	£40,603,272	9	44	£922,802	15	Graeme Souness
2004/05	£34,309,725	8	42	£816,898	15	Souness/Hughes
Average	**£37,029,578**	**10**	**48**	**£789,289**	**12**	**Graeme Souness**

Year	£XI	£XI Rank	Points	Cost Per Point	Position League	Manager
2004/05	£34,309,725	8	42	£816,898	15	Souness/Hughes
2005/06	£26,697,110	11	63	£423,764	6	Mark Hughes
2006/07	£28,380,195	10	52	£545,773	10	Mark Hughes
2007/08	£31,893,640	13	58	£549,890	7	Mark Hughes
Average	**£30,320,167**	**11**	**54**	**£584,081**	**10**	**Mark Hughes**
2008/09	£23,643,950	16	41	£576,682	15	Paul Ince/Sam Allardyce
Average	**£23,643,950**	**16**	**41**	**£576,682**	**15**	**Paul Ince**
2008/09	£23,643,950	16	41	£576,682	15	Ince/Allardyce
2009/10	£20,724,566	15	50	£414,491	10	Sam Allardyce
Average	**£22,184,258**	**16**	**46**	**£495,587**	**13**	**Sam Allardyce**

Top 5 Players Sold for a Profit

- Duff – Bought for: £0 (trainee), Sold for: £17m (£34.4m), Profit of: £17m (£34.4m)
- Bentley – Bought for: £1.5m (£2.8m), Sold for: £17m (£13.3m), Profit of: £15.5m (£10.5)
- Santa Cruz – Bought for: £3.5m (£4m), Sold for: £17.5m (£17.5m), Profit of: £14m (£13.5m)
- Shearer – Bought for: £3.3m (£22m), Sold for: £15m (£39.7), Profit of: f11.7m (£17.7m)
- Warnock – Bought for: £1.5m (£2.6m), Sold for: £8m (£8m), Profit of: £6.5m (£5.4)

Top 20 CTPP Purchases

#	Player	CTPP	Original fee	Year transferred	% of poss starts
1	Shearer A	£21,965,480	£3,300,000	1992/93	80%
2	Sutton C	£18,942,978	£5,000,000	1994/95	64%
3	Davies K	£17,759,465	£7,250,000	1998/99	24%
4	Batty D	£16,120,874	£2,700,000	1993/94	43%
5	Warhurst P	£15,822,339	£2,650,000	1993/94	19%
6	Ferguson B	£15,156,752	£7,500,000	2003/04	46%
7	Flowers T	£14,329,666	£2,400,000	1993/94	74%
8	Dailly C	£12,982,782	£5,300,000	1998/99	37%
9	Blake N	£10,410,721	£4,250,000	1998/99	12%
10	Ward A	£10,410,721	£4,250,000	1998/99	45%
11	Henchoz S	£10,128,237	£3,000,000	1997/98	70%
12	Jansen M	£10,043,284	£4,100,000	1998/99	25%
13	Gallacher K	£9,984,309	£1,500,000	1992/93	46%
14	Cole AA	£9,829,965	£7,500,000	2001/02	65%
15	McAteer J	£9,798,326	£4,000,000	1998/99	18%
16	Flitcroft G	£9,269,051	£3,525,000	1995/96	50%
17	Bellamy C	£9,123,766	£5,000,000	2005/06	58%
18	Grabbi C	£8,846,968	£6,750,000	2001/02	10%
19	Ripley S	£8,653,068	£1,300,000	1992/93	72%
20	Dahlin M	£8,440,197	£2,500,000	1997/98	17%

Expert View
Dan Clough (@danclough87)
www.roversreturn.footballunited.com

It's a common theory that Blackburn Rovers bought the Premier League title in 1995. Millionaire steel magnate Jack Walker swooped in as the club wallowed in Second Division mediocrity, pumped in millions and, within five years, his team was the best. But when you look at the figures, they weren't the only club spending big at that time.

Yes, on average, their squad was the most expensive in the league when they won the title (£87.5m), but the gap between theirs and other squads – less than £7million – is marginal compared with, for example, the difference between Chelsea and Manchester United in 2005/06, which was approximately £60m.

The Kenny Dalglish factor has more to do with Blackburn's success than money. When Dalglish stepped aside, his deputy, Ray Harford, took control. In 1995/96, Blackburn's average squad cost was higher than in the title-winning season, second only to Liverpool, but under less astute management they struggled to emulate the previous season's form and finished a disappointing 7th.

To further prove Dalglish was the key to Rovers' Premier League success, you only have to go back into the two seasons previous to 1995. In both, they punched above their weight, finishing higher up the league than sides with a higher average squad cost and a more expensive XI.

Despite his relative initial success, Roy Hodgson's big-money signings during the 1997/98 and 1998/99 seasons did not pay off. He was responsible for bringing in Kevin Davies from Southampton for £7.25m (CTPP £17.7m), the third-most expensive signing in Rovers' history and one of their most catastrophic flops. As well as Davies, Hodgson brought in flops such as Christian Dailly (CTPP £13m), Nathan Blake (CTPP £10.4m), Martin Dahlin (CTPP £8.4m), Callum Davidson (CTPP £5.9m) and Sébastien Pérez (CTPP £7.3m).

His successor, Brian Kidd, proved even more disastrous. In his short stint as manager, Rovers failed to halt the slide towards relegation and struggled in the First Division. To make matters worse, he brought in another expensive flop, signing Ashley Ward for £4.25m (CTPP £10.4m).

Astute management on the part of Mark Hughes and Sam Allardyce has continued to lead the way since the turn of the century, as the money dried up following Jack Walker's death. It's interesting to note that Blackburn's average squad cost has declined almost year on year, with the exception of a couple of seasons, and over the past decade, the squad that was Rovers' most expensive – that of the 2003/04 season – was the joint least successful (15th) since relegation.

Bolton Wanderers

Total Spend (Actual): £83.8m
Total Spend (CTPP): £134.8m
Average League Position: 13
Number of Managers: 6
Most Expensive Signing: Nicolas Anelka – £8m (CTPP £13.9m)
Best Value Signing: Jussi Jääskeläinen
Worst Value Signing: Heiðar Helguson

Player Signings Breakdown (data correct up to end of January transfer window 2010)

- UK: 41   EU: 19   Rest of Europe: 9   Rest of the World: 24

Major Trophies Won Since Premier League Began: 0

Premier League Statistics (correct to the end of the 2009/10 season)

Seasons: 11	Played: 418	
Won: 127	Drawn: 112	Lost:179
Goals Scored: 477	Goals Conceded: 612	Goal Difference: –135
Total Points: 493		

Overview

Bolton Wanderers have had three spells in the Premier League. Their first began in 1995, but the Trotters struggled amidst the upheaval of managerial changes and were relegated after just one season. They finished bottom, nine points from safety. They were back a year later, but again it was a brief sojourn; this time relegated on the fine margin of goal difference.

It would be three seasons before Bolton won promotion, beating Preston North End in the play-off final at the end of 2000/01 under Sam Allardyce. 2010/11 will be their 10th successive season in the Premier League.

With 71 seasons in England's highest division, Bolton have spent more time than any other club in the top flight without winning the league title.

Most Utilised Players

Finnish goalkeeper Jussi Jääskeläinen is Bolton's most utilised player in the Premier League, having started 326 out of a possible 342 league games, giving him a start ratio of 95%. Signed for £100,000 (£337,000) in 1997, Jääskeläinen has proven to be excellent value for the Trotters, having started all 38 league games in six out of the past nine seasons in the Premier League. He is clearly one of the league's best purchases in the past 18 years.

Kevin Davies is another player with a start ratio higher than 90%. Signed on a free transfer in 2003, Davies has started 243 out of 263 Premier League games for Bolton (91%). He has featured in at least 30 league games in every season for Bolton during his time at the club.

Least Utilised Players

Bolton have several players with 0% start ratios, but it is Daniel Braaten who proves to be the most expensive at £450k (£508k). Signed in August 2007, Braaten didn't start a single game for the Trotters before he was sold to Toulouse in June 2008, as part of the deal that brought Johan Elmander to the Reebok Stadium.

Managers

Year	£XI	£XI Rank	Points	Cost Per Point	Position League	Manager
1995/96	£13,903,192	20	29	£479,420	20	McFarland/Colin Todd
1997/98	£28,825,972	14	40	£720,649	18	Colin Todd
Average	**£21,364,582**	**17**	**34.5**	**£600,035**	**19**	**Colin Todd**
2001/02	£11,689,493	20	40	£292,237	16	Sam Allardyce
2002/03	£9,269,455	20	44	£210,669	17	Sam Allardyce
2003/04	£4,359,571	20	53	£82,256	8	Sam Allardyce
2004/05	£4,739,177	20	58	£81,710	6	Sam Allardyce
2005/06	£8,882,976	20	56	£158,625	8	Sam Allardyce
2006/07	£25,386,672	13	56	£453,333	7	Allardyce/Lee
Average	**£10,721,224**	**18.8**	**51.2**	**£213,138**	**10.3**	**Sam Allardyce**
2006/07	£25,386,672	13	56	£453,333	7	Allardyce/Sammy Lee
2007/08	£22,568,094	18	37	£609,948	16	Sammy Lee/Megson
Average	**£23,977,383**	**15.5**	**46.5**	**£531,641**	**11.5**	**Sammy Lee**
2007/08	£22,568,094	18	37	£609,948	16	Lee/Gary Megson
2008/09	£25,557,065	15	41	£623,343	13	Gary Megson
2009/10	£25,703,674	12	39	£659,069	14	Megson/Owen Coyle
Average	**£24,609,611**	**15**	**39**	**£630,787**	**14.3**	**Gary Megson**
2009/10	£25,703,674	12	39	£659,069	14	Megson/Owen Coyle
Average	**£25,703,674**	**12**	**39**	**£659,069**	**14**	**Owen Coyle**

Top 5 Players Sold for a Profit

- Anelka – Bought for: £8m (£13.9m), Sold for: £15m (£16.9m), Profit of: £7m (£3m)
- McAteer – Bought for: £0, Sold for: £4.5m (£11.8m), Profit of: £4.5m (£11.8m)
- Nolan – Bought for: £0 (trainee), Sold for: £4m (£3.1m), Profit of: £4m (£3.1m)
- Stubbs – Bought for: £0 (trainee), Sold for: £3.5m (£9.3m), Profit of: £3.5m (£9.3m)
- Blake – Bought for: £1.2m (£3.2m), Sold for: £4.3m (£10.4m), Profit of: £3.1m (£7.2m)

Top 20 CTPP Purchases

#	Player	CTPP	Original fee	Year transferred	% of poss starts
1	Anelka N	£13,902,567	£8,000,000	2006/07	70%
2	Holdsworth D	£11,816,276	£3,500,000	1997/98	27%
3	Elliott R	£8,440,197	£2,500,000	1997/98	11%
4	Elmander J	£7,818,931	£10,000,000	2008/09	59%
5	Fish M	£6,752,158	£2,000,000	1997/98	58%
6	Cahill G	£5,078,989	£4,500,000	2007/08	66%
7	Taylor M (IV)	£5,078,989	£4,500,000	2007/08	68%
8	Muamba F	£4,300,412	£5,500,000	2008/09	89%
9	Cox N	£4,051,295	£1,200,000	1997/98	53%
10	Pollock J	£3,968,305	d1500000	1996/97	66%
11	Steinsson G	£3,950,325	£3,500,000	2007/08	68%
12	Curčić S	£3,944,277	£1,500,000	1995/96	74%
13	Taggart G	£3,944,277	£1,500,000	1995/96	33%
14	Knight Z	£3,500,000	£3,500,000	2009/10	92%
15	Frandsen P	£3,306,920	d1250000	1996/97	78%
16	Johansen M (I)	£3,306,920	d1250000	1996/97	11%
17	Blake N	£3,155,422	£1,200,000	1995/96	64%
18	Gardner R	£2,449,581	£1,000,000	1998/99	60%
19	Hansen R	£2,449,581	d1000000	1998/99	26%
20	McAnespie S	£2,366,566	£900,000	1995/96	11%

Expert View

Richard McCormick (@ @MannyRoad)

Editor, Manny Road www.mannyroad.com

'Who needs Mourinho? We've got Sam Allardyce,' sang the fans, as Bolton came within a whisker of claiming a Champions League spot in 2005. It was the second of four consecutive top-eight finishes, a feat that Sam has never received sufficient credit for.

Recruitment was one factor. Youri Djorkaeff, Jay-Jay Okocha, Fernando Hierro, Iván Campo, Stelios Giannakopoulos, Bruno N'Gotty and Kevin Davies cost not a penny between them in transfer fees. Tal Ben Haim, Gary Speed and Abdoulaye Faye were picked up for the football equivalent of loose change.

But that was only part of the story. Allardyce's genius lay in taking players who were seen as past it, underperforming or simply unmanageable, and moulding them into a cohesive unit. Each one knew his job and (particularly in Davies's case) was willing to alter his natural game for the common cause.

Much has been made of long-ball tactics. The case was always overstated and it misses the point. Bolton could stifle the most talented of midfields (just ask Arsenal). It took organisation, hard work, high levels of fitness and commitment. Stop the other side playing and you're more than half-way there.

The formula didn't translate to Newcastle. Lack of time, a new owner, players who wouldn't buy into the plan and fans with delusions undimmed by over half a century of failure saw to that.

But don't let that detract from what Sam achieved at the Reebok. For an extended period, a little club from north-west England outperformed the likes of Spurs, Aston Villa, Newcastle and Manchester City who had far more resources. They ruffled the feathers of the big boys now and then too.

It was an extraordinary time.

Expert View
Michael Cox (@zonal_marking)
Editor, Zonal Marking www.zonalmarking.net

"I'm not suited to Bolton or Blackburn; I would be more suited to Inter or Real Madrid," Sam Allardyce recently said. "It wouldn't be a problem to me to go and manage those clubs because I would win the double or the league every time."

It was certainly tongue-in-cheek, but Allardyce doesn't receive due credit for his managerial achievements. Taking over Bolton in the old First Division, he guided them to an initial two seasons of mere Premiership survival, before recording finishes of 8th, 6th, 8th and 7th in his final four seasons at the club. Only the 'big four' of Arsenal, Chelsea, Liverpool and Manchester United finished in the top 10 in those four seasons, underlining how quickly Allardyce made Bolton an established Premier League club.

In stark contrast to his old-school, no-nonsense appearance in public, Allardyce is one of the greater innovators amongst current Premiership managers. He favours a huge backroom staff (generally around 20 coaches) and pays incredible attention to detail, both in terms of tactics and physical preparation. He is a strong advocate of using Prozone in order to analyse games and scout opponents, whilst his methods of improving players' fitness levels include pilates and yoga.

There has been strong criticism of his style of football – route one and unattractive – but his sides have generally included two or three genuinely technically gifted players. Players like Eiður Guðjohnsen, Jay-Jay Okocha, Stelios Giannakopoulos, Nicolas Anelka, El-Hadji Diouf, Hidetoshi Nakata, Youri Djorkaeff and Fernando Hierro played under Allardyce at Bolton.

His 'failure' at Newcastle has been slightly overstated. For a start, he was given just five months of the season to try and turn around a club that was in a terrible state upon his arrival. He left the club when they were comfortably mid-table in

11th place, having finished 13th the previous season.

At Blackburn he's been able to have more of an influence on the club as a whole. He took over the club midway through 2008/09 in 19th place and guided them to 15th place, before 10th in his first complete season, including being unbeaten at home to the 'big four'. Inter or Real might not come calling, but Allardyce's achievements deserve respect.

Bradford City

Total Spend (Actual): £8.4m
Total Spend (CTPP): £16.5m
Average League Position: 18.5
Number of Managers: 3
Most Expensive Signing: David Hopkin – £2.5m (CTPP £4.5m)
Best Value Signing: David Wetherall
Worst Value Signing: David Hopkin

Player Signings Breakdown (data correct up to end of January transfer window 2010)

- UK: 16   EU: 3   Rest of Europe: 1   Rest of the World: 0

Major Trophies Won Since Premier League Began: 0

Premier League Statistics (correct to the end of the 2009/10 season)

Seasons: 2	Played: 76	
Won: 14	Drawn: 20	Lost: 42
Goals Scored: 68	Goals Conceded: 138	Goal Difference: –70
Total Points: 62		

Overview

Before their promotion to the Premier League in 1999, via a 2nd-place finish in Division One, Bradford City had spent 77 years outside the top flight. Under Paul Jewell, they managed to defy the odds by surviving on the last day of the 1999/00 Premier League season with a 1-0 victory over Liverpool. The following season proved to be a more difficult one for the Bantams, and they were relegated from the Premier League; finishing in 20th place with 26 points, having scored the fewest goals (30), conceded the most (70) and lost more league games (22) than anyone else that season.

Managers

Year	£XI	£XI Rank	Points	Cost Per Point	Position League	Manager
1999/00	£10,243,172	19	36	£284,533	17	Paul Jewell
2000/01	£9,830,047	20	26	£378,079	20	Hutchings/Jefferies

Top 10 CTPP Purchases

#	Player	CTPP	Original fee	Year transferred	% of poss starts
1	Hopkin D	£4,449,689	£2,500,000	2000/01	21%
2	Wetherall D	£3,285,338	£1,400,000	1999/00	74%
3	Rankin I	£3,184,456	d1300000	1998/99	0%
4	Ward A	£2,669,813	£1,500,000	2000/01	63%
5	Mills L	£2,449,581	d1000000	1998/99	50%
6	Windass D	£2,327,102	d950000	1998/99	76%
7	Myers A	£1,877,336	£800,000	1999/00	33%
8	Petrescu D	£1,779,876	£1,000,000	2000/01	42%
9	Walsh G	£1,688,039	d500000	1997/98	39%
10	Whalley G	£1,469,749	d600000	1998/99	43%

Expert View

Benjamin Welby (@bmwelby)

Editor, Vital Bradford www.bradford.vitalfootball.co.uk

Bradford City started the 1998/99 season with five points from 21, but ended it with a 3-2 victory over Wolves and promotion to the Premier League. If getting there was far-fetched at the season's start, it had nothing on the chances of our survival in 1999/00. The next year we got what was expected. Perhaps the writing was on the wall from the moment Stuart McCall fell off the roof of that car. No sooner was promotion achieved than the agents of our heroes designated them top-flight stars. Ultimately that meant players like Robbie Blake and Darren Moore found themselves sidelined when they should have been integral.

Only Watford fielded a cheaper side that first year, with our most costly players having arrived whilst still in Division One. Then club-record signing Isaiah Rankin (£1.3m/£3.2m), Lee Mills (£1m/£2.4m) and Gareth Whalley (£0.6m/£1.5m) arrived in 1998, with Dean Windass (£0.95m/£2.3m) joining in March 1999. Jewell added to what he had as necessary and raided our nearest (though not dearest) neighbours, Leeds, for Lee Sharpe and Gunnar Halle for nominal fees, and captain David Wetherall (£1.4m/£3.3m). Jewell looked to the experience of Dean Saunders (on a free) and the youth of Andy O'Brien. He created a team on a shoestring budget, spending little before the season began.

Famously, of course, Rodney Marsh was so convinced we would go down that he offered to have his head shaved if we didn't. A last-day fixture against a Liverpool side on the verge of Champions League qualification suggested he'd be fine, only for record signing David Wetherall to head home a goal that prompted an appointment with the clippers.

We'd hung on by the skin of our teeth, but then Paul Jewell left. Chris Hutchings tried to consolidate, but behind the scenes we were in meltdown. These 'six weeks of madness' define our present and saw us break the club record to bring in David Hopkin (£2.5m/£4.4m - moved on to Crystal Palace for less than half that fee before the season was out) and other 'well-established' players like Ashley Ward (£1.5m/£2.7m), Dan Petrescu (£1m/£1.8m), Benito Carbone (free) and Stan Collymore (free). A small club from the grimy north was not an attractive proposition for Premier League superstars, so we enticed them with hefty wages and signing-on fees, and although the squad fractionally increased in value these players seldom delivered the quality we knew they possessed.

But the players tell only half the story. Valley Parade, shrine to those who lost their lives in 1985, stands as a testament to our folly. Instead of investing in training and youth facilities, money was spent on redeveloping the stadium in two phases. By the time the second phase was finished, we stood on the brink of relegation. The collapse of ITV Digital and the lack of parachute payments to cushion our fall meant relegation was only the start of things turning sour. After three relegations and two administrations, we've still not found a way to stop the rot.

Our dream became reality, but then we tried to push too far too soon. The Premier League, with its wealth, fame and glory, is not all bright lights. Blackpool seem to have learnt from our experience; Hull did not. History might record our sojourn as nothing more than a cameo, but those two seasons sit like a millstone around our necks to this day. Whilst little compares with home victories over Arsenal, Chelsea and Liverpool, we've had nothing to celebrate since David Wetherall's header. A hundred years on from lifting the FA Cup and five games into a new season, we find ourselves 90th of 92 clubs. Week in and week out we're living with the crushing disappointment of 10 years of decline. That's because of the Premier League; we didn't give it the respect it deserves. Would we rather have been one-season wonders?

Probably.

Burnley

Total Spend (Actual): £10.1m
Total Spend (CTPP): £10.1m
Average League Position: 18th
Number of Managers: 2
Most Expensive Signing: André Bikey & Steven Fletcher – £3m (CTPP £3m)
Best Value Signing: Tyrone Mears
Worst Value Signing: David Edgar

Player Signings Breakdown (data correct up to end of January transfer window 2010)

- UK: 4　　　　　　　EU: 0　　　Rest of Europe: 0　　　　　Rest of the World: 2

Major Trophies Won Since Premier League Began: 0

Premier League Statistics (correct to the end of the 2009/10 season)

Seasons: 1　　　　Played: 38
Won: 8　　　　　　Drawn: 6　　　　　　Lost:24
Goals Scored: 42　Goals Conceded: 82　　Goal Difference: –40
Total Points: 30

Overview

In 2009, Burnley clinched promotion to the Premier League following a 33-year absence. Despite a good start to the league campaign, including 1-0 home victories over both Manchester United and Everton, they were eventually relegated, finishing 18th on 30 points – the lowest ever tally for a team coming 3rd from bottom.

Despite having spent only one season in the Premier League, Burnley can claim a proud history having been crowned football league champions on two occasions (1920/21 and 1959/60) as well as winning the FA Cup in 1914. They are also one of only three clubs that have won all four of England's professional divisions. A less exceptional record is the one Burnley hold for most away losses (17) in the Premier League during a single season (2009/10).

Managers

Year	£XI	£XI Rank	Points	Cost Per Point	Position League	Manager
2009/10	£8,172,883	20	30	£272,429	18	Coyle/Laws

Top 10 CTPP Purchases

#	Player	CTPP	Original fee	Year transferred	% of poss starts
1	Mears T	£500,000	£500,000	2009/10	100%
2	Jensen B	£0	d0	2003/04	100%
3	Fletcher S	£3,000,000	£3,000,000	2009/10	92%
4	Elliot W	£0	d0	2005/06	89%
5	Alexander G	£112,866	d100000	2007/08	87%
6	Carlisle C	£225,733	d200000	2007/08	71%
7	Bikey A	£3,000,000	£3,000,000	2009/10	68%
8	Jordan S	£0	d0	2007/08	61%
9	Eagles C	£938,272	d1200000	2008/09	53%
10	Blake R	£282,166	d250000	2007/08	53%

Expert View

Kev Robinson (@kevr1990)

www.nonaynever.net

When Wade Elliott volleyed in the only goal in the 2009 Championship play-off final, he entered his club into a financial world that was both overwhelmingly alien and strikingly familiar. It had been dubbed the '£60m goal', because with promotion came all the riches that come with 21st-century life in England's top flight. To a club that just a couple of years earlier was forced to ask fans for donations in order to survive, a new-found wealth was a whole new world. And yet despite these riches, manager Owen Coyle would enjoy considerably the smallest budget in the league – a 'comforting' continuation of the known.

Chairman Barry Kilby has earned many admirers for his premiership at the club, overseeing and overcoming financial difficulties that were largely kickstarted by the collapse of ITV Digital. His strategy in this first season spearheading a Premier League club may have frustrated a number of supporters – and, so it seems, his manager – but many more respected his prudence.

Kilby had the long-term future of the club in mind when issuing a budget for Coyle to work with. With an eye undoubtedly on the likes of Derby County – who now face financial struggles following their flirtation with the top flight – he imposed a wage cap of £15k a week. The £3m signing of Steven Fletcher from Hibernian was the biggest expenditure of the summer – considered small in the context of the competition, but a world away from when the £30k signing of Michael Duff (who is actually still at the club after signing a new deal this summer) was considered risky.

Whilst the season ultimately ended in relegation, the club returns to the Football League in a great position – financially secure, the majority of the Premier League squad retained and, importantly, without the ticking time-bomb of a huge wage bill looming over our heads.

Charlton Athletic

Total Spend (Actual): £53.8m
Total Spend (CTPP): £95.1m
Average League Position: 12.8
Number of Managers: 3
Most Expensive Signing: Claus Jensen – £4m (CTPP £7.2m)
Best Value Signing: Darren Bent
Worst Value Signing: Madjid Bougherra

Player Signings Breakdown (data correct up to end of January transfer window 2010)

- UK: 23   EU: 11   Rest of Europe: 2   Rest of the World: 12

Major Trophies Won Since Premier League Began: 0

Premier League Statistics (correct to the end of the 2009/10 season)

Seasons: 8	Played: 304	
Won: 93	Drawn: 82	Lost:129
Goals Scored: 342	Goals Conceded: 442	Goal Difference: –100
Total Points: 361		

Overview

Charlton Athletic have had two spells in the Premier League, spanning a total of eight seasons. Their first inclusion lasted just one year – they were relegated at the end of 1998/99 upon finishing 18th, with 36 points. Their second spell was far more successful: seven consecutive seasons in England's top division, before suffering relegation at the end of the 2006/07 campaign.

Under Alan Curbishley Charlton established a reputation as being a solid mid–table side, with their highest finish – 7th place – coming in 2003/04. This was the Addicks' best performance in England's top division since 1953, when they finished 5th.

Most Utilised Players

Darren Bent is arguably Charlton's most successful purchase during their time in the Premier League. Signed for £3m (£5.5m) in June 2005, Bent started 68 out of a possible 76 league games for the Addicks, finishing as the club's top scorer in both of the seasons he spent at The Valley. He left Charlton with an 89% start ratio when he was sold to Tottenham in June 2007, for what would be £17.5m in today's money.

Another signing who figures highly in Charlton's utilisation charts is Hermann Hreiðarsson, signed from Ipswich Town in March 2003 for £800k (£1.3m). Hreiðarsson started 130 out of a possible 152 Premier League games for Charlton during his four seasons at the club, leaving with a start ratio of 86%.

Least Utilised Players

Madjid Bougherra joined Charlton from Sheffield Wednesday in January 2007 for £2.5m (£4.3m) but started only two league games (5%) for the Addicks, before being sold to Glasgow Rangers in July 2008. Another player with a low start ratio is Gary Rowett. Signed for £2.5m (£4m) in 2002, Rowett started 13 out of 76 Premier League games (17%) before he left Charlton in 2004.

Managers

Year	£XI	£XI Rank	Points	Cost Per Point	Position League	Manager
1998/99	£11,212,325	20	36	£311,453	18	Alan Curbishley
2000/01	£20,926,167	18	52	£402,426	9	Alan Curbishley
2001/02	£23,245,224	17	44	£528,301	14	Alan Curbishley
2002/03	£23,594,460	16	49	£481,520	12	Alan Curbishley
2003/04	£22,563,217	16	53	£425,721	7	Alan Curbishley
2004/05	£21,926,495	15	46	£476,663	11	Alan Curbishley
2005/06	£20,020,387	13	47	£425,966	13	Alan Curbishley
Average	£20,498,325	16.4	46.7	£436,007	12	**Alan Curbishley**
2006/07	£24,611,116	14	34	£723,856	19	**Dowie/Reed/Pardew**

Top 5 Players Sold for a Profit

- D. Bent – Bought for: £3m (£5.5m), Sold for: £15.5m (£17.5m), Profit of: £12.5m (£12m)
- Parker – Bought for: £0 (trainee), Sold for: £10m (£20.2m), Profit of: £10m (£20.2m)
- Mills – Bought for: £350,000 (£1.2m), Sold for: £4.37m (£10.3m), Profit of: £4.1m (£9.1m)
- Konchesky – Bought for: £0 (trainee), Sold for: £1.5m (£2.8m), Profit of: £1.5m (£2.8m)
- Reid – Bought for: £3m (£5.2m), Sold for: £4m (£4.5m), Profit of: £1m (£-700k)

Top 20 CTPP Purchases

#	Player	CTPP	Original fee	Year transferred	% of poss starts
1	Jensen C	£7,119,502	£4,000,000	2000/01	74%
2	Johansson J	£6,674,533	£3,750,000	2000/01	39%
3	Diawara S	£6,429,937	£3,700,000	2006/07	47%
4	Euell J	£6,225,644	£4,750,000	2001/02	54%
5	Bent D	£5,474,260	£3,000,000	2005/06	89%
6	Reid A	£5,213,463	£3,000,000	2006/07	39%
7	Jeffers F	£4,730,005	£2,600,000	2004/05	24%
8	Murphy D (I)	£4,548,082	£2,500,000	2004/05	71%
9	Bougherra M	£4,344,552	£2,500,000	2006/07	5%
10	Rowett G	£4,034,084	£2,500,000	2002/03	17%
11	Young L	£3,931,986	£3,000,000	2001/02	79%
12	Bent M	£3,649,506	£2,000,000	2005/06	38%
13	Rommedahl D	£3,638,465	£2,000,000	2004/05	50%
14	Traoré D	£3,475,642	£2,000,000	2006/07	29%
15	Faye A (II)	£3,475,642	£2,000,000	2006/07	66%
16	Stuart G	£2,694,540	£1,100,000	1998/99	45%

#	Player	CTPP	Original fee	Year transferred	% of poss starts
17	Redfearn N	£2,449,581	£1,000,000	1998/99	76%
18	Mendonca C	£2,363,255	d700000	1997/98	50%
19	Kiely D	£2,346,670	d1000000	1999/00	78%
20	Powell C	£2,020,905	£825,000	1998/99	77%

Expert View

Darryl Chamberlain (@darryl1974)

All Quiet in the East Stand: www.charlton.blogspot.com

For a few years, "doing things the Charlton way" was held up as the way to run a small football club in the Premier League. But the dream went sour after Alan Curbishley's departure – and the nightmares still reverberate around The Valley today.

A close bond between Curbishley, chairman Richard Murray and chief executive Peter Varney ensured success. After Charlton's first season in the Premier League ended in relegation, Curbishley was able to keep the bulk of his team together and charge back into the top flight.

The greatest buys were among the earliest. Chris Powell (£825,000/£2m CTPP) was among Curbishley's first Premier League signings in 1998 – with the hard-working left-back later being called up by England. ("Chris who?", sneered the *London Evening Standard*.) Goalkeeper Dean Kiely (£1m/£2.3m) was bought to steady Charlton after relegation, but helped the club stay up once they got back to the Premier League.

Goals from Jonatan Johansson (£3.25m/£6.67m) helped the Addicks reach 9th in 2001. Claus Jensen (£4m/£7.1m) brought flair while Jason Euell (£4.75m/£6.2m) provided more goals in a squad not known for its free scoring. A 4-2 win over Chelsea on Boxing Day 2003 was the high point. Then, while 4th in the table, Curbishley was forced to sell Scott Parker to the Blues amid acrimony. Many still feel Charlton would have qualified for Europe if Parker had stayed. Instead, that transfer started a gradual decline. Not that the ambition wasn't there – but Curbishley's eye for a player was waning. Dennis Rommedahl (£2m/ £3.6m) thrilled with his runs up the wing, but frustrated with his nerves in front of goal. Danny Murphy (£2.5m/£3.6m) brought dynamism to midfield – until he fell out with Curbishley over losing his place in the side. The less said about Francis Jeffers (£2.6m/£4.7m), the better.

Darren Bent (£3m/£5.5m) – supremely talented and modest with it – would have fitted in perfectly to Curbishley's earlier Premier League squads. But his final singing, Marcus Bent (£2.3m/£3.6m) – generously dubbed an "average player" by his old Everton boss David Moyes – rarely looked interested. The magician had run out of tricks. A minority of fans booed even mediocre performances and raced to berate the manager on radio phone-ins. A majority could agree, at least, that things were getting stale.

After Curbishley left in 2006, Iain Dowie was handed a huge sum to try to make life more exciting. Be careful what you wish for. Defender Souleymane Diawara (£3.7m/£6.4m) was even criticised by his own chairman once Dowie had been sacked after just 15 games. He could just as easily have turned his scorn on the hapless Djimi Traoré (£2m/£3.47m), Amdy Faye (£2m/£3.47m) or Jimmy Floyd Hasselbaink (free). Alan Pardew couldn't turn things around – and compounded issues with poor signings in the Championship, as the club was slowly strangled by a huge wage bill and sank to the third tier. For now, the Addicks live to fight on, but sadly, "doing things the Charlton way" ended up as a cautionary tale.

Chelsea

Total Spend (Actual): £579.8m
Total Spend (CTPP). £1068.8m
Average League Position: 5.17
Number of Managers: 11
Most Expensive Signing. Andrly Shevchenko – £30.8m (CTPP £53.6m)
Best Value Signing: Frank Lampard
Worst Value Signing: Juan Sebastián Verón

Player Signings Breakdown (data correct up to end of January transfer window 2010)

• UK: 31   EU: 50   Rest of Europe: 14   Rest of the World: 17

Major Trophies Won Since Premier League Began

Premier League Champions: 3 (2004/05, 2005/06, 2009/10)
FA Cup: 5 (1997, 2000, 2007, 2009, 2010)
League Cup: 3 (1998, 2005, 2007)
UEFA Cup Winners Cup: 1 (1998)

Premier League Statistics (correct to the end of the 2009/10 season)

Seasons: 18	Played: 696	
Won: 362	Drawn: 181	Lost:153
Goals Scored: 1148	Goals Conceded: 662	Goal Difference: +486
Total Points: 1267		

Overview

With 12 major trophies won, Chelsea are second only to Manchester United when it comes to lifting silverware since 1992. The majority of Chelsea's trophy-winning seasons have come since the arrival of Russian oligarch Roman Abramovich, with no fewer than eight pieces of silverware collected since he bought the club in 2003.

In three of the first four Premier League seasons, Chelsea finished in 11th place, with a 14th-place finish in 1993/94 marking their lowest league standing since they were relegated in 1988. Despite their relatively poor showing in the league, they did reach the 1994 FA Cup Final under Glenn Hoddle – where they lost 4-0 to Manchester United – and the semi-finals of the Cup Winners' Cup and FA Cup in 1995 and 1996 respectively. This relative success followed the appointment of Matthew Harding onto the board, the millionaire fan having invested £26.5m in the club. Tragically, Harding died in a helicopter accident in 1996 while flying back from a Chelsea away game; he therefore didn't live to see the trophies won in the next handful of years on the back of his financing.

It was with the appointment of Ruud Gullit as player/manager to replace Hoddle in 1996 that Chelsea started winning major honours. Gullit became the first overseas manager to lift the FA Cup when the Blues defeated Middlesbrough 2-0 – Chelsea's first major trophy since 1970. Gullit was replaced by Gianluca Vialli as player/manager in February 1998. Chelsea finished 1997/98 in 4th place and won both the League Cup (with another 2-0 victory over Middlesbrough) and European Cup Winners' Cup (with a 1-0 victory over VfB Stuttgart) that season. The Blues finished 3rd a year later, and then 5th in 1999/00, at the same time beating Aston Villa to win the FA Cup. Vialli was sacked just five games into 2000/01, with fellow Italian Claudio Ranieri taking his place. Chelsea finished 6th that year and the season after, before rising to 4th in 2002/03.

Roman Abramovich bought the club from Ken Bates in 2003, and invested heavily in the Chelsea squad. In an unprecedented spending spree, the Blues paid out over £100m (£222m CTPP) in the build-up to the 2003/04 season. Despite Ranieri leading Chelsea to a 2nd-place finish that season (at the time the club's best since 1954/55), the Italian was sacked and replaced with José Mourinho, who was fresh from leading Porto to Champions League glory. Chelsea once again flexed their unrivalled financial muscle, spending close to £100m (£180m) for the second summer running. This time their spending paid off: they won back-to-back Premier League titles in 2004/05 and 2005/06; a feat that has been achieved by only four other clubs (Portsmouth, Manchester United, Wolves and Liverpool) since the Second World War.

Chelsea finished 2nd in 2006/07, and, despite also adding the League Cup (2005) and FA Cup (2007), Mourinho and Chelsea parted company just weeks into the 2007/08 season. He was replaced by Israeli Avram Grant, who led the Blues to their first ever Champions League Final (which they lost to Manchester United on penalties after extra time). Despite this relative achievement, Grant was sacked just days after that defeat.

Brazilian World Cup-winning manager Phil Scolari took over for the 2008/09 season, but was sacked in February 2009 after a poor run of results. Guus Hiddink took charge on a temporary basis and led the Blues to a 3rd-place finish and a 2-1 FA Cup final victory over Everton. Hiddink honoured his contract with the Russian national side, and so Abramovich turned to Carlo Ancelotti. The Italian landed Chelsea their third Premier League title in 2010, and completed the club's first double by beating Portsmouth 1-0 in the 2010 FA Cup Final, becoming only the seventh side to win the League and FA Cup in the same season.

Below is a list of some of the Premier League records Chelsea currently hold:

- Most wins in a 38-game season: 29 (2004/05, 2005/06)
- Most home wins in a 38-game season: 18 (2005/06)
- Most away wins in a 38-game season: 15 (2004/05)
- Fewest draws in 38-game season: 3 (1997/98)
- Most goals scored in a 38-game season: 103 (2009/10)
- Fewest goals conceded in a 38-game season: 15 (2004/05)
- Best goal difference in a 38-game season: +71 (2009/10)
- Most consecutive wins at home: 19
- Most consecutive wins away: 11
- Most goals scored at home in a 38-game season: 68 (2009/10)
- Fewest goals conceded at home in a 38-game season: 6 (2004/05)
- Fewest goals conceded away in a 38-game season: 9 (2004/05)
- Most clean sheets in a 38-game season: 24 (2004/05)

Most Utilised Players

Frank Lampard is Chelsea's most utilised Premier League signing with a start ratio of 92% - phenomenal for an outfield player over almost a full decade. Signed from West Ham United in 2001 for £11m (£14.5m), Lampard has started 314 out of a possible 342 Premier League games for Chelsea. Petr Čech (81%) is next on the list, having been in the XI in 184 out of 228 Premier League games since his £8.5m (£17.2m) signing from Rennes in July 2004.

It is worth noting that three out of the top five Most Utilised Players for Chelsea were signed by Claudio Ranieri.

Least Utilised Players

There are a number of big-money signings that figure prominently in Chelsea's list of Least Utilised Players, with no fewer than five with a CTPP of over £20m having started less than 30% of the available fixtures. These are: Scott Parker (11%, £20.3m), Juan Verón (13%, £25.3m), Andriy Shevchenko (26%, £53.6m), Shaun Wright-Phillips (28%, £38.4m) and Adrian Mutu (28%, £32m). (Shevchenko was loaned out for some of his career at Chelsea, but as loans are conscious decisions by clubs to not make use of the player, that time still counts.)

Managers

Year	£XI	£XI Rank	Points	Cost Per Point	Position League	Manager
1992/93	£34,847,617	10	56	£622,279	11	Porterfield/Webb
1993/94	£32,175,544	12	51	£630,893	14	Glenn Hoddle
1994/95	£38,273,858	13	54	£708,775	11	Glenn Hoddle
1995/96	£32,901,859	14	50	£658,037	11	Glenn Hoddle
Average	£34,450,420	13	52	£665,902	12	Glenn Hoddle
1996-97	£44,558,534	12	59	£755,229	6	Ruud Gullit
1997/98	£59,061,096	7	63	£937,478	4	Gullit/Vialli
Average	£51,809,815	9.5	61	£846,354	5	Ruud Gullit
1997/98	£59,061,096	7	63	£937,478	4	Gullit/Vialli
1998/99	£79,770,946	4	75	£1,063,613	3	Gianluca Vialli
1999/00	£78,961,634	4	65	£1,214,794	5	Gianluca Vialli
2000/01	£87,051,048	3	61	£1,427,066	6	Vialli/Ranieri
Average	£76,211,181	4.5	66	£1,160,738	4.5	Gianluca Vialli
2000/01	£87,051,048	3	61	£1,427,066	6	Vialli/ Claudio Ranieri
2001/02	£97,619,495	3	64	£1,525,305	6	Claudio Ranieri
2002/03	£98,277,155	4	67	£1,466,823	4	Claudio Ranieri
2003/04	£153,144,833	1	79	£1,938,542	2	Claudio Ranieri
Average	£109,023,132	2.8	68	£1,589,434	4.5	Claudio Ranieri
2004/05	£195,163,150	1	95	£2,054,349	1	José Mourinho
2005/06	£229,619,425	1	91	£2,523,290	1	José Mourinho
2006/07	£255,266,748	1	83	£3,075,503	2	José Mourinho
2007/08	£201,709,707	1	85	£2,373,055	2	Mourinho/Avram Grant
Average	£220,439,757	1	89	£2,506,549	1.5	José Mourinho
2008/09	£168,193,359	1	83	£2,026,426	3	Scolari/Hiddink
2009/10	£187,436,346	1	86	£2,179,492	1	Carlo Ancelotti

Top 5 Players Sold for a Profit

- Flo – Bought for: £300k (£1m), Sold for: £14m (£25m), Profit of: £13.7m (£24m)
- Robben– Bought for: £13m (£23.7m), Sold for: £24m (£27.1m), Profit of: £11m (£3.4m)
- Huth – Bought for: £0 (trainee), Sold for: £6m (£10.5m), Profit of: £6m (£10.5m)
- Ben Haim – Bought for: £0 (free transfer), Sold for: £6m (£4.7m), Profit of: £6m (£4.7)
- Sidwell – Bought for: £0 (free transfer), Sold for: £5.5m (£4.3m), Profit of: £5.5m (£4.3m)

Top 20 CTPP Purchases

#	Player	CTPP	Original fee	Year transferred	% of poss starts
1	Shevchenko A	£53,524,884	£30,800,000	2006/07	26%
2	Essien M	£47,443,584	£26,000,000	2005/06	56%
3	Drogba D	£43,661,585	£24,000,000	2004/05	58%
4	Wright-Phillips S	£38,319,818	£21,000,000	2005/06	28%
5	Carvalho R	£36,111,770	£19,850,000	2004/05	57%
6	Duff D	£34,355,304	£17,000,000	2003/04	55%
7	Crespo H	£33,951,124	£16,800,000	2003/04	43%
8	Mutu A	£31,930,223	£15,800,000	2003/04	28%
9	Makélélé C	£28,090,513	£13,900,000	2003/04	69%

#	Player	CTPP	Original fee	Year transferred	% of poss starts
10	Cole A	£27,805,135	£16,000,000	2006/07	70%
11	Hasselbaink J	£26,698,133	£15,000,000	2000/01	78%
12	Verón J	£25,261,253	£12,500,000	2003/04	13%
13	Ferreira P	£24,013,872	£13,200,000	2004/05	40%
14	Robben A	£23,650,025	£13,000,000	2004/05	45%
15	Sutton C	£23,466,703	£10,000,000	1999/00	55%
16	Mikel J	£20,853,851	£12,000,000	2006/07	56%
17	Parker S	£20,209,002	£10,000,000	2003/04	11%
18	Bosingwa J	£18,284,361	£16,200,000	2007/08	55%
19	Tiago	£18,192,327	£10,000,000	2004/05	55%
20	Zhirkov Y	£18,000,000	£18,000,000	2009/10	26%

Expert View

Gabriele Marcotti (@Marcotti)

Writer/Broadcaster

BBC, ITV, The Times, Wall Street Journal, Sunday Herald, La Stampa, Sports Illustrated & Corriere dello Sport

When I was in school, my friends and I lived closer to Stamford Bridge than any other club, so that's where we went. Decrepit ground, the Shed End, Kerry Dixon, tickets for a fiver. Then we all went to university and returned to find Ruud Gullit and Gianfranco Zola and Ken Bates trying to take the club global. You can imagine the shock.

The seeds of Chelsea's "internationalism" were planted back in the mid-1990s. Ken Bates believed in rolling the dice and spending heavily – both on players and on the stadium – in an effort to capitalise on the Premier League's worldwide popularity. And in Matthew Harding, before his untimely death, he found a man with the pockets to make it happen. Critics would say the gamble failed: Chelsea were on the brink of financial oblivion by the summer of 2002. Then again, Bates might say it paid off, because he found an "exit strategy" in the shape of Roman Abramovich.

Bates wanted to turn Chelsea into a self-sustaining "super club" and borrowed heavily to do it. Abramovich's goal is the same; the difference is that he had the capital to fund the huge initial outlay himself, without the need to borrow. Time will tell whether Abramovich can take Chelsea to that point: there are many physiological reasons why it may never happen. Yet it's probably fair to say that without Bates' initial groundwork – however reckless – Abramovich would have started from a much lower rung.

Coventry City

Total Spend (Actual): £63.3m
Total Spend (CTPP): £170.6m
Average League Position: 14.89
Number of Managers: 4
Most Expensive Signing: Robbie Keane - £6m (CTPP £14.1m)
Best Value Signing: Robbie Keane
Worst Value Signing: Sandy Robertson

Player Signings Breakdown (data correct up to end of January transfer window 2010)

• UK: 39   EU: 14   Rest of Europe: 4   Rest of the World: 12

Major Trophies Won Since Premier League Began: 0

Premier League Statistics (correct to the end of the 2009/10 season)

Seasons: 9   Played: 354
Won: 99   Drawn: 112   Lost:143
Goals Scored: 387   Goals Conceded: 490   Goal Difference: -103
Total Points: 409

Overview

Coventry City were founding members of the Premier League and were present for the first nine seasons before they were relegated in 2001, ending a 34-year stay in England's top division. During their nine-year spell in the Premier League, Coventry's highest finish was 11th in both 1993/94 and 1997/98.

At the end of 1999/00, the Sky Blues became only the second Premier League club to fail to win a single away game all season, a 'feat' first achieved by Leeds United in 1992/93. Four other teams now jointly share that record (Wolves 03/04, Norwich 04/05, Derby 07/08 and Hull 09/10). Despite this unwanted record, Coventry finished 1999/00 in 14th place, thanks mainly to their home form, which was the sixth-best in the Premier League that season: won 12, drawn 1, lost 6.

Coventry's only major trophy to date is the 1987 FA Cup, which they won thanks to a 3-2 victory over Tottenham Hotspur - a game that is considered one of the best FA Cup finals in history.

Most Utilised Players

Two of Coventry's biggest signings in the Premier League figure highly in this category.

Craig Bellamy was a £5m (£8.9m) signing from Norwich City in 2000 as a replacement for Robbie Keane, who made the move to Serie A that same summer. Although Bellamy failed to match Keane's performances, he did start 33 league games (87% start ratio) for the Sky Blues during 2000/01, before being sold upon relegation.

Like Bellamy, Robbie Keane spent only one season with Coventry following his £6m (£14.1m) move from Wolves, aged 19 – a record fee for a teenager at that time. Unlike Bellamy, Keane made a big impact, scoring 12 league goals from 30 starts (79%) in 1999/00 before being sold to Inter Milan.

Least Utilised Players

Muhamed Konjić was signed by Gordon Strachan in 1999 for £2m (£4.9m), but started just 14 games (12%) before the Sky Blues were relegated at the end of the 2000/01 season.

Bobby Gould signed Mick Harford for £200k (£1.2m) in July 1993 but he failed to make a single start all season (0%) before he was sold to Wimbledon in August 1994.

Managers

Year	£XI	£XI Rank	Points	Cost Per Point	Position League	Manager
1992/93	£14,717,664	19	52	£283,032	15	Bobby Gould
1993/94	£14,068,024	19	56	£251,215	11	Bobby Gould/Phil Neal
Average	**£14,392,844**	**19**	**54**	**£267,123**	**13**	**Bobby Gould**
1993/94	£14,068,024	19	56	£251,215	11	Bobby Gould/Phil Neal
1994/95	£17,990,750	17	50	£359,815	16	Phil Neal/Ron Atkinson
Average	**£16,029,387**	**18**	**53**	**£305,515**	**13.5**	**Phil Neal**
1994/95	£17,990,750	17	50	£359,815	16	Phil Neal/Ron Atkinson
1995/96	£24,095,651	16	38	£634,096	16	Ron Atkinson
1996/97	£37,508,379	13	41	£914,839	17	Atkinson/Strachan
Average	**£26,531,593**	**15.3**	**43**	**£636,250**	**16.3**	**Ron Atkinson**
1996/97	£37,508,379	13	41	£914,839	17	Atkinson/Strachan
1997/98	£33,389,906	13	52	£642,114	11	Gordon Strachan
1998/99	£33,704,955	14	42	£802,499	15	Gordon Strachan
1999/00	£48,981,184	9	44	£1,113,209	14	Gordon Strachan
2000/01	£34,928,070	11	34	£1,027,296	19	Gordon Strachan
Average	**£37,702,499**	**12**	**42.6**	**£899,991**	**15.2**	**Gordon Strachan**

Top 5 Players Sold for a Profit

- Keane – Bought for: £6m (£14.1m), Sold for: £13m (£23.2m) Profit of: £7m (£9.1m)
- Kirkland – Bought for: £0 (trainee), Sold for: £6m (£7.9m), Profit of: £6m (£7.9m)
- Hartson – Bought for: £1m (£1.8m), Sold for: £6m (£7.9m), Profit of: £5m (£6.1m)
- Boateng – Bought for: £250k (£845k), Sold for: £4.5m (£10.6m), Profit of: £4.25m (£9.755m)
- McSheffrey – Bought for: £0 (trainee), Sold for: £4m (£7m), Profit of: £4m (£7m)

Top 20 CTPP Purchases

#	Player	CTPP	Original fee	Year transferred	% of poss starts
1	Keane R (II)	£14,080,022	£6,000,000	1999/00	79%
2	Hadji M	£9,386,681	£4,000,000	1999/00	80%
3	Bellamy C	£8,899,378	£5,000,000	2000/01	87%
4	McAllister G	£7,936,609	£3,000,000	1996/97	78%
5	Dublin D	£7,387,762	£1,950,000	1994/95	74%
6	Wegerle R	£6,656,206	£1,000,000	1992/93	37%
7	Breen G	£6,613,841	£2,500,000	1996/97	57%
8	Gallacher K	£5,990,586	D900000	1992/93	45%
9	Thompson D (I)	£5,339,627	£3,000,000	2000/01	58%
10	Whelan N	£5,259,036	£2,000,000	1995/96	67%
11	Konjić M	£4,899,163	£2,000,000	1998/99	12%
12	Jess E	£4,601,657	£1,750,000	1995/96	37%
13	Burrows D	£4,167,455	£1,100,000	1994/95	46%
14	Rosario R	£3,993,724	D600000	1992/93	67%
15	Salako J	£3,944,277	£1,500,000	1995/96	60%
16	Froggatt S	£3,674,372	£1,500,000	1998/99	58%
17	Babb P	£3,328,103	£500,000	1992/93	56%
18	Telfer P	£3,023,946	£1,150,000	1995/96	78%
19	Daish L	£2,892,470	£1,100,000	1995/96	41%
20	Roussel C	£2,816,004	£1,200,000	1999/00	37%

Expert View

Paul Knowles (@gmkonline)

www.gmkonline.com

It was once said that if the Titanic had been painted Sky Blue it would never have sunk, but just like the most expensive sea liner the world had ever seen, the most expensively assembled Coventry City squad (when converted to current prices) sank without a trace in the 2000/01 season.

Two major differences between the Sky Blues and the Titanic were that the captain of the Titanic wasn't responsible for how it was built, and if he had seen the iceberg he may well have tried to navigate around it.

The season before relegation we had the joys of seeing the very best of Robbie Keane, the most expensive teenager in English football at the time (£14m CTPP) up front, backed up by the invention and skills of Gary McAllister, Mustafa Hadji and Youssef Chippo (a combined £20m CTPP) in midfield. We were the entertainers; only Manchester United and Arsenal won more games at home than we did. If you had a season ticket you were treated to some wonderful games of football; if you went away you didn't see us win once.

However, that summer saw Robbie Keane depart for Internazionale and

McAllister leave for Liverpool. They were replaced with Craig Bellamy and David Thompson for £13m (CTPP). We started the season against Middlesbrough. Our best (and most expensive) centre-back, Gary Breen, was put at right-back to counter the attacking threat of Brian Deane; the midfield, without the probing of McAllister, was outfought and outthought; and David Thompson compounded a woeful debut by being sent off. The writing was on the wall. The great ship Coventry City had hit the iceberg and under the stewardship of Strachan it just lurched on to its destruction.

Based on the resources at his disposal, Strachan underachieved in all bar one of his seasons. His managerial ability was described back then as being like a B-movie where people are being brainwashed, but only those on the outside could see what was happening – except for us it was the other way round, we could see he was tactically inept but the press wouldn't believe us. You can give a manager money but if he can't spend it wisely, why bother?

One of the things I've noticed from the list of 20 most expensive signings made during the Premier League era is that only five actually lived up to the billing, with Dion Dublin an absolute steal. Of the rest, some had one good season but failed thereafter, and others were just woeful wastes of money. Where did spending lots of money get us? Treating water in the Championship, £60m in debt, wondering why we spent the equivalent of £4m on David Burrows.

Crystal Palace

Total Spend (Actual): £25.3m
Total Spend (CTPP): £80.4m
Average League Position: 19.25
Number of Managers: 5
Most Expensive Signing: Valérien Ismaël – £2.75m (CTPP £9.3m)
Best Value Signing: Kevin Miller
Worst Value Signing: Iván Kaviedes

Player Signings Breakdown (data correct up to end of January transfer window 2010)

• UK: 25   EU: 10   Rest of Europe: 3   Rest of the World: 3

Major Trophies Won Since Premier League Began: 0

Premier League Statistics (correct to the end of the 2009/10 season)

Seasons: 4   Played: 160
Won: 37   Drawn: 49   Lost:74
Goals Scored: 160   Goals Conceded: 243 Goal Difference: −83
Total Points: 160

Overview

Crystal Palace were founding members of the Premier League in 1992, only to be relegated at the end of that season, finishing in 20th place with 49 points – one point adrift from safety. Between 1992/93 and 2004/05, Crystal Palace were relegated from the Premier League on no fewer than four occasions (1992/93, 1994/95, 1997/98 and 2004/05) making them the most relegated team in Premier League history. They would never spend more than one consecutive season in England's top division during this period.

Despite the Eagles' relatively poor showing in the Premier League, they reached the semi-finals of both the League Cup and FA Cup in 1995. Palace lost both legs of the League Cup semi-final to Liverpool 1-0 and, to add to that heartbreak, lost the FA Cup semi-final 2-0 to Manchester United following a replay, after the first game ended 2-2. They also lost to Liverpool in the 2001 League Cup semi-final; winning the first leg 2-1, but then conceding five at Anfield.

Most Utilised Players

Crystal Palace have three players with 100% start ratios in three out of the four seasons spent in the Premier League, including goalkeeper Kevin Miller, signed in 1997 for £1m (£3.4m), and trainee Wayne Routledge, who featured during the 2004/05 campaign. One of Crystal Palace's more expensive signings also figures highly when it comes to utilisation. Chris Armstrong, signed from Millwall for £1m (£6.7m) in September 1992, featured in two of Palace's four seasons in the Premier League (1992/93 and 1994/95) before he left the Eagles, to join Tottenham, with an 89% start ratio.

Least Utilised Players

There are a number of players that were signed for £1m or more that have a start ratio lower than 30% for Crystal Palace in the Premier League. These include: Iván Kaviedes (3% start ratio), signed for £2m (£3.7m) in 2004; Itzik Zohar (5%), signed for £1m (£3.4m) in 1997; and Neil Emblen (21%), signed for £2m (£6.8m) in 1997.

Managers

Year	£XI	£XI Rank	Points	Cost Per Point	Position League	Manager
1992/93	£27,163,661	12	49	£554,360	20	Steve Coppell
1997/98	£27,301,685	15	33	£827,324	20	Coppell & 4 Others
Average	£27,232,673	13.5	41	£690,842	20	Steve Coppell

Year	£XI	£XI Rank	Points	Cost Per Point	Position League	Manager
1994/95	£20,719,726	15	45	£460,438	19	Alan Smith
2004/05	£5,313,507	19	33	£161,015	18	Iain Dowie

Top 20 CTPP Purchases

#	Player	CTPP	Original fee	Year transferred	% of poss starts
1	Ismaël V	£9,284,217	£2,750,000	1997/98	34%
2	Dyer B	£7,463,368	£1,250,000	1993/94	35%
3	Martyn N	£7,321,827	D1100000	1992/93	94%
4	Emblen N	£6,752,158	£2,000,000	1997/98	21%
5	Armstrong C (I)	£6,656,206	£1,000,000	1992/93	89%
6	Roberts A	£5,916,416	d2250000	1995/96	66%
7	Padovano M	£5,739,334	£1,700,000	1997/98	21%
8	Young E	£5,657,775	D850000	1992/93	61%
9	Lombardo A	£5,401,726	£1,600,000	1997/98	55%
10	Jansen M	£5,064,118	£1,500,000	1997/98	13%
11	Thorn A	£4,326,534	D650000	1992/93	81%
12	Warhurst P	£4,220,099	£1,250,000	1997/98	58%
13	Kaviedes I	£3,638,465	£2,000,000	2004/05	3%
14	Zohar I	£3,376,079	£1,000,000	1997/98	5%
15	Curčić S	£3,376,079	£1,000,000	1997/98	16%
16	Miller K (I)	£3,376,079	£1,000,000	1997/98	100%
17	Mortimer P	£3,328,103	D500000	1992/93	2%
18	Humphrey J	£2,662,482	d400000	1992/93	56%
19	Freedman D	£2,103,614	d800000	1995/96	16%
20	Shipperley N	£2,020,900	£1,000,000	2003/04	22%

Expert View

James Daly (@FYPFanzine)

Editor of Five Year Plan Fanzine, football writer Goal.com

Despite having spent only 13 of their 90 years in the Football League in the top flight, Palace's overspending to first try and stay there, and then return, has brought the club to the cusp of oblivion twice.

Suffice to say it probably wasn't worth it.

First Mark Goldberg gambled everything he had, and lots he didn't, to keep an unbalanced Eagles side up in 1998, claiming a 'five-year plan' to get Palace into the Champions League. They were in administration six months later.

Then in 2005 Simon Jordan threw all of his money at the club he owned (most of it going Andy Johnson's way) to return to the Premier League at the first attempt, but failed, and the club was sent on a downward spiral towards administration again in 2010.

It's not surprising that nearly half of the list of the club's most expensive

Premier League signings is made up of players from the ill-fated Goldberg era, including an equivalent of £9.2m by today's prices on Valérien Ismaël. That may sound like extortion for a defender who made only 13 appearances, but isn't much more than a lot of Premier League clubs today would throw at a player. He *did* go on to play in the Champions League, so maybe Goldberg wasn't totally wide of the mark in his prediction.

Rather heart-warmingly, though, some of Palace's greatest ever players are towards the bottom of the list with a more-than-reasonable £2.1m for Dougie Freedman in 1995, a striker who scored over 100 goals for the club; by today's standards, a snip.

Only one player comes from the 2005 relegation where Palace lost out on the last day of the season – £3.6m on Iván Kaviedes, who made only a handful of appearances – with the rest of the squad far cheaper. It perhaps makes Iain Dowie's efforts at trying to keep Palace up slightly more impressive. Maybe Eagles fans should cut him some slack....then again, maybe not.

Derby County

Total Spend (Actual): £58.4m
Total Spend (CTPP): £113.7m
Average League Position: 14.43
Number of Managers: 5
Most Expensive Signings: Three players tied: Craig Burley, Seth Johnson and Branko Strupar – £3m (CTPP £7.1m)
Best Value Signing: Jacob Laursen
Worst Value Signing: Robert Earnshaw

Player Signings Breakdown (data correct up to end of January transfer window 2010)

• UK: 28   EU: 17   Rest of Europe: 5   Rest of the World: 16

Major Trophies Won Since Premier League Began: 0

Premier League Statistics (correct to the end of the 2009/10 season)

Seasons: 7   Played: 266
Won: 68   Drawn: 70   Lost:128

Goals Scored: 271   Goals Conceded: 420   Goal Difference: -149
Total Points: 274

Overview

Derby County have spent seven seasons in the Premier League, including six consecutive campaigns in England's top division from 1996/97 to 2001/02, when they were relegated after finishing in 19th place with 30 points - 10 points away from safety. Their highest finish in the Premier League during this period was 8th, in 1998/99. The Rams would have to wait until 2007/08 before they experienced Premier League football again, although it would turn out to be a disastrous one as they set a number of unwanted Premier League records in a season that saw them finish in 20th place with just 11 points - 25 points from safety, and the lowest total in recent history.

The following are the unenviable Premier League records currently held by Derby County (all occurred during 2007/08):

- Fewest wins in a 38-game season: 1
- Fewest home wins in a 38-game season: 1 (shared with Sunderland)
- Fewest away wins in a 38-game season: 0 (shared with five other teams)
- Most consecutive games without a win during a 38-game season: 32
- Most league games lost in a 38- or 42-game season: 29 (shared with Ipswich and Sunderland)
- Fewest goals scored in a 38-game season: 20
- Fewest goals scored away in a 38-game season: 8 (shared with three other teams)
- Most goals conceded in a 38-game season: 89
- Most goals conceded at home in a 38 game season
- Worst goal difference in a 38-game season: -69

Despite the awful 2007/08 season, Derby have a proud history. They were crowned champions of England on two occasions (1972 and 1975), won the FA Cup in 1946 and reached the semi-finals of the European Cup in 1973.

Most Utilised Players

Jacob Laursen was one of Jim Smith's more astute signings during his six seasons in charge of the Rams. Derby paid £500k (£1.4m) to Danish side Silkeborg IF in July 1996. Laursen would go on to start 135 league games for the Rams, giving him an 89% start ratio before he returned to Denmark in 2000 on a free transfer.

Darryl Powell is another player who figures highly for Derby in the utilisation stakes. Powell joined Derby from Portsmouth in 1995 for a fee of £750k (£2m) and started 151 games (66%) for the Rams, before joining Birmingham in 2002 on a free transfer.

Least Utilised Players

Benny Feilhaber has Derby's lowest start ratio of the club's most expensive signings. Signed for £1m (£1.2m) from Hamburg in August 2007, Feilhaber would make just one start during Derby's ill-fated 2007/08 Premier League campaign before he was released at the end of that season.

Robert Earnshaw was signed for a club-record £3.5m (£6.1m) in June 2007 from Norwich City, but it would prove to be a poor season for the Welshman; he made just seven starts (18%) in a season that saw the Rams relegated. Earnshaw would be sold to Nottingham Forest not long after the 2007/08 season ended.

Managers

Year	£XI	£XI Rank	Points	Cost Per Point	Position League	Manager
1996/97	£16,918,782	19	46	£367,800	12	Jim Smith
1997/98	£17,134,462	19	55	£311,536	9	Jim Smith
1998/99	£20,336,645	18	52	£391,089	8	Jim Smith
1999/00	£28,058,404	15	38	£738,379	16	Jim Smith
2000/01	£27,972,160	14	42	£666,004	17	Jim Smith
2001/02	£17,296,489	18	30	£576,550	19	Smith/Todd/Gregory
Average	£21,286,157	17.2	43.8	£508,560	13.5	Jim Smith
2007/08	£12,363,429	19	11	£1,123,948	20	Davies/Jewell

Top 5 Players Sold for a Profit

- Dailly – Bought for: £1m (£2.7m), Sold for: £5.3m (£13m), Profit of: £4.3m (£10.3m)
- S Johnson – Bought for: £3m (£7m), Sold for: £7m (£9.2m), Profit of: £4m (£2.2m)
- Delap – Bought for: £500k (£1.7m), Sold for: £4m (£5.3m), Profit of: £3.5m (£3.6m)
- Carsley – Bought for: £0 (trainee), Sold for: £3.4m (£8.3m), Profit of: £3.4m (£8.3m)
- Christie – Bought for: £50k (£100k), Sold for: £3m (£4.9m), Profit of: £3m (£4.8m)

Top 20 CTPP Purchases

#	Player	CTPP	Original fee	Year transferred	% of poss starts
1	Johnson S	£7,040,011	£3,000,000	1999/00	64%
2	Burley C	£7,040,011	£3,000,000	1999/00	46%
3	Strupar B	£7,040,011	£3,000,000	1999/00	25%
4	Gabbiadini M	£6,656,206	D1000000	1991/92	13%
5	Carbonari H	£6,613,870	£2,700,000	1998/99	57%
6	Earnshaw R	£6,082,373	£3,500,000	2006/07	18%
7	Fuertes E	£5,397,342	£2,300,000	1999/00	21%
8	Bohinen L	£4,895,314	£1,450,000	1997/98	31%
9	Morris L	£4,224,007	£1,800,000	1999/00	13%
10	Štimac I	£4,128,343	£1,570,000	1995/96	50%
11	Grenet F	£3,931,986	£3,000,000	2001/02	32%
12	Higginbotham D	£3,559,751	£2,000,000	2000/01	79%
13	Miller K (II)	£3,385,993	£3,000,000	2007/08	79%
14	Burton D	£3,376,079	£1,000,000	1997/98	39%
15	Simpson P	£3,328,103	D500000	1991/92	1%
16	Davis C	£2,821,661	£2,500,000	2007/08	50%
17	Bragstad B	£2,669,813	£1,500,000	2000/01	26%
18	Dailly C	£2,645,536	£1,000,000	1996/97	54%
19	Ward A	£2,629,518	d1000000	1995/96	36%
20	Asanović A	£2,513,260	£950,000	1996/97	49%

Expert View
Peter Smith
Derby County season-ticket holder

From a dilapidated old ground to a brand new era fit for the Premier League: 1997 saw Derby County on the rise. Having said goodbye to the 100-year-old Baseball Ground after our first year in the Premier League, we rose to 9th in 1998 and then 8th in 1999 – the first two years in our spanking-new stadium. But by the turn of the millennium it was a case of ongoing relegation battles: two won, the third, in 2002, lost.

Jim Smith had done a brilliant job on a limited budget for the first few years, but investment in the team peaked in 1999/00. By 2002 it was an increasingly cheap side, and it showed. In current money, the record fee is no more than £7m.

Even cheaper was the £XI of 2007/08, after Billy Davies had led the Rams back to the top flight. Most fans sensed that we'd gone up too soon: a strange concept, I admit, after years of fighting to return – but a bit like going over the top from the trenches with a wooden spoon instead of a rifle. The less said about that season the better, but while too few points were won, the cost of the team had 'relegation' written all over it.

Currently the 121st-largest stadium in the whole of Europe, Pride Park now sees visits from the likes of Scunthorpe and Doncaster, rather than Manchester United and Liverpool.

Everton

Total Spend (Actual): £231.4m
Total Spend (CTPP): £447.9m
Average League Position: 11.33
Number of Managers: 5
Most Expensive Signing: Nick Barmby – £5.75m (CTPP £15.3m)
Best Value Signing: Tim Howard
Worst Value Signing: Per Krøldrup

Player Signings Breakdown (data correct up to end of January transfer window 2010)

- UK: 57   EU: 27   Rest of Europe: 6   Rest of the World: 13

Major Trophies Won Since Premier League Began

FA Cup: 1 (1995)

Premier League Statistics (correct to the end of the 2009/10 season)

Seasons: 18	Played: 696	
Won: 244	Drawn: 192	Lost:260
Goals Scored: 873	Goals Conceded: 894	Goal Difference: −21
Total Points: 924		

Overview

Founding members of both the Football League and Premier League, Everton are one of only seven teams to feature in all 18 Premier League seasons to date. However, their fortunes during that time have varied from battling relegation to fighting it out for European qualification, with a couple of cup final appearances thrown in along the way.

Everton's first season in the Premier League under Howard Kendall resulted in a 13th-place finish but, with the Toffees struggling the following season, Kendall and Everton parted ways; Mike Walker was named his successor. Everton continued to struggle and it would take an amazing escape on the last day of the season, which saw the Toffees come from 2–0 down to beat Wimbledon 3–2, to ensure their top–flight status. Walker's Everton continued to struggle into the 1994/95 season and he was replaced by Joe Royle in November 1994, who instantly improved their fortunes as they beat Liverpool 2–0 in the Merseyside derby – Royle's first game in charge. Everton went on to finish the season in 15th place, but the highlight of the campaign was the 1–0 FA Cup final victory over Manchester United. Royle led Everton to a 6th–place finish in 1995/96 before he resigned towards the end of the 1996/97 campaign, as his side finished in 16th place – just one point clear of the relegation zone.

Howard Kendall returned as manager for the third and final time in August 1997, but Everton survived on the final day of the 1997/98 season courtesy only of their superior goal difference over Bolton. Walter Smith replaced Kendall in time for the 1998/99 season, but during his first three campaigns in charge the Toffees could finish only in 14th, 13th and 16th. He was sacked in March 2002, with Everton struggling towards the bottom of the table. Fellow Scot David Moyes took over as Everton finished the 2001/02 season in 15th place.

Moyes' first full season in charge (2002/03) produced a 7th–place finish, but that was quickly followed by a 17th–place finish a year later. The 2004/05 campaign saw Everton finish 4th – an improvement of 13 places: a Premier League record, and enough to secure a place in the qualifying stages of the 2005/06 Champions League. Unfortunately for them, they failed to make it to the group stages after getting knocked out by Villarreal in the third qualifying round. Everton finished in a disappointing 11th place at the end of 2005/06.

The Toffees' form and consistency improved as they finished 2006/07 in 6th place, 2007/08 in 5th place (as well as reaching the semi-finals of the League Cup only to lose to Chelsea) and 2008/09 also in 5th place. Everton also reached their first final since 1995, when they lost 2-1 to Chelsea in the 2009 FA Cup. The Toffees finished the 2009/10 campaign (Moyes' eighth year in charge) in 8th place.

Correct to the end of the 2009/10 season, Everton have lost more Premier League games than any other club (260).

Most Utilised Players

Goalkeeper Tim Howard is Everton's most utilised player in the Premier League, with a 97% start ratio. Howard has failed to make the XI for only four league games (148 out of 152) since his £3m (£5.3m) move from Manchester United. Although he was initially on loan at Everton for the start of 2006/07, the deal was made permanent in February 2007. Another former Manchester United player, Phil Neville, ranks highly for Everton when it comes to utilisation. Signed for £3.5m (£6.4m) in August 2005, Neville has started 164 out of 190 Premier League games for the Toffees (86%), placing him third in Everton's overall list of Most Utilised Players.

Least Utilised Players

Per Krøldrup is a transfer David Moyes and most Evertonians would rather forget. Signed in June 2005 from Italian side Udinese for £5m (£9.2m), Krøldrup started only one league game (3%) before he left to join another Italian side, Fiorentina, in 2006.

Another less-than-successful overseas signing with a low utilisation ratio is Andy van der Meyde. Signed by David Moyes from Inter Milan in August 2005 for £1.5m (£2.8m), van der Meyde started just 12 Premier League games for Everton during his four seasons at the club. He was released in the summer of 2009 with a start ratio of 11%.

Managers

Year	£XI	£XI Rank	Points	Cost Per Point	Position League	Manager
1992/93	£49,154,498	5	53	£927,443	13	Howard Kendall
1993/94	£50,609,592	8	44	£1,150,218	17	Kendall//Mike Walker
1997/98	£59,995,559	6	40	£1,499,889	17	Howard Kendall
Average	**£53,253,216**	**6.3**	**45.7**	**£1,192,517**	**15.7**	**Howard Kendall**
1994/95	£49,725,461	11	50	£994,509	15	Mike Walker/Joe Royle
1995/96	£59,093,309	6	61	£968,743	6	Joe Royle
1996/97	£64,983,811	5	42	£1,547,234	15	Joe Royle/Dave Watson
Average	**£57,934,194**	**7.3**	**51**	**£1,170,162**	**12**	**Joe Royle**

Year	£XI	£XI Rank	Points	Cost Per Point	Position League	Manager
1998/99	£57,306,124	7	43	£1,332,701	14	Walter Smith
1999/00	£42,036,440	11	50	£840,729	13	Walter Smith
2000/01	£32,130,818	12	42	£765,019	16	Walter Smith
2001/02	£39,813,096	11	43	£925,886	15	Smith/Moyes
Average	**£42,821,620**	**10.3**	**44.5**	**£966,084**	**14.5**	**Walter Smith**
2001/02	£39,813,096	11	43	£925,886	15	Smith/Moyes
2002/03	£38,591,103	11	59	£654,086	7	David Moyes
2003/04	£37,835,043	10	39	£970,129	17	David Moyes
2004/05	£27,229,901	11	61	£446,392	4	David Moyes
2005/06	£39,988,801	8	50	£799,776	11	David Moyes
2006/07	£56,242,198	7	58	£969,693	6	David Moyes
2007/08	£56,726,407	7	65	£872,714	5	David Moyes
2008/09	£55,517,927	9	63	£881,237	5	David Moyes
2009/10	£52,788,697	8	61	£865,388	8	David Moyes
Average	**£44,970,353**	**9.1**	**55**	**£820,589**	**8.7**	**David Moyes**

Top 5 Players Sold for a Profit

- Rooney – Bought for: £0 (trainee), Sold for: £27m (£49.2m) Profit of: £27m (£49.2m)
- Lescott – Bought for: £5m (£8.7m), Sold for: £22m (£22m), Profit of: £17m (£13.3m)
- Jeffers – Bought for: £0 (trainee), Sold for: £10m (£13.2m), Profit of: £10m (£13.2m)
- Ball – Bought for: £0 (trainee), Sold for: £6.5m (£8.6m), Profit of: £6.5m (£8.6m)
- McFadden – Bought for: £1.25m (£2.6m), Sold for: £5.75m (£6.5m), Profit of: £4.5m (£3.9m)

Top 20 CTPP Purchases

#	Player	CTPP	Original fee	Year transferred	% of poss starts
1	Barmby N	£15,211,834	£5,750,000	1996/97	69%
2	Ferguson D (II)	£15,154,383	£4,000,000	1994/95	38%
3	Johnson A (I)	£14,945,260	£8,600,000	2006/07	68%
4	Cottee T	£14,643,654	D2200000	1992/93	51%
5	Kanchelskis A	£14,462,350	£5,500,000	1995/96	68%
6	Bilić S	£14,348,335	£4,250,000	1997/98	34%
7	Yakubu	£12,697,473	£11,250,000	2007/08	43%
8	Fellaini M	£11,728,397	£15,000,000	2008/09	63%
9	Amokachi D	£11,365,787	£3,000,000	1994/95	43%
10	Bakayoko I	£11,023,117	£4,500,000	1998/99	45%
11	Beattie J	£10,915,396	£6,000,000	2004/05	45%
12	Bilyaletdinov D	£10,000,000	£10,000,000	2009/10	42%
13	Johnston M	£9,984,309	D1500000	1992/93	17%
14	Dacourt O	£9,798,326	£4,000,000	1998/99	74%
15	Limpar A	£9,553,111	£1,600,000	1993/94	32%
16	Speed G	£9,259,377	£3,500,000	1996/97	76%
17	Krøldrup P	£9,123,766	£5,000,000	2005/06	3%
18	Lescott J	£8,689,105	£5,000,000	2006/07	72%
19	Ward M (I)	£8,653,068	D1300000	1992/93	54%
20	Samways V	£8,334,911	£2,200,000	1994/95	21%

Expert View

Ed Bottomley (@dixiessixty)

www.dixies60.com

We entered the Premier League era in a Bentley, and left the century on a pedal bike. Everton are a yo-yo club that haven't left the confines of one division; somehow travelling the million miles from title winners in '87 to near relegation in '94. We've been within minutes of the drop (twice), into the Champions League qualifiers, and lifted the FA Cup – and we've lost more Premier League games in total than any other team – but by God it has been exciting.

The gut-churning queasiness which stopped a friend of mine putting his lucky badge on his lapel because his hands were shaking too much is exactly the same feeling that a Man United fan has before a title clincher; nerves don't discern between relegation battles and trophy brawls.

Our first serious brush with relegation was in 1994 under Mike Walker's leadership. The man we poached from Norwich was all grey hair and gold chains, a sheep in spivs' clothing, but he did buy Anders Limpar (£1.6m/£9.5m) – who played a vital role in our last-day relegation escape against ornery mongrels Wimbledon (2-0 down, 3-2 up). Walker then splurged on Vinny Samways (£2.2m/£8.3m) and Daniel Amokachi (£3m/£11.7m) that summer – and was sacked shortly into the 1994/95 season.

Looking over our signings during the Premier League era, the first thing that strikes me is how little value we got from our priciest purchases. It isn't until we get 14 names down to Olivier Dacourt on the list of most expensive buys (CTPP) that we go over the 70% mark for percentage of possible starts. Of the 13 names above the Frenchman, only Andrei Kanchelskis (£5.5m/£14.5m) truly impressed. In fact, most of the expensive names failed both in terms of how well they played in an Everton shirt and in being utilised in the starting XI. It's startling to see, second from top, Duncan Ferguson – a hero to many Blues, with an astronomically high price tag, and an equally low percentage of possible starts. Ferguson's mark on the club was undeniable, but so is the fact that on paper he was a failure. Lots of teams sucking in the more refined air of top-four Premier League football seem as cold and calculating as Spock, and the Vulcan would definitely call Evertonians "emotionally compromised". Our love for Duncan Ferguson really cannot be explained; a few skyscraping headers and the fact that even now Tony Hibbert still larrups the ball up to the ghost of Big Dunc are poor returns for the money invested in him.

It's also interesting to dip into some of the names that have become bywords for failed signings amongst the Toffee cognoscenti. Alex Nyarko (£4.5m/£8m) and Per Krøldrup (£5m/£9.1m) are often mentioned, but most interesting is Andy van der Meyde. Many an attack on Moyes has been made because of his purchase of the Dutchman, but in reality he wasn't that much of a gamble in terms of spending (£1.5m/£2.7m).

The Premier League for Everton has been a queue of managers who didn't cut it, with two who did: Joe Royle and David Moyes. Our transfer spending during this period has swung wildly from bargains like Tim Cahill (£2m/£3.6m) to madcap spending like Ibrahima Bakayoko (£4.5m/£11m) – but as I've already touched on it's been exciting, and seldom has there been a calm season at Goodison; it's like experiencing lightning without the rain...

Fulham

Total Spend (Actual): £129m
Total Spend (CTPP): £161.8m
Average League Position: 12.56
Number of Managers: 4
Most Expensive Signing: Steve Marlet – £13.5m (CTPP £17.7m)
Best Value Signing: Mark Schwarzer
Worst Value Signing: Fredrik Stoor

Player Signings Breakdown (data correct up to end of January transfer window 2010)

- UK: 26   EU: 24   Rest of Europe: 5   Rest of the World: 22

Major Trophies Won Since Premier League Began: 0

Premier League Statistics (correct to the end of the 2009/10 season)

Seasons: 9	Played: 342	
Won: 105	Drawn: 95	Lost: 142
Goals Scored: 383	Goals Conceded: 458	Goal Difference: –75
Total Points: 410		

Overview

Fulham's top–flight history is still in its early stages. The club has spent a total of just 24 seasons in England's top division, with nine of those campaigns coming in the Premier

League from 2001/02 to the present-day. During Fulham's nine consecutive seasons in the Premier League, the Cottagers have come close to relegation on two occasions. First in 2006/07, when they finished one point clear of the relegation zone, then again the following season when they survived an even greater scare, staying up courtesy of a better goal difference than 18th-placed Reading. The 2008/09 campaign would turn out to be a remarkable one for Fulham as Roy Hodgson, on the back of keeping them up in 2007/08 against all the odds, led the Cottagers into 7th position and a place in Europe for only the second time in the club's history. They would also reach the quarter-finals of the FA Cup, only to be knocked out by Manchester United.

Fuham's 2009/10 campaign would prove to be one of their most successful seasons ever, reaching the quarter-finals of the FA Cup for the second season running, getting to the Europa League final and finishing 12th in the Premier League. They would end the season without silverware, but it was an unforgettable campaign for the Cottagers.

Most Utilised Players
Fulham have seven players with an 80% start ratio or higher in the Premier League, but it is Mark Schwarzer and Steve Finnan who lead the way. Schwarzer joined Fulham from Middlesbrough on a free transfer in 2008 and failed to start only one league game (99% start ratio) during his first two seasons with the Cottagers.

Steve Finnan was signed from Notts County for £500k (£1.3m) in November 1998, eventually helping Fulham reach England's top division in 2001/02. During the two seasons Finnan spent with Fulham in the Premier League, he failed to start only six matches (92% start ratio) out of 76 before he was sold to Liverpool in 2003.

Least Utilised Players
Fredrik Stoor was a £2m (£1.6m) signing from Rosenborg in 2008 but never started a Premier League game (0%) during his two seasons at the club. Another player with a low start ratio for Fulham is Jon Harley. Signed from Chelsea in August 2001 for £3.5m (£4.6m), Harley made just 19 Premier League starts (17% start ratio) for the Cottagers during his three seasons at the club.

Managers

Year	£XI	£XI Rank	Points	Cost Per Point	Position League	Manager
2001/02	£48,360,708	9	44	£1,099,107	13	Jean Tigana
2002/03	£44,196,262	7	48	£920,755	14	Jean/Chris
Average	**£46,278,485**	**8**	**46**	**£1,009,931**	**13.5**	**Jean Tigana**
2002/03	£44,196,262	7	48	£920,755	14	Tigana/Coleman
2003/04	£34,781,860	12	52	£668,882	9	Chris Coleman
2004/05	£26,422,741	12	44	£600,517	13	Chris Coleman
2005/06	£19,449,214	14	48	£405,192	12	Chris Coleman
2006/07	£16,643,952	17	39	£426,768	16	Coleman/Sanchez
Average	**£28,298,806**	**12.4**	**46.2**	**£604,423**	**12.8**	**Chris Coleman**

Year	£XI	£XI Rank	Points	Cost Per Point	Position League	Manager
2006/07	£16,643,952	17	39	£426,768	16	Coleman/Sanchez
2007/08	£27,910,126	17	36	£775,281	17	Sanchez/Hodgson
Average	**£22,277,039**	**17**	**37.5**	**£601,025**	**16.5**	**Lawrie Sanchez**
2007/08	£27,910,126	17	36	£775,281	17	Sanchez/Hodgson
2008/09	£28,856,017	13	53	£544,453	7	Roy Hodgson
2009/10	£22,465,156	14	46	£488,373	12	Roy Hodgson
Average	**£26,410,433**	**14.7**	**45**	**£602,702**	**12**	**Roy Hodgson**

Top 5 Players Sold for a Profit

- Saha – Bought for: £2.1m (£3.8m), Sold for: £12.85m (£26m), Profit of: £10.75m (£22.2m)
- Knight – Bought for: £0 (trainee), Sold for: £3.5m (£4m), Profit of: £3.5m (£4m)
- Boa Morte – Bought for: £1.6m (£2.1m), Sold for: £5m (£8.7m), Profit of: £3.4m (£6.6m)
- Finnan – Bought for: £500k (£1.3m), Sold for: £3.5m (£7.1m), Profit of: £3m (£5.8m)
- Davis – Bought for: £0 (trainee), Sold for: £3m (£5.5m), Profit of: £3m (£5.5m)

Top 20 CTPP Purchases

#	Player	CTPP	Original fee	Year transferred	% of poss starts
1	Marlet S	£17,693,937	£13,500,000	2001/02	44%
2	Van der Sar E	£9,174,634	£7,000,000	2001/02	83%
3	Johnson A (I)	£8,209,878	£10,500,000	2008/09	49%
4	Goma A	£7,119,502	d4000000	2000/01	59%
5	Clark L	£7,040,011	£3,000,000	1999/00	36%
6	Davies S (II)	£6,951,284	£4,000,000	2006/07	63%
7	Kamara D	£6,771,986	£6,000,000	2007/08	22%
8	Malbranque S	£6,553,310	£5,000,000	2001/02	84%
9	Davis S (II)	£5,925,487	£5,250,000	2007/08	58%
10	Hayles B	£4,899,163	£2,000,000	1998/99	36%
11	Harley J	£4,587,317	£3,500,000	2001/02	17%
12	Legwinski S	£4,587,317	£3,500,000	2001/02	61%
13	Zamora B	£4,534,980	£5,800,000	2008/09	78%
14	Bullard J	£4,344,552	£2,500,000	2006/07	32%
15	Duff D	£4,000,000	£4,000,000	2009/10	79%
16	Saha L	£3,737,739	£2,100,000	2000/01	54%
17	Diop P	£3,638,465	£2,000,000	2004/05	46%
18	Štolcers A	£3,559,751	d2000000	2000/01	0%
19	Collins J (I)	£3,559,751	d2000000	2000/01	38%
20	Queudrue F	£3,475,642	£2,000,000	2006/07	74%

Expert View
Richard Allen (@richallenfulham)

www.cravencottagenewsround.wordpress.com. Author of the annual "The Fulham Review"

The 5th of May 2007 and Fulham are in deep trouble. We're at home to Liverpool in the season's penultimate game. We really need a win. Caretaker manager Lawrie Sanchez is looking nervous.

Rafa Benítez has rested players ahead of the Champions League Final, Robbie

Fowler's radar is on the blink, and somehow it's still 0-0 with 20 minutes left. Here's Clint Dempsey, a £1.5m (£2.6m CTPP) Chris Coleman signing from whom we've seen nothing this season. Dempsey flips the ball wide to Liam Rosenior (£55k/£111k), bursts on into the area, then when the ball comes back bounces it past Pepe Reina for the winning goal. We're safe! Dempsey's goal is conservatively worth £30m.

Next season it happens again. All but relegated with five games left, the team (now led by Roy Hodgson after Sanchez's reign went badly wrong) strings together an improbable sequence of results and somehow survives. The resurrection is led by the extrovert play of Jimmy Bullard (£2.5m/£4.3m), the sheer drive of Brian McBride (£1m/£2.02) and a reborn Danny Murphy (undisclosed, minimal). And it wouldn't have happened without the otherwise far too expensive Diomansy Kamara (£6m/£6.8m), whose goals out of nothing to beat Man City in late April turned the season upside down.

At the time of writing, Fulham have been a Premier League club for 10 consecutive seasons. That's pretty impressive, so clearly something has gone right in our transfer work. We seem to have come up with the right player at the right time, and while there have been blips, even these have not been complete busts: Kamara saved our skin and our season at City, Andrew Johnson (£10.5m/£8.2m) was a key player in the team that got into Europe, and even Steve Marlet (£13.5m/£17.7m– oh dear....) helped us to win the Intertoto Cup.

The downs are far outweighed by the ups, with Roy Hodgson's last Fulham XI a perfect example. Our Europa League final side featured Mark Schwarzer (as good a 'keeper as we've seen) and Zoltan Gera (fans' player of the year), who both cost nothing. Our outstanding centre-backs, Aaron Hughes and Brede Hangeland, cost just over £3.5m (£3m) between them. Damien Duff, back to his Champions League best, cost £4m. Bobby Zamora, whose goals beat some fine sides on the way to the final, cost £5.8m (£4.5m). Phenomenal stuff.

Clubs like Fulham don't have much margin for error in the transfer market but, taking the last 10 years in their entirety, things couldn't realistically have gone much better. Long may it continue.

Hull City

Total Spend (Actual): £32.1m

Total Spend (CTPP): £27.5m

Average League Position: 18

Number of Managers: 2

Most Expensive Signing: Jimmy Bullard – £5m (CTPP £4m)

Best Value Signing: Stephen Hunt

Worst Value Signing: Péter Halmosi

Player Signings Breakdown (data correct up to end of January transfer window 2010)

- UK: 6   EU: 6   Rest of Europe: 0   Rest of the World: 8

Major Trophies Won Since Premier League Began: 0

Premier League Statistics (correct to the end of the 2009/10 season)

Seasons: 2   Played: 76

Won: 14   Drawn: 23   Lost:39

Goals Scored: 73   Goals Conceded: 139   Goal Difference: –66

Total Points: 65

Overview

Hull City won promotion to the Premier League for the first time in the club's history when they beat Bristol City 1–0 in the 2007/08 Championship play–off final. They managed to defy the odds and survive their first season in England's top flight by finishing in 17th place with 35 points – one point clear of the relegation zone. Unfortunately for the Tigers, they couldn't repeat the trick in 2009/10 and ended the season in 19th place with 30 points – five points adrift from safety.

When they ended the 2009/10 campaign without a single success on the road, Hull suffered the ignominy of becoming only the sixth team in Premier League history to record no away wins in a season.

Managers

Year	£XI	£XI Rank	Points	Cost Per Point	Position League	Manager
2008/09	£7,345,398	20	35	£209,869	17	Phil Brown
2009/10	£11,031,204	18	30	£367,707	19	Phil Brown/Iain Dowie
Average	£9,188,301	19	32.5	£288,788	18	Phil Brown

Top 10 CTPP Purchases

#	Player	CTPP	Original fee	Year transferred	% of poss starts
1	Bullard J	£3,909,466	£5,000,000	2008/09	17%
2	Cousin D	£3,127,573	£4,000,000	2008/09	25%
3	Olofinjana S	£3,000,000	£3,000,000	2009/10	29%
4	Zayatte K	£2,627,161	£3,360,000	2008/09	68%
5	Hunt S	£2,500,000	£2,500,000	2009/10	71%
6	Halmosi P	£2,345,679	£3,000,000	2008/09	11%
7	Ghilas K	£2,000,000	£2,000,000	2009/10	16%
8	Gardner A	£1,954,733	£2,500,000	2008/09	39%
9	Mouyokolo S	£1,800,000	£1,800,000	2009/10	50%
10	Marney D	£1,737,821	d1000000	2006/07	54%

Expert View

Ian Waterson

Editor, City Independent fanzine www.cityindependent.net

Hull City's stay in the Premier League may well have been fleeting, but it will be remembered for at least two reasons. Initially, a record-breaking and meteoric start to life in the top flight – the best ever by a newly promoted side – had the courageous Tigers down as the nation's second-favourite team. Well, for a limited time at least. More pertinently, it lasted a full 12 months longer than anybody could feasibly have envisaged. Our own fans included.

It is with incredible irony that of the £14m spent on players during our maiden season in the Premier League, our best player throughout our entire two-year sojourn was the one signed on a free. There is an unwritten top-flight rule of possessing a token Brazilian in your squad. In our case, Geovanni Deiberson Maurício Gómez (Geo to you and I) was snapped up from Manchester City and proved a real coup and fans' favourite.

Comfortably the worst buy undertaken by the club serves only to highlight the sheer perversity of the money-orientated Premier League. With just 28 minutes of football under his belt before a nine-month injury lay-off, take a bow club-record £5m signing Jimmy Bullard.

After a whole two years of Premier League exposure for Hull City, it is perhaps indicative of why the Tigers no longer figure in the top flight. Our star signing racked up a grand total of 13 appearances during our inaugural flirt with England's finest after being dogged with yet more injury problems.

In chasing the Holy Grail of Premier League football, Hull City committed the cardinal sin prone to all top-flight novices. Ambition overtook money, madness overtook reason and then Blackpool overtook us. Hmm...

Ipswich Town

Total Spend (Actual): £26.9m
Total Spend (CTPP): £60.7m
Average League Position: 16
Number of Managers: 2
Most Expensive Signing: Hermann Hreiðarsson – £4m (CTPP £7.2m)
Best Value Signing: Hreiðarsson
Worst Value Signing: Ulrich Le Pen

Player Signings Breakdown (data correct up to end of January transfer window 2010)

- UK: 18   EU: 7   Rest of Europe: 1   Rest of the World: 3

Major Trophies Won Since Premier League Began: 0

Premier League Statistics (correct to the end of the 2009/10 season)

Seasons: 5	Played: 202	
Won: 57	Drawn: 53	Lost:92
Goals Scored: 219	Goals Conceded: 312	Goal Difference: –93
Total Points: 224		

Overview

Ipswich Town have enjoyed two spells in the Premier League, and both have been notable for drastically different reasons. Their first spell began in 1992/93 when they finished 16th, despite being in 4th place at the turn of the year. Their fortunes would decline the following season as they ended 1993/94 in 19th place – one point clear of the relegation zone. The Tractor Boys suffered an awful campaign in 1994/95, losing 29 league games (a joint Premier League record shared with three other teams), including a 9-0 defeat to Manchester United (a Premier League record), and conceding 59 league goals away from home (a Premier League record for a 42-game season) as they finished bottom with 27 points – a massive 21 points from safety.

Ipswich's second spell in the Premier League, beginning in 2000/01, initially proved more successful, but they would spend just two seasons in England's top division. Remarkably, their first season back in the top flight saw Ipswich finish in 5th place, earning the Tractor Boys a spot in the following season's Uefa Cup. The 2001/02 campaign saw the Portman Road club win just one of their first 17 Premier League games before a sequence of seven wins from eight games saw Ipswich move as high as 12th in the table. Following a 2-1 victory over Everton at Goodison Park on February 2, Ipswich would win just one of their remaining 13 league games, culminating in a 5-0 defeat to 2nd-placed Liverpool, which confirmed the club's relegation on the final day of the season.

Most Utilised Players

Herman Hreiðarsson became Ipswich Town's record signing in 2000, when George Burley signed him for £4m (£7.2m) from Wimbledon. Hreiðarsson started 73 out of a possible 76 games for the Tractor Boys, giving him a start ratio of 96%, before Ipswich's relegation from the Premier League at the end of 2001/02. Hreiðarsson holds the record for being relegated the most times, having gone down with every single team he's played for in the Premier League: Crystal Palace, Wimbledon, Ipswich, Charlton and Portsmouth.

Least Utilised Players

Ulrich Le Pen was a £1.4m (£1.9m) signing from French side Lorient in 2001. He didn't start a single game for Ipswich during 2001/02 and returned to France in 2002.

Managers

Year	£XI	£XI Rank	Points	Cost Per Point	Position League	Manager
1992/93	£8,007,258	22	52	£153,986	16	John Lyall
1993/94	£14,245,674	18	43	£331,295	19	John Lyall
1994/95	£16,312,836	20	27	£604,179	22	Lyall/Burley
Average	**£12,855,256**	**20**	**40.7**	**£363,153**	**19**	**John Lyall**
1994/95	£16,312,836	20	27	£604,179	22	Lyall/Burley
2000/01	£21,868,403	17	66	£331,339	5	George Burley
2001/02	£28,521,423	14	36	£792,262	18	George Burley
Average	**£22,234,221**	**17**	**43**	**£575,927**	**15**	**George Burley**

Top 10 CTPP Purchases

#	Player	CTPP	Original fee	Year transferred	% of poss starts
1	Hreiðarsson H	£7,119,502	£4,000,000	2000/01	96%
2	Sereni M	£5,897,979	£4,500,000	2001/02	66%
3	Stewart M (II)	£5,866,676	d2500000	1999/00	70%
4	Slater S	£4,776,555	£800,000	1993/94	60%
5	Marshall I	£4,478,021	£750,000	1993/94	50%
6	Williams G (I)	£4,326,534	£650,000	1992/93	87%
7	George F	£4,063,052	£3,100,000	2001/02	55%
8	Bent M	£3,931,986	£3,000,000	2001/02	58%
9	Paz A	£3,788,596	£1,000,000	1994/95	31%
10	Sedgley S	£3,788,596	£1,000,000	1994/95	62%

Expert View

Graham Saunders

Ipswich Town season–ticket holder

Seasons of relative brilliance, and seasons of relegation. Looking back, to finish 16th with 52 points in 1992/93 seems somehow wrong. Yes, there were two extra teams back then, but such a total would have seen a team finish 9th in 2010.

To get 52 points with the only £XI in the division to cost under £10m some 18 seasons ago was some achievement. But 52 points fell to 43, which dropped to 27;

and we disappeared out of the top flight.

Finishing 5th in 2000/01 was another minor miracle. Spending £4m on Herman Hreiðarsson (our record purchase in CTPP terms: £7.1m) still looks fairly good business, given that the player was still a regular in the Premier League (for Portsmouth) in 2009/10, at the age of 36. But selling him for just £800,000 (£1.3m) in 2003 doesn't look quite so clever in retrospect.

The biggest success was a striker born as Billy Tubbs. Marcus Stewart, as he later became known, was the Premier League's second-top goalscorer during 2000/01, with 19 goals. At £5.9m in today's money, Stewart was a veritable bargain. But he only scored six the following season, as part of a struggling team that returned to the second tier of English football – all from a campaign that began in the UEFA Cup. And with that, our dreams crashed and burned.

Leeds United

Total Spend (Actual): £141.2m
Total Spend (CTPP): £339.1m
Average League Position: 8.83
Number of Managers: 5
Most Expensive Signing: Rio Ferdinand – £18m (CTPP £32.1m)
Best Value Signing: Nigel Martyn
Worst Value Signing: David Rocastle

Player Signings Breakdown (data correct up to end of January transfer window 2010)

- UK: 33   EU: 10   Rest of Europe: 4   Rest of the World: 7

Major Trophies Won Since Premier League Began: 0

Premier League Statistics (correct to the end of the 2009/10 season)

Seasons: 12	Played: 468	
Won: 189	Drawn: 125	Lost:154
Goals Scored: 641	Goals Conceded: 573	Goal Difference: +68
Total Points: 692		

Overview
Leeds United's fall from Premier League grace was as sharp as their sudden return to

the top. When Leeds were promoted back to the top flight in 1990, it took them just two seasons to be crowned champions of England for the third time in their history, making them the final team to win the old First Division before the change in 1992/93. Their first season in the Premier League saw Leeds go the entire campaign without winning a single away game (a Premier League record that is now shared by five other teams), finishing in 17th place, a difference of 16 places and a drop of 31 points from the previous season's total.

Leeds finished the next two seasons (1993/94 and 1994/95) in 5th place, before two seasons in mid-table were followed by five top-five finishes in a row, finishing as high as 3rd (1999/00) and as low as 5th (1997/98 and 2001/02), with two 4th-place finishes (1998/99 and 2000/01) thrown in for good measure. It was between 1999 and 2001 that Leeds set the scene for what would be their near fatal decline in 2004.

Under David O'Leary, Leeds reached the UEFA Cup semi-final in 1999/00 and finished the Premier League season in 3rd place, earning the Whites a place in the Champions League the following season. Backed with some big-money signings such as Rio Ferdinand, signed for £18m (£32.1m) In November 2000 (then a world-record fee for a defender), Leeds reached their second consecutive European semi-final, where they lost to Valencia over two legs in the 2000/01 Champions League.

Leeds finished 2000/01 outside the places that earned Champions League qualification for 2001/02, and had to settle for a spot in the less lucrative UEFA Cup after finishing the season in 4th, losing out to 3rd-placed Liverpool by a single point.

Leeds again spent big in an attempt to qualify for the Champions League via the top four league places (2001/02 was the first season that saw four places awarded to English teams) but finished the season in 5th and had to again make do with the UEFA Cup, resulting in O'Leary being sacked in the summer of 2002. Things would soon spiral out of control for Leeds, as crippling debt built up from loans used to buy players in a bid to sustain regular Champions League football. This forced the Elland Road outfit to sell star players such as Robbie Keane, Robbie Fowler and Jonathan Woodgate in 2002/03 as Leeds finished in 15th place.

Things would go from bad to disastrous in 2003/04 as Leeds' crippling debts saw more players leave the club, which was relegated from England's top division after finishing in 19th place – six points adrift of safety. A further exodus of players followed as Leeds were faced with insolvency, before their training ground and stadium were both sold in 2004. The club would eventually enter into administration in 2007, which confirmed their relegation to England's third division (now known as League One) for the first time in their history.

Despite all of their problems on and off the pitch during the 2000s, Leeds United have a history and fan base that is befitting of a major Premier League club, having won three league titles (1968/69, 1973/74 and 1991/92), one FA Cup (1972), one League Cup (1968) and two Uefa Cups (1968 and 1971).

Most Utilised Players

Goalkeeper Nigel Martyn ranks as Leeds United's most utilised player signed in the Premier League. Bought for £2.25m (£6m) from Crystal Palace in 1996, Martyn started 207 games (91% start ratio) for the Whites during his seven seasons at Elland Road. Only Gary McAllister has a higher start ratio (92%) for Leeds, but he was signed before the Premier League was formed.

Jimmy Floyd Hasselbaink is another player that figures highly. Signed for £2m (£6.8m) in June 1997, Hasselbaink spent two seasons at Leeds. He started 66 league games, giving him an 87% start ratio before he was sold to Atlético Madrid in 1999.

Least Utilised Players

There are four players that were signed by Leeds United for CTPP £10m or more with a start ratio of 30% or less. These include the late David Rocastle, who was signed from Arsenal in 1992 for £2m (£13.4m), a then club record. Rocastle started just 17 league games (20% start ratio) before he was sold to Manchester City in 1993.

David White was another big-money signing who failed to make the most of his career at Elland Road. Signed for £2m (£12m) from Manchester City in 1993 (before Rocastle went the other way), White made just 28 starts (23% start ratio) for Leeds before he was sold to Sheffield United in 1995.

Managers

Year	£XI	£XI Rank	Points	Cost Per Point	Position League	Manager
1992/93	£43,562,492	9	51	£854,167	17	Howard Wilkinson
1993/94	£54,585,789	6	70	£779,797	5	Howard Wilkinson
1994/95	£61,410,086	5	73	£841,234	5	Howard Wilkinson
1995/96	£57,179,904	7	43	£1,329,765	13	Howard Wilkinson
1996/97	£52,342,499	8	46	£1,137,880	11	Wilkinson/Graham
Average	**£53,816,154**	**7**	**56.6**	**£988,569**	**10.2**	**Howard Wilkinson**
1996/97	£52,342,499	8	46	£1,137,880	11	Wilkinson/Graham
1997/98	£40,524,693	11	59	£686,859	5	George Graham
1998/99	£40,975,998	12	67	£611,582	4	Graham/O'Leary
Average	**£44,614,397**	**10.3**	**57.3**	**£812,107**	**6.7**	**George Graham**
1998/99	£40,975,998	12	67	£611,582	4	Graham/O'Leary
1999/00	£45,206,309	10	69	£655,164	3	David O'Leary
2000/01	£73,885,223	7	68	£1,086,547	4	David O'Leary
2001/02	£95,297,942	4	66	£1,443,908	5	David O'Leary
Average	**£63,841,368**	**8.25**	**67.5**	**£949,300**	**4**	**David O'Leary**
2002/03	£39,064,624	10	47	£831,162	15	Venables/Peter Reid
2003/04	£31,674,835	13	33	£959,843	19	Peter Reid/Eddie Gray
Average	**£35,369,730**	**11.5**	**40**	**£895,503**	**17**	**Peter Reid**

Top 5 Players Sold for a Profit

- R Ferdinand – Bought for: £18m (£32m), Sold for: £30m (£48.4m) Profit of: £12m (£16.4m)
- Hasselbaink – Bought for: £2m (£6.8m), Sold for: £12m (£28.2m), Profit of: £10m (£21.4m)
- Woodgate – Bought for: £0 (trainee), Sold for: £9m (£14.5m), Profit of: £9m (£14.5m)
- A Smith – Bought for: £0 (trainee), Sold for: £7m (£12.8m), Profit of: £7m (£12.8m)
- Kewell – Bought for: £0 (trainee), Sold for: £5m (£10.1m), Profit of: £5m (£10.1m)

Top 20 CTPP Purchases

#	Player	CTPP	Original fee	Year transferred	% of poss starts
1	Ferdinand R	£32,037,760	£18,000,000	2000/01	71%
2	Deane B	£16,120,874	£2,700,000	1993/94	82%
3	Fowler R	£14,417,282	£11,000,000	2001/02	32%
4	Rocastle D	£13,312,412	£2,000,000	1992/93	20%
5	Yeboah A	£12,881,225	£3,400,000	1994/95	37%
6	Dacourt O	£12,815,104	£7,200,000	2000/01	46%
7	White D (I)	£11,941,388	£2,000,000	1993/94	23%
8	Sharpe L	£11,904,914	£4,500,000	1996/97	37%
9	Brolin T	£11,832,831	£4,500,000	1995/96	45%
10	Bridges M	£11,733,352	£5,000,000	1999/00	26%
11	Hopkin D	£10,972,256	£3,250,000	1997/98	56%
12	Viduka M	£10,679,253	£6,000,000	2000/01	83%
13	Wallace R (II)	£10,649,930	D1600000	1992/93	64%
14	Duberry M	£10,560,017	£4,500,000	1999/00	26%
15	Mills D	£10,254,949	£4,370,000	1999/00	64%
16	Palmer C	£9,850,349	£2,600,000	1994/95	85%
17	Huckerby D	£9,386,681	£4,000,000	1999/00	14%
18	Johnson S	£9,174,634	£7,000,000	2001/02	22%
19	Dorigo T	£8,653,068	D1300000	1992/93	64%
20	Matteo D	£8,454,409	£4,750,000	2000/01	76%

Expert View

Anthony Clavane

Sunday Mirror / author of "Promised Land: The Reinvention of Leeds United"

www.anthonyclavane.com

Leeds United should have been the team of the noughties. Top of the Premiership on the first day of 2000, 3rd at the end of the season and Uefa Cup semi-finalists. I remember Nelson Mandela opening the new Millennium Square, introduced by Leeds captain Lucas Radebe. Mandela called The Chief his "hero". For both the city and its football team, the only way was up.

And then came The Fall. An Asian student was beaten up outside a nightclub. Criminal charges were pressed against two stars – Lee Bowyer and Jonathan Woodgate – and the club began to unravel. 'Bowyergate' was a contributory factor, but the real reason the mighty Whites suffered one of the most spectacular meltdowns in footballing history was the board's infamous "living the dream" strategy.

During the course of the decade, Leeds went from threatening to win the Champions League – losing the semi-final to Valencia in 2002 – to threatening to win the old third division. They disappeared from the spotlight in a decade when the Premier League conquered the globe. When broadcast contracts, transfer budgets and wages all reached galactic levels. When the top flight attracted some of the best footballers on the planet. David O'Leary's babies: the team that never was.

Looking at Leeds' top 20 signings, from Rio Ferdinand (£32m in today's money) to Dom Matteo (£8.5m), you have to ask the question: "What if?" What if there had been no spend, spend, spend? Critics claim that they bought success, but they reached the Champions League quarter-final without Ferdinand. Thorp Arch, their acclaimed, and envied, conveyor-belt of home-grown talent, had produced the likes of Woodgate, Alan Smith, Paul Robinson and Harry Kewell. It went on to produce the likes of Aaron Lennon, James Milner and Fabian Delph. United worked their way up the table with a fairly inexpensive team. And, whisper it softly, they were quite liked. At one stage, the babies were the darlings of the media.

As a fan, I didn't complain when they had six top-class strikers on their books. Of course, I didn't know chairman Peter Ridsdale's profligate regime had taken out a £60m bond, gambling recklessly on continuing Champions League qualification. And I was kept in the dark about Publicity Pete's goldfish. The policy of speculating to accumulate unravelled because the team finished 5th in 2002, missing out on the elite tournament.

After finishing in the top five for five consecutive years, Leeds imploded. The only way was down. Devoured from within by a toxic combination of excessive debt and bitter in-fighting, they suffered two relegations, went into administration and plummeted, like a stone in the well, until they hit rock bottom. Separated from the golden umbilical cord of the TV largesse, they were locked into a dive; a fast-moving, downward vortex in which losses and high wages fed debts, which in turn produced yet more losses and yet more debts. At the end of the noughties, they were indeed the footballing story of our times. But for all the wrong reasons.

Leicester City

Total Spend (Actual): £46.5m
Total Spend (CTPP): £102.2m
Average League Position: 13.63
Number of Managers: 6
Most Expensive Signing: Ade Akinbiyi – £5m (CTPP £8.9m)
Best Value Signing: Ian Walker
Worst Value Signing: Arnar Gunnlaugsson

Player Signings Breakdown (data correct up to end of January transfer window 2010)

- UK: 46   EU: 6   Rest of Europe: 2   Rest of the World: 4

Major Trophies Won Since Premier League Began

League Cup: 2 (1996/97 and 1999/00)

Premier League Statistics (correct to the end of the 2009/10 season)

Seasons: 8	Played: 308	
Won: 84	Drawn: 90	Lost:134
Goals Scored: 354	Goals Conceded: 456	Goal Difference: –102
Total Points: 342		

Overview

Leicester City have had three separate spells in the Premier League, along with three relegations (1994/95, 2001/02 and 2003/04), but their most successful period came between 1996/97 and 2000/01 under the leadership of Martin O'Neill. Indeed, it was Leicester's most successful period since the 1960s – a time when they reached five cup finals, finishing as runners up in the FA Cup on three occasions (1961, 1963 and 1969), winning one League Cup (1964) and losing the final of the same competition a season later (1965).

Under Martin O'Neill, Leicester reached three League Cup finals in four seasons – a phenomenal achievement. They won two (1997 and 2000), earning the Foxes a place in the Uefa Cup in both 1997/98 and 2000/01. In 1997, it was the first time Leicester had qualified for a European competition since 1961/62. O'Neill also led the Foxes to four consecutive top-10 finishes in the Premier League before he left to take over at Celtic in June 2000.

After O'Neill's departure, Peter Taylor was appointed manager, but he couldn't build on the Ulsterman's success, as Leicester finished 13th in his first season in charge

(2000/01). The following season saw Leicester struggle further, with Taylor replaced by the duo of Dave Bassett and Micky Adams. They couldn't prevent the Foxes being relegated, as the club finished in 20th place with 28 points – 12 points from safety. Adams would ensure Leicester spent just one season in England's second tier, winning promotion at the first time of asking. But their third spell in the Premier League would prove equally as brief, ending 2003/04 in 18th place with 33 points – six adrift from 17th place.

Leicester City jointly hold the record of most home draws in a 38–game Premier League season, having drawn 10 times in 1997/98 and again in 2003/04.

Most Utilised Players

Ian Walker and Mark Draper top the list of Most Utilised Players for Leicester in the Premier League. Walker signed from Spurs for £2.5m (£3.3m) in July 2001 and would go on to start 72 Premier League games (95%) before he left to join Bolton in 2005. Draper was signed in 1994 for £1.25m (£4.8m) and would fail to start only three league games (93%) in the single season he spent at Filbert Street before he was sold to Aston Villa.

Least Utilised Players

Arnar Gunnlaugsson was signed by Martin O'Neill for £2m (£4.9m) from Bolton Wanderers in 1999, but he failed to establish himself in the team and left to join Dundee United in 2002 having made just 10 Premier League starts (7%). Graham Fenton was another disappointing signing for Martin O'Neill. Signed for £1m (£3.4m) in August 1997, Fenton made just 13 league starts (11%) for the Foxes during the three seasons he spent at the club.

Managers

Year	£XI	£XI Rank	Points	Cost Per Point	Position League	Manager
1994/95	£15,477,234	21	29	£533,698	21	Little/McGhee
1996/97	£17,489,007	17	47	£372,107	9	Martin O'Neill
1997/98	£21,380,985	16	53	£403,415	10	Martin O'Neill
1998/99	£24,523,983	17	49	£500,489	10	Martin O'Neill
1999/00	£24,961,687	16	55	£453,849	8	Martin O'Neill
Average	**£22,088,916**	**16.5**	**51**	**£432,465**	**9.25**	**Martin O'Neill**
2000/01	£35,242,875	10	48	£734,227	13	Peter Taylor
2001/02	£28,145,447	15	28	£1,005,195	20	Taylor/Bassett/Adams
Average	**£31,694,161**	**12.5**	**38**	**£869,711**	**16.5**	**Peter Taylor**
2001/02	£28,145,447	15	28	£1,005,195	20	Taylor/Bassett/Adams
2003/04	£12,268,172	19	33	£371,763	18	Micky Adams
Average	**£20,206,810**	**17**	**30.5**	**£688,479**	**19**	**Micky Adams**

Top 5 Players Sold for a Profit

- Heskey – Bought for: £0 (trainee), Sold for: £11m (£25.9m) Profit of: £11m (£25.9m)
- Lennon – Bought for: d750k (£2m), Sold for: £5.75m (£10.3m), Profit of: £5m (£8.3m)
- Piper – Bought for: £0 (trainee), Sold for: £3.5m (£5.7m), Profit of: £3.5m (£5.7m)
- Savage – Bought for: £400k (£1.4m), Sold for: £2.5m (£4.1m), Profit of: £2.1m (£2.7m)
- Draper – Bought for: £1.25m (£4.8m), Sold for: £3.25m (£8.6m), Profit of: £2m (£3.8m)

Top 20 CTPP Purchases

#	Player	CTPP	Original fee	Year transferred	% of poss starts
1	Akinbiyi A	£8,899,378	£5,000,000	2000/01	64%
2	Eadie D	£7,040,011	£3,000,000	1999/00	41%
3	Jones M	£5,784,596	£3,250,000	2000/01	21%
4	Rowett G	£5,339,627	£3,000,000	2000/01	62%
5	Gunnlaugsson A	£4,899,163	£2,000,000	1998/99	7%
6	Sinclair F	£4,899,163	£2,000,000	1998/99	64%
7	Draper M	£4,735,745	£1,250,000	1994/95	93%
8	Elliott M	£4,232,858	£1,600,000	1996/97	73%
9	Scowcroft J	£3,931,986	£3,000,000	2001/02	71%
10	Impey A	£3,919,330	£1,600,000	1998/99	55%
11	Robins M	£3,788,596	£1,000,000	1994/95	26%
12	Fenton G	£3,376,079	£1,000,000	1997/98	11%
13	Walker I	£3,276,655	£2,500,000	2001/02	95%
14	Claridge S	£3,155,422	d1200000	1995/96	51%
15	Davidson C	£3,025,788	£1,700,000	2000/01	54%
16	Flowers T	£2,581,337	£1,100,000	1999/00	47%
17	Zagorakis T	£2,532,059	£750,000	1997/98	30%
18	Keller K	£2,380,983	£900,000	1996/97	87%
19	Philpott L	£2,329,672	d350000	1992/93	45%
20	Guppy S	£2,248,706	£850,000	1996/97	62%

Expert View

David Bevan (@The72football)
Leicester Mercury Newspaper, and Football League blog The 72 – www.theseventytwo.wordpress.com

Leicester City's seven seasons in the Premier League can be divided into three very different periods: the 1994/95 season under Brian Little and then Mark McGhee, which ended in relegation; the glorious four years with Martin O'Neill in charge from 1996 to 2000; and the subsequent fall from grace when Peter Taylor took over as manager.

The figures produced by the Transfer Price Index will present few surprises to City fans in the sense that they reflect the incredible value O'Neill found on the market and, equally, just how poorly Taylor spent the money gained by O'Neill's success. Discovering that Ade Akinbiyi's record transfer in 2000 is the equivalent to an £8.9m purchase in today's money is particularly galling. Indeed, none of

City's five most expensive Premier League players became terrace heroes, and two − Darren Eadie and Matthew Jones − retired from professional football due to injury.

Of the top 15, only Matt Elliott and Steve Claridge, both O'Neill buys, can reasonably claim to be City legends. City fans can reflect with satisfaction on the bargains that characterised the O'Neill years. In today's market, the fees City paid for key men Neil Lennon and Muzzy Izzet both equate to under £2m apiece.

Interestingly, Peter Taylor's 2000/01 side should have finished 9th in the Premier League based on the cost of each squad that season. City started superbly, but lost eight games in a row towards the end of the campaign and ended in 13th place. When the following season kicked off, Taylor's squad was valued six places lower, as the 15th costliest in the league.

In contrast, O'Neill's City were never expected to finish above 16th position based on squad cost, but achieved a top-half finish in each of their four Premier League seasons.

Liverpool

Total Spend (Actual): £404.5m
Total Spend (CTPP): £729.8m
Average League Position: 4.28
Number of Managers: 4
Most Expensive Signing: Djibril Cissé − £14.2m (CTPP £25.9m)
Best Value Signing: José Reina
Worst Value Signing: Bernard Diomède

Player Signings Breakdown (data correct up to end of January transfer window 2010)

- UK: 21   EU: 47   Rest of Europe: 10   Rest of the World: 18

Major Trophies Won Since Premier League Began

FA Cup: 2 (2001 and 2006)
League Cup: 3 (1995, 2001 and 2003)
Champions League: 1 (2005)
UEFA Cup: 1 (2001)

Premier League Statistics (correct to the end of the 2009/10 season)

Seasons: 18   Played: 696

Won: 349   Drawn: 177   Lost:170

Goals Scored: 1,130   Goals Conceded: 669   Goal Difference: +461

Total Points: 1,224

Overview

Despite being England's most successful club, Liverpool have found it difficult to challenge for the Premier League title and have not been crowned champions of England since 1989/90, although only Manchester United (20), Chelsea (12) and Arsenal (10) have won more trophies than Liverpool (seven) since the Premier League was formed.

The first two Premier League seasons saw Graeme Souness' Liverpool finish 6th in 1992/93 and 8th in 1993/94 – a campaign that saw the Scot replaced by Roy Evans in January 1994 following a humiliating FA Cup defeat to Bristol City.

Although Roy Evans improved the atmosphere and quality of football at Anfield post-Souness, he had only the 1995 League Cup triumph over Bolton Wanderers to show for his efforts. Evans did lead Liverpool to two 4th-place finishes (1994/95 with 74 points and 1996/97 with 68 points) and two 3rd-place finishes (1995/96 with 71 points and 1997/98 with 65 points) before he was replaced by Gérard Houllier in November 1998.

Houllier's first season at the club in 1998/99 (a campaign that saw Evans and Houllier appointed as joint managers before Evans resigned in November, leaving the Frenchman in sole charge) saw Liverpool finish 7th, but the Reds' fortunes steadily rose as Houllier led them to a 4th-place finish in 1999/00 and then 3rd in 2000/01. The latter season saw Liverpool achieve an historic cup treble: the Merseysiders won the League Cup, FA Cup and UEFA Cup, becoming the first team to do so in the same season. The League Cup and FA Cup double also saw Liverpool become only the second side (after Arsenal in 1993) to achieve such a feat, although Chelsea have since joined the elite club by winning both cups in 2007. Houllier followed up the cup success of 2001 by leading the Reds to 2nd in 2001/02 with 80 points, both firsts for Liverpool in the Premier League. Houllier missed a large chunk of that season after undergoing heart surgery, leaving his assistant Phil Thompson in charge of team affairs.

Liverpool couldn't maintain the upward momentum and ended 2002/03 in 5th place, with a League Cup Final victory over Manchester United the highlight of the season, before finishing 2003/04 in 4th place, as the quality of football hit a new low. Houllier was sacked at the end of that season and replaced by Rafa Benítez for the start of 2004/05.

Benítez made an instant impact during his first two seasons at Liverpool, leading the Reds to the Champions League/European Cup Final for the first time since 1984/85. His side, 3–0 down at half-time, came back to beat AC Milan on penalties, after the game ended 3–3, and Liverpool lifted the trophy for the fifth time. The league form suffered, however, and Liverpool could finish the season only in 5th place with 58 points. A year later, the Anfield outfit ended 2005/06 in 3rd place with 82 points (their highest tally in the Premier League at the time) and won another trophy on penalties, this time beating West Ham following a thrilling FA Cup Final that also finished 3–3 after extra time.

The following season saw Liverpool again finish 3rd, but this time with 68 points – 14 fewer than the previous campaign. The Reds would also reach their second Champions League Final in three seasons, but despite the Reds being the better team this time, AC Milan gained revenge with a 2–1 victory. In 2007/08, Liverpool earned eight more points than the previous campaign, but their total of 76 was enough to finish only 4th.

By finishing 2008/09 in 2nd place with 86 points (Liverpool's highest points tally since 1987/88 and good enough to be crowned champions in eight out of the first 18 Premier League seasons), the Reds produced their finest league showing since their last title triumph of 1989/90. Like 2002/03, Liverpool couldn't build on their 2nd-place finish and ended the 2009/10 campaign in 7th place with 63 points – 23 fewer than the previous season. This poor performance contributed towards Benítez leaving Liverpool shortly after the end of the season, with Roy Hodgson named as his replacement.

Most Utilised Players
Pepe Reina tops Liverpool's Most Utilised Players list with a 96% start ratio, having missed just eight league games since his £6m (£11m) arrival from Villareal in July 2005.

Sami Hyypiä was a £2.6m (£6.1m) signing by Houllier from Willem II in May 1999 and ranks fourth in the list, having started 310 Premier League games (82% start ratio) during a Liverpool career that spanned a decade.

Least Utilised Players
Five of the top 10 players in the least utilised list are Gérard Houllier signings, with two each signed by Souness and Benítez, and one by Roy Evans. The two most expensive players that feature in the top 10 are Mark Kennedy (Evans) and Bernard Diomède (Houllier).

Kennedy was signed by Roy Evans from Milwall in March 1995 for what was then a British-record £2.3m (£8.8m) deal for a teenager. He would start only five Premier League games for Liverpool before he was sold to Manchester City in 1999. Diomède proved to be Houllier's most expensive failure, making just one league start for Liverpool following his £3m (£5.4m) move from Auxerre in July 2003. This equates to the World Cup winner costing Liverpool £3m (£5.4m) per start before he returned to France in 2003.

Managers

Year	£XI	£XI Rank	Points	Cost Per Point	Position League	Manager
1992/93	£63,386,101	2	59	£1,074,341	6	Graeme Souness
1993/94	£75,596,708	2	60	£1,259,945	8	Souness/Roy Evans
Average	**£69,491,405**	**2**	**59.5**	**£1,167,143**	**7**	**Graeme Souness**
1993/94	£75,596,708	2	60	£1,259,945	8	Souness/Roy Evans
1994/95	£79,006,929	3	74	£1,067,661	4	Roy Evans
1995/96	£89,313,515	1	71	£1,257,937	3	Roy Evans
1996/97	£81,099,634	2	68	£1,192,642	4	Roy Evans
1997/98	£52,311,762	10	65	£804,796	3	Roy Evans
1998/99	£53,575,564	10	54	£992,140	7	Evans/Gérard Houllier
Average	**£71,817,352**	**4.7**	**65.3**	**£1,095,854**	**4.8**	**Roy Evans**
1998/99	£53,575,564	10	54	£992,140	7	Evans/Gérard Houllier
1999/00	£66,752,063	5	67	£996,299	4	Gérard Houllier
2000/01	£78,358,412	5	69	£1,135,629	3	Gérard Houllier
2001/02	£72,439,177	6	80	£905,490	2	Gérard Houllier
2002/03	£75,690,207	5	64	£1,182,659	5	Gérard Houllier
2003/04	£87,479,159	5	60	£1,457,986	4	Gérard Houllier
Average	**£72,382,430**	**6**	**65.7**	**£1,111,701**	**4.2**	**Gérard Houllier**
2004/05	£75,171,147	4	58	£1,296,054	5	Rafael Benítez
2005/06	£93,220,381	4	82	£1,136,834	3	Rafael Benítez
2006/07	£84,110,888	3	68	£1,236,925	3	Rafael Benítez
2007/08	£96,562,289	3	76	£1,270,556	4	Rafael Benítez
2008/09	£96,049,949	3	86	£1,116,860	2	Rafael Benítez
2009/10	£90,993,156	4	63	£1,444,336	7	Rafael Benítez
Average	**£89,351,302**	**3.5**	**72.2**	**£1,250,261**	**4**	**Rafael Benítez**

Top 5 Players Sold for a Profit

- Alonso – Bought for: £10.5m (£19.1m), Sold for: £30m (£30m), Profit of: £19.5m (£10.9m)
- Fowler – Bought for: £0 (trainee), Sold for: £11m (£14.5m), Profit of: £11m (£14.5m)
- Owen – Bought for: £0 (trainee), Sold for: £8m (£14.6m), Profit of: £8m (£14.6m)
- Matteo – Bought for: £0 (trainee), Sold for: £4.75m (£8.5m), Profit of: £4.75m (£8.5m)
- Crouch – Bought for: £7m (£12.8m), Sold for: £11m (£8.6m), Profit of: £4m (£-4.2m)

Top 20 CTPP Purchases

#	Player	CTPP	Original fee	Year transferred	% of poss starts
1	Cissé D	£25,833,105	£14,200,000	2004/05	38%
2	Heskey E	£25,813,374	£11,000,000	1999/00	62%
3	Torres F	£22,573,285	£20,000,000	2007/08	61%
4	Collymore S	£22,350,904	£8,500,000	1995/96	72%
5	Mascherano J	£20,993,155	£18,200,000	2006/07	59%
6	Aquilani A	£20,000,000	£20,000,000	2009/10	24%
7	Saunders D	£19,302,998	D2900000	1992/93	N/A
8	Alonso X	£19,101,944	£10,500,000	2004/05	64%
9	Hamann D	£18,773,363	£8,000,000	1999/00	65%
10	Rush I	£18,637,377	D2800000	1992/93	72%
11	Johnson G (I)	£18,000,000	£18,000,000	2009/10	63%
12	Diouf E	£16,136,338	£10,000,000	2002/03	54%

#	Player	CTPP	Original fee	Year transferred	% of poss starts
13	Stewart P	£15,309,274	£2,300,000	1992/93	33%
14	Ruddock N	£14,926,735	£2,500,000	1993/94	56%
15	Keane R (II)	£14,855,969	£19,000,000	2008/09	42%
16	Wright M	£14,643,654	D2200000	1992/93	56%
17	Ince P	£14,179,531	£4,200,000	1997/98	86%
18	Babb P	£13,638,944	£3,600,000	1994/95	64%
19	Clough N	£13,583,329	£2,275,000	1993/94	24%
20	Scales J	£13,260,085	£3,500,000	1994/95	55%

Expert View

Oliver Kay (@oliverkaytimes)

Football Correspondent, The Times

The Premier League era was only a few weeks old when Liverpool, champions of England only two years earlier, found themselves doing something that would happen many times over the years to come: selling a big-money signing at a loss. Dean Saunders had been a British record acquisition when he joined from Derby County for £2.9m (£19.3m CTPP) in 1991, but, after a fitful first season, he was sold to Aston Villa at a £600,000 loss (£4m), with Graeme Souness admitting that "it didn't work out."

On reflection, it has been a familiar lament at Anfield during the Premier League era, in which the league title has been at times tantalisingly close but more often far out of reach. Paul Stewart (£15.3m CTPP), Nigel Clough (£13.6m), Stan Collymore (£22.4m), Paul Ince (£14.2m), Christian Ziege (£14.2m), Nick Barmby (£10.7m), El-Hadji Diouf (£16.1m), Djibril Cissé (£25.8m), Robbie Keane (£15m), Alberto Aquilani (£17m) – again and again, big-money signings have come and gone, some of them without even making a short-term impact. And that is before we get to players such as István Kozma, Sean Dundee, Bernard Diomède and Antonio Núñez, who offer a reminder that "cut-price" does not necessarily mean "bargain".

There have also been some outstanding purchases – Sami Hyypiä (£6.1m CTPP), Dietmar Hamann (£18.8m), Xabi Alonso (£19.1m), José Reina (£10.9m) and Fernando Torres (£22.6m), to name but five – but, when a club is constantly trying to bridge a gap, the margin for error is small. There have been too many mistakes when Liverpool needed to get it spot-on.

One thing that strikes me when examining Liverpool's transfer record is how many of the signings appear to have been poorly researched. Every manager makes mistakes, but, when Souness confessed to an error of judgement over Saunders, admitting that the forward did not fit into Liverpool's "more calculated, less direct" style, it did not stop such mistakes being repeated with players such as

Diouf and Cissé, who lacked the sophistication even to fit into what was, by then, a slightly less patient style of play.

For the most part, the club's lack of revenue, combined with a lack of productivity from the youth academy, has led to a situation where sizeable transfer budgets have been spread thinner than elsewhere, leading Rafael Benítez, in particular, to invest in players who were only ever going to be squad-fillers or short-term signings. While it is certainly true that Sir Alex Ferguson and Arsène Wenger would not have signed Sotiris Kyrgiakos, Jan Kromkamp and Andriy Voronin, it is also true that they would not have been required to fill gaps in their squad with imports of such dubious quality.

For all the criticism of Liverpool's academy, it is worth wondering how much worse things would have been in the Premier League era but for the emergence of Steve McManaman, Robbie Fowler, Jamie Carragher, Michael Owen and Steven Gerrard. The disappointment is that this production line slowed almost to a standstill during the 2000s, meaning that the focus on transfers for Houllier, Benítez and now Hodgson became ever sharper.

Expert View
Roy Henderson (@royhendo)
Writer, www.redandwhitekop.net & www.royhendo.com

The Fall of Liverpool

In an interview ahead of his testimonial in September 2010, Jamie Carragher, when asked what he would say to Alex Ferguson if he ever met him, said "I'd say he never 'knocked Liverpool off their f*cking perch'. That's nonsense that. Graeme Souness did that. United were competing with Norwich and Aston Villa for their first title. They weren't competing with Liverpool, were they?"

Carragher's statement raises an interesting question. What was it that triggered Liverpool Football Club's decline from domination of domestic and European football to relative also-rans on both fronts? There are many factors to consider, but in 2010, possibly more than ever before, the fundamental one is clear. To dominate, you need economic muscle. If you want to be sat on your perch, it's nigh on impossible to stay there for too long without it.

But what if you no longer have that economic muscle? What if other sides have more economic muscle than you do? If you have any hope of being successful in that context, you need some miraculous combination of reasonable investment, organisational vision (with congruence at all levels), commitment, patience, and last but not least, a knack for investing your money well – at least as well if not better than your competitors.

In fact, if your competitors are better funded than you are, you better pray they lack some or all of those things.

So where does that leave Graeme Souness? When he took over at Liverpool in the Spring of 1991, economic muscle wasn't a problem. The club was still something of a juggernaut with a momentum all of its own. While it was maybe beginning its relative decline in both financial and strategic terms, it was still one of the biggest spenders in English football, and adding to an already phenomenal playing staff. It's not too outrageous a statement to suggest that without dramatic changes in the transfer market, Liverpool could have sustained its momentum for several more years without suffering too much.

Though now ageing, the team Souness inherited had won the league the year before, and his first handful of games saw the side clinch a close second in the league to winners Arsenal despite the sudden departure of Kenny Dalglish – a massive shock to the club and to the city as a whole. So while the squad was no doubt experiencing turmoil following Kenny's departure, it might have been wiser not to disrupt things too much, and to keep the juggernaut on the rails a little longer while a few tweaks were made.

As it was, we saw a sage lesson in how to squander economic muscle, and how to dissipate a juggernaut's momentum. Souness started out with rich resources at his disposal. He inherited a squad of proven winners, a club with the ability to consistently nurture its own players and relatively cheap buys from lower divisions through to first team duty, and an ability to go toe-to-toe with anyone in the transfer market at the time.

It's fair to say the prayers of poorer-funded competitors came true. Souness failed to invest his resources wisely. The club itself developed a habit of doing the same, and the two compounded each other to the extent that Liverpool has been playing catch-up ever since.

Certain transfers are emblematic of each manager's tenure at Liverpool. For Souness, names like Julian Dicks, Torben Piechnik and Paul Stewart showcase an awful judgement of talent. On top of that, truly world-class players were replaced with those of a lesser standard, such as Dean Saunders, Nigel Clough, Mark Wright and Mark Walters, often for huge fees approaching the British transfer record.

In today's prices, Souness paid £127.3m for 13 players (almost £10m each). Also in today's money, the total raised when those players left the club was just £33.5m (almost half of which came from the sale of Saunders); meaning a loss of almost £100m by current-day standards. Of these 13 signings, only Rob Jones (£2m

CTPP) was an enduring success, with Mark Wright (£14.6m) eventually showing some form towards his mid-30s. In short, truly awful business.

Others have been blamed for Liverpool's relative demise. Overall, however, the club's decline both on and off the pitch began with Souness, and was compounded by men in suits behind the scenes – a situation that continues to this day.

Manchester City

Total Spend (Actual): £392m
Total Spend (CTPP): £493.6m
Average League Position: 12.62
Number of Managers: 9
Most Expensive Signing: Carlos Tévez – £25.5m (CTPP £25.5m)
Best Value Signing: Sylvain Distin
Worst Value Signing: Valeri Bojinov

Player Signings Breakdown (data correct up to end of January transfer window 2010)

- UK: 41   EU: 32   Rest of Europe: 8   Rest of the World: 20

Major Trophies Won Since Premier League Began: 0

Premier League Statistics (correct to the end of the 2009/10 season)

Seasons: 13	Played: 506	
Won: 162	Drawn: 138	Lost:206
Goals Scored: 618	Goals Conceded: 674	Goal Difference: –56
Total Points: 624		

Overview

Manchester City entered the Premier League era on the back of two 5th-place finishes in England's top division, but they could manage only 9th in 1992/93. In 1993/94, Brian Horton's City side finished in 16th, joining Sheffield United in drawing 18 league games – a joint Premier League record for most draws in a 42-game season (Southampton also drew 18 games the following season to equal the record). Worse was to come for the Blues as they ended 1994/95 in 17th place and 1995/96 in 18th place, sealing their relegation to England's second tier. They would return to the Premier League in 2000/01, but an 18th-place finish saw them once again relegated to the First Division.

City would return to the Premier League at the first time of asking under the guidance of Kevin Keegan, finishing 9th in 2002/03 in what would be the club's last season at Maine Road before moving to the newly built City of Manchester Stadium. The Blues also qualified for the UEFA Cup via the Fair Play ranking (the first time City had qualified for a European competition in 25 years). A 16th-place finish followed in 2003/04 and 8th place was secured in 2004/05. Keegan decided to retire from football during the latter campaign, leaving the relatively inexperienced Stuart Pearce to fill the void for the last two months of the season.

Under Pearce, City managed to finish the next two seasons only in 15th (2005/06) and 16th (2006/07), leading to the appointment of former England boss Sven-Göran Eriksson. The Swede led City to a 9th-place finish in 2007/08, which included a league double over local rivals Manchester United (for the first time since 1969/70). City also qualified for the UEFA Cup through the Fair Play ranking, but this wasn't enough to prevent Eriksson from losing his job as Mark Hughes replaced him during the close season.

Hughes' first season in charge saw City go the entire 2008/09 campaign without drawing a single league game at home (a Premier League record) as they finished in 10th. City could only reach the UEFA Cup quarter-finals, despite large investment in the playing squad, including breaking the British transfer record with the £32.5m (£25.4m) signing of Robinho from Real Madrid.

Following more investment in new players during the pre-season, City started the 2009/10 campaign in good form, winning five out of the first six Premier League games, before a run of seven consecutive draws (a joint Premier League record shared with two other teams) between October 5 and November 21 contributed towards Hughes being sacked in December. Despite leading the Blues to their first cup semi-final appearance since 1981, Hughes was replaced by Roberto Mancini. Mancini's City lost the League Cup semi-final to Manchester United over two legs, but they managed to finish 5th in the league to qualify for the 2010/11 Europa League. With further investment undertaken, a lot more is now expected.

Most Utilised Players

Kit Symons and Eike Immel are top of the list of Manchester City's Most Utilised Players in the Premier League with 100% start ratios, both obtained during 1995/96. Symons was a £1.2m (£3.2m) signing in 1995, with Immel costing £400k (£1.1m) from VfB Stuttgart that same summer.

A £4m (£6.5m) capture from Paris Saint-Germain in 2002, Sylvain Distin is arguably one of Kevin Keegan's best signings for Manchester City. Distin failed to start just 12 league games (94% start ratio) during his five seasons at the club before he left to join Portsmouth in May 2007.

Least Utilised Players

Sven-Göran Eriksson signed Valeri Bojinov from Fiorentina for £5.75m (£6.5m) in August 2007, but the Bulgarian made only three Premier League starts (4% start ratio) before returning to Italy to join Parma in a permanent deal in July 2010.

Two recent big-money signings also figure highly in this category, with both Jo (£19m) and Roque Santa Cruz (£17.5m) currently holding start ratios of 16% after failing to hold down a regular place in the City first team following their moves from CSKA Moscow (July 2008) and Blackburn Rovers (June 2009) respectively.

Managers

Year	£XI	£XI Rank	Points	Cost Per Point	Position League	Manager
1992/93	£54,951,737	4	57	£964,066	9	Peter Reid
1993/94	£57,091,337	5	45	£1,268,696	16	Brian Horton
1994/95	£54,021,591	8	49	£1,102,481	17	Brian Horton
Average	£55,556,464	6.5	47	£1,185,589	16.5	Brian Horton
1995/96	£43,779,635	11	38	£1,152,096	18	Alan Ball
2000/01	£24,776,768	16	34	£728,728	18	Joe Royle
2002/03	£43,635,853	8	51	£855,605	9	Kevin Keegan
2003/04	£45,510,620	6	41	£1,110,015	16	Kevin Keegan
2004/05	£34,427,471	7	52	£662,067	8	Keegan/Stuart Pearce
Average	£41,191,315	7	48	£875,896	11	
2004/05	£34,427,471	7	52	£662,067	8	Keegan/Stuart Pearce
2005/06	£29,085,345	10	43	£676,403	15	Stuart Pearce
2006/07	£26,589,063	12	42	£633,073	14	Stuart Pearce
Average	£30,033,960	9.7	45.7	£657,181	12.3	Stuart Pearce
2007/08	£36,546,872	10	55	£664,489	9	Sven-Göran Eriksson
2008/09	£65,296,040	5	50	£1,305,921	10	Mark Hughes
2009/10	£121,147,357	3	67	£1,808,170	5	Hughes/Mancini
Average	£93,221,699	4	58.5	£1,557,045	7.5	Mark Hughes

Top 5 Players Sold for a Profit

- Wright-Phillips – Bought for: £0 (trainee), Sold for: £21m (£38.4m) Profit of: £21m (£38.4m)
- Barton – Bought for: £0 (trainee), Sold for: £5.8m (£6.6m), Profit of: £5.8m (£6.6m)
- Sturridge – Bought for: £0 (trainee), Sold for: £5m (£5m), Profit of: £5m (£5m)
- Flitcroft – Bought for: £0 (trainee), Sold for: £3.6m (£9.3m), Profit of: £3.6m (£9.3m)
- Evans – Bought for: £0 (trainee), Sold for: £3m (£3m), Profit of: £3m (£3m)

Top 20 CTPP Purchases

#	Player	CTPP	Original fee	Year transferred	% of poss starts
1	Tévez C	£25,500,000	£25,500,000	2009/10	84%
2	Robinho	£25,411,527	£32,500,000	2008/09	47%
3	Adebayor E	£25,000,000	£25,000,000	2009/10	66%
4	Lescott J	£22,000,000	£22,000,000	2009/10	45%
5	Anelka N	£20,977,239	£13,000,000	2002/03	76%
6	Santa Cruz R	£17,500,000	£17,500,000	2009/10	16%
7	Curle K	£16,640,516	D2500000	1992/93	80%
8	Phelan T	£16,640,516	£2,500,000	1992/93	62%
9	Touré K	£16,000,000	£16,000,000	2009/10	82%
10	Jo	£14,855,969	£19,000,000	2008/09	16%
11	de Jong N	£13,292,183	£17,000,000	2008/09	61%
12	Barry G	£12,000,000	£12,000,000	2009/10	89%
13	Rocastle D	£11,941,388	£2,000,000	1993/94	50%
14	Samaras G	£10,948,519	£6,000,000	2005/06	25%
15	Bellamy C	£10,946,504	£14,000,000	2008/09	43%
16	Bianchi R	£9,932,246	£8,800,000	2007/08	18%
17	Kernaghan A	£9,553,111	£1,600,000	1993/94	37%
18	Bridge W	£9,382,718	£12,000,000	2008/09	51%
19	Elano	£9,029,314	£8,000,000	2007/08	66%
20	Ćorluka V	£9,029,314	£8,000,000	2007/08	49%

Expert View

Danny Pugsley (@danny_pugsley)

www.bitterandblue.com

The 2009/10 season was the campaign in which the club was supposed to be ready to take the next step; the leap to the promised land of the Champions League and the riches on offer. Having backed Mark Hughes the previous January in the transfer market (when the likes of Nigel de Jong, Wayne Bridge, Shay Given and Craig Bellamy were added to the 'gift' of Robinho – as it is doubtful Hughes actively pursued the Brazilian) the new board opened up the chequebook in some style.

In came Kolo Touré, Joleon Lescott, Carlos Tévez and Emmanuel Adebayor. Big names on big money. Expectations were high and, with a squad value of £242.6m (CTPP), they had every reason to be.

Results didn't quite live up to expectations, however, and although Mark Hughes had the side handily placed around Christmas he was handed his marching orders, and Roberto Mancini took the reins. As we all know, Mancini came up just short and many believed that fifth place was a respectable finish – but with the squad costing 92% of that of the champions (Chelsea), the points return of 78% of Chelsea's total was not good enough, and they should have been able to take the extra step given the resources placed at the disposal of Hughes and Mancini.

As disappointing as this season was, it was nothing in comparison to some of the underachieving sides of days gone by.

In the wake of the Peter Reid era (who was controversially sacked just four games into the season), Brian Horton (remember Brian Who?) was handed the reins by an increasingly unpopular Peter Swales. The 1993/94 season saw a Sq£ of £103.7m, which ranked fifth amongst all clubs that season. The return, however, did not match the talent at the club's disposal – which included Tony Coton, Terry Phelan, Keith Curle, David White and Niall Quinn – and only a late season rally (helped by the additions of David Rocastle, Uwe Rösler, Peter Beagrie and Paul Walsh) staved off relegation.

Despite the squad cost being 90% of that of champions Manchester United, the 45 points gained were just 49% of United's haul. Scant return for a side that was not far removed from fifth-place finishes. The following season did not bring happier times either. The Sq£ was reduced – to 60% of champions Blackburn Rovers – but this still ranked ninth in the division, and a mere four-point improvement on the preceding year resulted in a disappointing 17th-place finish.

Horton was sacked following this season, and it is interesting that fan sentiment considers him to have been harshly treated by the club (not being Francis Lee's 'man') and that his side played some of the most attractive and attacking football of City's modern history. There may be some degree of truth within this viewpoint, but it is interesting that the weight of evidence suggests that Horton grossly underachieved when you consider what he had at his disposal during those two seasons.

It is now two years or so since the Abu Dhabi United Group (ADUG) takeover that changed the landscape of the club forever, with seemingly unlimited pots of cash to help deliver the expectations of the new owners. It is perhaps easy then to forget quite how much trouble the club found itself in during the mid-2000s in the aftermath of the Kevin Keegan era. Stuart Pearce was the man who took charge when Keegan walked away and the 2006/07 season saw the club in dire straits. There was no money in the coffers, which forced Pearce to bring in a string of free transfers and loans in an attempt to bolster the squad. A squad cost of £48.7m (CTPP) paled into insignificance (just 20%) compared with champions Chelsea, who were lavishing millions in their pursuit of success. The fact that Pearce guided the side to the relative comfort of 11th position, achieving 47% of the total points Chelsea amassed, should perhaps be applauded.

The end of the season saw the Thaksin Shinawatra era arrive with its brash promises and ambitions. And what was Pearce's reward for navigating the club through these choppy waters? The sack, with Mark Hughes handed the millions.

Until very recently, City were not known for throwing their money (or weight) around. That of course changed with the arrival of ADUG and their oil money (and to a lesser degree Thaksin Shinawatra's arrival that preceded it). The early 1990s saw the arrival of Tony Coton, Keith Curle, Terry Phelan and Niall Quinn at a similar time. The quartet were purchased for a total sum of £6.8m – the £2.5m shelled out for both Curle and Phelan considerable amounts at the time. All four gave great value to the club (it is astonishing that both Coton and Curle didn't collect numerous England caps). In current terms, Quinn (bought from Arsenal for £800,000) cost £5.3m, Coton £6.6m and Curle and Phelan £16.6m each.

At Blackburn, and even to some extent at City, Mark Hughes made some savvy purchases on what you would class a 'mid-level' basis. The same, however, could not be said for those times where he was handed the keys to the vault to bring in players on an unlimited budget. It is not just the outlay on certain players – given that Carlos Tévez has almost 'paid back' his £25.5m fee – but in terms of their eventual utilisation.

You could be forgiven for thinking that many of the big-money signings that Hughes made have had only 12-18 months at the club, and have opportunities of success ahead of them; by and large, though, this is not the case. Whilst Vincent Kompany and Nigel de Jong will surely go on to be excellent purchases for the money it took to land them, there are a number of players brought in by Hughes whose careers at the club are all but dead in the water. Being charitable, you could consider Jo to have been in place when Hughes was arriving at the club, but starting just 16% of games after paying a £19m fee is a terrible piece of business – even if it does look as though by default he is back in and around the fringes of the squad. Robinho, a British transfer record at £32.5m (£25.4) in 2008, at around the time Hughes was due to start work, started only 47% of games and left for just £14.9m two years later.

Most definitely on Hughes's watch though were Roque Santa Cruz (£17.5m), who began just 16% of Premier League games; Joleon Lescott (£22m) – 45%; Craig Bellamy (£10.9m) – 43%; Wayne Bridge (£9.3m) – 51%; and Adebayor (£25m) – 66%. All players who are either now elsewhere or who have been usurped from the line-up, and despite talk of rotation, are realistically costly back-ups.

Following Roberto Mancini's arrival, there has been a clear shift in strategy to landing younger, hungrier players primarily from aboard, at a lower cost than Hughes was spending to land more proven, veteran Premier League players.

Perhaps this, as much as concern over results, weighed on the minds of the powers that be when they brought an end to his time in charge at the club.

So how do we feel about this new-found wealth? Fans were a little guilty of turning a blind eye to Thaksin Shinawatra's reputation. At the time of his arrival, the club had struggled without money for a number of seasons and were floundering around the wrong end of the table. Once Sheikh Mansour and ADUG arrived, there was a degree of reticence, but he cleverly said the right things and backed this up with his actions; taking his time to implement changes and in general taking a sensible approach – although there has been the odd cringeworthy statement from the chief executive, Garry Cook.

What fans have been pleased to see is that amidst all of the lavishing huge sums on players in terms of transfers and salaries, they appear to have kept supporters' interests at the forefront of many initiatives – be that the changes to the website and social media interaction, fan forums, implementation of the match-day experience and the charitable initiatives that have been undertaken.

Obviously the owners did not purchase the club solely for the fans' benefit, but they appear to be taking a very sensible view and approach in terms of their investment. That feeling of security shouldn't be underestimated and fans are viewing their involvement as a very long-term one.

Manchester United

Total Spend (Actual): £417.8m
Total Spend (CTPP): £699.1m
Average League Position: 2.14
Number of Managers: 1
Most Expensive Signing: Wayne Rooney – £27m (CTPP £49.2m)
Best Value Signing: Edwin van der Sar
Worst Value Signing: Zoran Tošić

Player Signings Breakdown (data correct up to end of January transfer window 2010)

- UK: 14   EU: 25   Rest of Europe: 6   Rest of the World: 18

Major Trophies Won Since Premier League Began

Premier League Champions: 11 (1992/93, 1993/94, 1995/96, 1996/97, 1998/99, 1999/2000, 2000/01, 2002/03, 2006/07, 2007/08, 2008/09)
FA Cup: 4 (1993/94, 1995/96, 1998/99, 2003/04)
League Cup: 3 (2005/06, 2008/09, 2009/10)
Champions League: 2 (1998/99, 2007/08)

Premier League Statistics (correct to the end of the 2009/10 season)

Seasons: 18	Played: 696	
Won: 449	Drawn: 147	Lost:100
Goals Scored: 1,374	Goals Conceded: 590	Goal Difference: +784
Total Points: 1494		

Overview

Manchester United's record since the inception of the Premier League is phenomenal, with 11 league titles and a host of domestic and European cup competitions won since 1992. Unlike Liverpool, Arsenal and Leeds (the last three teams to win the old First Division before it became the Premier League), United hit the ground running and were crowned champions at the end of the inaugural Premier League season (1992/93), finishing ahead of 2nd-placed Aston Villa by 10 points. This was the Red Devils' first league title since 1967. The following season (1993/94) saw United go one better, winning back-to-back league titles (for the first time since 1957) and the FA Cup as they completed the double for the first time in the club's history.

United again won back-to-back league titles a couple of years later, finishing four points clear of 2nd-placed Newcastle United in 1995/96 and finishing eight points clear of Newcastle, Arsenal and Liverpool (who all recorded 68 points) in 1996/97.

Arsenal's emergence under the leadership of Arsène Wenger in 1997 would produce one of the great modern-day rivalries between the two clubs and their managers. Arsenal pipped United to the title by just one point in 1997/98, while the roles were reversed the following season (1998/99) as the Red Devils won the title ahead of the Gunners by a single point. United and Arsenal would also clash in an FA Cup semi-final that produced one of the great FA Cup goals, scored by Ryan Giggs (in extra time in the replay), to send United to the final, where they beat Newcastle United 2-0. Just four days after completing their third double, the Red Devils completed an historic treble as they defeated Bayern Munich 2-1 in the European Cup final (their first for 31 years) thanks to two goals in second-half injury time.

Manchester United also won the Premier League in 1999/00 and 2000/01 (scoring 47 away goals in the league that season - a Premier League record), making them just the fourth team in English football history to win three consecutive league titles. They finished third in 2001/02 (their lowest league position since 1990/91), before regaining their title in 2002/03 by finishing five points ahead of 2nd-placed Arsenal. The next three seasons saw United win the FA Cup and finish 3rd in 2003/04, secure another 3rd-place finish in 2004/05 and then finish 2nd in 2005/06, before the Red Devils once again won three consecutive Premier League titles in 2006/07, 2007/08 and 2008/09 (the first English side to achieve this feat twice).

In 2007/08, Manchester United won the Champions League for the second time in nine seasons after they beat fellow English side Chelsea on penalties. It was the first time two English teams had met in the final in the history of the tournament.

The 2009/10 campaign saw United lift the League Cup following a 2-1 victory over Aston Villa, and they would end the Premier League season in 2nd place behind Chelsea.

United hold the Premier League records for biggest home win (9-0 v Ipswich Town in March 1995) and biggest away win (8-1 v Nottingham Forest in February 1999).

Most Utilised Players

Three players have start ratios of over 90% for Manchester United, but all three were signed before the Premier League began (Paul Ince - 92%, Peter Schmeichel - 91% and Steve Bruce - 90%). Of the players signed during the Premier League era, only Fabien Barthez (92 starts; 81%) and Edwin van der Sar (153 starts; 81%) have start ratios of over 80%.

Barthez was signed in 2000 for £7.8m (£13.9m). The flamboyant Frenchman left the Red Devils in January 2004 following mixed fortunes in the United goal. Van der Sar moved to Old Trafford in June 2005 for £2m (£3.7m) from Fulham and has come the closest to filling the gloves of the legendary Schmeichel.

Least Utilised Players

Zoran Tošić joined Manchester United from Serbia's FK Partizan for £16.3m (£12.8m) in January 2009, but he did not start a single Premier League game for the club - making him one of the most expensive players to have a zero start percentage. He was sold in the summer of 2010 to CSKA Moscow, for a fee believed to be £8m.

(Note: Tošić was originally supposed to be part of a double deal including Adem Ljajić, but the younger Serb never finalised a move to Old Trafford; as such, the transfer fee is open to debate. But any discrepancy will not affect United's £XI figures, as he never made the starting XI.)

Diego Forlán failed to make an impact during his career in Manchester, but he has gone on to prominence in Spain. Ferguson signed the Uruguayan for £7.5m (£9.9m) from Argentine side Independiente in January 2002, but Forlán started only 23 Premier League games (15%) before he was sold to Villarreal in August 2004.

Managers

Year	£XI	£XI Rank	Points	Cost Per Point	Position League	Manager
1992/93	£73,379,127	1	84	£873,561	1	Alex Ferguson
1993/94	£92,208,897	1	92	£1,002,271	1	Alex Ferguson
1994/95	£81,691,903	2	88	£928,317	2	Alex Ferguson
1995/96	£70,776,892	5	82	£863,133	1	Alex Ferguson
1996/97	£59,611,462	6	75	£794,819	1	Alex Ferguson
1997/98	£70,995,161	4	77	£922,015	2	Alex Ferguson
1998/99	£106,197,289	1	79	£1,344,269	1	Alex Ferguson
1999/00	£104,323,670	2	91	£1,146,414	1	Alex Ferguson
2000/01	£80,534,293	4	80	£1,006,679	1	Alex Ferguson
2001/02	£95,175,852	5	77	£1,236,050	3	Alex Ferguson
2002/03	£113,757,434	1	83	£1,370,571	1	Alex Ferguson
2003/04	£99,223,823	3	75	£1,322,984	3	Alex Ferguson
2004/05	£149,992,332	2	77	£1,947,952	3	Alex Ferguson
2005/06	£161,688,549	2	83	£1,948,055	2	Alex Ferguson
2006/07	£171,702,282	2	89	£1,929,239	1	Alex Ferguson
2007/08	£171,806,255	2	87	£1,974,785	1	Alex Ferguson
2008/09	£158,436,770	2	90	£1,760,409	1	Alex Ferguson
2009/10	£141,384,155	2	85	£1,663,343	2	Alex Ferguson
Average	**£111,271,453**	**2.6**	**83**	**£1,335,270**	**1.6**	**Alex Ferguson**

Top 5 Players Sold for a Profit

- Ronaldo – Bought for: £12.24m (£24.8m), Sold for: £80m (£80m) Profit of: £67.76m (£55.2m)
- Beckham – Bought for: £0 (trainee), Sold for: £25m (£50.6m), Profit of: £25m (£50.6m)
- Rossi – Bought for: £0 (trainee), Sold for: £9m (£10.2m), Profit of: £9m (£10.2m)
- Stam – Bought for: £10.5m (£25.8m), Sold for: £16.5m (£21.7m), Profit of: £6m (£-4.1m)
- Richardson – Bought for: £0 (trainee), Sold for: £5.5m (£6.2m), Profit of: £5.5m (£6.2m)

Top 20 CTPP Purchases

#	Player	CTPP	Original fee	Year transferred	% of poss starts
1	Rooney W	£49,119,283	£27,000,000	2004/05	76%
2	Ferdinand R	£48,409,013	£30,000,000	2002/03	72%
3	Verón J	£36,829,602	£28,100,000	2001/02	59%
4	Carrick M	£32,323,469	£18,600,000	2006/07	65%
5	Yorke D	£30,864,726	£12,600,000	1998/99	53%
6	Cole AA	£26,520,170	£7,000,000	1994/95	52%
7	Saha L	£25,968,568	£12,850,000	2003/04	27%
8	Stam J	£25,720,605	£10,500,000	1998/99	52%
9	van Nistelrooy R	£24,902,578	£19,000,000	2001/02	72%
10	Ronaldo C	£24,735,819	£12,240,000	2003/04	69%
11	Berbatov D	£23,847,740	£30,500,000	2008/09	70%
12	Keane R (I)	£22,390,103	£3,750,000	1993/94	62%
13	Anderson	£20,315,957	£18,000,000	2007/08	32%
14	Hargreaves O	£19,187,293	£17,000,000	2007/08	15%
15	Nani	£19,187,293	£17,000,000	2007/08	37%
16	Berg H	£16,880,394	£5,000,000	1997/98	32%
17	Valencia L	£16,000,000	£16,000,000	2009/10	76%
18	Pallister G	£15,309,274	D2300000	1992/93	86%
19	Barthez F	£13,883,029	£7,800,000	2000/01	81%
20	Parker P	£13,312,412	D2000000	1992/93	46%

Expert View
William Abbs (@WilliamAbbs)
www.sahafromthemaddingcrowd.blogspot.com

Manchester United have not always bought their success

For all the riches at Sir Alex Ferguson's disposal as boss, Manchester United have succeeded in winning the title with both a lower squad cost and, on average, a cheaper £XI than any other side to have won the Premier League since its inception in 1992/1993. With all player values reconciled with current transfer purchase prices (CTPP), it is noted that United won the league in 1996 with a squad that cost a relatively modest £54.1m. Furthermore, they were triumphant the following season, too, with a starting XI that, on average, was worth a respectable £59.6m.

Roman Abramovich's billions completely changed the complexion of the English transfer market in 2003, but even before the Russian's arrival on the scene it was apparent that a team had to spend big if they were to outdo Ferguson's men. The average value of a Chelsea Premier League-winning starting eleven is £204.1m, but Arsène Wenger's three championships with Arsenal, two of which were won prior to the Chelsea takeover, have been achieved with squads costing £145m on average. Back in the mid '90s, Kenny Dalglish still had to pay the equivalent of £94.9m to assemble the Blackburn Rovers squad that wrested the title across Lancashire in 1995.

United's 1996 and 1997 titles were achieved with relative frugality because, after the club had failed to win a trophy in 1995, Paul Ince, Andrei Kanchelskis and Mark Hughes were sold for a combined figure of roughly £13.5m (£50m). They were replaced not by players from other clubs but the group of youngsters emerging from the club's youth team: David Beckham, Paul Scholes et al. After breaking the British transfer record to buy Andy Cole in early 1995, the next two seasons saw Ferguson spend big on only one player: Karel Poborský. The Czech midfielder cost £3.5m (£9.2m) in the wake of his performances at Euro 96, most notably his iconic goal against Portugal. Ole Gunnar Solskjær arrived that summer, too, for a mere £1.5m (£5m), while Ronny Johnsen and Jordi Cruyff cost even less.

Verón was a failure but van Nistelrooy failed the team

In a list of Manchester United's most expensive purchases, Juan Sebastián Verón perches near the summit like a monument to transfer folly and serves as a reminder to those clubs that scale the heights of the transfer market to be careful how they spend their money. United had just won a third successive Premier League crown when they paid Lazio £28.1m (£36.8m) for Verón in 2001. The transfer smashed the British record set when Rio Ferdinand had joined Leeds United from West Ham for £18m (£32m) just eight months earlier. Although the reasons why Verón appealed to Sir Alex Ferguson were sound – he was an established international with Argentina who had enjoyed a successful period in Serie A and who, at 26, was entering his prime – the midfielder lasted only two seasons at Old Trafford, starting just 59% of the games in that time, before being sold to Chelsea for just over half what United had originally paid.

Verón left Manchester United in the same subdued manner that had characterised most of his performances for the club. Despite starting well in both of his seasons at Old Trafford, Verón's influence lowered considerably in each as he struggled first with form and then with injury (the latter helping to explain the disappointing percentage of games that he started). In truth, his standing with the club's fans was complicated from the beginning because his arrival compromised the attacking role that Paul Scholes performed in midfield. While it was hardly Verón's fault that he should be in competition with a player who was (and still is) adored at Old Trafford, Scholes' unhappiness at being overlooked in favour of the Argentine for a match against Liverpool in the autumn of 2001 saw the ginger-haired midfielder refuse to travel to the following game, a League Cup tie with Arsenal, his selection for which he perceived as another snub.

It is worth recalling, however, that United did win the Premier League in 2003 while Verón was still at the club. That title was also the only one that Ferguson won with Ruud van Nistelrooy in the side, the Dutchman being a £19m (£24.9m) purchase made in the same summer as Verón and a player whose time in Manchester is remembered as being far more of a success than his former teammate's. Van Nistelrooy scored 150 goals during his five years at United – 95 of them in the league – but such personal triumphs did not bring sustained success to the club. Before he was sold to Real Madrid in 2006, van Nistelrooy's goals helped United to win only three major honours. The Dutchman scored twice in the 2004 FA Cup final as he added that trophy to his league title the previous season, but the Carling Cup winner's medal he received during his final season in England was picked up as an unused substitute. Although he was a magnificent goalscorer, van Nistelrooy had begun to clash with his teammates (Cristiano Ronaldo reportedly being the most notable example) and his sale gave rise to a run of three successive league titles for United – mirroring the sequence that had preceded his and Verón's arrival in 2001.

United get busy in the transfer market when success is interrupted

Historically, a summer of significant transfer activity for Manchester United follows their failure to win the league the season before. In the summer of 1995, after the club had lost its league crown to Blackburn Rovers and the FA Cup final to Everton, Alex Ferguson chose to jettison Paul Ince, Andrei Kanchelskis and Mark Hughes. Already filtering up from the club's youth system, Nicky Butt, David Beckham and Paul Scholes were almost direct replacements for the three players sold, but usually Ferguson addresses United's shortfalls from the previous year by spending big during the summer months.

To have had so many good young players break through at a similar age in the mid-'90s was a freak occurrence that is highly unlikely to be repeated. So, after Arsenal won the double in 1998, Ferguson was moved to buy Jaap Stam, Dwight Yorke and Jesper Blomqvist for a combined sum of £27.5m, a figure that now equates to almost £70m. After Arsenal won another double in 2002, Ferguson responded by paying Leeds United a then British-record fee of £30m – or a still-whopping £48.4m at current prices – for Rio Ferdinand, making him the most expensive defender in the world at the time. Ferdinand's transfer fee was almost three times that for Jaap Stam, which was also a world record for a defender in 1998, but the Leeds man's value had been inflated by an exceptional World Cup, whereas the purchase of Stam was agreed prior to France 98. (However, in CTPP terms, Stam cost more than half the amount paid for Ferdinand.)

In 1996, 1999 and 2003, United succeeded in reclaiming the Premier League title at the first attempt, but this run was eventually broken. Ferguson had reacted to the success of Arsène Wenger's 'invincibles' in 2004 by acquiring Alan Smith, Gabriel Heinze and Wayne Rooney, but even the most expensively assembled squad in the club's history (worth £265.6m at current prices) could not stop José Mourinho from earning Chelsea their first league title in half a century – with a squad costing over £100m more than United's.

Middlesbrough

Total Spend (Actual): £168.2m
Total Spend (CTPP): £298.9m
Average League Position: 13.29
Number of Managers: 5
Most Expensive Signing: Fabrizio Ravanelli – £7m (CTPP £23.7m)
Best Value Signing: Mark Schwarzer
Worst Value Signing: Carlos Marinelli

Player Signings Breakdown (data correct up to end of January transfer window 2010)

• UK: 30   EU: 23   Rest of Europe: 2   Rest of the World: 19

Major Trophies Won Since Premier League Began

League Cup: 1 (2003/04)

Premier League Statistics (correct to the end of the 2009/10 season)

Seasons: 14   Played: 536
Won: 160   Drawn: 156   Lost:220
Goals Scored: 621   Goals Conceded: 741   Goal Difference: –120
Total Points: 633

Overview

Middlesbrough's 14 seasons in the Premier League have produced three relegations, five cup finals, one trophy, one points deduction and, impressively, just five managers. The 1992/93 campaign was Boro's first in the top flight since 1988/89 and, like that season, the Teessiders ended up relegated.

Under the management of Bryan Robson, Boro returned to the Premier League in 1995/96 and a strong early showing, where they lost just two of the opening 13 games, compensated for an awful end to the season as they won just two of their final 19 league games to end up in 12th place. The 1996/97 season was one of the most eventful in the club's history. They reached the final of both the FA and League Cups for the first time, but they would lose both: the League Cup Final 1–0 to Leicester and the FA Cup Final 2–0 to Chelsea.

Despite reaching both domestic cup finals, it was Boro's league campaign that brought controversy, as they cancelled their match away to Blackburn in December, claiming they didn't have enough players to take to the field after the club had been hit by a virus. The FA took a dim view of this and deducted Boro three points as punishment. This sanction was to prove decisive as it meant Boro were relegated in 19th place instead of finishing safe in 14th.

Chairman Steve Gibson kept faith with Robson, however, and he led Middlesbrough back to the Premier League for the 1998/99 season. Boro were as high as 4th in the league by mid-December after losing just two of their opening 18 games, which included a 3-2 victory over Manchester United at Old Trafford, but their form tailed off and they finished in 9th place.

The 1999/00 campaign saw Boro finish 12th. It proved to be Robson's penultimate season with the Teesiders as Steve Gibson appointed Terry Venables as co-manager in December 2000, with Boro struggling after winning just two of their opening 17 league games. They ended the season 14th, but both Robson and Venables departed in June 2001, which resulted in Gibson naming Steve McLaren as the club's new manager.

McLaren spent five seasons with Middlesbrough, but his first two were underwhelming as the club finished in 12th in 2001/02 and 11th in 2002/03. There was yet another mid-table finish in 2003/04 (11th place) but McLaren would make history as Middlesbrough lifted their first (and only) major trophy by beating Bolton 2-1 in the League Cup Final. This also meant the club qualified for the UEFA Cup for the first time in their history. The 2004/05 season saw Middlesbrough finish 7th (their highest top-flight finish since 1974/75) – gaining them UEFA Cup qualification for the second consecutive season. In 2005/06, the Teesiders finished a disappointing 14th in the Premier League, but McLaren took them to the UEFA Cup Final where they lost 4-0 to Seville. (Yet another example of an outstanding cup run affecting league form.) McLaren left after that game to take over as England manager.

Gareth Southgate replaced McLaren, and he led Middlesbrough to the quarter-finals of the FA Cup in 2006/07 and a 12th-place finish. Boro once again reached the quarter-finals of the FA Cup in 2007/08, but could finish only in 13th place in the league. The 2008/09 season saw the Teessiders reach the quarter-finals of the FA Cup for the third consecutive season, but their top-flight status came to an end after an 11-year run as they finished in 19th place with 32 points – just three points adrift from safety.

Most Utilised Players

Two of Middlesbrough's most expensive signings figure prominently when it comes to having high start ratios in the Premier League for the club. Bryan Robson paid Juventus £7m (£23.7m) for Fabrizio Ravanelli in 1996, and he made an immediate impact by scoring a hat-trick on his debut in Boro's 3-3 draw with Liverpool on the opening day of 1996/97. Ravanelli scored 16 Premier League goals from 33 starts (87% start ratio) that season but it wasn't good enough to keep Boro in the Premier League.

Signed by Steve McLaren in 2001 from Aston Villa for £6.5m (£8.6m), Gareth Southgate started 160 Premier League games for Boro during his five years as a player, earning him an 84% start ratio before he succeeded McLaren as manager in 2006. Southgate is Middlesbrough's fifth-most expensive signing in standard terms, and ranks 11th for CTPP.

Least Utilised Players

Bryan Robson signed Carlos Marinelli from Boca Juniors in October 1999 for £1.5m (£3.6m) but, despite joining a long list of Argentine footballers to be dubbed the 'new Maradona', Marinelli made just 18 Premier League starts (9%) for Boro before returning to Boca in 2004.

Steve McLaren paid Derby County £3m (£4.9m) for the services of Malcolm Christie in January 2003, but the striker was dogged by injuries throughout his time at the Riverside; he started just 27 Premier League games (14%). Christie left Middlesbrough in June 2007 after his contract expired and without the club offering him a new deal.

Managers

Year	£XI	£XI Rank	Points	Cost Per Point	Position League	Manager
1992/93	£21,527,280	13	44	£489,256	21	Lenny Lawrence
1995/96	£40,458,312	12	43	£940,891	12	Bryan Robson
1996/97	£54,361,357	7	39	£1,393,881	19	Bryan Robson
1998/99	£41,633,291	11	51	£816,339	9	Bryan Robson
1999/00	£40,401,814	12	52	£776,958	12	Bryan Robson
2000/01	£35,699,250	9	42	£849,982	14	Robson/Venables
Average	**£42,510,805**	**10.2**	**45.4**	**£955,610**	**13.2**	**Bryan Robson**
2001/02	£33,535,044	13	45	£745,223	12	Steve McClaren
2002/03	£48,280,186	6	49	£985,310	11	Steve McClaren
2003/04	£43,439,831	7	48	£904,996	11	Steve McClaren
2004/05	£29,767,392	10	55	£541,225	7	Steve McClaren
2005/06	£41,802,628	7	45	£928,947	14	Steve McClaren
Average	**£39,365,016**	**8.6**	**48.4**	**£821,140**	**11**	**Steve McClaren**
2006/07	£38,931,084	9	46	£846,328	12	Gareth Southgate
2007/08	£36,524,437	11	42	£869,629	13	Gareth Southgate
2008/09	£28,496,787	14	32	£890,525	19	Gareth Southgate
Average	**£34,650,769**	**11.3**	**40**	**£868,827**	**14.7**	**Gareth Southgate**

Top 5 Players Sold for a Profit

- Downing – Bought for: £0 (trainee), Sold for: £12m (£12m), Profit of: £12m (£12m)
- Tuncay – Bought for: £0 (free transfer), Sold for: £5m (£5m) Profit of: £5m (£5m)
- Yakubu – Bought for: £7.5m (£13.7m), Sold for: £11.25m (£12.7m), Profit of: £3.75m (£-1m)
- Cattermole – Bought for: £0 (free transfer), Sold for: £3.5m (£2.8m), Profit of: £3.5m (£2.8m)
- Young – Bought for: £2.5m (£2.9m), Sold for: £5m (£4m), Profit of: £2.5m (£1.1m)

Top 20 CTPP Purchases

#	Player	CTPP	Original fee	Year transferred	% of poss starts
1	Ravanelli F	£23,632,552	£7,000,000	1997/98	87%
2	Merson P	£15,192,355	d4500000	1997/98	8%
3	Barmby N	£13,804,970	£5,250,000	1995/96	55%
4	Yakubu	£13,685,649	£7,500,000	2005/06	59%
5	Alves A	£13,543,971	£12,000,000	2007/08	41%
6	Juninho Paulista	£12,490,211	£4,750,000	1995/96	59%
7	Gascoigne P	£11,647,472	d3450000	1997/98	42%
8	Maccarone M	£10,488,620	£6,500,000	2002/03	30%
9	Huth R	£10,426,926	£6,000,000	2006/07	35%
10	Ziege C	£9,386,681	£4,000,000	1999/00	76%
11	Southgate G	£8,519,303	£6,500,000	2001/02	84%
12	Viduka M	£8,186,547	£4,500,000	2004/05	49%
13	Boateng G	£8,068,169	£5,000,000	2002/03	78%
14	Deane B	£7,348,744	£3,000,000	1998/99	47%
15	Festa G	£7,142,948	£2,700,000	1996/97	49%
16	Mido A	£6,771,986	£6,000,000	2007/08	17%
17	Ehiogu U	£6,255,145	£8,000,000	2008/09	54%
18	Cooper C	£6,123,954	£2,500,000	1998/99	46%
19	Pallister G	£6,123,954	£2,500,000	1998/99	48%
20	Whyte D	£5,990,586	£900,000	1992/93	66%

Expert View

Anthony Vickers

The Evening Gazette, Middlesbrough

At heart, Boro fans know that their golden era was always about Steve Gibson's financial muscle. It would be nice to think that the decade and more in the top flight, the three Wembley appearances in just over a year, the first ever trophy and two successive Uefa Cup campaigns culminating in a pulsating, but ultimately painful, charge to the final was about us finally claiming our birth right as a big club, or that we had earned it through shrewd strategic planning and careful husbandry of talent allied to managerial nous.

But the truth is we gained entry to the elite because the chairman plonked a massive bag of cash on the table. And did it at just the right time. Just how much money is mind-boggling. The figures adjusted for inflation are quite staggering, especially when you consider the current business model involves scouring Scotland for bargain buys.

Ravanelli arrived straight from scoring the winner in the Champions League for what today would be £23.6m; Juninho arrived as the Brazilian player of the year for what would now be £12.5m; troubled Paul Merson for £15.1m; Nick Barmby for £13.8m. Boro even forked out what would now be £11.6m for the fading shell of Gazza.

None of those came because of a burning love for Teesside, but because Boro could afford the fees and were riding the wages curve. For the first time in history, Boro were a side who household names could say "matched my ambitions." From provincial makeweights in a crumbling stadium to nouveau riche top-table wannabees in a shiny new home, the transformation was unbelievable. And unsustainable. Boro's entry to the big time came when Gibson's incremental annual investments could blow our rivals – Coventry, Norwich, Southampton, maybe then an ailing Aston Villa too – out of the water.

But as the Sky money poured in and the wages and transfer fees nudged beyond Gibson's pocket, Boro hit the skids. They couldn't compete in the market. Momentum was lost ... then as the plane touched down from the Uefa Cup final in Eindhoven, you could feel the sickening lurch as the club started to roll backwards.

Cost-cutting has hurt Boro. Ultimately it cost us a place in the Premier League as the talent headed for the exit to be replaced by cheaper models in the Championship. Brash Boro burst into the big time in 1996/97 as Bryan Robson assembled a squad costing £76.43m (CTPP), and had the eighth-most expensive £XI, at £52.3m. The club's high point came as Steve McClaren's men delivered the Carling Cup and European qualification in 2003/04 with a Sq£ valued at £107.42m in today's money. With a massive downsizing of finances and ambition underway, the £XI Gareth Southgate led meekly to relegation in 2008/09 cost just £28.4m.

Newcastle United

Total Spend (Actual): £322.8m
Total Spend (CTPP): £652.1m
Average League Position: 8.56
Number of Managers: 9
Most Expensive Signing: Alan Shearer – £15m (CTPP £39.7m)
Best Value Signing: Shay Given
Worst Value Signing: Stéphane Guivarc'h

Player Signings Breakdown (data correct up to end of January transfer window 2010)

- UK: 48   EU: 33   Rest of Europe: 5   Rest of the World: 23

Major Trophies Won Since Premier League Began: 0

Premier League Statistics (correct to the end of the 2009/10 season)

Seasons: 16	Played: 616	
Won: 247	Drawn: 165	Lost:204
Goals Scored: 884	Goals Conceded: 777	Goal Difference: +107
Total Points: 906		

Overview

Newcastle United entered the Premier League in 1993/94 without a league title to their name since 1926/27 and without a major trophy of any kind since the 1968/69 Inter-Cities Fairs Cup (which became known as the UEFA Cup in 1971) won after defeating Hungarian side Újpest. Kevin Keegan made an instant impact with Newcastle in the Premier League, finishing 1993/94 in 3rd place and ending the season as top scorers with 82 goals. Newcastle followed this by starting 1994/95 in top form by winning nine of their opening 11 games, scoring 29 goals and conceding 10 as they ended October top of the league. Following a 2-0 defeat away to Manchester United at the end of October, Newcastle's form dipped, and an inconsistent run of results saw the Magpies end the season in 6th place. They also reached the quarter-finals of the FA Cup that season, losing 1-0 to eventual winners Everton.

The 1995/96 season featured Newcastle United at their attacking best, as they lost just three of their first 25 league games. The Toon Army were top of the league in mid-March and it seemed their long wait for a trophy was about to come to an end, but a 2-0 defeat to Arsenal and an enthralling 4-3 last-minute defeat to Liverpool at Anfield - a game which was voted Match of the Decade at the Premier League's Ten Seasons Awards in April 2003   resulted in Newcastle dropping down to 2nd place, where they stayed until the end of the season.

Newcastle signalled their intentions for 1996/97 by paying a world-record £15m (£39.7m) for Blackburn and England striker Alan Shearer, but Keegan resigned in January 1997 to be replaced by Kenny Dalglish. The Scot led Newcastle to a 2nd-place finish with 68 points - the lowest tally by runners-up in the 18 seasons of the Premier League.

Newcastle had a poor league campaign under Dalglish in 1997/98 but they did reach their first FA Cup Final since 1974, only to lose 2-0 to Arsenal. Dalglish lasted just two games into 1998/99, with his replacement, Ruud Gullit, repeating Dalglish's 13th-place league finish and FA Cup Final appearance. Another 2-0 defeat followed at Wembley - this time to Manchester United.

Newcastle's poor start to the 1999/00 season saw Gullit replaced with Bobby Robson, whose first home game saw the team record an 8-0 victory over Sheffield Wednesday;

how's that for a start? The Magpies ended the league campaign in 11th and reached the semi-finals of the FA Cup for the third season in a row, only to lose 2-1 to Chelsea. There was another 11th-place Premier League finish in 2000/01, but Newcastle's fortunes were on an upward trajectory as they ended 2001/02 in 4th place and reached the quarter-finals of the FA Cup.

The 2002/03 season saw Newcastle make it to the second group stages of the Champions League (their first appearance in the competition) and finish 3rd in the Premier League. The following campaign got off to a poor start, though, as they failed to make it to the Champions League group stages after losing the 3rd qualifying round play-off to FK Partizan on penalties, resulting in them entering the UEFA Cup instead. The league campaign also began badly as Newcastle failed to win any of their opening six league games. They recovered to finish the season in 5th place but, despite Newcastle reaching the semi-finals of the UEFA Cup, Robson was sacked in August 2004 after another poor start to the Premier League campaign.

Graeme Souness was named as Robson's successor, but the Magpies continued to struggle in 2004/05. They finished in 14th place, although they did reach the semi-finals of the FA Cup and quarter-finals of the UEFA Cup, losing to Manchester United and Sporting Lisbon respectively. Newcastle continued to struggle during 2005/06, despite spending a club-record £17m (£31.1m) on Michael Owen; they were 15th by early February and Souness was sacked. Glenn Roeder took over from the Scot and he guided the Magpies to a 7th-place finish by winning six of their remaining seven league games. The 2006/07 campaign ended badly for Roeder as Newcastle finished in 13th place and the former West Ham boss was given his P45. Sam Allardyce was next in the hot seat, arriving in May 2007, but he would last only until January 2008, when his sacking resulted in the shock re-appointment of Kevin Keegan. The Magpies ended 2007/08 in 12th place, but worse was to come.

Keegan resigned in controversial circumstances in September 2008, releasing a statement saying that, in his opinion, "...a manager must have the right to manage and that clubs should not impose upon any manager any player that he does not want". This implied that Keegan did not have the final say on player transfers, and a Premier League arbitration panel ruled in his favour in October 2009, after it was revealed that the loan signing of Ignacio González was made against Keegan's wishes after Dennis Wise had recommended the player to the manager based on a YouTube compilation. Keegan was awarded £2m after the tribunal ruled in favour of a constructive dismissal verdict. Joe Kinnear took over from Keegan in September 2008, but he suffered serious heart problems for the second time in his career. Terrace idol Alan Shearer became temporary Newcastle manager in April 2008, but he was unable to save the club from relegation as the Magpies ended the season with just two wins from 20 league games - one win from eight under Shearer.

Most Utilised Players

Kenny Dalglish signed Shay Given on a free transfer while he was manager of Blackburn Rovers in 1994 and he raided his old club for Given's services in July 1997, paying £1.5m (£5.1m) for the talented goalkeeper. Given started 354 Premier League games for the Magpies (more than any other Newcastle player) giving him a 78% start ratio before being sold to Manchester City in February 2009 for £8m (£6.3m).

Alan Shearer also has a 78% ratio, and is second only to Shay Given when it comes to players who have made the most Premier League starts for Newcastle United. Keegan signed Shearer from Blackburn Rovers for a then world-record £15m (£39.7m) in July 1996. Shearer spent a decade with Newcastle, starting 295 Premier League games and scoring 148 league goals in the process. He retired in 2006 as Newcastle's highest goal scorer of all time, having scored 206 times in all competitions.

Least Utilised Players

Diego Gavilán became the first Paraguayan to play in the Premier League when Ruud Gullit paid Paraguay's Cerro Porteño £2m (£4.7m) for his services in 1999. Unfortunately for Gavilán, he was unable to settle in England, starting just two Premier League games (2%) during his time with the Magpies.

A more expensive and bigger-name signing who failed to settle was Stéphane Guivarc'h, who won the 1998 World Cup with France. Kenny Dalglish signed Guivarc'h for £3.5m (£8.6m) from French side Auxerre and, despite scoring on his debut in a 4-1 defeat to Liverpool, Guivarc'h found himself out of favour with Gullit (who had replaced Dalglish just two games into 1998/99) and he was sold to Glasgow Rangers for the exact same fee, having started just two Premier League games (5%) for the Magpies.

Managers

Year	£XI	£XI Rank	Points	Cost Per Point	Position League	Manager
1993/94	£44,674,648	11	77	£580,190	3	Kevin Keegan
1994/95	£63,595,172	4	72	£883,266	6	Kevin Keegan
1995/96	£80,903,917	3	78	£1,037,230	2	Kevin Keegan
1996/97	£107,815,548	1	68	£1,585,523	2	Kevin/Dalglish
2007/08	£61,362,190	6	43	£1,427,028	12	Allardyce//Keegan
2008/09	£63,534,985	6	34	£1,868,676	18	Keegan//Kinnear
Average	**£70,314,410**	**5.2**	**62**	**£1,230,319**	**7.2**	**Kevin Keegan**
1996/97	£107,815,548	1	68	£1,585,523	2	Keegan/Dalglish
1997/98	£86,288,655	1	44	£1,961,106	13	Kenny Dalglish
Average	**£97,052,102**	**1**	**56**	**£1,773,314**	**7.5**	**Kenny Dalglish**
1998/99	£94,802,568	2	46	£2,060,925	13	Ruud Gullit
1999/00	£118,233,197	1	52	£2,273,715	11	Gullit/Robson
Average	**£106,517,883**	**1.5**	**49**	**£2,167,320**	**12**	**Ruud Gullit**
1999/00	£118,233,197	1	52	£2,273,715	11	Gullit/Robson
2000/01	£90,123,779	2	51	£1,767,133	11	Bobby Robson

Year	£XI	£XI Rank	Points	Cost Per Point	Position League	Manager
2001/02	£101,678,125	2	71	£1,432,086	4	Bobby Robson
2002/03	£107,202,951	3	69	£1,553,666	3	Bobby Robson
2003/04	£108,983,681	2	56	£1,946,137	5	Bobby Robson
Average	**£105,244,347**	**2**	**59.8**	**£1,794,548**	**6.8**	**Bobby Robson**
2004/05	£70,322,499	5	44	£1,598,239	14	Graeme Souness
2005/06	£74,364,866	5	58	£1,282,153	7	Souness/Roeder
Average	**£72,343,683**	**5**	**51**	**£1,440,196**	**10.5**	**Graeme Souness**
2005/06	£74,364,866	5	58	£1,282,153	7	Souness/Roeder
2006/07	£62,673,539	6	43	£1,457,524	13	Glenn Roeder
Average	**£68,519,203**	**5.5**	**50.5**	**£1,369,839**	**10**	**Glenn Roeder**
2007/08	£61,362,190	6	43	£1,427,028	12	**Allardyce/Keegan**

Top 5 Players Sold for a Profit

- Milner – Bought for: £3.6m (£6.6m), Sold for: £12m (£9.4m), Profit of: £8.4m (£2.8m)
- Given – Bought for: £1.5m (£5.1m), Sold for: £8m (£6.3m), Profit of: £6.5m (£1.2m)
- Bassong – Bought for: £1.8m (£1.4m), Sold for: £8m (£8m), Profit of: £6.2m (£6.6m)
- N'Zogbia – Bought for: £0 (trainee), Sold for: £6m (£4.7m), Profit of: £6m (£4.7m)
- Andy Cole – Bought for: d1.75m (£11.7m), Sold for: £7m (£26.6m) Profit of: £5.25m (£14.9m)

Top 20 CTPP Purchases

#	Player	CTPP	Original fee	Year transferred	% of poss starts
1	Shearer A	£39,683,045	£15,000,000	1996/97	78%
2	Owen M	£31,020,805	£17,000,000	2005/06	38%
3	Asprilla F	£19,721,386	£7,500,000	1995/96	32%
4	Speed G	£18,568,434	£5,500,000	1997/98	77%
5	Luque A	£17,517,631	£9,600,000	2005/06	8%
6	Martins O	£17,378,209	£10,000,000	2006/07	67%
7	Ferguson D (II)	£17,147,070	£7,000,000	1998/99	32%
8	Peacock D	£16,120,874	£2,700,000	1993/94	66%
9	Ferdinand L	£15,777,109	£6,000,000	1995/96	88%
10	Pistone A	£15,192,355	£4,500,000	1997/98	39%
11	Boumsong J A	£14,917,710	£8,200,000	2005/06	58%
12	Woodgate J	£14,522,704	£9,000,000	2002/03	37%
13	Dyer K	£14,080,022	£6,000,000	1999/00	56%
14	Robert L	£13,761,951	£10,500,000	2001/02	72%
15	Hugo	£13,715,887	£8,500,000	2002/03	21%
16	Marcelino E	£13,610,688	£5,800,000	1999/00	20%
17	Fox R	£13,434,062	£2,250,000	1993/94	46%
18	Hamann D	£12,860,303	£5,250,000	1998/99	58%
19	Cort C	£12,459,129	£7,000,000	2000/01	17%
20	Andersson A (II)	£12,153,884	£3,600,000	1997/98	28%

Expert View
Paul Wakefield and Ben Woolhead
Black & White & Read All Over www.blackandwhiteandreadallover.blogspot.com

Surveying the priciest purchases during Newcastle's tenure in the Premier League, it's fair to say that they represent a fairly mixed bag. For every outstanding performer, there's a similarly priced flop, a yang to every yin, an Owen (over £31m CTPP) to every Shearer (over £39m).

Though Kenny Dalglish bequeathed the club a clutch of good signings – most notably Gary Speed (£18.6m), but also Shay Given and Nobby Solano (an astonishing combined total of just over £3m in yesterday's money) – it's telling that the players we'd consider greats were, by and large, the ones who played during the halcyon days of King Kev and Sir Bobby Robson.

What that illustrates is that, in reality, it isn't about the fee so much as the other qualities of the player you bring in that make them stand out. A hefty price tag does little to assist players in their quest to enter the pantheon of greats, whose members grandparents hazily describe to grandchildren many years hence.

The players signed in recent seasons broadly fall into three categories: those who, whatever the price, represented good value; those who were (or have the potential to be) decent servants; and those who were overpriced dross.

No one outside a padded cell could possibly argue that Alan Shearer was a bad signing, even if we originally let the sheet-metal worker's son from Gosforth slip through our fingers and it ended up costing us a world-record fee to rectify the mistake. Peter Beardsley (£8.9m) justified Keegan's decision to let top scorers David Kelly and Gavin Peacock leave just as we returned to the top flight, while Robson took a brave punt on Craig Bellamy (£7.9m), to the guffaws of Coventry fans. In truth, though, three of our best Premier League players – Andy Cole, Rob Lee and John Beresford – were all recruited during the 1992/93 promotion season.

Otherwise it's all too often been a case of either bad luck – Michael Owen sustaining that terrible injury while playing for England; much-coveted European talents like Jon Dahl Tomasson (£8.4m), Hugo Viana (£13.7m) and Alessandro Pistone (£15.2m) failing to settle – or just rank bad judgement. Our many crimes against common sense include Silvio Marić (£8.9m), Marcelino (£13.6m), Albert Luque (£17.5m), Andreas Andersson (£12.2m) and, perhaps worst of all, Stéphane Guivarc'h (£8.6m), who dared to call himself a World Cup winner.

And let's not forget the ill-timed sales. Les Ferdinand (£15.8m), for instance – deemed over the hill at 30 after a superb 41 goals in 68 games and flogged to Spurs, just as Shearer picked up a long-term injury, leaving the wet-behind-the-ears Tomasson to carry the attack. Or Jonathan Woodgate (£14.5m), admittedly injury-prone but the classiest defender most of us have ever seen at St James', sold to Real Madrid. Freddie Shepherd promised an exciting signing to appease the fans; we bid £24m for Wayne Rooney (almost £50m CTPP), he promptly moved to Man United and we were left woefully short in defence. That's us all over.

What the numbers highlight is that Newcastle have spent a lot of money in the transfer market but without any silverware to show for the investment. People criticise clubs like Manchester City for trying to buy the title, but it remains infinitely worse to spend all the cash and be left with nothing but memories of great games and "what ifs".

Norwich City

Total Spend (Actual): £11.7m
Total Spend (CTPP): £38m
Average League Position: 13.50
Number of Managers: 3
Most Expensive Signing: Darren Beckford – D925k (CTPP £6.2m)
Best Value Signing: Darren Huckerby
Worst Value Signing: Scott Howie

Player Signings Breakdown (data correct up to end of January transfer window 2010)

• UK: 17   EU: 4   Rest of Europe: 0   Rest of the World: 2

Major Trophies Won Since Premier League Began: 0

Premier League Statistics (correct to the end of the 2009/10 season)

Seasons: 4	Played: 164	
Won: 50	Drawn: 51	Lost:63
Goals Scored: 205	Goals Conceded: 257	Goal Difference: –52
Total Points: 201		

Overview

Norwich City's spells in the Premier League have been both spectacular and short. The inaugural 1992/93 season turned out to be one to remember for the club as they led the table for much of the campaign ahead of eventual champions Manchester United. The Canaries finished the season in 3rd place, earning a spot in the UEFA Cup for the first time in the club's history. This 3rd-place finish was made all the more surprising as they had ended the 1991/92 season in 18th place.

Norwich made a promising start in 1993/94, including victories over Blackburn (who finished 2nd) and Leeds United (who finished 5th), and found themselves as high as 2nd at the start of November. Fortunes would take a nosedive, however, following Mike Walker's decision to quit in January 1994 to take over at Everton. Norwich won just two out of their remaining 20 Premier League games, including seven consecutive draws (a joint Premier League record), to finish the campaign in 12th place.

The Canaries' first venture onto European soil that season saw them defeat Vitesse Arnhem in the first round and, memorably, record a famous 2-1 victory over German giants Bayern Munich at the Olympic Stadium in Munich in round two. That defeat to Norwich remains the only time Bayern Munich have lost at home to English opponents. Their shock victory took Norwich to the third round, where eventual winners Inter Milan eliminated them 2-0 on aggregate.

John Deehan, who replaced Walker in January 1994, was unable to prevent the second-half decline from 1993/94 being repeated in 1994/95; flying high at Christmas, Norwich won just one out of their last 20 Premier League games, resulting in a 20th-place finish - two points adrift from safety.

It was a decade before Norwich City returned to the Premier League, as Nigel Worthington led the Canaries to the 2003/04 First Division championship. The 2004/05 Premier League campaign would prove a disappointing one, though. Norwich failed to win any of their opening 13 Premier League fixtures and went the entire season without winning a single away game (another joint Premier League record). A late-season surge that saw the Canaries win four out of their final seven league games (including a 2-0 win over Manchester United) was not enough to ensure their safety, as they finished in 19th place and returned swiftly to what was now known as The Championship.

Most Utilised Players
Darren Huckerby proved to be an influential signing by Nigel Worthington following his £750k (£1.6m) arrival from Manchester City in 2003, helping The Canaries to win the 2003/04 First Division and get back to the Premier League. Huckerby would miss just two Premier League games (95% start ratio) for the Canaries in 2004/05, but he was unable to prevent them going straight back down.

Least Utilised Players
Scott Howie was signed for £100k (£600k) in August 1993 from Scottish side Clyde, but made just one Premier League start during 1993/94 as Bryan Gunn remained first choice 'keeper. Howie returned to Scotland to join Motherwell in October 1994, leaving behind a start ratio of just 2% at Norwich.

Managers

Year	£XI	£XI Rank	Points	Cost Per Point	Position League	Manager
1992/93	£15,263,156	18	72	£211,988	3	Mike Walker
1993/94	£12,026,451	21	53	£226,914	12	Walker/John Deehan
Average	**£13,644,803**	**19.5**	**62.5**	**£219,451**	**7.5**	**Mike Walker**
1993/94	£12,026,451	21	53	£226,914	12	Walker/John Deehan
1994/95	£17,191,422	18	43	£399,801	20	John Deehan
Average	**£14,608,936**	**19.5**	**48**	**£313,357**	**16**	**John Deehan**
2004/05	£9,007,504	18	33	£272,955	19	**Nigel Worthington**

Top 10 CTPP Purchases

#	Player	CTPP	Original fee	Year transferred	% of poss starts
1	Beckford D	£6,156,991	D925000	1992/93	17%
2	Ashton D	£5,457,698	£3,000,000	2004/05	42%
3	Robins M	£5,324,965	£800,000	1992/93	45%
4	Ekoku E	£5,091,998	£765,000	1992/93	21%
5	Newman R (II)	£3,993,724	D600000	1992/93	56%
6	Newsome J	£3,788,596	£1,000,000	1994/95	83%
7	Phillips D	£3,494,508	D525000	1992/93	100%
8	Milligan M	£3,220,306	£850,000	1994/95	60%
9	Sheron M	£3,030,877	£800,000	1994/95	40%
10	Fleming C (II)	£2,025,647	d600000	1997/98	100%

Expert View

Sam McDonnell (@littlenorwich)

Little Norwich www.littlenorwich.com

Norwich City FC and the Premier League may not be a match made in heaven but the Canaries are a side that, despite only two short tenures, have provided memorable moments and inspiring performances.

The opening season of the Premier League was indeed the dawn of new era, and early on it was led by an unusually plucky canary. Mike Walker's side were the early pace-setters, thanks in part to the goals of Mark Robins, signed for a CTPP of around £5.3m; from the moment he was introduced, it appeared to be money well spent. He led the opening-day comeback at Highbury which saw a 2-0 half time lead for Arsenal dominantly reversed into an unfathomable 4-2 victory. Robins' cool head on relatively young shoulders was the vital addition that turned the good team Dave Stringer left behind into Mike Walker's title challengers. A feat made all the more impressive when you remember that, in the pre-season,

Norwich had lost star player Robert Fleck to Chelsea. The title was a step too far, but a 3rd-place finish saw Norwich qualify for European football for the first time. The team wasn't made up of stars, just hard working professionals organised and playing at the top of their game.

After the European adventure of 1993/94, Norwich's secret was out and clubs came calling for the players who had propelled them to such dizzy heights. City were relegated at Elland Road in the May of 1995. The holes left by the sales of key players had become too large to cover, and the dream was over. So began a summer of optimism. "On Loan to the Endsleigh" as it was known at the time; sadly the loan was one with significant interest, as Norwich didn't return to the promised land for another nine seasons.

New manager Nigel Worthington benefitted from brilliantly timed investment in his playing squad from the board. Darren Huckerby, originally on loan and subsequently unveiled as a late Christmas present, was the driving force behind a City side that seemed destined for promotion back to the top tier. In the form of his life, Huckerby made a good team great at that level, and they strolled to the league title and a return to the Premier League.

Modest investment was made again in the summer with the club publicly announcing they were budgeting for finishing bottom of the division. This negative (albeit sensible) strategy still allowed for one high-profile signing, Dean Ashton, who arrived halfway through the season. At a club record £3.5m (£5.5m CTPP), Ashton was an incredible piece of business; his adjustment to Premier League football seamless. Had he signed in the summer, as was originally the plan, it is highly plausible that City would have found the additional couple of points needed to reaffirm top-flight status.

City's brief return to the top level eventually set the club back a couple of years, leading fans to question its benefit. To heap any more "what ifs" on Ashton, whose short career is now lost to possibility, would be unfair but Norwich were relegated by a narrow margin. They then went on to struggle considerably and have only recently appeared to recover. Despite their pragmatic outlook on a season in the sun, City are now a cautionary tale to other well-run ambitious clubs trying to make it to the top level.

Nottingham Forest

Total Spend (Actual): £25.4m
Total Spend (CTPP): £74.7m
Average League Position: 14.80
Number of Managers: 5
Most Expensive Signing: Teddy Sheringham – D£2m (CTPP £13.3m)
Best Value Signing: Dean Saunders
Worst Value Signing: Andrea Silenzi

Player Signings Breakdown (data correct up to end of January transfer window 2010)

• UK: 18   EU: 5   Rest of Europe: 1   Rest of the World: 1

Major Trophies Won Since Premier League Began: 0

Premier League Statistics (correct to the end of the 2009/10 season)

Seasons: 5   Played: 198
Won: 60   Drawn: 59   Lost:79
Goals Scored: 229   Goals Conceded: 287   Goal Difference: –58
Total Points: 239

Overview

Nottingham Forest entered the Premier League era on the back of three successive top–10 finishes in the old First Division, but their fortunes under legendary manager Brian Clough would hit their lowest point since he took charge of the club back in 1975. Despite opening 1992/93 with a 1–0 victory over Liverpool (the first live game broadcast on Sky Sports), Forest would lose their next six league games, and by the end of December the team had won just three out of their first 21 games. Despite winning five of the next seven following the turn of the year, Forest crashed out of both the FA Cup and League Cup to Arsenal at the fifth–round stage, losing both games 2–0, while they won just two of their remaining 14 league games; ending the season in 22nd place with 40 points, and sealing their relegation to the First Division.

Nottingham Forest quickly returned to the Premier League for 1994/95 under Frank Clark. Not only did they consolidate their place in England's top division, but they finished in 3rd place with 77 points (a joint record highest finish for a newly promoted club), earning a spot in the UEFA Cup for the first time since the European ban on English clubs had been lifted. The 1995/96 campaign wasn't as successful on the domestic front for Forest: they finished 9th in the Premier League and suffered an FA Cup quarter–final exit at the hands of Aston Villa. Forest did, however, produce the best performance of any British club in Europe that season, as they reached the UEFA Cup quarter–finals;

losing to eventual winners Bayern Munich 7–2 on aggregate.

That would be as good as it got for Nottingham Forest in the Premier League. The club were relegated for the second time at the end of 1996/97, finishing with 34 points. Despite winning their opening game 3–0 against Coventry, Forest failed to win any of their next 16 league games. Clark parted company with the club in December 1996 following a 4–2 defeat to Liverpool but, despite a mini revival that saw the Midlanders win four out of the next six games under the guidance of newly appointed player/ manager Stuart Pearce, another slump in form followed and they would end the season with seven draws and four defeats from their remaining 11 Premier League games.

Nottingham Forest returned to the Premier League once again in 1998/99 – this time under former Wimbledon manager Dave Bassett. Forest started the season with two victories from their first three games, putting them in 2nd place at the end of August, but a disastrous run of results (resulting in Bassett being sacked in January 1999) saw them go 19 league games without a win. Bassett's replacement, Ron Atkinson, couldn't prevent Forest's third relegation from the Premier League; they won their final three games, but ended the campaign with 30 points, and just seven wins all season.

Atkinson didn't endear himself to Forest supporters after their 8–1 thrashing at home to Manchester United on 6 February 1999, saying his team had "just played in a nine-goal thriller". That scoreline remains the biggest home defeat for any club in the Premier League to date.

Most Utilised Players
Assured defender Colin Cooper cost £1.8m (£10.7m) in 1993, and started 108 of the 118 games (92%) that Forest played in the top flight over the next five years. In 1998 he was sold to Middlesbrough for £2.5m (£6.1m), a veritable bargain for the Teessiders.

Least Utilised Players
Striker Andrea Silenzi became the first Italian footballer to play in the Premier League when he was signed by Frank Clark for £1.8m (£4.73m) from Italian side Torino in the summer of 1995. Silenzi started just four league games (5%) and failed to find the net in the league during his time with Forest. He returned to Italy in 1996, joining Venezia on loan. It is believed that Dave Bassett tore up Silenzi's contract after he refused to return from his loan spell at Venezia.

Managers

Year	£XI	£XI Rank	Points	Cost Per Point	Position League	Manager
1992/93	£18,308,529	15	40	£457,713	22	Brian Clough
1994/95	£38,686,634	12	77	£502,424	3	Frank Clark
1995/96	£33,301,087	13	58	£574,157	9	Frank Clark
1996/97	£30,751,938	15	34	£904,469	20	Clark/Pearce

Year	£XI	£XI Rank	Points	Cost Per Point	Position League	Manager
Average	£34,246,553	13.3	56.3	£660,350	10.7	Frank Clark
1998/99	£26,128,582	16	30	£870,953	20	Bassett/Adams/Atkinson

Top 5 Players Sold for a Profit

- Collymore – Bought for: d2m (£11.95m), Sold for: £8.5m (£22.35m) Profit of: £6.5m (£10.4m)
- Stone – Bought for: £0 (trainee), Sold for: £5.5m (£13.48m), Profit of: £5.5m (£13.48m)
- Keane – Bought for: D10,000 (£66.5k), Sold for: £3.75m (£22.4m), Profit of: £3.74m (£22.3m)
- Clough – Bought for: £0 (trainee), Sold for: £2.3m (£13.6m), Profit of: £2.3m (£13.6m)
- Charles – Bought for: £0 (trainee), Sold for: £1.45m (£5.5m), Profit of: £1.45m (£5.5m)

Top 20 CTPP Purchases

#	Player	CTPP	Original fee	Year transferred	% of poss starts
1	Sheringham T	£13,312,412	D2000000	1992/93	*
2	Collymore S	£11,941,388	d2000000	1993/94	88%
3	Cooper C	£10,747,249	d1800000	1993/94	92%
4	Black K	£9,984,309	D1500000	1992/93	20%
5	Roy B	£9,471,489	£2,500,000	1994/95	59%
6	Tiler C	£9,318,689	D1400000	1992/93	48%
7	Van Hooijdonk P	£9,259,377	£3,500,000	1996/97	36%
8	Johnson A (III)	£7,427,373	d2200000	1997/98	66%
9	Campbell K	£7,362,651	£2,800,000	1995/96	49%
10	Rogers A	£6,752,158	d2000000	1997/98	89%
11	Bart–Williams C	£6,573,795	£2,500,000	1995/96	61%
12	Quashie N	£6,123,954	£2,500,000	1998/99	32%
13	Webb N	£5,324,965	£800,000	1992/93	21%
14	McKinnon R	£4,992,155	£750,000	1992/93	12%
15	Silenzi A	£4,733,133	£1,800,000	1995/96	5%
16	Shipperley N	£3,674,372	£1,500,000	1998/99	32%
17	Phillips D	£2,985,347	d500000	1993/94	64%
18	Palmer C	£2,694,540	£1,100,000	1998/99	34%
19	Bohinen L	£2,686,812	d450000	1993/94	46%
20	Wright T (II)	£2,686,812	d450000	1993/94	3%

* Sold three games into Premier League era.

Expert View
Daniel Taylor (@DTguardian)

Football Writer, The Guardian

'Too good to go down'. That phrase stuck to Nottingham Forest during 1992/93 like a tick on the side of a dog. 'Too bad to stay up' would have been more accurate, but it is easy to understand why it was applied. This was the team managed by Brian Clough, including his son Nigel, Stuart Pearce and a young Roy Keane. We had big-name players, often on reasonably big wages. Yet the logic was flawed,

Forest went down and the lesson is of what can happen when mistakes are made in the transfer market – specifically, when good players are replaced by bad ones, or not replaced at all.

The club's Premier League years form a wild graph of exhilarating highs and excruciating lows, though mostly the latter. We have been promoted twice and relegated three times, finishing bottom every time. A modern-day yo-yo club, except the string appears to have snapped now.

If we are being generous, there were mitigating circumstances about that first relegation, namely that Clough was ravaged by the excesses of alcohol and his judgement was inevitably blurred. Des Walker, regarded as the finest defender the club has ever produced, moved to Sampdoria and his replacement, Carl Tiler (£9.3m in today's money), was simply not up to it. Three games in, our most prolific forward, Teddy Sheringham, went to Spurs. Clough passed up the chance to sign a young Southend United striker by the name of Stan Collymore and brought in Robert Rosario (£400,000; CTPP £2.7m), with just 31 league goals in 10 years to his name. The mistakes were fatal.

The subsequent rise and fall tells the story of how influential one major signing can be, and Collymore was undoubtedly a superstar in Nottingham once Clough's replacement, Frank Clark, made him one of his first recruits (for £11.9m CTPP). Forest not only came back up at the first attempt but were the last promoted side to mount an authentic title challenge the following year, eventually finishing third with Collymore scoring 25 goals. Were it not for a bad November, when the team did not score a goal, we could conceivably have won the league.

The flipside is that a club of Forest's size always lose their better players. In 1994/95, we were the last English side left in Europe. The following season, Collymore left for Liverpool (£8.5m; CTPP £22.3m), Bryan Roy and Lars Bohinen also moved and were not replaced adequately, and the club dropped out of the top division like a stone in the well.

Again, the team bounced straight back, this time with Kevin Campbell (£2.8m; CTPP £7.4m) and Pierre van Hooijdonk (£3.5m; CTPP £9.3m) a cut above the average striker in the second tier. But what followed in 1998/99 was little short of a farce. Campbell was sold in pre-season, followed by the club's best centre-half, Colin Cooper. Van Hooijdonk subsequently went on strike in protest and suddenly the three players who had probably done the most to get the club promoted were gone. Nobody used the phrase 'too good to go down' *that* year.

Oldham Athletic

Total Spend (Actual): £2.8m

Total Spend (CTPP): £17m

Average League Position: 20

Number of Managers: 1

Most Expensive Signing: Ian Olney – d700k (CTPP £4.7m)

Best Value Signing: Mike Milligan

Worst Value Signing: Tore Pedersen

Player Signings Breakdown (data correct up to end of January transfer window 2010)

- UK: 6   EU: 1   Rest of Europe: 1   Rest of the World: 0

Major Trophies Won Since Premier League Began: 0

Premier League Statistics (correct to the end of the 2009/10 season)

Seasons: 2   Played: 84

Won: 22   Drawn: 23   Lost:39

Goals Scored: 105   Goals Conceded: 142   Goal Difference: –37

Total Points: 89

Overview

Despite being founder members of the Premier League, Oldham Athletic have spent only two seasons in England's top division, and have not featured in the Premier League since they were relegated at the end of the 1993/94 – after finishing in 21st place with 40 points, three points away from safety.

During their second season in the Premier League Oldham reached the semi-finals of the FA Cup and were minutes away from recording a famous victory over Manchester United before Mark Hughes equalised during extra time. Manchester United went on to win the replay 4–1.

Managers

Year	£XI	£XI Rank	Points	Cost Per Point	Position League	Manager
1992/93	£19,817,269	14	49	£404,434	19	Joe Royle
1993/94	£19,155,372	15	40	£478,884	21	Joe Royle
Average	£19,486,321	15	44.5	£441,659	20	Joe Royle

Top 15 CTPP Purchases

#	Player	CTPP	Original fee	Year transferred	% of poss starts
1	Olney I	£4,659,344	D700000	1992/93	50%
2	Pointon N	£3,993,724	£600,000	1992/93	68%
3	Milligan M	£3,993,724	D600000	1992/93	96%
4	McDonald N	£3,328,103	D500000	1992/93	6%
5	Sharp G	£3,328,103	D500000	1992/93	61%
6	Jobson R	£3,061,855	D460000	1992/93	92%
7	Pedersen T	£2,985,347	£500,000	1993/94	17%
8	McCarthy S	£2,985,347	£500,000	1993/94	45%
9	Holden R	£2,686,812	£450,000	1993/94	67%
10	Beckford D	£1,996,862	£300,000	1992/93	23%
11	Halle G	£1,863,738	D280000	1992/93	75%
12	Keeley J	£1,597,489	D240000	1992/93	2%
13	Moulden P	£1,497,646	D225000	1992/93	2%
14	Brennan M	£1,331,241	£200,000	1992/93	30%
15	Tolson N	£998,431	D150000	1992/93	0%

Expert View

Charlie Davidson

Oldham fan

Joe Royle did a great job in getting us to the top division the season before it became known as the Premier League, but between 1992 and 1994 the Latics actually underachieved in relation to the cost of the team.

However, the real drama was in the cups: a League Cup Final, and two FA Cup semi-finals, between 1990 and 1994. In between, we spent three seasons in the top flight, steadily declining from 17th to 19th to 21st – and a return to relative obscurity.

Rather than the players who were bought, the story is more about those who were sold. Denis Irwin left to join Manchester United for £625,000 (£4.3m) on the eve of the new era; and Earl Barrett moved to Aston Villa in February 1992, for a staggering £11.3m in today's money. That was half of a top-class defence, and it's no wonder we failed to survive at that level for too long after.

Spending £4.7m in today's money on an honest plodder like Ian Olney perhaps captures the essence of our demise.

Portsmouth

Total Spend (Actual): £106m
Total Spend (CTPP): £140.8m
Average League Position: 13.86
Number of Managers: 6
Most Expensive Signing: Peter Crouch – £11m (CTPP £8.6m)
Best Value Signing: David James
Worst Value Signing: David Nugent

Player Signings Breakdown (data correct up to end of January transfer window 2010)

- UK: 22   EU: 25   Rest of Europe: 8   Rest of the World: 20

Major Trophies Won Since Premier League Began

FA Cup: 1 (2007/08)

Premier League Statistics (correct to the end of the 2009/10 season)

Seasons: 7	Played: 266	
Won: 79	Drawn: 65	Lost:122
Goals Scored: 292	Goals Conceded: 380	Goal Difference: –88
Total Points: 293		

Overview

Portsmouth's promotion to the Premier League for 2003/04 ended an absence of 16 seasons from England's top division. Backed by the funds of flamboyant chairman Milan Mandarić, manager Harry Redknapp led Portsmouth to a 13th-place finish that season, which included 1–0 victories over both Liverpool and Manchester United at Fratton Park. Redknapp would shock the Fratton Park faithful the following season (2004/05) as he and assistant Jim Smith resigned from Portsmouth in November 2004 to take over local rivals Southampton. The duo disagreed with Mandarić over his appointment of Velimir Zajec in a Director of Football role. Zajec took over as manager but he then reverted back to his original role following Alain Perrin's arrival in April 2005. In an ironic twist, Portsmouth finished the season 16th, seven points ahead of Redknapp's Southampton, who were relegated in bottom place.

Perrin's Portsmouth made a dreadful start to the 2005/06 campaign, winning just two of their opening 16 league games. The Frenchman was subsequently sacked in December 2005 to be replaced by – you guessed it – Harry Redknapp, who some supporters still hadn't forgiven for joining Southampton just over a year earlier. Pompey would eventually escape the relegation dogfight, winning six of their final 10 league games to finish in 17th place. In 2006/07, Redknapp led Portsmouth to their highest league finish since

3rd in 1954/55, as the team finished 8th.

In 2006 Redknapp began to invest some of new owner Alexandre Gaydamak's money, bringing in players such as Glen Johnson (from Chelsea), Lassana Diarra (Arsenal), Sulley Muntari (Udinese) and Jermain Defoe (Tottenham). In 2007/08, Portsmouth bettered the performances of the previous season as they finished in 8th place and beat Cardiff City 1-0 at Wembley to become the first club outside of the 'big four' to win the FA Cup since Everton defeated Manchester United in 1995.

The 2008/09 season saw the arrival of Peter Crouch from Liverpool for a club record £11m (£8.6m). Redknapp wouldn't stick around, however, as he left to take over at Tottenham in October 2008. Tony Adams was promoted to manager, but Portsmouth's financial problems would begin to show as both Defoe (£15.75m) and Diarra (£20m) were sold during the January transfer window with very little of the proceeds re-invested in the squad. Adams was sacked in February 2009 after winning just two games from 16. Paul Hart, like Adams, was promoted from within as he was named manager not long after Adams' departure. Portsmouth ended the season in 14th place, seven points clear of the drop zone.

Portsmouth's dire financial situation would result in the sales of Peter Crouch, Sylvain Distin, Niko Kranjčar and Glen Johnson before the start of the 2009/10 campaign, in a bid to lower the wage bill, but the club's finances did not improve; some players and staff went unpaid during October and November. Paul Hart was sacked in November 2009 with the team bottom of the league, having won just two games. Avram Grant took over and, despite the ownership of the club changing hands on no fewer than four occasions during the course of the season, Portsmouth entered into administration, resulting in a mandatory nine-point deduction in March 2010 - all but guaranteeing their relegation. Portsmouth's demotion to the Championship was confirmed the following month but, despite the turmoil surrounding the club, Grant led Portsmouth to their second FA Cup Final in three seasons, where they lost to 1-0 to the Israeli's former side, Chelsea.

Most Utilised Players
Peter Crouch is the only Portsmouth player with a 100% start ratio, but he spent just one Premier League season (2008/09) at Fratton Park following his £11m (£8.6m) transfer from Liverpool in July 2008. David James started more Premier League games (134) than any other Portsmouth player during his four seasons at the club. Signed by Harry Redknapp for £1.2m (£2.1m), James left Pompey as a free agent following their relegation, with an 88% start ratio.

Least Utilised Players
One signing that Harry Redknapp didn't get right was that of striker David Nugent, who joined the club in July 2007 for £4.5m (£5.1m) from Preston North End. Nugent started just 18 Premier League games for Portsmouth (giving him a 16% start ratio), scoring only three league goals, before he was sent on loan to Burnley for the 2009/10 campaign.

John Utaka cost a fairly hefty £7m (£7.9m) by Portsmouth's standards, but started only 34% of games.

Managers

Year	£XI	£XI Rank	Points	Cost Per Point	Position League	Manager
2003/04	£13,829,508	18	45	£307,322	13	Harry Redknapp
2004/05	£15,422,996	17	39	£395,461	16	Redknapp/Zajec/Perrin
2005/06	£18,007,799	17	38	£473,889	17	Perrin/Jordan/Redknapp
2006/07	£21,246,017	15	54	£393,445	9	Harry Redknapp
2007/08	£36,082,368	12	57	£633,024	8	Harry Redknapp
2008/09	£33,826,136	11	41	£825,028	14	Redknapp/Adams/Hart
Average	**£23,069,137**	**15**	**45.7**	**£504,695**	**12.8**	**Harry Redknapp**
2004/05	£15,422,996	17	39	£395,461	16	Redknapp/Zajec/Perrin
2005/06	£18,007,799	17	38	£473,889	17	Perrin/Jordan/Redknapp
Average	**£16,715,398**	**17**	**38.5**	**£434,675**	**16.5**	**Alain Perrin**
2009/10	£10,823,811	19	19	£569,674	20	**Paul Hart/Avram Grant**

Top 5 Players Sold for a Profit

- Diarra – Bought for: £5.5m (£6.2m), Sold for: £20m (£15.7m), Profit of: £14.5m (£9.5m)
- Johnson – Bought for: £4m (£4.5m), Sold for: £18m (£18m) Profit of: £14m (£13.5m)
- Defoe – Bought for: £7.5m (£8.5m), Sold for: £15.75m (£12.4m), Profit of: £8.25m (£3.9m)
- Distin – Bought for: £0 (free transfer), Sold for: £5.7m (£5.7m), Profit of: £5.7m (£5.7m)
- Muntari – Bought for: £7m (£7.9m), Sold for: £12.7m (£10m), Profit of: £5.7m (£2.1m)

Top 20 CTPP Purchases

#	Player	CTPP	Original fee	Year transferred	% of poss starts
1	Crouch P	£8,600,824	£11,000,000	2008/09	100%
2	Yakubu	£8,471,577	£5,250,000	2002/03	84%
3	Defoe J	£8,464,982	£7,500,000	2007/08	38%
4	Muntari S	£7,900,650	£7,000,000	2007/08	71%
5	Utaka J	£7,900,650	£7,000,000	2007/08	34%
6	Benjani	£7,481,488	£4,100,000	2005/06	54%
7	Diarra L (II)	£6,207,653	£5,500,000	2007/08	29%
8	Kranjčar N	£6,082,373	£3,500,000	2006/07	41%
9	Nugent D	£5,078,989	£4,500,000	2007/08	16%
10	Davis S (I)	£4,257,757	£2,333,333	2005/06	62%
11	Mendes P	£4,257,757	£2,333,333	2005/06	46%
12	Pamarot N	£4,257,757	£2,333,333	2005/06	33%
13	Boateng KP	£4,000,000	£4,000,000	2009/10	53%
14	Kaboul Y	£3,909,466	£5,000,000	2008/09	47%
15	Stefanović D	£3,738,665	£1,850,000	2003/04	73%
16	O'Brien A (I)	£3,649,506	£2,000,000	2005/06	39%
17	Kamara D	£3,638,465	£2,000,000	2004/05	39%
18	Belhadj N	£3,440,330	£4,400,000	2008/09	49%
19	Faye A (II)	£3,031,350	£1,500,000	2003/04	58%
20	Silva D	£2,737,130	£1,500,000	2005/06	34%

Expert View
Nick Szczepanik (@NickSzczepanik)

Covered Portsmouth's Premier League years as a football writer for The Times

In the beginning, it was all so simple. Harry Redknapp took Portsmouth into the Premier League in 2003 with a team of free transfers and loanees, and carried on in the same vein once the club was in the top flight. He used his wheeling and dealing skills – however much he may now disavow them – to secure bargain signings such as Patrik Berger, Teddy Sheringham and Amdy Faye, while Milan Mandarić, the owner, kept the total outlay within manageable proportions.

Then, in 2006, came Alexandre "Sacha" Gaydamak, who bought out Mandarić in two stages. Huge wages started to be paid, to players such as Sol Campbell and David James, and big transfer fees followed. A £25m loan taken out with Standard Bank of South Africa financed the arrivals of record signing Sulley Ali Muntari (£7m/£7.9m CTPP), along with John Utaka (£7m/£7.9m) and David Nugent, in summer 2007.

Portsmouth fans had seldom had it so good, and they revelled in the 2008 FA Cup victory and the bold new signings that kept turning up – Glen Johnson, Jermain Defoe, Peter Crouch. Few of them wondered how a small provincial club could possibly afford them, and Redknapp, suddenly given the chance to build a team of his dreams and secure the first trophy of his career, did not seem to care.

Journalists on the Portsmouth beat who investigated Gaydamak found a distant, aloof figure with no visible means of financing the signings he did. Of course, his father, Arkady, an Israeli businessman wanted by Interpol in connection with arms deals – and therefore highly unlikely to pass a fit-and-proper-persons test – was very wealthy, but the club always denied that he was indirectly bankrolling the project. It was just coincidence, then, that when Gaydamak Senior's Israeli businesses ran into trouble, Portsmouth's money dried up.

Redknapp sniffed the wind and left for Tottenham. On transfer fees alone, he had done well enough. For every flop such as Utaka and Nugent, whose fees will never be recouped, there was a Lassana Diarra, Johnson or Muntari, sold on at a handsome profit. But the contracts that he and Peter Storrie, the chief executive, had offered had holed the club below the waterline.

The club hit the buffers over the summer and autumn of 2009. It changed hands a number of times, bank loans were called in, player wages and outstanding transfer debts to other clubs could not be paid, and HMRC issued a winding-up order.

Only then did the fans realise that player contracts had included some ludicrous wages and bonuses – mostly triggered by fanciful outcomes such as FA Cup wins and European qualification. Unfortunately, both happened, and club insiders were warning of the consequences even while the FA Cup was being paraded at Wembley. The inevitable relegation was bad enough, but the true shame of the club was the betrayal of its own community in the form of a trail of debts to local businesses that the club had left across Hampshire. Portsmouth and their fans had lived the dream, in the words of a previous profligate owner of another club, and woke up to a nightmare.

Queens Park Rangers

Total Spend (Actual): £6m
Total Spend (CTPP): £21.4m
Average League Position: 10.25
Number of Managers: 2
Most Expensive Signing: Trevor Sinclair – £750k (CTPP £4.5m)
Best Value Signing: Trevor Sinclair
Worst Value Signing: Ned Zelić

Player Signings Breakdown (data correct up to end of January transfer window 2010)

• UK: 9   EU: 1   Rest of Europe: 0   Rest of the World: 3

Major Trophies Won Since Premier League Began: 0

Premier League Statistics (correct to the end of the 2009/10 season)

Seasons: 4	Played: 164	
Won: 59	Drawn: 39	Lost:66
Goals Scored: 224	Goals Conceded: 232	Goal Difference: −8
Total Points: 216		

Overview

Queens Park Rangers were founding members of the Premier League in 1992 and they started life in the division by finishing in 5th place with 63 points: their highest league placing since 1987/88. Rangers finished ahead of Liverpool (6th), Arsenal (10th) and Chelsea (11th) in 1992/93, thanks mainly to Les Ferdinand's 20 Premier League goals, making him the second–highest scorer in the league that season.

The 1993/94 Premier League campaign wasn't quite as successful for QPR as they finished 9th, albeit with just three points fewer (60) than in 1992/93. Les Ferdinand's goals were again a feature of that season as he found the net 16 times.

In 1994/95, the Loftus Road outfit got off to a poor start in the Premier League, winning just one of their first 11 games before manager Gerry Francis resigned to take over at Tottenham. Ray Wilkins became player-manager and the club recovered from that poor start to finish in 8th place with 60 points. Rangers also reached the quarter-finals of the FA Cup, where they lost 2-0 to Manchester United. Les Ferdinand enjoyed another prolific campaign, bagging 24 Premier League goals.

Star striker Ferdinand – originally bought from non-league Hayes – was sold to Newcastle United prior to the start of 1995/96 for £6m (£15.8m, with over a million in today's money going to the club that originally found him). His goals would prove a big miss for QPR as they were relegated – finishing in 19th place with 33 points. Ferdinand scored 25 Premier League goals for Newcastle that season, and his absence, and the failure to sign a suitable replacement, cost QPR dear: their 13-year run in England's top division came to an end.

Most Utilised Players
Trevor Sinclair was signed from Blackpool for £750k (£4.5m) by Gerry Francis in 1993, and he went on to cement his place in the QPR team over the next four years. Sinclair started 99 Premier League games for Rangers (81%) and won October's Premier League Player of the Month award in 1995 (making him the only QPR player to have won the award).

Least Utilised Players
Australian international defender Ned Zelić was signed by Ray Wilkins from Borussia Dortmund in 1995 for £1.25m (£3.3m). Zelić's career in England never took off, though; he made just three Premier League starts (8%) during his time with QPR before returning to Germany in 1996.

Managers

Year	£XI	£XI Rank	Points	Cost Per Point	Position League	Manager
1992/93	£14,485,173	20	63	£229,923	5	Gerry Francis
1993/94	£20,247,595	13	60	£337,460	9	Gerry Francis
Average	£17,366,384	16.5	61.5	£283,692	7	Gerry Francis
1994/95	£15,373,795	22	60	£256,230	8	Francis/Wilkins
1995/96	£16,373,975	19	33	£496,181	19	Ray Wilkins
Average	£15,873,885	20.5	46.5	£376,205	13.5	Ray Wilkins

Top 15 CTPP Purchases

#	Player	CTPP	Original fee	Year transferred	% of poss starts
1	Sinclair T	£4,478,021	£750,000	1993/94	81%
2	Penrice G	£4,160,129	D625000	1992/93	26%
3	Stejskal J	£3,993,724	D600000	1992/93	48%
4	Yates S	£3,880,951	£650,000	1993/94	65%
5	Zelić N	£3,286,898	£1,250,000	1995/96	8%
6	Wilson C	£2,995,293	D450000	1992/93	94%
7	Barker S	£2,662,482	D400000	1992/93	77%
8	Hateley M	£2,629,518	£1,000,000	1995/96	26%
9	Bardsley D	£2,496,077	D375000	1992/93	79%
10	Peacock D	£2,329,672	D350000	1992/93	77%
11	Sinton A	£1,996,862	D300000	1992/93	86%
12	Brevett R	£1,664,052	D250000	1992/93	37%
13	Osborn S	£1,577,711	£600,000	1995/96	16%
14	Sommer J	£1,577,711	£600,000	1995/96	87%
15	Holloway I	£1,497,646	D225000	1992/93	59%

Expert View

Richard Ormerod

QPR season ticket holder

Strange as it may seem these days, QPR were a well-established top-flight club when the Premier League was founded. Having enjoyed nine consecutive and relatively successful seasons in the old Division One, we continued this form into the early years of the 'whole new ball game'.

Before the current era of financial insanity, smaller clubs still had a chance of competing at the top level if they had an eye for a bargain, after the inevitable process of selling on their best players. This was no better illustrated than our remarkable 5th-place finish under Gerry Francis in the inaugural Premier League season. With a squad assembled for less than £5m (cheap even at the time) and playing occasionally scintillating football, we finished as the top London club. How times have changed.

Subsequent finishes of 9th in 1994 and 8th in 1995 were almost considered a disappointment at the time. Many fans felt we should have pushed on to compete for the much-vaunted European places, even after Gerry Francis departed for Spurs and the veteran player but novice manager Ray Wilkins replaced him.

Andy Sinton bought for £350k (£2m), sold for £2.75m (£14.4m); Darren Peacock bought for £200k (£2.3m), sold for £2.7m (£13.8m); Les Ferdinand bought for £35k, sold for £6m (£15.7m). All classic examples of how we profited handsomely on players bought before and sold during the early Premier League era. But a club can't keep doing this forever and the last of these proved to be our undoing. The

Ferdinand money was squandered on scandalously poor signings (Ned Zelić, Mark Hateley, Simon Osborn and Juergen Sommer the pick of the bunch), and without Sir Les' 20-plus goals we were comfortably relegated.

Fifteen seasons, a further relegation and subsequent promotion, six chairmen and 19 changes of manager later, we are still waiting and hoping for a return to the big time...

Reading

Total Spend (Actual): £13.1m
Total Spend (CTPP): £18.8m
Average League Position: 13
Number of Managers: 1
Most Expensive Signing: Greg Halford – £2.5m (CTPP £4.35m)
Best Value Signing: Kevin Doyle
Worst Value Signing: Emerse Faé

Player Signings Breakdown (data correct up to end of January transfer window 2010)

- UK: 5   EU: 2   Rest of Europe: 1   Rest of the World: 6

Major Trophies Won Since Premier League Began: 0

Premier League Statistics (correct to the end of the 2009/10 season)

Seasons: 2	Played: 76	
Won: 26	Drawn: 13	Lost:37
Goals Scored: 93	Goals Conceded: 113	Goal Difference: –20
Total Points: 91		

Overview
Despite being one of the oldest football clubs in England (formed in 1871), Reading had to wait until 2006/07 for their first taste of top-flight football. Hot on the heels of winning the 2005/06 Football League Championship, which earned the Royals automatic promotion to the Premier League for 2006/07, Steve Coppell defied overwhelming odds and many critics who believed Reading would be relegated, and led the team to an impressive 8th-place finish. Their total of 56 points was just one behind the tally that earned 7th-place Bolton a place in the following season's Uefa Cup.

Reading's second season in the Premier League would end up being a poor one and, despite home victories over Liverpool (3–1) and Everton (1–0), who finished 4th and 5th respectively, the Royals never recovered from a spell that saw them lose eight consecutive league games. They finished the season in 18th place with 36 points – level on points with Fulham but with an inferior goal difference that brought their short stay in the Premier League to an end.

Reading's 7–4 defeat away to Portsmouth on 29 September 2007 is the highest-scoring match in the Premier League to date.

Most Utilised Players
Kevin Doyle was signed for just £103k (CTPP £188k) from Cork City in June 2005 and scored 13 Premier League goals in his and Reading's debut season in the Premier League. Doyle scored just six times the following season as the Royals were relegated, but his total of 62 Premier League starts made him Reading's fifth-most utilised player during this time.

Least Utilised Players
Ivory Coast international midfielder Emerse Faé was signed from French outfit Nantes for £2.5m (CTPP £2.9m) in August 2007. Faé started just three Premier League games (8% start ratio) for Reading in 2007/08, and, following a refusal to play for the reserve team towards the end of the season, he was suspended and eventually sent back to France where he joined Nice on loan in June 2008, before completing a permanent deal later that year.

Managers

Year	£XI	£XI Rank	Points	Cost Per Point	Position League	Manager
2006/07	£6,140,190	20	55	£111,640	8	Steve Coppell
2007/08	£6,089,682	20	36	£169,158	18	Steve Coppell
Average	**£6,114,936**	**20**	**45.5**	**£140,399**	**13**	**Steve Coppell**

Top 10 CTPP Purchases

#	Player	CTPP	Original fee	Year transferred	% of poss starts
1	Halford G	£4,344,552	£2,500,000	2006/07	5%
2	Faé E	£2,821,661	£2,500,000	2007/08	8%
3	Seol K	£2,606,731	£1,500,000	2006/07	32%
4	Lita L	£1,824,753	d1000000	2005/06	42%
5	Bikey A	£1,737,821	£1,000,000	2006/07	28%
6	Murty G	£1,714,707	d700000	1998/99	67%
7	Rosenior L	£1,692,996	£1,500,000	2007/08	39%
8	Matějovský M	£1,580,130	£1,400,000	2007/08	26%
9	Duberry M	£1,390,257	£800,000	2006/07	26%
10	Cissé K	£733,632	£650,000	2007/08	29%

Record-breaking Reading stormed the Championship with an emphatic 106 points when they finally broke into the top-flight for the first time in their 134-year history in 2007.

Wary of the fate of clubs such as Southampton, Derby County, Bradford City and Leeds United before them, Royals were cautious in their spending. With Steve Coppell at the helm and prudent chairman Sir John Madejski holding the purse strings, fans knew there would not be a transfer war chest to splash on reaching the Premier League. And why was there much of a need?

Top clubs had already been chasing the likes of Kevin Doyle, plucked from Cork City for just £75,000, and Dave Kitson, brought to Madejski Stadium from Cambridge United for just £150,000.

Ironically, the man who was instrumental in the signings of half of Reading's squad during the Premier League years of 2006/07 and 2007/08, chief scout Brian McDermott, is now in charge as manager as we try and get back into the top flight. Coppell knew how to get the best out of players who wanted to play and had a point to prove, but in the transfer market itself he was somewhat unsuccessful when signing cheques of more than £1m.

Emerse Faé became the club's record signing in 2007 when he joined for £2.5m from Nantes, but he never settled and was quickly bombed out after failing to establish himself. Seol Ki-Hyeon was effective for his first season after his £1.5m switch from Wolves, but he was swapped for Liam Rosenior with Fulham as he flopped in the second season with Royals. And Greg Halford was another player who, at a cost of £2.4m, could not justify his price tag. With pocket change, Coppell was a master, but give him much more and he failed to make it count.

Chairman Sir John was quick to berate the wages paid to Premier League stars, and Coppell joined in the debate as Royals missed out on a host of players in 2007, including Joleon Lescott and John Mensah. Needless to say, Reading's 8th-place finish during their first season in the top flight was a result of astronomical standing, with most of Coppell's so called "big-name signings" failing to impress. That in itself makes Reading's rollercoaster top-flight stay seem even more impressive, but also hints towards why second-season syndrome hit them so badly.

However, a current lasting legacy for Coppell at Reading is Jimmy Kébé. The Mali winger was scouted by McDermott, a former Arsenal wide man. The chief scout went to watch Kébé twice in France when he was playing for Boulogne.

At first glance McDermott picked the phone up and told Coppell he had to sign the 26-year-old, but Coppell remained unsure and sent McDermott back out to check on the player. This time round, by his own words, McDermott said Kébé's performance was awful, but that didn't stop him sticking to his guns. Royals finally signed the Malian in January 2008 as they looked to fight the spectre of relegation to the Championship, and to this day he remains their most prized asset.

Reading can also boast a certain nous in bringing in players for nominal fees and selling them in multi-million-pound deals, as in the cases of Doyle (£6.5m), Kitson (£5.5m), Stephen Hunt (£3.5m) and Nicky Shorey (£3m).

Sheffield United

Total Spend (Actual): £13.7m
Total Spend (CTPP): £33.4m
Average League Position: 17.33
Number of Managers: 2
Most Expensive Signing: Brian Gayle – D700k (CTPP £4.7m)
Best Value Signing: Alan Kelly
Worst Value Signing: Luton Shelton

Player Signings Breakdown (data correct up to end of January transfer window 2010)

- UK: 15   EU: 4   Rest of Europe: 3   Rest of the World: 3

Major Trophies Won Since Premier League Began: 0

Premier League Statistics (correct to the end of the 2009/10 season)

Seasons: 3	Played: 122	
Won: 32	Drawn: 36	Lost:54
Goals Scored: 128	Goals Conceded: 168	Goal Difference: −40
Total Points: 132		

Overview

Sheffield United were founding members of the Premier League in 1992, but their first spell in the rebaptised top flight would last only two seasons. The 1992/93 campaign saw the Blades finish in 14th place with 52 points, just three points clear of the relegation zone. There were some notable results for Dave Bassett's team, including a 2-1 defeat of Manchester United on the opening day, with Blades striker Brian Deane scoring the first ever Premier League goal. That season also saw Sheffield United record victories over Liverpool (1-0), Tottenham (6-0) and Leeds United (2-1), and league 'doubles' over Chelsea (2-1 and 4-2) and Everton (1-0 and 2-0). Sheffield United also reached the semi-final of the FA Cup, where they lost to local rivals Sheffield Wednesday 2-1 after extra time, putting an end to United's hopes of adding to their four previous FA Cup wins.

In 1993/94, the Blades were relegated on the last day of the season. Despite needing just one point against Chelsea to secure their survival, United were sent down as their opponents scored two goals in the closing stages to overturn a 2-1 deficit. This failure to secure a point was somewhat ironic given that the Blades recorded the most draws during a 42-game season (18 - a record shared by two other teams).

It wasn't until 2006/07 that Sheffield United returned to the Premier League - this time led by Neil Warnock - but it would be a short-lived reacquaintance with the top flight. Despite recording victories over Arsenal (1-0), who finished 4th, and Tottenham (2-1), who finished 5th, the Blades were relegated on goal difference. Sheffield United ended up just one place and one goal behind 17th-place Wigan, who finished with a goal difference of -22.

Most Utilised Players
Alan Kelly was signed for £150k (£1m) from Preston North End in July 1992 and featured in the first two seasons that Sheffield United were present in the Premier League. Goalkeeper Kelly made 61 starts (73%) over the two seasons and played a major role in Sheffield United having the seventh-best defensive record in 1992/93.

Least Utilised Players
Luton Shelton arrived in January 2007 for £1.85m (£3.3m) from Helsingborg, but he had to wait until April before he started his first game for the Blades. Shelton would make just two starts in total for Sheffield United (5%) as they failed in their bid to avoid relegation from the Premier League.

Managers

Year	£XI	£XI Rank	Points	Cost Per Point	Position League	Manager
1992/93	£12,254,551	21	52	£235,664	14	Dave Bassett
1993/94	£13,500,963	20	42	£321,452	20	Dave Bassett
Average	£12,877,757	20.5	47	£278,558	17	Dave Bassett
2006/07	£7,482,720	18	38	£196,914	18	Neil Warnock

Top 15 CTPP Purchases

#	Player	CTPP	Original fee	Year transferred	% of poss starts
1	Gayle B	£4,659,344	D700000	1992/93	52%
2	Davis C	£4,344,552	£2,500,000	2006/07	47%
3	Hulse R	£3,823,206	£2,200,000	2006/07	74%
4	Nilsen R	£3,283,882	£550,000	1993/94	50%
5	Shelton L	£3,214,969	£1,850,000	2006/07	5%
6	Akinbiyi A	£3,193,318	d1750000	2005/06	5%
7	Kilgallon M	£3,041,187	£1,750,000	2006/07	16%
8	Hodges G	£2,995,293	D450000	1992/93	56%
9	Falconer W	£2,388,278	£400,000	1993/94	50%
10	Flo J	£2,388,278	£400,000	1993/94	76%
11	Cowan T	£2,329,672	D350000	1992/93	30%
12	Tuttle D	£2,089,743	£350,000	1993/94	74%
13	Beesley P	£1,996,862	D300000	1992/93	73%
14	Pemberton J	£1,996,862	D300000	1992/93	32%
15	Blake N	£1,791,208	£300,000	1993/94	17%

Expert View

John Ashdown (@John_Ashdown)

Sheffield United fan and journalist for The Guardian

After back-to-back promotions, Dave Bassett arrived in the top flight with Sheffield United having already proved he was happier unearthing rough diamonds than buying the finished product. By the time the Premier League kicked off in 1992 his shortcomings when handed larger sums of cash were all too obvious. Brian Gayle, a transfer record £750,000 (£4.7m) in 1991, was a flop, but goalkeeper Alan Kelly, £150,000 (£1m) from Preston a year later (and the most expensive signing of that summer), was up there with Bassett's best bargains.

But in truth, the biggest transfer in terms of impact during that first spell in the Premier League was an outgoing one. Brian Deane's £2.9m (£16.1m) move to Leeds in the summer of 1993 funded a steady season-long spending spree but it was a jolting reminder of United's place in the pecking order, a hammer blow to the collective psyche. Deane's replacement, Jostein Flo (£400,000/£2.4m from Sogndal) was memorable but inadequate. In all, United spent almost £2m on the likes of Flo, Nathan Blake (£300,000/£1.8m), Willie Falconer (£400,000 /£2.4m) and the commendable Roger Nilsen (£550,000/£3.3m) in an attempt to stave off relegation. It failed. But only just.

Neil Warnock was equally hit-and-miss in 2006/07. For every Rob Hulse (excellent value at £2.2m/£3.8m from Leeds), there was a Claude Davis (a Bambi-on-ice waste at £2.5m/£4.3m from Preston). For every disastrous Luton Shelton (£1.85m/£3.2m from Helsingborg), there was a brilliant Matthew Kilgallon

(£1.75m/£3m from Elland Road and a delicious role reversal of the Deane situation 13 years earlier).

Yet again, defeat on the final day, when the Blades' fate was in their own hands, meant relegation. But the very nature of those painful small-margin finales makes it difficult to label United's transfer dealings an outright failure, particularly as convenient excuses for the drop existed outside the club – Hans Segers in 1994 and Carlos Tévez in 2007. Still, it would clearly be too generous to say they were a success. At times, though, they were fun.

Sheffield Wednesday

Total Spend (Actual): £53.1m
Total Spend (CTPP): £183.5m
Average League Position: 12
Number of Managers: 4
Most Expensive Signing: Andy Sinton – £2.75m (CTPP £16.5m)
Best Value Signing: Peter Atherton
Worst Value Signing: Klas Ingesson

Player Signings Breakdown (data correct up to end of January transfer window 2010)

- UK: 29   EU. 14   Rest of Europe: 3   Rest of the World: 3

Major Trophies Won Since Premier League Began: 0

Premier League Statistics (correct to the end of the 2009/10 season)

Seasons: 8	Played: 316	
Won: 101	Drawn: 89	Lost:126
Goals Scored: 409	Goals Conceded: 453	Goal Difference: –44
Total Points: 392		

Overview

Sheffield Wednesday remain the last club outside the top division to win a major English trophy – when they lifted the League Cup in 1990/91 as a Second Division club (Wednesday also gained promotion back to the top flight that season). However, life in the Premier League didn't begin well for the Owls as they won just four of their opening 19 league games, leaving them deep in relegation trouble. Things began to look up by the end of February, though, as they won eight out of nine games and progressed to the semi-final of the League Cup and quarter-final of the FA Cup. Their form in the league became inconsistent (resulting in a 7th-place finish) as they reached the finals of both domestic cups (beating local rivals Sheffield United in the semi-finals of the FA Cup). The Owls would ultimately end the season trophyless, however, as Arsenal claimed 2-1 victories in both finals.

The 1993/94 season saw a similar poor start for the Owls, with just one win from their opening 13 league games, once again putting them in the thick of the relegation mix. Wednesday would soon earn a reputation for being entertainers that season as they smashed five goals past West Ham, Everton and Ipswich, while also suffering a 5-0 defeat away to Manchester United. The Owls ended the season in 7th place, with only Manchester United (80 goals) and Newcastle United (82 goals) outscoring their goal tally of 76.

Wednesday finished the next two seasons in 13th (which led to Trevor Francis being dismissed) and 15th place (under his replacement David Pleat), before they secured their third 7th-place finish in the Premier League at the end of 1996/97 - this despite drawing 10 league games at home (a joint Premier League record). Wednesday suffered a disastrous start to the following season, which included a 7-2 defeat away to Blackburn, a 5-2 loss at home to Derby County and a 6-1 mauling away to Manchester United, which resulted in Pleat being sacked in November 1997 to be replaced by Ron Atkinson (who had previously led the Owls to the 1991 League Cup triumph over Manchester United). Although Atkinson, employed on a short-term deal, secured survival courtesy of a 16th-place finish, the team played inconsistently throughout and he wasn't kept on at the end of the season. Danny Wilson (who played under Atkinson in 1990/91) was given the job in the summer of 1998.

Unfortunately for Wilson and Wednesday, a 12th-place finish in 1998/99 was followed by a 19th-place finish in 1999/00, sealing the Hillsborough club's second relegation in 14 seasons. The low point of Wilson's reign came during a sequence that saw the Owls win just one of their opening 17 league games, which included an 8-0 thrashing by Newcastle United at St James' Park.

Most Utilised Players
Trevor Francis paid Coventry City £800k (£3.1m) for Peter Atherton in 1994, and he would go on to captain the club. Atherton started 214 Premier League games for the Owls, giving him a 92% starting ratio. Only Des Walker, signed for £2.7m (£16.2m) from Sampdoria in 1993 (also by Francis), has a higher starting ratio (96%), also having started more league games (264).

Least Utilised Players
Unlike Atherton and Walker, former Swedish international Klas Ingesson turned out to be one of Francis' poorest forays into the transfer market, following his £2m (£7.6m) transfer from Dutch giants PSV Eindhoven in 1994. Ingesson started just 12 Premier League games during the two seasons he spent with the Owls, giving him a lowly 15%

starting ratio. Following his departure from Hillsborough in 1996, Ingesson went on to have a more successful career in Italy, first with Bari and then Bologna.

Managers

Year	£XI	£XI Rank	Points	Cost Per Point	Position League	Manager
1992/93	£33,232,694	11	59	£563,266	7	Trevor Francis
1993/94	£49,203,605	9	64	£768,806	7	Trevor Francis
1994/95	£51,525,412	10	51	£1,010,302	13	Trevor Francis
Average	**£44,653,904**	**10**	**58.0**	**£780,792**	**9.0**	**Trevor Francis**
1995/96	£45,960,362	10	40	£1,149,009	15	David Pleat
1996/97	£47,423,694	11	57	£831,995	7	David Pleat
1997/98	£64,675,132	5	44	£1,469,889	16	Pleat/Shreeves/Atkinson
Average	**£52,686,396**	**8.7**	**47.0**	**£1,150,298**	**12.7**	**David Pleat**
1998/99	£56,196,808	8	46	£1,221,670	12	Danny Wilson
1999/00	£52,526,867	7	31	£1,694,415	19	Wilson/Shreeves
Average	**£54,361,838**	**7.5**	**38.5**	**£1,458,042**	**15.5**	**Danny Wilson**

Top 5 Players Sold for a Profit

- Kovačević – Bought for: £2m (£5.3m), Sold for: £7m (£18.6m) Profit of: £5m (£13.3m)
- Thome – Bought for: £0 (free transfer), Sold for: £2.7m (£6.4m), Profit of: £2.7m (£6.4m)
- Bart-Williams – Bought for: D275k (£1.9m), Sold for: £2.5m (£6.6m), Profit of: £2.25m (£4.7m)
- Warhurst – Bought for: D750k (£5m), Sold for: £2.65m (£15.9m), Profit of: £1.9m (£10.9m)
- Hirst – Bought for: D250k (£1.7m), Sold for: £2m (£6.8m), Profit of: £1.75m (£5.1m)

Top 20 CTPP Purchases

#	Player	CTPP	Original fee	Year transferred	% of poss starts
1	Sinton A	£16,419,409	£2,750,000	1993/94	44%
2	Walker D	£16,120,874	£2,700,000	1993/94	96%
3	Di Canio P	£15,192,355	£4,500,000	1997/98	51%
4	Carbone B	£10,128,237	£3,000,000	1997/98	57%
5	Hinchcliffe A	£10,128,237	£3,000,000	1997/98	67%
6	Woods C	£7,987,447	D1200000	1992/93	40%
7	Ingesson K	£7,577,191	£2,000,000	1994/95	15%
8	Booth A	£7,142,948	£2,700,000	1996/97	70%
9	De Bilde G	£7,040,011	£3,000,000	1999/00	97%
10	Waddle C	£6,656,206	£1,000,000	1992/93	57%
11	Jonk W	£6,123,954	£2,500,000	1998/99	88%
12	Blondeau P	£6,076,942	£1,800,000	1997/98	13%
13	Nolan I	£5,682,894	£1,500,000	1994/95	85%
14	Palmer C	£5,657,775	D850000	1992/93	83%
15	Magilton J	£5,401,726	£1,600,000	1997/98	18%
16	Jemson N	£5,324,965	D800000	1992/93	18%
17	Kovačević D	£5,259,036	£2,000,000	1995/96	21%
18	Stefanović D	£5,259,036	£2,000,000	1995/96	39%
19	Warhurst P	£4,992,155	D750000	1992/93	35%
20	Petrescu D	£4,925,174	£1,300,000	1994/95	35%

Expert View
David Taylor
Sheffield Wednesday season–ticket holder

From big spenders and fairly major players in the '90s to the third tier of English football and on the brink of a winding-up order from Her Majesty's Revenue & Customs over £600,000 in unpaid tax in late 2010. I'm guessing that Sheffield Wednesday are not the only club to be experiencing such a journey.

It started well, with the club overperforming in those early years, under the leadership of Trevor Francis. But by the time we had the fifth-costliest £XI in the Premier League (1997/98), we were finishing 16th in the table; throwing money at three different managers that season. Respite was brief – up to 12th under Danny Wilson (with the 8th-most expensive £XI), then relegation a year later, when ranking 7th.

Paying the equivalent of £16.4m for Andy Sinton and £10.1m for Andy Hinchcliffe sums up the madness; at least Benito Carbone (£10.1m) and Paolo Di Canio (£15.2m) provided some welcome glamour and excitement. Wim Jonk at £2.5m (£6.1m), however, was another costly flop; Wednesday fans voiced dissent about a clause in his contract which stipulated that he would automatically receive £5,000 per game missed through injury. He racked up quite a lot of money this way. At least Des Walker had some serious international pedigree, and proved his long-term worth at £16.1m CTPP. Though probably better remembered as a Nottingham Forest player, he actually played almost 50 more games for Wednesday.

Southampton

Total Spend (Actual): £65m
Total Spend (CTPP): £160.4m
Average League Position: 14.15
Number of Managers: 12
Most Expensive Signing: David Hirst – £2m (CTPP £6.8m)
Best Value Signing: Claus Lundekvam
Worst Value Signing: Agustín Delgado

Player Signings Breakdown (data correct up to end of January transfer window 2010)

• UK: 60   EU: 20   Rest of Europe: 7   Rest of the World: 7

Major Trophies Won Since Premier League Began: 0

Premier League Statistics (correct to the end of the 2009/10 season)

Seasons: 13	Played: 506	
Won: 150	Drawn: 137	Lost:219
Goals Scored: 598	Goals Conceded: 738	Goal Difference: −140
Total Points: 587		

Overview

Southampton were founding members of the Premier League and entered 1992/93 on the back of 14 consecutive campaigns in England's top division. Their top-flight status almost came to an end in 1992/93 (under Ian Branfoot), and again in 1993/94; avoiding relegation by just a single point on both occasions. The latter season saw the deeply unpopular Branfoot resign in January 1994 with Southampton in the relegation zone, to be replaced by Alan Ball, who turned around Saints' fortunes by the end of the season. The team scored 15 goals in their final six league games (eight scored by Matt Le Tissier) to ensure their Premier League status once again.

Southampton finished 10th during Ball's only full season in charge (1994/95), but he left to join Manchester City in the summer of 1995. Dave Merrington took over from Ball for the start of 1995/96, but Southampton struggled for most of the season before three wins in April (which earned Merrington the April Manager of the Month award) secured Southampton's survival. The Saints finished in 17th place - level on points with Ball's 18th-place Manchester City but prevailing courtesy of a better goal difference. Southampton also reached the quarter-finals of the FA Cup that season, only to lose 2–0 to Manchester United. Once again, Southampton's managerial revolving door was in full swing as Merrington left at the end of the season to care for his ill wife. Graeme Souness was appointed as his successor, but he lasted only one season as the Saints finished in 16th place.

Southampton finished the next three seasons in 12th, 17th and 15th under Dave Jones, although he was suspended from the club in January 2000 (to be replaced by Glenn Hoddle) as he struggled to manage the team amid an ongoing court case. Hoddle left just over a year later to take over at Tottenham, with Southampton in the top half of the table. First-team coach Stuart Gray replaced Hoddle and, despite a drop in form, Southampton won their last two league games against esteemed opposition: a 2–1 victory against Manchester United and a 3–2 triumph over Arsenal in the last ever competitive game played at The Dell. In true Roy of the Rovers fashion, Southampton legend Matt Le Tissier came off the bench to score a late volley to secure all three points for the Saints and a 10th-place finish - a fitting end as the club moved to the new St Mary's stadium for the start of 2001/02.

Gordon Strachan replaced Gray just three months into 2001/02, which ended with an

11th-place finish. The following season proved Southampton's most successful in the Premier League as they finished in 8th place (their highest position since 1989/90). They also reached the 2003 FA Cup Final in Cardiff, where they lost 1-0 to Arsenal. Southampton finished 2003/04 in 12th place, but Strachan resigned in March 2004 to spend more time with his family. The Scot's departure saw three managers swap places over the next 10 months. Paul Sturrock arrived in March 2004 but was relieved of his duties no less than one month into 2004/05 as Steve Wigley was named as his successor. Wigley lasted until December 2004 before he was sacked, as chairman Rupert Lowe decided Harry Redknapp was the man to save Southampton from relegation. This plan backfired, however, as Saints ended the season rock bottom with 32 points – two points adrift from safety – to bring their 27-year status as a top-flight club to a close.

Most Utilised Players

Graeme Souness signed Claus Lundekvam from Norwegian side SK Brann in 1996 for £400k (£1.1m). Lundekvam started 283 Premier League games for Southampton (83%) but, despite the high number of appearances, the defender scored only two goals during 12 years at the club. No player has a higher start ratio or has played more Premier League games for the Saints than the Norwegian.

Least Utilised Players

Ecuador striker Agustín Delgado joined Southampton in 2001 for £3.5m (£4.6m) from Mexican side Necaxa. Unfortunately for Delgado and Southampton, his time with the south-coast club was dogged by injuries as he started just two Premier League games during his three years in England. He left Southampton with a 2% start ratio to return to Ecuador in 2004. Gordon Strachan, when asked about his plans for Delgado, said: "I've got more important things to think about. I've got a yoghurt to eat, the expiry date is today. That can be my priority rather than Agustín Delgado."

Managers

Year	£XI	£XI Rank	Points	Cost Per Point	Position League	Manager
1992/93	£15,707,854	17	50	£314,157	18	Ian Branfoot
1993/94	£16,828,329	17	43	£391,356	18	Ian Branfoot/Alan Ball
Average	£16,268,092	17	46.5	£352,757	18	Ian Branfoot
1993/94	£16,828,329	17	43	£391,356	18	Ian Branfoot/Alan Ball
1994/95	£16,337,887	19	54	£302,553	10	Alan Ball
Average	£16,583,108	18	48.5	£346,955	14	Alan Ball
1995/96	£19,737,670	18	38	£519,412	17	Dave Merrington
1996/97	£17,363,053	18	41	£423,489	16	Graeme Souness
1997/98	£21,105,564	17	48	£439,699	12	Dave Jones
1998/99	£15,231,079	19	41	£371,490	17	Dave Jones
1999/00	£11,137,623	18	44	£253,128	15	Jones/Glenn Hoddle
Average	£15,824,755	18	44.3	£354,772	14.7	Dave Jones

Year	£XI	£XI Rank	Points	Cost Per Point	Position League	Manager
1999/00	£11,137,623	18	44	£253,128	15	Jones/Glenn Hoddle
2000/01	£11,295,243	19	52	£217,216	10	Hoddle/Stuart Gray
Average	**£11,216,433**	**18.5**	**48**	**£235,172**	**12.5**	**Glenn Hoddle**
2000/01	£11,295,243	19	52	£217,216	10	Hoddle/Stuart Gray
2001/02	£14,025,241	19	45	£311,672	11	Gray/Strachan
Average	**£12,660,242**	**19**	**48.5**	**£264,444**	**10.5**	**Stuart Gray**
2002/03	£19,030,480	18	52	£365,971	8	Gordon Strachan
2003/04	£24,903,708	15	47	£529,866	12	Strachan/Wigley/Sturrock
Average	**£21,967,094**	**16.5**	**49.5**	**£447,918**	**10**	**Gordon Strachan**
2003/04	£24,903,708	15	47	£529,866	12	Strachan/Wigley/Sturrock
2004/05	£23,285,695	14	32	£727,678	20	Sturrock/Wigley/Redknapp
Average	**£24,094,702**	**14.5**	**39.5**	**£628,772**	**16**	**Paul Sturrock**

Top 5 Players Sold for a Profit

- Richards – Bought for: £0 (free transfer), Sold for: £8.1m (£10.7m), Profit of: £8.1m (£10.7m)
- Bridge – Bought for: £0 (trainee), Sold for: £7m (£14.2m) Profit of: £7m (£14.2m)
- K Davies – Bought for: £750k (£2.5m), Sold for: £7.25m (£17.8m), Profit of: £6.5m (£15.3m)
- K Jones – Bought for: £0 (free transfer), Sold for: £6m (£6.8m), Profit of: £6m (£6.8m)
- Crouch – Bought for: £2m (£3.7m), Sold for: £7m (£12.8m), Profit of: £5m (£9.1m)

Top 20 CTPP Purchases

#	Player	CTPP	Original fee	Year transferred	% of poss starts
1	Hirst D	£6,752,158	£2,000,000	1997/98	37%
2	Phillips K	£6,567,926	£3,250,000	2003/04	64%
3	Delap R	£5,242,648	£4,000,000	2001/02	70%
4	Beresford J	£5,064,118	£1,500,000	1997/98	10%
6	Monkou K	£4,992,155	£750,000	1992/93	68%
5	Groves P	£4,992,155	£750,000	1992/93	31%
7	Delgado A	£4,587,317	£3,500,000	2001/02	2%
8	Van Damme J	£4,548,082	£2,500,000	2004/05	11%
9	Watson G	£4,546,315	£1,200,000	1994/95	31%
10	Shipperley N	£4,546,315	£1,200,000	1994/95	55%
11	van Gobbel U	£4,388,902	£1,300,000	1997/98	33%
12	Prutton D	£4,034,084	£2,500,000	2002/03	44%
13	Dixon K	£3,827,319	£575,000	1992/93	19%
14	Quashie N	£3,820,389	£2,100,000	2004/05	34%
15	Ripley S	£3,674,372	£1,500,000	1998/99	24%
16	Crouch P	£3,638,465	£2,000,000	2004/05	47%
17	Magilton J	£3,582,416	£600,000	1993/94	63%
18	Palmer C	£3,376,079	£1,000,000	1997/98	58%
19	Dowie I	£3,328,103	D500000	1992/93	71%
20	Allen P	£3,283,882	£550,000	1993/94	48%

Looking at the figures, it quickly becomes clear that Dave Jones spent particularly well during his two and a half seasons with the club. Between the summer of 1997 and January 2000, he brought in a handful of the players that went on to form the crux of the team that reached the FA Cup Final in 2003, at relatively low prices. The likes of James Beattie and Marian Pahars (with CTPP valuations of £2.4m and £2m respectively) became two of the club's major goalscorers of the Premier League era and represent particularly good value for money.

Although Jones spent the club's limited transfer budget fairly astutely, the same can't really be said for Glenn Hoddle and Gordon Strachan who, despite gradually improving Southampton's performance on the field, seemed not to have a focused transfer policy.

The sizeable amounts spent on Agustín Delgado, Jelle Van Damme, Neil McCann and Nigel Quashie – players who either made very few appearances for the club or disappointed with the level of their performances – were never fully justified and characterised the confused financial practices of the club during the latter part of the Rupert Lowe era.

Stoke City

Total Spend (Actual): £44.9m
Total Spend (CTPP): £39.2m
Average League Position: 11.5
Number of Managers: 1
Most Expensive Signings: Robert Huth and Tuncay – £5m (CTPP £5m)
Best Value Signing: Rory Delap
Worst Value Signing: Michael Tonge

Player Signings Breakdown (data correct up to end of January transfer window 2010)

• UK: 10   EU: 3   Rest of Europe: 1   Rest of the World: 6

Major Trophies Won Since Premier League Began: 0

Premier League Statistics (correct to the end of the 2009/10 season)

Seasons: 2	Played: 76	
Won: 23	Drawn: 23	Lost:30
Goals Scored: 72	Goals Conceded: 103	Goal Difference: −31
Total Points: 92		

Overview

Stoke City are currently the oldest club in the Premier League (founded in 1863), but the 2010/11 campaign will be just their third in England's top division since 1984/85. Stoke's first season in the Premier League in 2008/09 produced some notable victories at the Britannia Stadium over more fashionable clubs such as Aston Villa (3–2), Spurs (2–1), Arsenal (2–1) and Manchester City (1–0), which played a significant role in achieving a 12th–place finish. Stoke had the eighth–best home record that season.

The following season saw Stoke finish one place higher (11th) with two points more (47) than the previous season. The Potters also had a good run in the FA Cup, defeating Arsenal 3–1 in the fourth round and Manchester City 3–1 (following a replay) in the fifth round before losing 2–0 to the eventual winners Chelsea in the quarter–finals.

The only major trophy that Stoke has won to date is the League Cup in 1971/72, when they defeated Chelsea 2–1.

Most Utilised Players

Two players who didn't cost a fee top Stoke's Most Utilised Players list. Thomas Sorensen, who was released by Aston Villa at the end of the 2007/08 campaign, and Rory Delap, who initially joined on loan from Sunderland in October 2006, both have start ratios of 89%, having started 68 league games during Stoke's two seasons in the Premier League up to the end of the 2009/10 campaign.

Least Utilised Players

Michael Tonge signed for Stoke City in September 2008 for £2m (£1.6m) from Sheffield United, but he would make just one Premier League start for the Potters (3%) before he was sent on loan, first to Preston North End and then Derby County.

Managers

Year	£XI	£XI Rank	Points	Cost Per Point	Position League	Manager
2008/09	£10,047,765	19	45	£223,284	12	Tony Pulis
2009/10	£17,420,065	16	47	£370,640	11	Tony Pulis
Average	£13,733,915	18	46	£296,962	12	Tony Pulis

Top 10 CTPP Purchases

#	Player	CTPP	Original fee	Year transferred	% of poss starts
1	Huth R	£5,000,000	£5,000,000	2009/10	79%
2	Sanli T	£5,000,000	£5,000,000	2009/10	34%
3	Kitson D	£4,300,412	£5,500,000	2008/09	26%
4	Begović A	£3,250,000	£3,250,000	2009/10	8%
5	Whitehead D	£3,000,000	£3,000,000	2009/10	87%
6	Collins D	£2,750,000	£2,750,000	2009/10	58%
7	Olofinjana S	£2,345,679	£3,000,000	2008/09	37%
8	Higginbotham D	£1,954,733	£2,500,000	2008/09	67%
9	Faye A (I)	£1,759,260	£2,250,000	2008/09	87%
10	Faye A (II)	£1,759,260	£2,250,000	2008/09	47%

Expert View

Martin Spinks

The Stoke Sentinel

Stoke City's recent history essentially dates back to the summer of 2006, when there was a change of ownership and manager.

Out went the Icelanders after seven years of shrinking budgets and increasingly bizarre decision-making. In came former owner Peter Coates, but this time far richer than during his first spell at the helm, and in too came Tony Pulis for a second stint as manager after being sacked by the Icelanders 12 months earlier.

Pulis got off to a rocky start, but he began re-establishing his reputation and popularity with the fans thanks to a string of inspired loan signings. The policy of bringing in expensive players for a limited period of time paid dividends as the likes of Lee Hendrie, Salif Diao and even Patrik Berger were hired for varying lengths of time. Longer-term seeds were also sown with the permanent signings of Ricardo Fuller (£500k/£868k), Liam Lawrence (£500k/£868k) and Rory Delap (free). The loan policy returned in the latter stages of Pulis's second season back with Stoke as Stephen Pearson, Shola Ameobi, Carlo Nash, Chris Riggott and Jay Bothroyd were all recruited to give The Potters' promotion push one last shove over the line in 2008.

Pulis bought big ahead of Stoke's Premier League debut as no fewer than 10 new faces arrived at the Britannia by the end of August 2008. There was one spectacular failure – record £5.5m signing Dave Kitson – while others like Andrew Davies, Michael Tonge and Tom Soares melted into the background. But there were always bound to be casualties after buying in bulk, while the likes of Thomas Sorensen and Abdoulaye Faye more than outweighed the failures. And there was still money up the sleeve by the following January to finance the inspired signings of James Beattie and Matthew Etherington.

Beattie would fall disappointingly by the wayside after a blistering start to keep Stoke up, but Etherington continued to prosper as Pulis raised the bar elsewhere in the team. Etherington, like Fuller before him and Eiður Guðjohnsen and Jermaine Pennant after him, illustrates the Pulis tendency to acquire quality players on a downer in the hope and belief of raising them back towards their former glories. His 2010 signing of Kenwyne Jones for a club record £8m is also an indication of his patience in signing players he has pursued for a year or more.

And while quality and experience has largely been his mantra in the transfer market, we mustn't forget his willingness to gamble on the younger potential of a Ryan Shawcross or an Asmir Begović. Pulis has made intermittent mistakes in the market, but one look at Stoke's league positions since his return in 2006 more than vindicates both his judgement and his valuations – not to mention the decision to bring him back to Stoke in the first place.

Sunderland

Total Spend (Actual): £169.5m
Total Spend (CTPP): £218.6m
Average League Position: 14.78
Number of Managers: 6
Most Expensive Signing: Tore André Flo – £8m (CTPP £13m)
Best Value Signing: Kevin Phillips
Worst Value Signing: John Oster

Player Signings Breakdown (data correct up to end of January transfer window 2010)

• UK: 39   EU: 30   Rest of Europe: 4   Rest of the World: 9

Major Trophies Won Since Premier League Began: 0

Premier League Statistics (correct to the end of the 2009/10 season)

Seasons: 9   Played: 342
Won: 89   Drawn: 81   Lost:172
Goals Scored: 332   Goals Conceded: 504   Goal Difference: –172
Total Points: 348

Overview
Sunderland's nine seasons in the Premier League have included three relegations, two

top-eight finishes, two of the worst seasons by any club side since 1992/93 and a host of unwanted Premier League records.

Their first season in the Premier League in 1996/97 ended with relegation as they finished in 19th place with 40 points, just one point adrift from safety. Despite the failure to survive, Sunderland were able to claim some surprise results against the teams that made up the top six that season: champions Manchester United (2-1 at home), 2nd-placed Newcastle (1-1 away) 3rd-placed Arsenal (1-0 at home), 4th-placed Liverpool (0-0 away), 5th-placed Aston Villa (1-0 at home) and 6th-placed Chelsea (3-0 at home).

Sunderland's second spell in the Premier League encompassed four seasons and, initially at least, was far more successful. The 1999/00 season saw the Black Cats - spearheaded by Kevin Phillips (who scored 30 Premier League goals that season to become the first and only English winner of the Golden Shoe, awarded to Europe's top goalscorer) - finish in 7th place with 58 points. This was Sunderland's highest top-flight finish since 1954/55. The Black Cats once again finished 7th in 2000/01, with 57 points, and at one point in mid-January they were as high as 2nd following a 2-0 win away at West Ham United. A run of just three victories from their final 15 league games saw Sunderland finish just four points outside the European qualification places.

2001/02 saw a highly inconsistent Sunderland side finish in 17th place with 40 points, four points clear of the relegation zone. This was followed up in 2002/03 by what was then the worst league performance by any team in the Premier League, as Sunderland ended the season rock bottom with just four victories and 19 points. Peter Reid parted company with Sunderland in October 2002, but his replacement Howard Wilkinson won just two league games (2-0 against Spurs and 2-1 versus Liverpool) before he was sacked and replaced by Mick McCarthy in March 2003. By that stage, relegation was inevitable and Sunderland ended the season losing 15 consecutive games, which is a Premier League record.

Sunderland gained promotion back to the Premier League for 2005/06, but the campaign got off to an awful start as they lost the first five games. This meant that the club had lost 20 consecutive Premier League games over two seasons (a Premier League record). Things would go from bad to worse that season. The Mackems must have thought they'd run over the world's entire population of black cats by the time the campaign was finished; they ended with just three league wins (just one at home - a Premier League record) and 29 defeats (a joint Premier League record).

Sunderland were absent from the Premier League for just one season, coming back up for the 2007/08 campaign with Roy Keane at the helm, and finishing in 15th place. The Irishman departed midway through the 2008/09 campaign, leaving Ricky Sbragia to lead them to a 16th-place finish with 36 points, just two points clear of the relegation zone. Steve Bruce was then named as Sunderland's third manager in as many years, and he secured a 13th-place finish in his first season in charge at the Stadium of Light.

As of the end of the 2009/10 campaign, Sunderland had the worst overall goal difference (−172) of any club that has competed in the Premier League since its inception.

Most Utilised Players

Sunderland have two players with 100% start ratios in the form of Paul Bracewell (signed for £50k; CTPP £132k) and Darren Bent (signed for £10m; CTPP £10m), but both have featured only during a single Premier League season (the 2010/11 campaign will be Bent's second with Sunderland). It is Kevin Phillips who has started the most Premier League games for Sunderland (139), giving him a start ratio of 91% following his £525k (£1.8m) arrival from Watford in 1997. Phillips scored 61 Premier League goals during the four seasons he spent with Sunderland in the top flight.

Least Utilised Players

Peter Reid signed John Oster in 1999 from Everton for £1m (£2.4m), but the player suffered a torrid time with the Black Cats, starting just seven Premier League games. He had loan spells with Barnsley, Grimsby (twice) and Leeds United between 2001 and 2005, before being released by Sunderland in 2005. Oster left the Black Cats with a 6% start ratio.

Managers

Year	£XI	£XI Rank	Points	Cost Per Point	Position League	Manager
1996/97	£10,410,540	20	40	£260,264	18	Peter Reid
1999/00	£23,968,182	17	58	£413,245	7	Peter Reid
2000/01	£31,875,119	13	57	£559,213	7	Peter Reid
2001/02	£26,216,892	16	40	£655,422	17	Peter Reid
2002/03	£26,718,540	14	19	£1,406,239	20	Reid/Wilkinson/McCarthy
Average	**£23,837,855**	**16**	**42.8**	**£658,876**	**13.8**	**Peter Reid**
2002/03	£26,718,540	14	19	£1,406,239	20	Reid/Wilkinson/McCarthy
2005/06	£9,014,820	19	15	£600,988	20	McCarthy/Kevin Ball
Average	**£17,866,680**	**16.5**	**17**	**£1,003,613**	**20**	**Mick McCarthy**
2007/08	£29,163,759	15	39	£747,789	15	Roy Keane
2008/09	£30,979,607	12	36	£860,545	16	Keane/Sbragia
Average	**£30,071,683**	**13.5**	**37.5**	**£804,167**	**15.5**	**Roy Keane**
2009/10	**£51,778,219**	**9**	**44**	**£1,176,778**	**13**	**Steve Bruce**

Top 5 Players Sold for a Profit

- Bridges – Bought for: £0 (trainee), Sold for: £5m (£11.8m) Profit of: £5m (£11.8m)
- Whitehead – Bought for: d150k (£273k), Sold for: £3m (£3m), Profit of: £2.85m (£2.73m)
- Phillips – Bought for: £525k (£1.8m), Sold for: £3.25m (£6.6m), Profit of: £2.7m (£4.8m)
- Leadbitter – Bought for: £0 (trainee), Sold for: £2.65m (£2.65m), Profit of: £2.65m (£2.65m)
- Collins – Bought for: d140k (£255k), Sold for: £2.75m (£2.75m), Profit of: £2.61m (£2.5m)

Top 20 CTPP Purchases

#	Player	CTPP	Original fee	Year transferred	% of poss starts
1	Flo T	£12,909,070	£8,000,000	2002/03	61%
2	Gordon C	£10,157,978	£9,000,000	2007/08	63%
3	Bent D	£10,000,000	£10,000,000	2009/10	100%
4	Schwarz S	£8,213,346	£3,500,000	1999/00	54%
5	Thome E	£8,009,440	£4,500,000	2000/01	38%
6	Turner M	£8,000,000	£8,000,000	2009/10	76%
7	Jones K (II)	£6,771,986	£6,000,000	2007/08	72%
8	Ferdinand A	£6,255,145	£8,000,000	2008/09	66%
9	Arca J	£6,229,564	£3,500,000	2000/01	49%
10	Richardson K (II)	£6,207,653	£5,500,000	2007/08	65%
11	Cattermole L	£6,000,000	£6,000,000	2009/10	50%
12	Reyna C	£5,897,979	£4,500,000	2001/02	37%
13	Kilbane K	£5,866,676	£2,500,000	1999/00	64%
14	Piper M	£5,647,718	£3,500,000	2002/03	21%
15	Chopra M	£5,643,321	£5,000,000	2007/08	29%
16	Stewart M (II)	£5,244,310	£3,250,000	2002/03	24%
17	Cana L	£5,000,000	£5,000,000	2009/10	76%
18	Wright S	£4,840,901	£3,000,000	2002/03	36%
19	Laslandes L	£4,718,383	£3,600,000	2001/02	13%
20	Reid A	£4,514,657	£4,000,000	2007/08	43%

Expert View

Jonathan Wilson (@jonawils)

Columnist for The Guardian and Sports Illustrated

Author of "Inverting The Pyramid" and "Sunderland: A Club Transformed".

The £XI results are fascinating for how closely they fit to the 'feel' of each season. So 1999/00 and 2000/01, in both of which Sunderland finished 7th, felt like huge overachievements, and sure enough they were 10 and six places above expected levels respectively. What's interesting then is that in 2001/02, when they slumped to 17th, although it felt like a great come down, it was only actually one place below expected – a sign of how Sunderland failed to keep up with the spending of others.

Then in 2007/08, the first season up under Roy Keane, there was a sense that 15th was about right – avoid relegation, consolidate – and it turns out that matches expectations exactly. The following year, though, as investment continued and Sunderland fell a place in the table, dissatisfaction set in, and sure enough they were four places lower than expected.

Looking at the Current Transfer Purchase Prices of the club's Premier League players, it's shaming that Tore André Flo (£12.9m) should be Sunderland's record signing – a disaster, even if he did come into the club at a difficult time. Craig

Gordon and Darren Bent have clearly proved themselves worth the money, but the eye-catching aspect of that table is how many good players Peter Reid picked up on the cheap. Steve Agnew, Jody Craddock, Gavin McCann, Allan Johnston, Thomas Sorensen, Paul Butler, Martin Scott, Chris Makin and Kevin Phillips were all excellent players bought for under £2m in today's prices. Reid's reputation is tainted by the savaging he received in Tom Bower's *"Broken Dreams"*, and clearly players like Milton Núñez and Carsten Fredgaard were errors, but early on his record is superb.

Swindon Town

Total Spend (Actual): £1.8m
Total Spend (CTPP): £11m
Average League Position: 22
Number of Managers: 1
Most Expensive Signings: Adrian Whitbread and Jan Åge Fjørtoft - £500k (CTPP £3m)
Best Value Signing: Adrian Whitbread
Worst Value Signing: Jan Åge Fjørtoft

Player Signings Breakdown (data correct up to end of January transfer window 2010)

• UK: 9 • EU: 1 • Rest of Europe: 1 • Rest of World: 0

Major Trophies Won Since Premier League Began: 0

Premier League Statistics (correct to the end of the 2009/10 season)

Seasons: 1	Played: 42	
Won: 5	Drawn: 15	Lost: 22
Goals Scored: 47	Goals Conceded: 100	Goal Difference: –53
Total Points: 30		

Overview
Swindon Town were promoted to England's top division for the one and only time in their history after they beat Leicester City in the 1993 play-off final. Manager Glenn Hoddle left to take over as Chelsea manager prior to the start of the 1993/94 Premier League season, and Swindon found life in the top flight difficult under Hoddle's replacement, John Gorman. They were relegated, finishing in 22nd place with 30 points.

It was a season of unwanted records for the Robins as they conceded 100 league goals, 45 of them at home. Both are still Premier League records, although they did occur during a 42–game season.

Managers

Year	£XI	£XI Rank	Points	Cost Per Point	Position League	Manager
1993/94	£9,710,377	22	30	£323,679	22	John Gorman

Top 10 CTPP Purchases

#	Player	CTPP	Original fee	Year transferred	% of poss starts
1	Whitbread A	£2,985,347	£500,000	1993/94	81%
2	Fjørtoft J	£2,985,347	£500,000	1993/94	62%
3	Scott K (I)	£1,791,208	£300,000	1993/94	52%
4	Mutch A	£1,492,674	£250,000	1993/94	64%
5	Taylor S (III)	£1,331,241	d200000	1991/92	100%
6	Nijholt L	£1,044,871	£175,000	1993/94	74%
7	MacLaren R	£998,431	D150000	1988–89	24%
8	Hazard M	£865,307	d130000	1990/91	17%
9	Kilcline B	£537,362	£90,000	1993/94	24%
10	Moncur J	£532,496	d80000	1991/92	98%

Expert View

Brian McDowell

Swindon Town season–ticket holder

It all seems so long ago. Perhaps because it was. Despite inflation, no player cost more than £3m in current money, and the £XI of the season was under £10m. This was never going to be a rags to riches story; it was rags to rags all the way.

But there was good football on show. Micky Hazard and John Moncur – we had some good ex-Spurs midfielders back then. We'd also had another – Glenn Hoddle – who had led us to promotion as player-manager, before making a swift exit. Even if he'd stayed, and not defected to Chelsea, we would probably have struggled. As it was, we were condemned from the start. John Gorman – another ex-Spur – took charge for the season. But Hoddle, at 36, hadn't just steered us from close to the third tier of English football to the top flight; he had also been our best player.

Still, we were belatedly where we wanted to be; where we were so close to being just three years earlier. Unlike some other clubs, Swindon Town undertook their financial misconduct just before the Premier League began: managed by

Ossie Ardiles (that's right, an ex-Spurs midfielder), the 1990 play-offs were won, but the club later admitted 36 charges of breaching league rules, 35 due to illegal payments made to players. Chairman Brian Hillier was given a six-month prison sentence and chief accountant Vince Farrar was put on probation. Swindon stayed in the old Second Division.

And after the wait? An early 5-0 defeat by Liverpool at home showed us that perhaps we didn't belong in the big time after all. But better to have been there – just briefly – than not at all.

Tottenham Hotspur

Total Spend (Actual): £411.1m
Total Spend (CTPP): £652.2m
Average League Position: 9.44
Number of Managers: 11
Most Expensive Signing: Les Ferdinand – £6m (CTPP £20.3m)
Best Value Signing: Teddy Sheringham
Worst Value Signing: Hélder Postiga

Player Signings Breakdown (data correct up to end of January transfer window 2010)

• UK: 50 • EU: 36 • Rest of Europe: 13 • Rest of World: 18

Major Trophies Won Since Premier League Began

League Cup: 2 (1998/99, 2007/08)

Premier League Statistics (correct to the end of the 2009/10 season)

Seasons: 18	Played: 696	
Won: 258	Drawn: 181	Lost:257
Goals Scored: 951	Goals Conceded: 933	Goal Difference: +18
Total Points: 955		

Overview
Tottenham Hotspur were founding members of the Premier League in 1992 and, as of the end of the 2009/10 campaign, they have conceded 933 Premier League goals, more

than any other side. The 1992/93 season saw a Tottenham side led by Doug Livermore finish in 8th place, despite some heavy defeats at the hands of Leeds United (5–0), QPR (4–1), Manchester United (4–1), Sheffield United (6–0) and Liverpool (6–2). Spurs also reached the FA Cup semi-finals that season, losing 1–0 to Arsenal. Ossie Ardiles was appointed manager in 1993, but an awful sequence that saw Tottenham win just two from 23 league games – including seven consecutive defeats that spanned all of January and February – resulted in a 15th-place finish, just three points above the drop zone.

In what would become a recurring theme for Spurs – changing managers – Gerry Francis replaced Ardiles in November 1994. The North London club had an inconsistent season, never stringing more than three league wins together but reaching the semi-finals of the FA Cup – where they lost 4–1 to Everton – and finishing in 7th place.

In a rarity for a Spurs manager, Francis then had two full seasons, which produced an 8th-place finish in 1995/96 and a 10th-place finish in 1996/97. An inconsistent start to 1997/98 saw Francis and Spurs part company, with Christian Gross named as his replacement in November 1997. Spurs remained inconsistent and could finish only 14th, just four points clear of the relegation zone. Gross never completed a full season with Spurs; former Arsenal manager George Graham was named his successor in October 1998. Tottenham ended the Premier League season in 11th place, but they had more success in the cups. They reached the semi-finals of the FA Cup (losing 2–0 to Newcastle) and went one better by reaching the League Cup Final, which they won 1–0 against Leicester. Spurs couldn't build on this success, however, and finished 1999/00 in 10th place. Graham was sacked in March 2001, as new chairman Daniel Levy appointed erstwhile hero Glenn Hoddle to the White Hart Lane hot seat. Spurs lost their FA Cup semi-final to Arsenal (2–1) and finished 2000/01 in 12th place – their fifth consecutive mid-table finish.

Hoddle's Spurs then finished 2001/02 in 9th, reaching the League Cup final (losing to Blackburn 2–1) along the way, which was followed by a 10th-place finish in 2002/03. Hoddle was sacked early in 2003/04 as Spurs lost four of their opening six games. David Pleat was named as Hoddle's successor until the end of the season, but Spurs could finish only 14th.

Former French national coach Jacques Santini was named as Tottenham's new manager, but he resigned in November 2004 after less than five months in the job. His assistant and replacement Martin Jol would immediately improve Spurs' league form. He won five consecutive league games – the club's best winning sequence since 1992/93 – to be named December Manager of the Month. Spurs ended 2004/05 in 9th place, and Jol would lead them to successive 5th-place finishes in 2005/06 and 2006/07 – their highest league placing since coming 3rd in 1989/90. Spurs also reached the quarter-finals of the FA Cup and Uefa Cup, losing to Chelsea (following a replay) and Seville respectively, as well as the semi-final of the League Cup, where they lost to Arsenal, in 2006/07.

Despite attaining Tottenham's highest league placing for almost 20 years, Jol was sacked in October 2007 and was replaced by the man who masterminded Seville's defeat of Spurs in the previous season's Uefa Cup – Juande Ramos. Spurs lifted the League Cup, beating Chelsea 2–1 after extra time, but they once again slipped down into mid-table obscurity in the league, finishing in 11th place. A sequence of six defeats and two draws from Tottenham's opening eight league games of the 2008/09 campaign resulted in Ramos being sacked, with Harry Redknapp named as his successor in October 2008. Spurs recovered from the poor start to finish the season in 8th place and they reached their fourth League Cup final in 10 seasons, only to lose to Manchester United on penalties. The 2009/10 campaign saw Spurs reach their highest points total since 1986/87 as they finished in 4th place with 70 points, earning them a place in the Champions League Third Qualifying Round for the first time.

Most Utilised Players
Only Darren Anderton (273; 58% start ratio) has started more Premier League games for Spurs than Teddy Sheringham, although Sheringham has a far superior start ratio of 83%. Doug Livermore signed Sheringham for £2.1m (£14m) very early in the 1992/93 season, and it would prove to be a shrewd signing as the striker scored 21 Premier League goals for Spurs (adding to the goal he scored for Nottingham Forest on the opening day of the campaign), making him the league's top scorer that season. Sheringham spent five seasons with Spurs, scoring 69 Premier League goals before joining Manchester United in July 1997 for £3.5m (£11.9m).

Gerry Francis signed French winger David Ginola for £2.5m (£8.5m) from Newcastle United in July 1997, and he produced his best form while playing for Spurs, winning both the PFA Players' Player of the Year and the Football Writers' Association Footballer of the Year awards in 1998/99. Ginola scored 13 league goals in the three seasons he spent with Spurs and started 100 league games (88%).

Least Utilised Players
Glenn Hoddle signed Portuguese striker Hélder Postiga from FC Porto in July 2003 for £6.25m (£12.7m). Despite making a name for himself in Portugal under then Porto manager José Mourinho, Postiga started just nine Premier League games for Spurs (24%), scoring one league goal, before returning to Porto after just one season in England.

Algerian midfielder Moussa Saïb joined George Graham's Tottenham in 1998 for £2.3m (£7.8m) from Spanish side Valencia. Although Saïb picked up a League Cup winner's medal in 1999, he started just three Premier League games (4%), scoring once, before he joined Saudi Arabian side Al-Nassr in 2000.

Managers

Year	£XI	£XI Rank	Points	Cost Per Point	Position League	Manager
1992/93	£47,929,439	6	59	£812,363	8	Doug Livermore
1993/94	£45,121,429	10	45	£1,002,698	15	Ossie Ardiles
1994/95	£53,964,209	9	62	£870,390	7	Ardiles/Gerry Francis
Average	**£49,542,819**	**9.5**	**53.5**	**£936,544**	**11**	**Ossie Ardiles**
1994/95	£53,964,209	9	62	£870,390	7	Ardiles/Gerry Francis
1995/96	£53,312,942	8	61	£873,983	8	Gerry Francis
1996/97	£50,013,727	10	46	£1,087,255	10	Gerry Francis
1997/98	£53,184,324	9	44	£1,208,735	14	Francis/Christian Gross
Average	**£52,618,801**	**9**	**53.3**	**£1,010,091**	**9.75**	**Gerry Francis**
1997/98	£53,184,324	9	44	£1,208,735	14	Francis/Christian Gross
1998/99	£63,994,422	6	47	£1,361,583	11	Gross/Graham
Average	**£58,589,373**	**7.5**	**45.5**	**£1,285,159**	**12.5**	**Christian Gross**
1998/99	£63,994,422	6	47	£1,361,583	11	Gross/Graham
1999/00	£61,512,490	6	53	£1,160,613	10	George Graham
2000/01	£66,144,462	8	49	£1,349,887	12	Graham/Glenn Hoddle
Average	**£63,883,791**	**6.7**	**49.7**	**£1,290,694**	**11**	**George Graham**
2000/01	£66,144,462	8	49	£1,349,887	12	Graham/Glenn Hoddle
2001/02	£64,290,271	7	50	£1,285,805	9	Glenn Hoddle
2002/03	£42,584,548	9	50	£851,691	10	Glenn Hoddle
2003/04	£43,315,868	8	45	£962,575	14	Hoddle/David Pleat
Average	**£54,083,787**	**8**	**48.5**	**£1,112,490**	**11.25**	**Glenn Hoddle**
2004/05	£42,241,107	6	52	£812,329	9	Jacques Santini/Jol
2005/06	£46,594,380	6	65	£716,837	5	Martin Jol
2006/07	£75,417,340	4	60	£1,256,956	5	Martin Jol
2007/08	£86,504,982	4	46	£1,880,543	11	Jol/Juande Ramos
Average	**£62,689,452**	**5.0**	**55.8**	**£1,166,666**	**8**	**Martin Jol**
2007/08	£86,504,982	4	46	£1,880,543	11	Jol/Juande Ramos
2008/09	£93,623,149	4	51	£1,835,748	8	Ramos/Redknapp
Average	**£90,064,066**	**4**	**48.5**	**£1,858,146**	**9.5**	**Juande Ramos**
2008/09	£93,623,149	4	51	£1,835,748	8	Ramos/Redknapp
2009/10	£78,370,565	5	70	£1,119,580	4	Harry Redknapp
Average	**£85,996,857**	**4.5**	**60.5**	**£1,477,664**	**6**	**Harry Redknapp**

Top 5 Players Sold for a Profit

- Berbatov – Bought for: £10.9m (£19m), Sold for: £30.5m (£23.9m), Profit of: £19.6m (£4.9m)
- Carrick – Bought for: £3m (£5.5m), Sold for: £18.6m (£32.4m) Profit of: £15.6m (£26.9m)
- Robbie Keane – Bought for: £7m (£11.3m), Sold for: £19m (£14.9m), Profit of: £12m (£3.6m)
- Barmby – Bought for: £0 (trainee), Sold for: £5.25m (£13.9m), Profit of: £5.25m (£13.9m)
- Tainio – Bought for: £0 (free transfer), Sold for: £3.5m (£2.8m), Profit of: £3.5m (£2.8m)

Top 20 CTPP Purchases

#	Player	CTPP	Original fee	Year transferred	% of poss starts
1	Ferdinand L	£20,256,473	£6,000,000	1997/98	43%
2	Rebrov S	£19,578,631	£11,000,000	2000/01	49%
3	Berbatov D	£18,924,870	£10,890,000	2006/07	55%
4	Bent D	£17,494,296	£15,500,000	2007/08	42%
5	Durie G	£14,643,654	D2200000	1992/93	32%
6	Zokora D	£14,250,132	£8,200,000	2006/07	66%
7	Defoe J	£14,146,302	£7,000,000	2003/04	47%
8	Sheringham T	£13,978,033	£2,100,000	1992/93	83%
9	Anderton D	£13,312,412	D2000000	1992/93	58%
10	Bentley D	£13,292,183	£17,000,000	2008/09	41%
11	Modrić L	£13,135,805	£16,800,000	2008/09	72%
12	Jenas J	£12,773,273	£7,000,000	2005/06	63%
13	Postiga H	£12,630,626	£6,250,000	2003/04	24%
14	Armstrong C (I)	£11,832,831	£4,500,000	1995/96	51%
15	Dozzell J	£11,344,319	£1,900,000	1993/94	43%
16	Keane R (II)	£11,295,436	£7,000,000	2002/03	62%
17	Fox R	£11,043,976	£4,200,000	1995/96	50%
18	Popescu G	£10,986,927	£2,900,000	1994/95	55%
19	Pavlyuchenko R	£10,946,504	£14,000,000	2008/09	36%
20	Richards D	£10,616,362	£8,100,000	2001/02	64%

Expert View

Ewan Roberts (@EwanRoberts)

"One In The Hole" www.oneinthehole.wordpress.com

The inaugural Premier League season was a microcosm of what Spurs fans could come to expect: the sale of star players (Gary Lineker and Paul Gascoigne in the off-season), tumultuous relations between chairman and manager (the sacking of Peter Shreeves, the dismissal of Chief Executive Terry Venables), the capture of highly rated players – Teddy Sheringham from Nottingham Forest for £2.1m (£13.9m in today's money) – and, often against better judgment, hope. This could be our year.

Invariably, barring two League Cups and a 4th-place finish last season, it has never been our year. But not for want of trying – few teams have invested so heavily, but reaped as little reward. Often the gates of White Hart Lane have seemed more like revolving doors, but big spending has generally always been facilitated by the sale of star players – a two steps back, one step forward policy that has continually hampered performance.

After narrowly missing out on a place in Europe in the 1994/95 season,

FWA Footballer of the Year Jürgen Klinsmann left for Bayern Munich and was replaced by the mediocre Chris Armstrong (£4.5m/£11.8m CTPP), with Nick Barmby replaced by Ruel Fox (£4.2m/£11m), a player whose ability defied his 106 league appearances. It took 11 years before we bettered our 7th-place finish in 1994/95 – a run that saw us become the very definition of mid-table mediocrity.

The Tottenham hierarchy's inability to successfully replace our best players was still evident a decade later – a decade, incidentally, in which we splashed out on flops such as Serhiy Rebrov (£11m/£19.5m), Hélder Postiga (£6.25m/£12.6m) and Ramon Vega (£3.75m/£9.9m). In 2005/06, Michael Carrick left for Manchester United to be replaced by the disappointing Didier Zokora (£8.2m/£14.25m). While money was reinvested in the squad and our ranks bolstered, the quality within it was diluted. Two years later, the formidable strike partnership of Dimitar Berbatov and Robbie Keane left for Manchester United and Liverpool respectively. Spurs' frontline in 2008/09 thus consisted of Frazier Campbell, Darren Bent and Roman Pavlyuchenko. We earned two points from our opening eight games.

Harry Redknapp, our saviour from that season, was the 10th Spurs manager across the Premier League's 18 seasons. As with many of the managers before him, Redknapp initially froze out several of the misguided signings from the previous regimes (David Bentley, Adel Taarabt, Darren Bent) and sought to forge his own squad (Jermain Defoe, Wilson Palacios) – a process that had until that time contributed to a constant state of rebuilding and instability.

Interestingly, last year's 4th-place finish came off the back of transfer windows in which relatively little was spent, and few players were sold – a rarity indeed. But Redknapp still had a massive and valuable squad at his disposal which he utilised to great effect – it was Younes Kaboul (a player considered a failing of the ill-fated Director of Football system) that provided the cross that brought Champions League football to White Hart Lane. Finally, selling good players actually helped Spurs prosper: without the money raised from selling Carrick and Berbatov, the subsequent success might never have followed.

Watford

Total Spend (Actual): £10.9m
Total Spend (CTPP): £21.3m
Average League Position: 20
Number of Managers: 2
Most Expensive Signing: Heiðar Helguson – £1.65m (CTPP £3.6m)
Best Value Signing: Steve Palmer
Worst Value Signing: Tamás Priskin

Player Signings Breakdown (data correct up to end of January transfer window 2010)

• UK: 11 • EU: 7 • Rest of Europe: 4 • Rest of World: 2

Major Trophies Won Since Premier League Began: 0

Premier League Statistics (correct to the end of the 2009/10 season)

Seasons: 2	Played: 76	
Won: 11	Drawn: 19	Lost:46
Goals Scored: 64	Goals Conceded: 136	Goal Difference: –72
Total Points: 52		

Overview

Watford's first taste of life in the Premier League in 1999/00 ended in the same fashion as when they were last in England's top division in 1987/88: a 20th-place finish with 24 points and relegation. Although the Hornets won only six Premier League games all season, they did record a surprise 1–0 win over Liverpool at Anfield on August 14, which was followed by a 1–0 victory over Chelsea at Vicarage Road the following month. Watford were unable to build on such promising results and would win just three out of their next 30 Premier League games. Watford also experienced third-round exits in both the FA Cup and League Cup that season.

Under Aidy Boothroyd, Watford's second season in the Premier League in 2006/07 produced a similar fate: 20th place and relegation. Despite winning one fewer game than in 1999/00, Watford finished the season with four more points (28), but the Hornets still finished 10 points adrift from safety. The Hertfordshire club suffered an early fourth-round exit in the League Cup to Newcastle United but defied all the odds and reached the semi-finals of the FA Cup, where they lost 4–1 to Manchester United.

Most Utilised Players
Steve Palmer is the only Watford player that can boast a 100% start ratio in the Premier

League, although he participated in only one of the two seasons the Hornets have spent in the Premier League. Signed from Ipswich Town in 1995 for £135k (£355k), Palmer started all 38 Premier League games for Watford during 1999/00 and was instrumental in shutting out both Liverpool and Chelsea that season.

Least Utilised Players

Tamás Priskin was signed for £1m (£1.8m) in August 2006 from Hungarian side Győri ETO. Despite setting up Watford's first goal of the 2006/07 Premier League season, he was unable to hold down a place in the side and ended the campaign with just seven Premier League starts, giving him a start ratio of 18%.

Managers

Year	£XI	£XI Rank	Points	Cost Per Point	Position League	Manager
1999/00	£4,569,906	20	24	£190,413	20	Graham Taylor
2006/07	£6,665,000	19	28	£238,036	20	Adrian Boothroyd

Top 10 CTPP Purchases

#	Player	CTPP	Original fee	Year transferred	% of poss starts
1	Helguson H	£3,520,006	£1,500,000	1999/00	37%
2	Shittu D	£2,780,513	£1,600,000	2006/07	71%
3	Francis D	£2,606,731	£1,500,000	2006/07	74%
4	Wooter N	£2,229,337	£950,000	1999/00	42%
5	Williams G (II)	£1,737,821	£1,000,000	2006/07	5%
6	Priskin T	£1,737,821	£1,000,000	2006/07	18%
7	Cox N	£1,173,335	£500,000	1999/00	53%
8	Williamson L	£1,042,693	£600,000	2006/07	11%
9	King M	£912,377	d500000	2005/06	32%
10	Hoskins W	£868,910	£500,000	2006/07	11%

Expert View

Matt Rowson

http://bhappy.wordpress.com

Each of Watford's seasons in the top flight resulted in a 20th-place finish; as such, neither can be deemed 'successful' by the most obvious metric. However, both need to be evaluated in the context of two unexpected promotion campaigns achieved with relatively modest outlay on the back of a little good luck with injuries. Neither squad was equipped for Premier League football; the Sq£ listed in each case rate the two groups of players amongst the cheapest seven (out of 366) assembled in the Premier League's history. However, the squads that actually earned promotion, including post-promotion departures, would be valued at roughly £2.5m (1999/2000) and £4m (2006/07) in terms of CTPP.

These figures illustrate the quandary facing smaller clubs promoted via the play-offs; often with demonstrably inferior squads to their new opponents, already a month behind their fellow new boys, how do they play it? Do they gamble, and risk turning the financial boon of promotion into a millstone with unsustainable contracts if relegated, or do they go for prudence, and with it the likely hammerings, accusations of lack of ambition and nagging suspicion of a missed opportunity?

Above all, who do they sign? Established top-flight players will generally have better options, so they are often recruiting from relegated sides or from the top of the Championship in August; by January, if struggling, even this set of candidates will consider themselves to have preferable alternatives. Other than Damien Francis (£2.6m CTPP) and Gareth Williams (£1.7m), both of whose careers were ultimately wrecked by injury, the most obvious 'wastes of money' amongst Watford's relatively modest list were desperate gambles in January 2007. Will Hoskins (£900k) and Steve Kabba (£900k) never justified their fees, although both were understandable punts in the context of Marlon King's injury and Ashley Young's sale. In the case of each season, the more dramatic financial idiocy came post-relegation back in the second tier, chasing another bite of the cherry.

Of the other individuals near the top of the CTPP Purchases list, all proved decent value by recouping much or in excess of their original cost and/or, as in the case of Helguson, by defiantly and persistently demonstrating their value on the pitch; £1.5m quickly felt like good value at the time, £3.5m in today's money no less so. The best bargains, of course, are those marked 'trainee', which you'll find next to 30% of the names in Watford's Premier League roster – a strategy that the Hornets pursue profitably to this day.

West Bromwich Albion

Total Spend (Actual): £52.6m
Total Spend (CTPP): £71.7m
Average League Position: 18.75
Number of Managers: 3
Most Expensive Signing: Robert Earnshaw – £3.6m (CTPP £6.6m)
Best Value Signing: Jonathan Greening
Worst Value Signing: Lee Chaplow

Player Signings Breakdown (data correct up to end of January transfer window 2010)

• UK: 22 • EU: 12 • Rest of Europe: 2 • Rest of World: 5

Major Trophies Won Since Premier League Began: 0

Premier League Statistics (correct to the end of the 2009/10 season)

Seasons: 4	Played: 152	
Won: 27	Drawn: 41	Lost:84
Goals Scored: 132	Goals Conceded: 251	Goal Difference: –119
Total Points: 122		

Overview

West Bromwich Albion brought to an end an absence of 16 seasons when they won promotion back to England's top division at the end of 2001/02. The Baggies have had three different spells in the Premier League and been relegated on all three occasions (2002/03, 2005/06 and 2008/09). The start of the 2002/03 Premier League season saw West Brom face three of the top five from the previous campaign – Manchester United (3rd), Leeds United (5th) and Arsenal (1st) – in their opening three games, and Gary Megson's men lost all three. Despite winning their next three games (all 1–0) following the tough start, the Baggies gained maximum points from just three out of their remaining 32 league games, ending the season with 26 points – a mammoth 18 points adrift from safety.

West Brom were soon promoted back to the Premier League for the start of 2004/05, when a dreadful start to the season saw them fail to win any of their opening seven league games, and pick up maximum points from just one of their first 23 fixtures (during this period, Gary Megson was sacked to be replaced by Bryan Robson). Despite this awful sequence of results, Albion produced an unlikely escape on the final day of the season, finishing one point ahead of 18th–placed Crystal Palace (indeed, just one point separated 20th and 17th. The Baggies thus became the first team since the Premier League began to survive after being bottom at Christmas.

Bryan Robson's first full season in charge of West Brom (2005/06) saw the club unable to consolidate their position in the Premier League following their great escape of the previous campaign. Once again, the Baggies made a poor start to the season, winning just two of their opening 12 league games (including a 2–1 victory over Arsenal at The Hawthorns), and ending the season as they began, without winning any of their final 13 games. They finished in 19th place with 30 points, eight points away from safety.

It would take West Brom another two seasons before they returned to the Premier League, this time under the guidance of Tony Mowbray, but the 2008/09 campaign would follow a similar pattern for the Baggies: a fight for survival. After a reasonable start that saw them claim three wins and a draw from their opening seven league games, they failed to pick up maximum points from any of their next 10 games, which resulted in the Baggies falling into the relegation zone where they would stay for the remainder of the season.

Most Utilised Players

Left-sided midfielder Jonathan Greening joined the Baggies from Middlesbrough in the summer of 2004 for £1.25m (£2.3m), quickly establishing himself as an integral part of the West Brom side that avoided relegation in 2004/05. Greening has made the most starts for West Brom in the Premier League era. His 102 appearances over three seasons give him an 89% start ratio. Greening's consistent performances saw him named club captain in 2007, but he handed in a transfer request after suffering his second relegation with the Baggies in 2009. He was eventually sold to Fulham in 2010 following a season-long loan spell.

Least Utilised Players

Tony Mowbray signed Slovakian international defender Marek Čech for £2m (£1.6m) from Portuguese giants FC Porto in July 2008, to add competition at left-back with Paul Robinson. Čech started just three Premier League games (8%) during the Baggies' relegation season of 2008/09. It took the departure of both Mowbray and Robinson before Čech established himself in the West Brom side during 2009/10, which saw the Midlanders win promotion back to the Premier League under Roberto Di Matteo.

Managers

Year	£XI	£XI Rank	Points	Cost Per Point	Position League	Manager
2002/03	£16,110,691	19	26	£619,642	19	Gary Megson
2004/05	£16,188,399	16	34	£476,129	17	Megson/Robson
Average	**£16,149,545**	**17.5**	**30**	**£547,886**	**18**	**Gary Megson**
2004/05	£16,188,399	16	34	£476,129	17	Megson/Robson
2005/06	£19,337,852	15	30	£644,595	19	Bryan Robson
Average	**£17,763,126**	**15.5**	**32**	**£560,362**	**18**	**Bryan Robson**
2008/09	£16,929,210	18	32	£529,038	20	**Tony Mowbray**

Top 10 CTPP Purchases

#	Player	CTPP	Original fee	Year transferred	% of poss starts
1	Earnshaw R	£6,549,238	£3,600,000	2004/05	29%
2	Ellington N	£5,474,260	£3,000,000	2005/06	39%
3	Davies C	£5,474,260	£3,000,000	2005/06	87%
4	Albrechtsen M	£4,911,928	£2,700,000	2004/05	61%
5	Hughes L	£4,034,084	£2,500,000	2002/03	37%
6	Valero B	£3,674,898	£4,700,000	2008/09	71%
7	Koumas J	£3,630,675	£2,250,000	2002/03	42%
8	Roberts J	£3,559,751	d2000000	2000/01	82%
9	Brunt C	£3,385,993	d3000000	2007/08	74%
10	Barnett L	£2,821,661	d2500000	2007/08	26%

We're told there is a correlation between spending and achievement when it comes to the Premier League. On that basis, you could say that Albion have overachieved in most of their previous Premier League campaigns. Each time, until now, they've had the lowest wage bill. They've finished bottom just once. But in terms of the expense of the team, Albion have never finished far from expectations: 19th (£XI rank) resulted in 19th place; 16th and 17th (£XI rank) resulted in 15th and 19th in the table; and in 2008/09, 18th (£XI) resulted in 20th.

The promotion summer of 2002 wasn't a pleasant one at The Hawthorns. The departure of chairman Paul Thompson following his fall-out with Gary Megson brought unnecessary instability when the club needed it least. New chairman Jeremy Peace effectively ripped up the player bonus scheme introduced by his predecessor – which had been £5,000 for a first-team appearance, £7,500 for each point and £15,000 for a victory.

Peace maintained this was the road to ruin and broke the news during Albion's pre-season tour of Devon. Players revolted, holding an impromptu press conference in the car park of their Exeter hotel where a senior player read out the statement, which included: "For winning promotion an Albion player received an average of £4,000 in bonuses. At our West Midland rivals Birmingham, each player received an average of £35,000 and it's well known Wolves players would have received between £50,000 and £100,000 had we not stopped them getting promoted ... It is clear the club is now offering us First Division basic pay with First Division bonuses. This is the attitude of a First Division club."

Strike action was tenuously mentioned, but common sense prevailed and they got on with it. Jason Koumas was the record signing at £2.25m (£3.6m) for all of 24 hours, with Lee Hughes (£4m) returning to the club for £250,000 above that. A total of £8.1m on six players with only one loan, Ife Udeze, being brought in during the inaugural January transfer window. Albion were relegated. The wage bill rose steadily until the 2004/05 season when Albion started their second top-flight campaign.

The Baggies have, traditionally, adopted a 'flex-down policy' on Premier League wages – meaning that all players take a drop in pay in the event of relegation. The one exception to this norm was Kanu, who arrived on a free transfer in summer 2004. On a basic wage of £16k per week, the Nigerian's wages rose to way over £20k based on various bonuses and bolt-ons. Coincidentally, or not, Albion stayed up in 2004/05, for the only time. Once again they had the lowest wage bill, thanks in the main to Norwich's spending during the campaign; however, the £XI correctly suggests that Albion should have avoided the drop.

Survival gave Bryan Robson an unprecedented transfer kitty. Nathan Ellington and Curtis Davies each cost £3m (£5.5m), with both players eventually leaving for a profit (Ellington just under £4m, Davies for £11m). Kanu exercised his get-out clause, saving Albion the hassle of paying Premier League wages for a Championship player and potential resentment among the other players who had all 'flexed down' with their salaries. Albion were relegated with a wage bill of around £11m, but their highest £XI ranking, at 15th.

Tony Mowbray went for a bold policy of his own – young players, on higher transfer fees but lower wages. By now, Luke Moore was the highest earner at just under £22k a week. Mowbray was to spend just shy of £15m – although that was partly balanced by the sale of Davies – with Borja Valero, at £4.7m, becoming Albion's record signing. Significantly, Borja, who came from Real Mallorca, was on relatively low wages. Again only players willing to 'flex down' would be signed. Again, Albion were relegated in 20th. For once, the team with the lowest wage bill finished lowest in the top flight. The £XI was also consistent with relegation.

The yo-yo club bounced back up in 2010 under Roberto Di Matteo. This time the policy was altered. Low transfer fees, competitive wages. Albion would be willing to bring in Bosmans or players on lower transfer fees but pay more in salaries. The Baggies have not disclosed any fees this summer but their spending is understood to be in the region of £7m – with their wage bill being above Blackpool. For once, Albion are not the lowest payers.

West Ham United

Total Spend (Actual): £169.9m
Total Spend (CTPP): £318.1m
Average League Position: 11.53
Number of Managers: 8
Most Expensive Signing: Matthew Upson – £7.5m (CTPP £13.1m)
Best Value Signing: Robert Green
Worst Value Signing: Marco Boogers

Player Signings Breakdown (data correct up to end of January transfer window 2010)

• UK: 61 • EU: 24 • Rest of Europe: 9 • Rest of World: 22

Major Trophies Won Since Premier League Began: 0

Premier League Statistics (correct to the end of the 2009/10 season)

Seasons: 15   Played: 578
Won: 195   Drawn: 146   Lost:237
Goals Scored: 680   Goals Conceded: 810   Goal Difference: –130
Total Points: 731

Overview

West Ham missed the start of the Premier League courtesy of being relegated in 1992, but the Hammers would make a swift return to the top flight, finishing 1993/94 in 13th place under Billy Bonds. The board felt a change was needed so Bonds' assistant Harry Redknapp was promoted to the role of manager. Redknapp's Hammers finished 1994/95 in 14th place, the following campaign in 10th place and 1996/97 back in 14th.

West Ham's fortunes improved the following season, as highly promising youth players such as Frank Lampard and Rio Ferdinand began to make a name for themselves; helping the Hammers to finish in 8th place and reach the quarter-finals of the FA Cup. The 1998/99 season saw West Ham attain their highest league placing since coming 3rd in 1985/86, as they finished in 5th place. By this stage, more products of West Ham's youth system – such as Joe Cole and Michael Carrick – were beginning to break into the first team, but 8th in 1999/00 was followed by 15th in 2000/01. Redknapp was due to sign a new contract at Upton Park but, following some ill-advised comments he made to a fanzine, he was sacked with just one game remaining at the end of 2000/01.

(Despite continuing to deny taking illegal payments, Redknapp's transfer dealings at West Ham were called into question in Tom Bower's book "Broken Dreams – Vanity, Greed and the Souring of British Football", while his later dealings as manager at Portsmouth were put under the microscope – and on hidden camera – on the BBC's long-running investigative show, "Panorama".)

Glenn Roeder stepped up to replace Redknapp and, on the back of some big-name and big-money signings, the Hammers finished 2001/02 in 7th place. West Ham struggled in 2002/03 and finished the campaign in 18th place. Roeder left his post in April 2003 after he was diagnosed with a brain tumour. Trevor Brooking took over for the remainder of the season, but he couldn't prevent West Ham's relegation.

The Hammers returned to the Premier League in 2005/06 under Alan Pardew, finishing the season in 9th place with an FA Cup Final (their first since 1980) against Liverpool to come. Unfortunately for the Hammers, they lost 3-1 on penalties after an entertaining game finished 3-3 in extra time. The 2006/07 season saw new owners take over the club, and a poor run of form resulted in the dismissal of Pardew in December 2006.

Alan Curbishley was named his successor, but the Hammers continued to struggle until the final weeks of the season; it took a sequence of seven wins from the final nine games, including away victories over Arsenal (1-0), and Manchester United (1-0) on the last day of the season, to see West Ham retain their Premier League status - in 15th, three points clear of the drop zone. Curbishley led the East Enders to a 10th-place finish in 2007/08, but a disagreement with the board amidst claims they had sold players behind his back resulted in the boss resigning in September 2008. Gianfranco Zola became West Ham's first overseas manager when he replaced Curbishley, and he led the Hammers to a 9th-place finish, despite being just one place above the relegation zone on Boxing Day. The Hammers struggled in 2009/10 as they finished in 17th place with 35 points - five points clear of the relegation places. Zola was sacked at the end of the season, with Avram Grant named as his successor in June 2010.

Most Utilised Players
Robert Green (signed by Alan Pardew) has the highest start ratio (92%) for West Ham in the Premier League, having started 140 Premier League games for the Hammers since his £2m (£3.5m) move from Norwich City in August 2006. Green started all 38 Premier League games in 2007/08, 2008/09 and 2009/10.

Trevor Sinclair currently holds the record for most Premier League starts for West Ham, having been in the side at kick off 175 times during his five-year spell with the club. Harry Redknapp signed Sinclair from QPR for £2.3m (£7.8m) in January 1998, and only Paolo Di Canio (48) has scored more Premier League goals for the club.

Least Utilised Players
Redknapp also signed the aptly named Marco Boogers in July 1995 from Dutch side Sparta Rotterdam for £1m (£2.7m). It would turn out to be one of Redknapp's worst pieces of business in the transfer market, as Boogers failed to start a single game (0%) before he returned to Holland in 1996. Another one of Harry Redknapp's signings figures prominently in the form of Gary Charles, who joined West Ham for £1.2m (£2.9m) in October 1999 following an unsuccessful spell with Portuguese side Benfica. Charles suffered with alcohol abuse during his time with the Hammers, and spent the majority of his time battling injuries. He started just two Premier League games (3%) for West Ham before his career came to an end in 2002.

Managers

Year	£XI	£XI Rank	Points	Cost Per Point	Position League	Manager
1993/94	£20,240,743	14	52	£389,245	13	Billy Bonds
1994/95	£26,479,505	14	50	£529,590	14	Harry Redknapp
1995/96	£25,466,868	15	51	£499,350	10	Harry Redknapp
1996/97	£31,555,340	14	42	£751,318	14	Harry Redknapp
1997/98	£36,624,199	12	56	£654,004	8	Harry Redknapp
1998/99	£36,590,883	13	57	£641,945	5	Harry Redknapp
1999/00	£35,937,087	13	55	£653,402	9	Harry Redknapp
2000/01	£25,539,885	15	42	£608,093	15	Harry Redknapp
Average	£31,170,538	13.7	50.4	£619,672	10.7	Harry Redknapp

Year	£XI	£XI Rank	Points	Cost Per Point	Position League	Manager
2001/02	£39,917,617	10	53	£753,163	7	Glenn Roeder
2002/03	£33,210,297	13	42	£790,721	18	Roeder/Brooking
Average	**£36,563,957**	**11.5**	**47.5**	**£771,942**	**12.5**	**Glenn Roeder**
2005/06	£18,390,112	16	55	£334,366	9	Alan Pardew
2006/07	£18,590,693	16	41	£453,432	15	Pardew/Curbishley
Average	**£18,490,402.50**	**16**	**48**	**£393,899**	**12**	**Alan Pardew**
2006/07	£18,590,693	16	41	£453,432	15	Pardew/Curbishley
2007/08	£39,481,513	9	49	£805,745	10	Alan Curbishley
2008/09	£43,121,938	10	51	£845,528	9	Curbishley/Zola
Average	**£33,731,381**	**11.7**	**47**	**£701,568**	**11.3**	**Alan Curbishley**
2008/09	£43,121,938	10	51	£845,528	9	Curbishley/Zola
2009/10	£37,948,146	10	35	£1,084,233	17	Gianfranco Zola
Average	**£40,535,042**	**10**	**43**	**£964,880**	**13**	**Gianfranco Zola**

Top 5 Players Sold for a Profit

• Rio Ferdinand – Bought for: £0 (trainee), Sold for: £18m (£32.1m), Profit of: £18m (£32.1m)
• Lampard – Bought for: £0 (trainee), Sold for: £11m (£14.5m), Profit of: £11m (£14.5m)
• Anton Ferdinand – Bought for: £0 (trainee), Sold for: £8m (£6.3m) Profit of: £8m (£6.3m)
• Defoe – Bought for: £0 (trainee), Sold for: £7m (£14.2m), Profit of: £7m (£14.2m)
• Reo Coker – Bought for: d575k (£1.1m), Sold for: £8.5m (£9.6m), Profit of: £7.925m (£8.5m)

Top 20 CTPP Purchases

#	Player	CTPP	Original fee	Year transferred	% of poss starts
1	Upson M	£13,033,657	£7,500,000	2006/07	66%
2	Ashton D	£12,773,273	£7,000,000	2005/06	29%
3	Foé M	£10,288,242	£4,200,000	1998/99	50%
4	Dicks J	£9,471,489	£2,500,000	1994/95	56%
5	Kanouté F	£9,386,681	£4,000,000	1999/00	52%
6	Boa Morte L	£8,689,105	£5,000,000	2006/07	26%
7	Hartson J	£8,465,716	£3,200,000	1996/97	52%
8	Bellamy C	£8,464,982	£7,500,000	2007/08	26%
9	Parker S	£7,900,650	£7,000,000	2007/08	66%
10	Sinclair T	£7,764,981	£2,300,000	1997/98	77%
11	Wanchope P	£7,626,679	£3,250,000	1999/00	87%
12	Řepka T	£7,208,641	£5,500,000	2001/02	72%
13	Nsereko S	£7,037,038	£9,000,000	2008/09	3%
14	Faubert J	£6,884,852	£6,100,000	2007/08	45%
15	Dyer K	£6,771,986	£6,000,000	2007/08	6%
16	Răducioiu F	£6,349,287	£2,400,000	1996/97	16%
17	Kitson P	£6,084,734	£2,300,000	1996/97	20%
18	Diamanti A	£6,000,000	£6,000,000	2009/10	47%
19	Berkovic E	£5,739,334	£1,700,000	1997/98	82%
20	Hutchison D	£5,682,894	£1,500,000	1994/95	35%

Expert View

Tom Victor (@tomvictor)
Freelance journalist, www.peleconfidential.com

West Ham United have rarely been big spenders, often preferring to fall back on their impressive youth system, and this is demonstrated by the fact that only three of their signings (Matthew Upson, Dean Ashton and Marc-Vivien Foé) have a CTPP of more than £10m.

Still, things have changed a little since the club's promotion back to the Premier League in 2005, and particularly since Terence Brown's departure as chairman midway through the 2006/07 season. While big-money signings Upson and Julien Faubert have eventually proved their worth, Eggert Magnusson's tenure also saw the club spend millions on the likes of Kieron Dyer, Craig Bellamy and Savio Nsereko, none of whom managed more than 20 starts in claret and blue. Indeed, Nsereko, who cost the club somewhere between £5.5m and £9m (the amount paid in add-ons is unknown) started only one of a possible 38 games for the club.

Interestingly, West Ham's highest league finish (5th in 1998/99) was achieved with a squad whose cost totalled just over £71m (adjusted with CTPP), less than half the cost of the Blackburn Rovers team relegated that season. Then-manager Harry Redknapp generally spent shrewdly and effectively, forking out £750,000 on top scorer Ian Wright in the summer (equivalent to £1.8m now), along with flops Scott Minto and Javier Margas, before augmenting his squad in January with the signings of Foé and Paolo Di Canio for a combined £5.9m (around £14.4m in today's money). Even after the sales of Rio Ferdinand and Eyal Berkovic the following season, the Irons' most expensive purchase in 1999/2000 was Fredi Kanouté, for £4m.

With the notable exceptions of Dyer and Nsereko, West Ham have, by-and-large, got full value out of their more expensive signings, either through financial profit or performances on the pitch (and sometimes, as with John Hartson, both). It is perhaps this past record which has encouraged new owners David Sullivan and David Gold to shell out just under £10m on new signings Pablo Barrera, Winston Reid and Frédéric Piquionne without feeling the need to recoup any of that money through sales.

Wigan Athletic

Total Spend (Actual): £83.2m
Total Spend (CTPP): £104.2m
Average League Position: 13.6
Number of Managers: 4
Most Expensive Signing: Emile Heskey – £5.5m (CTPP £9.6m)
Best Value Signing: Chris Kirkland
Worst Value Signing: Olivier Kapo

Player Signings Breakdown (data correct up to end of January transfer window 2010)

• UK: 18 • EU: 16 • Rest of Europe: 1 • Rest of World: 15

Major Trophies Won Since Premier League Began: 0

Premier League Statistics (correct to the end of the 2009/10 season)

Seasons: 5	Played: 190	
Won: 56	Drawn: 42	Lost:92
Goals Scored: 187	Goals Conceded: 286	Goal Difference: –99
Total Points: 210		

Overview

Wigan Athletic are currently enjoying their first spell in England's top division, having gained promotion from the Championship as runners-up in 2005. Their first ever season in the Premier League (2005/06) didn't have the best of starts – losing their first two games – but they quickly hit their stride and won eight of their next nine games, putting them in 2nd place by the middle of November. A fixture list from Hades saw Wigan face Arsenal, Spurs, Liverpool, Chelsea and Manchester United in consecutive games, which resulted in five straight defeats for the Latics. Wigan recovered from this setback to finish the season in a very respectable 10th place. They reached their first major cup final in February 2006 when they played Manchester United for the League Cup, but the fairytale was brought to a cruel end as Wigan lost the game 4-0.

Wigan's second season in the top flight saw them escape relegation by the narrowest of margins on the last day of the season. They beat Sheffield United 2-1 at Bramall Lane, which meant the Yorkshiremen were demoted in place of Wigan owing to an inferior goal difference (–23 versus –22).

Wigan once again left it late to ensure their survival the following season. They lost eight consecutive league games between 22 September and 1 December 2007 – leaving them struggling in 19th place. They had to wait until the penultimate game of the season to guarantee their status, which came as a result of a 2-0 victory over 6th-placed Aston Villa. The 2008/09 season saw Wigan return to the safety of mid-table with an 11th-place finish.

Wigan once again returned to struggling ways in 2009/10 as they finished just six points clear of the relegation zone. The Latics claimed some notable scalps that season, recording their first ever Premier League victories over Chelsea (3-1), Liverpool (1-0) and Arsenal (3-2). However, this was tempered by some humiliating defeats, including a club-record 9-1 mauling away to Tottenham (eight of those goals came in the second half), a 5-0 defeat away to Manchester United and an 8-0 hammering at Chelsea on the last day of the season. Those three heavy defeats ensured Wigan set a new record for most goals conceded away from home in a Premier League season: 55.

Most Utilised Players

For a player with a reputation for being injury prone, Chris Kirkland has a surprisingly high starting ratio of 84%, having missed just 25 Premier League games since he joined Wigan for £2m (£3.5m) in October 2006. He initially joined from West Bromwich Albion on loan in July 2006, but the deal was made permanent just three months later, having quickly established himself as Wigan's first-choice goalkeeper.

Least Utilised Players

Steve Bruce signed French midfielder Olivier Kapo for £3.5m (£2.8m) from his former club Birmingham City in July 2008. Despite Kapo playing for Bruce during their time at St Andrew's, he started just 10 Premier League games at Wigan before joining French side Boulogne on a six-month loan deal in January 2010. Kapo was released from his Wigan contract in August 2010, having started just 13% of Wigan's matches.

Managers

Year	£XI	£XI Rank	Points	Cost Per Point	Position League	Manager
2005/06	£13,028,010	18	51	£255,451	10	Paul Jewell
2006/07	£28,280,551	11	38	£744,225	17	Paul Jewell
Average	**£20,654,281**	**14.5**	**44.5**	**£499,838**	**13.5**	**Paul Jewell**
2007/08	£28,353,106	16	40	£708,828	14	Hutchings/Barlow/Bruce
2008/09	£23,306,044	17	45	£517,912	11	Steve Bruce
Average	**£25,829,575**	**16.5**	**42.5**	**£613,370**	**12.5**	**Steve Bruce**
2009/10	£23,779,041	13	36	£660,529	16	**Roberto Martínez**

Top 5 Players Sold for a Profit

- Valencia - Bought for: £1.5m (£1.7m), Sold for: £16m (£16m) Profit of: £14.5m (£14.3m)
- Palacios - Bought for: £1m (£1.2m), Sold for: £12m (£9.4m), Profit of: £11m (£8.2m)
- Baines - Bought for: £0 (trainee), Sold for: £6m (£6.8m), Profit of: £6m (£6.8m)
- Taylor - Bought for: £750k (£1.4m), Sold for: £6m (£4.7m), Profit of: £5.25m (£3.3m)
- Chimbonda - Bought for: £500k (£900k), Sold for: £4.5m (£7.9m), Profit of: £4m (£7m)

Top 10 CTPP Purchases

#	Player	CTPP	Original fee	Year transferred	% of poss starts
1	Heskey E	£9,558,015	£5,500,000	2006/07	70%
2	Koumas J	£5,981,921	£5,300,000	2007/08	28%
3	King M	£5,643,321	£5,000,000	2007/08	11%
4	Camara H	£5,474,260	£3,000,000	2005/06	40%
5	Hall F	£5,213,463	£3,000,000	2006/07	29%
6	N'Zogbia C	£4,691,359	£6,000,000	2008/09	63%
7	McCarthy J	£3,000,000	£3,000,000	2009/10	50%
8	Landzaat D	£4,344,552	£2,500,000	2006/07	63%
9	Connolly D	£3,649,506	£2,000,000	2005/06	5%
10	Aghahowa J	£3,649,424	£2,100,000	2006/07	7%

Expert View

Martin Tarbuck (@mudhutter)
Author, Editor of The Mudhutter fanzine www.mudhutter.co.uk

I doubt that when he has retired from football, anyone will refer to him as "Emile Heskey, the former Wigan player" but he probably has been our most prominent, high-profile signing to date (£5.5m/£9.6m CTPP). He gave us good service in today's terms – two and a half years is probably testimonial territory the way WAFC turn over players nowadays. It was a mutually beneficial arrangement; he resurrected his career to a certain extent, and we acquired a centre-forward who didn't score that many for us, but contributed in the unselfish way he did everywhere else. I remember a 3-2 home defeat to Chelsea where their backline found him completely unplayable; he scored a brace and we lost undeservedly in the last minute. If he could run the champions ragged, you'd expect him to get a panful against the Readings and Watfords, but as I'm sure you know it never happened. He will be best remembered for his second-half performance as a centre-half to keep us up against Sheffield United in the 2006/07 season, which is still a source of mirth for the Heskey knockers.

By contrast, Jason Koumas (£5.3m/£6m) was undoubtedly the biggest waste of space at the club, and the greatest drain on the wage bill since the last lazy Welshman we signed, Simon Haworth. There's nothing more criminal than a footballer with great natural ability but a shocking attitude to go with it. He was perceived as a flagship signing at the beginning of our third season, as £5.3m was more or less our entire summer transfer budget, but 32 starts in three years says it all. Every manager has tried him out and given him a chance only to dump him a couple of games later.

Then there's Marlon King. He was generally perceived as a panic buy by Steve Bruce when he signed, and obviously caused the chairman to say 'he's left us with some bad players' when Bruce left the following season. In terms of his ability, apart from a fleeting spell at Watford – and to be fair to him he suffered a terrible cruciate injury – he had never really cut it in the top flight and scored one solitary goal for Latics, a penalty at that! His off-field problems have been well documented, but he'd already been in jail before he signed for Latics and racked up a string of other offences; so I think that our cuddly chairman Mr Whelan, employer of thousands of people, is trying to pull the wool over people's eyes saying that the club should have checked his record before signing him. He wouldn't give someone a job in a warehouse if they'd been done for handling stolen cars, let alone pay them £30,000-40,000 a week.

Wimbledon

Total Spend (Actual): £33.9m
Total Spend (CTPP): £101.5m
Average League Position: 12.25
Number of Managers: 2
Most Expensive Signing: John Hartson – £7.5m (CTPP £18.4m)
Best Value Signing: Kenny Cunningham
Worst Value Signing: Gareth Ainsworth

Player Signings Breakdown (data correct up to end of January transfer window 2010)

• UK: 20 • EU: 3 • Rest of Europe: 8 • Rest of World: 1

Major Trophies Won Since Premier League Began: 0

Premier League Statistics (correct to the end of the 2009/10 season)

Seasons: 8	Played: 316	
Won: 99	Drawn: 94	Lost:123
Goals Scored: 384	Goals Conceded: 472	Goal Difference: –88
Total Points: 391		

Overview
Wimbledon finished the inaugural Premier League season in 12th place (one place lower than the previous campaign), having enjoyed some surprising victories – which included doing the league 'double' over Arsenal (3-2 away, 1-0 at home) and Liverpool (3-2 away, 2-0 at home). The Dons also secured victories over reigning champions Leeds United (1-0 at home) and eventual champions Manchester United (1-0 at Old Trafford).

The 1993/94 season would be Wimbledon's most successful campaign in the Premier League, with 6th place their joint-highest finish in England's top division. Once again, they lived up to their reputation of being a bogey team against the bigger clubs with a victory over 5th-placed Leeds United (1-0 at home), a draw against 4th-placed Arsenal (1-1 away), beating 3rd-placed Newcastle (4-2 at home), beating 2nd-placed Blackburn (4-1 at home) and claiming a surprise victory over champions Manchester United (1-0 at home). Wimbledon also claimed two draws against Liverpool (1-1 home and away) and eliminated them from the League Cup in round four.

The 1994/95 season resulted in a 9th-place finish. However, they dropped five places the following campaign to finish 14th with 41 points, just three points clear of the relegation zone. The following season the Dons once again claimed some surprising victories, beating Liverpool (who finished 4th) 1-0 at home and claiming successive away wins against Chelsea (2-1) and Arsenal (3-1). The Dons produced a strong showing on all three domestic fronts during 1996/97.

However, the next three seasons saw their fortunes suffer a turn for the worse. They finished 1997/98 in 15th, just four points clear of the relegation zone. A 16th-place finish followed in 1998/99, despite the Dons being as high as 6th in mid-January – a month that also saw the arrival of John Hartson for a club-record £7.5m (£18.4m).

Joe Kinnear suffered a heart attack prior to Wimbledon's game with Sheffield Wednesday on 3 March 1999; the Dons won that match 2-1, but they failed to win any of their remaining 11 league games, losing nine. Kinnear resigned as manager of Wimbledon at the end of the season due to ill health. His successor, Egil Olsen, failed to halt the downward spiral as the club started 1999/2000 by winning just one of their opening 10 fixtures. An end-of-season collapse followed an inconsistent run of results up to March as Wimbledon lost nine of their last 10 games, sealing their relegation to the First Division after 16 seasons in England's top flight.

The Dons' finest moment was undoubtedly the 1988 FA Cup final, which produced one of the great upsets of English football with the defeat of league champions Liverpool. But Wimbledon FC can add no further trophies to the cabinet; in 2004, they became Milton Keynes Dons. While MK Dons are legally a continuation of Wimbledon FC, the new club makes no claim to the history of the previous one.

Most Utilised Players
Former Republic of Ireland international defender Kenny Cunningham moved to Wimbledon from Millwall in November 1994 in a deal that included his team-mate Don Goodman joining him at the Dons for a combined price of £1.3m (£4.92m); Cunningham's fee was believed to be £650k (£2.46m). Cunningham enjoyed a successful spell with Wimbledon, starting 200 Premier League games (86%) before their relegation at the end of 1998/99.

Least Utilised Players

Gareth Ainsworth joined Wimbledon from Port Vale in November 1998 for a then club record £2m (£4.9m), but despite the large outlay (by Wimbledon's standards), Ainsworth started just five Premier League games (7%) during the two seasons he represented them in the Premier League. Loan spells with Preston North End and Walsall followed before he signed for Cardiff City in 2003.

Managers

Year	£XI	£XI Rank	Points	Cost Per Point	Position League	Manager
1992/93	£16,389,323	16	54	£303,506	12	Joe Kinnear
1993/94	£19,131,042	16	65	£294,324	6	Joe Kinnear
1994/95	£18,332,749	16	56	£327,371	9	Joe Kinnear
1995/96	£21,416,399	17	41	£522,351	14	Joe Kinnear
1996/97	£18,710,301	16	56	£334,113	8	Joe Kinnear
1997/98	£18,985,433	18	44	£431,487	15	Joe Kinnear
1998/99	£27,899,843	15	42	£664,282	16	Joe Kinnear
Average	£20,123,584	16.3	51.1	£411,062	11.4	Joe Kinnear
1999/00	£32,588,009	14	33	£987,515	18	Egil Olsen

Top 5 Players Sold for a Profit

- Cort – Bought for: £0 (trainee), Sold for: £7m (£12.5m) Profit of: £7m (£12.5m)
- Euell – Bought for: £0 (trainee), Sold for: £4.75m (£6.23m), Profit of: £4.75m (£6.23m)
- Perry – Bought for: £0 (trainee), Sold for: £4m (£9.4m), Profit of: £4m (£9.4m)
- Barton – Bought for: D300k (£2m), Sold for: £4m (£10.5m), Profit of: £3.7m (£8.5m)
- Scales – Bought for: D70k (£466k), Sold for: £3.5m (£13.26m), Profit of: £3.43m (£12.8m)

Top 20 CTPP Purchases

#	Player	CTPP	Original fee	Year transferred	% of poss starts
1	Hartson J	£18,371,861	£7,500,000	1998/99	36%
2	Kennedy M	£6,752,158	£2,000,000	1997/98	14%
3	Roberts A	£6,752,158	£2,000,000	1997/98	43%
4	Lund A	£5,866,676	£2,500,000	1999/00	26%
5	Hreiðarsson H	£5,866,676	£2,500,000	1999/00	63%
6	Andersen T	£5,866,676	£2,500,000	1999/00	92%
7	Earle R	£5,158,560	D775000	1992/93	76%
8	Ainsworth G	£4,899,163	£2,000,000	1998/99	7%
9	Holdsworth D	£4,792,468	£720,000	1992/93	62%
10	Jones V	£4,659,344	£700,000	1992/93	71%
11	Thatcher B	£4,497,412	£1,700,000	1996/97	54%
12	Andresen M	£4,224,007	£1,800,000	1999/00	11%
13	Ekoku E	£3,485,508	£920,000	1994/95	53%
14	Hughes M (II)	£2,700,863	£800,000	1997/98	61%
15	Goodman J	£2,462,587	£650,000	1994/95	18%
16	Cunningham K	£2,462,587	£650,000	1994/95	86%
17	Badir W	£2,346,670	£1,000,000	1999/00	32%
18	Blissett G	£2,089,743	£350,000	1993/94	8%
19	Barton W	£1,996,862	D300000	1992/93	79%
20	Berry G	£1,664,052	£250,000	1992/93	7%

Expert View
Robert Dunford (@repd)
Wimbledon fan

In one of his famous press conference quips, Joe Kinnear proudly stated that Wimbledon bought players at Woolworths and sold them at Harrods. The club certainly built a reputation for developing the likes of Chris Perry, and selling on for huge fees. But spending-wise, the club didn't always shop in the bargain basement.

Wimbledon often broke their own transfer record during the mid-90s, although modern-day valuations for the likes of Robbie Earle (£5.2m) and Ben Thatcher (£4.5m) make them look like veritable steals. Yet the club's best signing was one it didn't initially intend to make. When Kenny Cunningham moved across South London from Millwall, he joined as a makeweight in the deal that also took Jon Goodman to Selhurst. However, as Goodman's injuries took hold, the Irish right-back went on to gain respect for both club and country.

It is hard to believe that Cunningham stayed at the Dons for eight years, let alone costing just £2.5m in modern money. Yet John Hartson failed as much as Cunningham succeeded. The Welshman's purchase shocked even the keenest observer – the Premier League's paupers had money after all. However, Hartson failed to live up to his price tag, and speculation quickly surfaced about his fitness and motivation. The squad cost more than ever, yet was spending more time looking downwards instead of up.

Matters changed after Kinnear suffered a heart attack in March 1999. The new manager was former Norwegian boss Egil Olsen, a disciple of the Crazy Gang ethos. Olsen continued his predecessor's approach to spending, albeit more Scandinavian in accent. However, a mixture of new ownership issues, political wrangling behind the scenes and the dreaded "player power" plunged the club into crisis – relegation in May 2000 was inevitable, if a relief for fans.

Today, buying at Woolworths is not an option, as poor management and failure to adapt to a changed market saw to that. For the same reasons, nobody else can purchase from the now-'extinct' Wimbledon FC.

Wolverhampton Wanderers

Total Spend (Actual): £22.1m
Total Spend (CTPP): £28.7m
Average League Position: 17.5
Number of Managers: 2
Most Expensive Signing: Kevin Doyle – £6.5m (CTPP £6.5m)
Best Value Signing: Jody Craddock
Worst Value Signing: Stefan Maierhofer

Player Signings Breakdown (data correct up to end of January transfer window 2010)

• UK: 4 • EU: 4 • Rest of Europe: 3 • Rest of World: 4

Major Trophies Won Since Premier League Began: 0

Premier League Statistics (correct to the end of the 2009/10 season)

Seasons: 2	Played: 76	
Won: 16	Drawn: 23	Lost:37
Goals Scored: 70	Goals Conceded: 133	Goal Difference. –63
Total Points: 71		

Overview
Despite Wolverhampton Wanderers having a proud history, which includes being crowned champions of England three times (1953/54, 1957/58 and 1958/59), four FA Cup wins (1892/93, 1907/08, 1948/49 and 1959/60) and two League Cup wins (1973/74 and 1979/80), the club has struggled in the Premier League, spending only two seasons (prior to 2010/11) in England's top division since they were relegated back in 1981/82.

Wolves' first season in the Premier League – 2003/04 – didn't end well. Despite recording home victories over Manchester City (1–0), Leeds United (3–1), Manchester United (1–0) and Everton (1–0), Dave Jones' side failed to win a single away game and ended the campaign relegated, in 20th place.

Wolves' second season in the Premier League – 2009/10 – was more successful. They finished 15th, eight points clear of the drop zone. Despite winning just nine Premier League games all season, Wolves did complete the league 'double' over 4th–placed Tottenham Hotspur.

Most Utilised Players
Jody Craddock featured in both of Wolves' Premier League seasons, and is seen as one

of Dave Jones's best signings. Purchased for £1.75m (£3.6m) from Sunderland in 2003, Craddock has started 64 Premier League games (84%) for Wolves, and was voted their Player of the Season in 2009/10.

Least Utilised Players
Austrian striker Stefan Maierhofer was signed from Rapid Vienna for £1.8m in August 2009, but despite scoring on his league debut in a 3–1 defeat to Blackburn Rovers, he started only one Premier League game for Wolves during the 2009/10 campaign. Maierhofer currently has a 3% start ratio, which is unlikely to be improved upon as he is due to spend the 2010/11 campaign on a season–long loan with MSV Duisburg.

Managers

Year	£XI	£XI Rank	Points	Cost Per Point	Position League	Manager
2003/04	£16,371,073	17	33	£496,093	20	Dave Jones
2009/10	£15,042,447	17	38	£395,854	15	Mick McCarthy

Top 20 CTPP Purchases

#	Player	CTPP	Original fee	Year transferred	% of poss starts
1	Doyle K	£6,500,000	£6,500,000	2009/10	87%
2	Cort C	£4,041,800	£2,000,000	2003/04	34%
3	Miller K (II)	£3,931,986	d3000000	2001/02	45%
4	Craddock J	£3,536,575	£1,750,000	2003/04	84%
5	Camara H	£3,031,350	£1,500,000	2003/04	76%
6	Milijaš N	£2,600,000	£2,600,000	2009/10	32%
7	Kennedy M	£2,359,192	d1800000	2001/02	74%
8	Cameron C	£2,293,658	d1750000	2001/02	66%
9	Silas	£2,020,900	£1,000,000	2003/04	5%
10	Halford G	£2,000,000	£2,000,000	2009/10	32%

Expert View
Thomas Baugh (@thomasbaugh)
www.wolvesblog.com

In 2003, Wolves were promoted to the Premier League for the first time in their proud history. A 19-year absence from England's top tier was finally at an end thanks to a resounding 3-0 play-off final victory over Sheffield United.

With Sir Jack Hayward's millions and the riches that come from being part of supposedly the greatest league in the world, the supporters expected major investment and extended residence amongst the elite. The club, unfortunately, had other ideas, and unwisely went about populating the squad with a collection of unknown Johnny foreigners and Premier League has-beens.

One million pounds (£2m CTPP) was wasted on Silas (Jorge Manuel Rebelo

Fernandes), perhaps the most cowardly footballer ever to turn out in the domestic game. He started just two matches, flinched, ducked and dived every time the ball came near him and then vanished into thin air, never to be seen at Molineux again. Veteran full-back Oleg 'The Horse' Luzhny was brought in on a free transfer having been released from Arsenal, although witnessing his traumatic four starts for the club, you'd be forgiven for thinking he'd taken early retirement.

Isaac Okoronkwo was an equally uninspired freebie, starting just seven games and contributing zip to our season. Steffen Iversen, also free, faired marginally better, scoring four goals in 16 appearances, but ended up very much on the periphery in the second half of the campaign. Semi-serious cash was splashed out only on three players. Defender Jody Craddock, relegated the previous season with Sunderland, came in for £1.75m (£3.5m CTPP), Henri Camara joined for £1.5m (£3m) and, later in the season, Carl Cort arrived from Newcastle for £2m (£4m).

Craddock endured a torrid season and was frequently singled out as a weak link as Wolves shipped 77 goals, giving them the second-weakest defence in the league. By contrast, the Cort-Camara partnership thrived, having come together at the halfway stage; their effective forward play signalling a positive upturn in our fortunes. It was all too late though, and Wolves were relegated, finishing rock bottom of the table, with the club rightly accused by supporters of trying to 'do it on the cheap'.

It took Wolverhampton Wanderers five years to bounce back, but lessons were learned from 2003, and whilst still prudent, the £6.5m capture of Kevin Doyle from Reading demonstrated the necessary level of ambition. Wolves finished 15th in 2009/10, with the energetic forward playing a key role. However, Doyle narrowly missed out on the club's Player of the Season award – a certain Jody Craddock, described as a waste of money back in 2003, taking home the gong.

It's funny how things can go full circle.

Part Three
Seasons: 1992–2010

1992/93

Average transfer value (actual): £594,309   **+8.5% compared with 1991/92**

Highest Sqf:	£131,360,229	**Liverpool**
Highest £XI:	£73,379,127	**Manchester United**
Average £XI:	£33,186,616	
Highest gross spend (CTPP):	£57,300,000	**Blackburn**
Highest net spend (CTPP):	£47,991,216	**Blackburn**

The inaugural Premier League season, 1992/93, saw a new era ushered in with success for what to this day remains the club to benefit most from the revamp: Manchester United. After 26 years without a title, they landed the first of what, to date, is 11 championships since the old First Division gave way to its rebranded successor (before the newer old First Division became the Championship, just to further muddy the lexicon).

With a nod towards things to come, the Premier League era kicked off with the most expensive side winning the title. But that's about where the predictability ended. As we will see when we come to more recent campaigns, the correlation between the expense of a side and the level of its success had yet to be quite as clear cut. On average, teams finished just over five places away from their ranking according to their £XI.

The second-most expensive side, Liverpool, finished way back in 6th as Graeme Souness tried to rebuild Kenny Dalglish's successful but ageing side, and failed spectacularly, racking up just 59 points. Aston Villa took advantage of Liverpool's woes, and finished 2nd in the league with the third-highest £XI. But next comes the first major surprise package of the Premier League: Norwich City. Despite having the 18th-most expensive £XI, they finished 3rd under Mike Walker. The East Anglian club would end up beating Bayern Munich in the UEFA Cup early the following season (before losing to Inter Milan in the next round), but by the end of that campaign found themselves relegated. That's how quickly, and how far, teams could rise and fall at that point in time; something almost unthinkable now.

Just behind Norwich in terms of radical overachievement were Queens Park Rangers; indeed, they also enjoyed a finish 15 places above their £XI rank. Gerry Francis is another managerial name hardly uttered in reverential tones these days, but his team finished above Liverpool, Spurs and Arsenal. Unlike Norwich, QPR maintained a top-nine position for the next two seasons, and were only relegated a year later, when Francis had left to take charge of Spurs.

Of those underachieving to alarming levels in 1992/93, Everton, with erstwhile hero

Howard Kendall in charge, were a full eight places below their expected position, and Leeds, in defending their title, slipped to a shocking 17th place; again, such a slide unthinkable in 2010. In fairness to Howard Wilkinson, the £XI ranked at 9th, so this was not a team bankrolled to the title in 1992. Even so, they surely should not have fallen so far, so fast. Arsenal were another recent title winner (League Champions in 1991) who soon found themselves struggling, finishing in 10th place just 24 months later.

Major transfers

Season	Buying club	Player	Original fee	CTPP
1992/93	Blackburn	Shearer A	£3,300,000	£21,965,480
1992/93	Man City	Phelan T	£2,500,000	£16,640,516
1992/93	Aston Villa	Saunders D	£2,300,000	£15,309,274
1992/93	Liverpool	Stewart P	£2,300,000	£15,309,274
1992/93	Chelsea	Fleck R	£2,100,000	£13,978,033
1992/93	Spurs	Sheringham T	£2,100,000	£13,978,033

Managers

Remarkably, only one manager was replaced over the course of the first Premier League season: Ian Porterfield was released from his duties in February to be replaced by David Webb, with Chelsea in 11th place, just six points off 4th. However, given the effects of the post-Heysel ban, England was entitled to only four places in Europe, one of these being through the FA Cup. Chelsea were 11 points behind 3rd-placed Norwich at the time of the managerial casualty. The change had little overall effect, with Chelsea finishing in 11th position with the 10th-highest £XI – thereby only marginally underperforming in terms of the expected placings.

Finances

The groundbreaking deal with Sky and the BBC, signed on 18 May 1992, was initially worth £304m, covering the seasons 1992/93 through to 1996/97. This equates to £60.8m per season, or just under £3m per club per season. In reality, clubs were guaranteed a minimum of only £1m per season, although appearance and prize money were expected to double this amount for each club. This was a significant increase over previous broadcasting deals in order to secure exclusive rights for Sky.

Other

The Champions League had been reorganised for the 1992/93 season, but still featured only the champions of the top-ranked 32 countries. In England's case, Leeds, as champions in 1991/92, were entered; after struggling past VfB Stuttgart following a replay, they were eliminated by Rangers in the second round – and so failed to qualify for the lucrative group stages. By the time of their November elimination, they were already 12th in the Premier League, some nine points off the top after just 14 games. It would seem that this participation, combined with the reduced spend on the squad and now being 'the team to beat', had cost Leeds any chance of successfully defending their title.

1993/94

Average transfer value (actual): £662,543   +11.5% compared with 1992/93

Highest Sq£:	£150,112,450	Liverpool
Highest £XI:	£92,208,897	Manchester United
Average £XI:	£38,421,388	
Highest gross spend (CTPP):	£8,200,000	Blackburn
Highest net spend (CTPP):	£44,720,499	Blackburn

Manchester United followed up their 1992/93 success by winning a second consecutive title. This was achieved with an £XI of £92.2m, some 25.7% higher than the previous season's record. This compares with a 15.7% overall increase of the £XI value for the 22 clubs; in part caused by the squad values of the teams that were relegated and promoted. Crystal Palace (£36.7m), Middlesbrough (£32.5m) and Nottingham Forest (£50.0m) were replaced by the more expensive combined teams of Newcastle (£79.1m), Swindon (£14.9m) and West Ham (£48.0m), resulting in a total increase in value of £22.7m.

The overall final positions of teams had become slightly more aligned with their £XI values. On average, teams were roughly four places away from their expected positions based on utilisation. Liverpool again had the second-most expensive team (and, indeed, the most expensive squad), although the gap to Manchester United had grown from £10m to almost £17m. Similar to the previous season, Liverpool underperformed by six places in finishing 8th picking up one point more, but now finding themselves a massive 32 adrift of the champions.

Third in the list of £XI was Blackburn. Rovers chased Manchester United all the way, ultimately finishing in 2nd place under the leadership of Kenny Dalglish. Newly promoted Newcastle finished 3rd with the 11th-most expensive £XI, an excellent performance by Kevin Keegan. Coventry also finished eight places higher than expected, in 11th, although this was surpassed by Norwich, whose overachievement, in finishing 12th, was nine places. However, the best-performing team over the course of the season was Wimbledon. Ranked only 16th in terms of £XI at £19.1m (20.7% of Manchester United's) and 19th in value for the overall squad, Joe Kinnear steered the Dons to 6th place in the league, their joint-highest ever league position.

The two worst-performing teams were Everton and Manchester City, who ended the season in 17th and 16th place respectively. Everton finished nine places lower than expected, while Manchester City, whose £XI suggested they should have finished 5th, ended up 11 places lower. Indeed, in the previous season both of these major clubs would have been relegated with their 1993/94 points haul. However, thanks to Sheffield

United's and Oldham's low points totals (with Swindon cut well adrift), and Everton's second-half comeback in their final match of the season, both would survive.

Major transfers

Season	Buying club	Player	Original fee	CTPP
1993/94	Man United	Keane R (I)	£3,750,000	£22,390,103
1993/94	Sheff Wed	Sinton A	£2,750,000	£16,419,409
1993/94	Blackburn	Batty D	£2,700,000	£16,120,874
1993/94	Leeds	Deane B	£2,700,000	£16,120,874
1993/94	Newcastle	Peacock D	£2,700,000	£16,120,874
1993/94	Sheff Wed	Walker D	£2,700,000	£16,120,874

Managers

Three clubs replaced their managers before the start of the season: Chelsea, who appointed Glenn Hoddle; Spurs, who went with Hoddle's ex-team-mate, Ossie Ardiles; and Manchester City, who chose Brian Horton. All three teams finished below their expected placing based on £XI, with Manchester City coming out worst.

A further five teams changed manager during the season: Coventry, Norwich, Liverpool, Everton and Southampton. Coventry and Norwich, as we have seen, were two of the major successes of the season, with Norwich's managerial change occurring due to Mike Walker's switch to Everton. Liverpool, Everton and Southampton all finished below where expected, and, in the case of the Merseyside teams, significantly below. Souness had taken Liverpool – a club that had finished in the top two in almost every season for 20 years, and whose £XI and Sq£ ranked in the top two – down to sixth (twice) and then eighth.

Finances

A new four-year sponsorship deal was signed with brewers Carling, who paid £12m for its first four-year deal, rising to £36m when they renewed in 1997.

Attendances rose by almost 9% compared with 1992/93, generating the highest attendance figures in the top flight for over a decade. Given the increased stadia sizes in the new millennium, it is worth considering the relatively low capacities of some of the clubs in the second season of the Premier League: Arsenal 38,500, Manchester United 43,500, Newcastle 32,536, Spurs 26,153 (during re-construction). However, Everton, Liverpool, Aston Villa and Chelsea, have only marginally increased their capacities in the last 20 or so years.

1994/95

Average transfer value (actual): £1,044,144   **+57.6% compared with 1993/94**

Highest Sqf:	£144,330,148	**Liverpool**
Highest £XI:	£87,541,696	**Blackburn**
Average £XI:	£42,458,253	
Highest gross spend (CTPP):	£44,326,570	**Everton**
Highest net spend (CTPP):	£37,507,097	**Everton**

The major story of 1994/95 was Jack Walker's Blackburn Rovers. In current terms their squad cost £141.7m, an increase of 13.5% on the season before. This was only marginally lower than that of Liverpool, who still had the highest Sqf; although this would be the final time they could claim this distinction.

Blackburn unquestionably used their squad to maximum effect. They had the highest £XI for the only time in the Premier League era and finished a single point ahead of defending champions Manchester United, to claim their first title in 81 years. This was achieved in no small part due to their continued spending. In July 1994 they smashed the British transfer record, raising it by 33% when buying Chris Sutton from Norwich. Rovers had the second-most expensive squad, but it was only marginally more costly than United's, who ranked third. Rovers' biggest achievement was in overcoming a team now used to winning titles, with only a slightly higher £XI.

Average £XIs across the division were some 10.5% higher than in the previous year. Again there was a net gain from promotions – Sheffield United (£13.5m), Oldham (£19.2m) and Swindon (£9.7m) replaced by Nottingham Forest (£38.7m), Crystal Palace (£20.7m) and Leicester (£15.5m) – this time to the tune of £32.4m.

The top two finished in the expected order based on £XI, and the top seven in the league all ranked in the top eight £XI. The exception to this was newly promoted Nottingham Forest, who finished 3rd. This new success was achieved with a relatively small squad, with no fewer than 10 players playing at least 35 of the 42 games. This entitled them to entry in the UEFA Cup for 1995/96, where they performed exceptionally well before being eliminated in the quarter-final by eventual winners Bayern Munich.

The average difference to a team's expected placing dropped again, to exactly four places; league position was more closely remembling £XI.

Forest's achievement was surpassed by QPR, who by all rights should have been bottom based on their utilisation, but finished 14 places higher in 8th. This meant that a team with an £XI of just £15.4m was competing with teams almost four times as expensive.

Just behind QPR came two further overachievers in Wimbledon and Southampton, both of whom should have been struggling against relegation but found themselves comfortably mid-table.

Only two teams underperformed significantly: Manchester City finished 17th, nine places worse than their £XI would have suggested; and Aston Villa, who, in ranking 18th, finished 12 places lower than anticipated. To date, this represents the second-worst underachievement in Premier League history based on league placings.

The overall utilisation showed a table split into three distinct groups. The 'Big Three' - which at this time included Blackburn, Manchester United and Liverpool - had an average £XI of about £80m. The middle group included 10 teams with an £XI of between £40m-£60m, while the bottom group with the remaining nine teams had a combined utilisation total of just under £30m.

Major transfers

Season	Buying club	Player	Original fee	CTPP
1994/95	Man United	Cole AA	£7,000,000	£26,520,170
1994/95	Blackburn	Sutton C	£5,000,000	£18,942,978
1994/95	Everton	Ferguson D (II)	£4,000,000	£15,154,383
1994/95	Liverpool	Babb P	£3,600,000	£13,638,944
1994/95	Liverpool	Scales J	£3,500,000	£13,260,085

Managers

No fewer than eight clubs changed managers during the course of the season, with varying degrees of success. QPR replaced Gerry Francis - who moved to Spurs to replace Ossie Ardiles - with Ray Wilkins. George Graham was sacked by Arsenal after allegations that he received illegal payments, and they ultimately finished five places lower than expected. Mike Walker - so good at Norwich - was replaced at Everton by former club favourite Joe Royle. At Ipswich, John Lyall, and then Paul Goddard, gave way to a joint managerial team of John Wark and George Burley; relegation still ensued.

Aston Villa replaced Ron Atkinson with Brian Little, finishing just three points ahead of the relegation zone (due to restructuring, four teams were relegated and the Premier League played with 20 teams from the following season). Villa, with an £XI of £55.7m, were mixing it with teams ranked below £20m. They finished 18th, a whopping 12 places below their £XI ranking.

Finances

With no new TV or sponsorship deals, the major financial talking point was the fine imposed on Spurs. This arose from financial irregularities during the previous decade, and was ultimately settled at £1.5m (£5.7m in today's terms). Attendances increased for the ninth successive year, 5.3% higher than 1993/94.

Other

Due to the relatively low fee paid for Eric Cantona, Manchester United's £XI was barely impacted by his suspension from January until September of the following season. This followed his infamous karate kick on a spectator at Crystal Palace, and may well have cost United a third consecutive title.

1995/96

Average transfer value (actual): £1,504,397   **+44.1% compared with 1994/95**

Highest Sq£:	£171,184,692	**Blackburn**
Highest £XI:	£89,313,515	**Liverpool**
Average £XI:	£47,316,666	
Highest gross spend (CTPP):	£67,907,305	**Newcastle**
Highest net spend (CTPP):	£49,237,727	**Newcastle**

Manchester United regained their title in 1995/96, as their youth policy began to bear fruit. They had used (on average) just under two home-grown players per game in 1994/95. This rose to over four in 1995/96, and would see their success continue until the new century. (Remarkably, a decade and a half later, Paul Scholes and Ryan Giggs are regulars in United's match-day squad.)

As a result, their £XI dropped quite markedly, from the second- to the fifth-highest in the division. Such was the quality of the youngsters, the title was won with a cost per point of just £863,133.

The number of teams in the top flight of English football was reduced to 20 from this season onwards. This concentrated the spending power of the clubs even further. The converse of this was that the average variation between league placing and £XI was reduced from four places in 1994/95 to just 2.6 places in 1995/96.

In short, clubs were now beginning to be placed very close to their ranking in the overall utilisation table. This made it harder for smaller sides to break the stranglehold of the bigger-spending clubs. Of the top nine spenders, only one team could not finish in the top nine: Leeds, who fell away to 13th place. The top nine teams ranked by £XI all had utilisation values of over £53m; after a gap of £8m comes the bottom half of the table.

The four clubs relegated at the end of the previous season had £XIs of £20m or below. The two clubs replacing them were low-spending Bolton (£13m) and Middlesbrough

(£41m), thereby increasing the average £XI by 4.1%.

The highest £XI belonged to Liverpool, who broke the transfer record for the first time in four years when signing Stan Collymore. However, even with this new record utilisation figure, and a crop of 'free' young stars, Liverpool could manage only 3rd place in the league. It would also prove to be the last occasion on which Liverpool could boast the most expensive £XI.

Manchester United, in comparison, had only the fifth-most expensive £XI, but finished top of the pile. Interestingly, United didn't field a single player whom they had bought in the close season; every player was already on the books or had come through the youth system.

The biggest climbers in the £XI table were Newcastle, who spent very heavily during the season; finishing 2nd with the third-most expensive £XI. Second in the ranking were Blackburn, who, now without Kenny Dalglish, finished way back in 7th place.

The worst underachievers were Manchester City. With an £XI only marginally below the average, the club had a terrible campaign, and were relegated in 18th place. It took them five years to recover their place in the top flight, having fallen to the third tier.

Major transfers

Season	Buying club	Player	Original fee	CTPP
1995/96	Liverpool	Collymore S	£8,500,000	£22,350,904
1995/96	Arsenal	Bergkamp D	£7,500,000	£19,721,386
1995/96	Newcastle	Asprilla H	£7,500,000	£19,721,386
1995/96	Newcastle	Ferdinand L	£6,000,000	£15,777,109
1995/96	Everton	Kanchelskis A	£5,500,000	£14,462,350

Managers
Four clubs introduced new managers before the season. Bruce Rioch (Arsenal) and Dave Merrington (Southampton) subsequently led their teams to positions on a par with expectation based on the £XI. Ray Harford (Blackburn) and David Pleat (Sheffield Wednesday) both finished five places below their utilisation ranking.

The only team who changed their manager during the season was Bolton, who finished bottom of the table (three places below expectation), well adrift of safety.

Finances
The end of the season saw the first major tournament to be staged in England since the 1966 World Cup finals. With football "coming home", the clubs of the Premier League enjoyed the financial rewards of staging the European Football Championship. Average attendance per game increased by 13.5%.

Other

Manchester United not only won the league with an impressive late run, but captured the FA Cup as well, thereby becoming the first team to win the 'double' twice.

Blackburn, as defending champions, entered the Champions League for the first time, but it's best remembered for their own players trading blows during an away game.

Nottingham Forest performed heroics in Europe to reach the quarter-finals of the UEFA Cup. However, all of the other participants were eliminated in the first two rounds, leaving England struggling in the overall UEFA rankings in 7th place.

Note: total gross spend was £443m, just 1% higher than the previous year. However, this was achieved with two fewer clubs, meaning the average per club was 11% higher.

1996/97

Average transfer value (actual): £1,495,288   **-0.6% compared with 1995/96**

Highest Sq£:	£165,304,916	Newcastle
Highest £XI:	£107,815,548	Newcastle
Average £XI:	£47,056,000	
Highest gross spend (CTPP):	£39,881,461	Newcastle
Highest net spend (CTPP):	£24,074,381	Spurs

The Premier League apparently took a deep breath following the inflationary pressures of the previous two campaigns, with a slight reduction in average transfer value. The average difference between expected and actual position increased to 4.6 places, with two of the promoted sides performing particularly well. Derby would have been expected to finish in the relegation places, but were comfortably above the trapdoor in 12th, six points ahead of relegated Sunderland. By finishing in 9th place, some eight places above expectation, Leicester fared even better. Wimbledon, too, were star performers, also finishing eight places above where the £XI rankings would have forecast, in 8th.

Buoyed by their second-place finish in 1995/96, Newcastle seemed determined to buy their way to the title the following season, taking almost the opposite approach to champions Manchester United, who continued with their youth policy (by contrast,

Kevin Keegan disbanded his club's reserve team). Although United bought four players this season, the amounts that changed hands were relatively modest; only Ole Gunnar Solksjær amongst the signings would make a lasting impression.

The result of the Geordies' largesse was to increase their utilisation to £107.8m, making Newcastle the first club to smash through the £100m barrier for £XI; this figure would not be surpassed until 1999/2000.

Nevertheless, Newcastle could not sustain a title challenge, finishing seven points behind Manchester United. Remarkably, despite winning the title again, Manchester United slipped to sixth place in utilisation, on which basis they would have been struggling to capture a UEFA Cup place. The policy of long-term youth development introduced by Alex Ferguson was clearly paying dividends, even if such a trick is virtually impossible to repeat. United used 23 players, of whom 22 started; seven of these started fewer than a dozen games, leaving a core of 15 who rotated throughout the season – there were no ever-presents.

Three teams performed particularly badly this season: Blackburn, Everton and Middlesbrough. Rovers could not recover from the loss of Alan Shearer to Newcastle, reflected in their 20% drop in £XI.

The Toffees had the fifth-most expensive £XI, higher even than champions Manchester United, but finished in 15th place, just two points safe from relegation. Middlesbrough, however, suffered a worse fate; the seventh-most expensive £XI, who should in theory have been battling for a European place, found themselves in the bottom two under the management of former England captain Bryan Robson. Without a settled side, 30 players were used in the league, and ultimately this, combined with the exertions of two extended cup runs and the docking of points, led to their downfall.

Overall, utilisation remained static, despite the loss of comparatively wealthy Manchester City the previous season. The relegated teams (City £43.8m, QPR £16.4m and Bolton £13.9m) were replaced by Leicester (£17.5m), Derby (£16.8m) and Sunderland (£10.4m) for a combined reduction in the league's £XI of £39.2m, but this gap was closed by the other 17 teams.

Major transfers

Season	Buying club	Player	Original fee	CTPP
1996/97	Newcastle	Shearer A	£15,000,000	£39,683,045
1996/97	Middlesbrough	Ravanelli F	£7,000,000	£23,632,552
1996/97	Everton	Barmby N	£5,750,000	£15,211,834
1996/97	Chelsea	Di Matteo R	£4,900,000	£12,963,128
1996/97	Chelsea	Zola G	£4,500,000	£11,904,914
1996/97	Leeds	Sharpe L	£4,500,000	£11,904,914

Managers

Two new managers started the season: Ruud Gullit at Chelsea and Graeme Souness at Southampton. Both teams performed slightly better than expected, with Chelsea winning the FA Cup in the process.

Seven teams changed managers in mid-season, and none of them went on to finish higher than the £XI suggested. Newcastle replaced Kevin Keegan with Kenny Dalglish in January, and although he steered them to second place, the gap to the leaders was still quite large.

Arsenal had waited to get their man, with Arsène Wenger appointed as full-time coach in September whilst waiting for the Japanese season to finish. This would provide the Gunners with longer-term success. Two of the clubs to change manager performed disastrously. Blackburn's poor showing following Shearer's departure led to their replacing Ray Harford with long-time coach Tony Parkes. The fourth-highest team in the utilisation rankings finished just two points ahead of relegation. Worst of all however was Everton, with Joe Royle resigning in March, to be replaced by Dave Watson. The Toffees survived relegation by the narrowest of margins. Changing manager mid-season certainly did not pay dividends.

Finances

Attendances increased by 4% on the previous season. This was in part down to Manchester United, whose ground development programme allowed them to be the only team to exceed an average of 40,000 – in their case, just over 55,000.

Other

UEFA revamped the Champions League at the end of this season, with England gaining a second place for 1997/98; the beneficiaries of this change were Newcastle, who secured their spot on the final day, under challenge from Arsenal and Liverpool; goal difference separating 2nd from 4th. This meant that England would have seven representatives the following season in European competition.

Middlesbrough failed to fulfil their fixture at Blackburn just before Christmas due to injuries and illness; although the match was replayed at a later date, Middlesbrough had three points deducted, which proved crucial at the end of the season; the extra points would have seen Boro finish 14th and escape relegation. Coventry were the beneficiaries, as they would have been sent down in Boro's place.

1997/98

Average transfer value (actual): £1,171,726   −21.6% compared with 1996/97

Highest Sq£:	£200,390,055	Newcastle
Highest £XI:	£86,288,655	Newcastle
Average £XI:	£46,060,649	
Highest gross spend (CTPP):	£76,299,382	Newcastle
Highest net spend (CTPP):	£36,039,642	Crystal Palace

The 1997/98 season was a period of comparative austerity. For the first time, the average value paid on transfers actually decreased year on year. The teams promoted and relegated during the close season played a significant part in this. Middlesbrough, who had spent large sums of money on star signings, were one of the clubs replaced by Barnsley, Bolton and Crystal Palace.

With Alan Shearer injured in a pre-season friendly, Newcastle's record high £XI dropped by some 20% compared with the previous season, resulting in the top teams being much more closely bunched together on utilisation. Nevertheless, Newcastle still came out on top of both £XI and Sq£. Their reliance on Shearer was highlighted by their final league position of 13th, which represents one of the biggest ever variances from expectation.

The reduced spending seems to have caused a greater variability throughout the division, with an average difference of final placing to expectation of over five places for the first (and so far only) time. As noted earlier in the book, the late '90s was the last time that the league's competitive balance was roughly in check.

The three biggest successes this season were Liverpool (+7 places), Leeds (+6 places) and Derby (+10 places). With the departures of players like Stan Collymore, John Scales and Ian Rush, and the emergence of yet more talented trainees (an average in the XI of 3.4, up from 2.4 a year earlier), Liverpool had dropped in £XI ranking to 10th place, only just above the divisional average. Leeds had not yet started on their investment campaign, so they were more than happy to finish in the top five. Derby, with the second-lowest £XI and third-lowest Sq£, took advantage of the plight of some of the more illustrious clubs to finish a comfortable 9th, enjoying life in their new Pride Park home.

Three teams stand out above all others in their underperformance: Newcastle, Sheffield Wednesday and Everton. Newcastle and their lack of goals (35 in 38 games) can be larguely attributed to the loss of Alan Shearer until February, although his return did enable them to reach the final of the FA Cup. Sheffield Wednesday performed poorly with the fifth-highest utilisation, and were saved by a change of manager in October after a dreadful start. Even worse, Everton survived relegation only on goal difference, despite having the sixth-most expensive £XI in the division.

Major transfers

Season	Buying club	Player	Original fee	CTPP
1997/98	Aston Villa	Collymore S	£7,000,000	£23,632,552
1997/98	Spurs	Ferdinand L	£6,000,000	£20,256,473
1997/98	Newcastle	Speed G	£5,500,000	£18,568,434
1997/98	Arsenal	Overmars M	£5,000,000	£16,880,394
1997/98	Chelsea	Le Saux G	£5,000,000	£16,880,394

Managers

Three new managers had been installed for the start of the season. Dave Jones steered Southampton to a respectable 12th position, five places above where they would be expected to finish based on £XI. However, Howard Kendall, who returned to Goodison Park, could lead Everton only to finishing amongst teams costing roughly one third of their £XI. After Tony Parkes' brief caretaker spell had come to an end, Blackburn Rovers appointed Roy Hodgson and finished 6th, despite boasting the third-most expensive Sq£ (although it was an improvement on the 13th-placed finish a year earlier).

Five other teams changed manager during the course of the campaign; for Chelsea and Aston Villa this had little overall impact. Sheffield Wednesday replaced David Pleat with Ron Atkinson in October, and he steered Wednesday to safety, but only just. Despite this rescue act, Atkinson was not offered a new contract and was replaced during the summer.

Crystal Palace seemed unsure as to who should be their manager, starting the season with Steve Coppell at the helm. However, with the club on the verge of a takeover he moved onto the board and was replaced by joint managers Attilio Lombardo and Tomas Brolin. With the club already doomed, they too resigned and Ray Lewington, assisted by chairman Ron Noades, sailed Palace home in bottom place. Lack of stability on and off the field cost Palace their Premier League life.

At Spurs, Gerry Francis suffered a terrible start to the season; he was replaced by Christian Gross with the team sitting in the relegation zone. Gross managed to pull things around and Spurs survived with just four points to spare, some 11 places lower than their utilisation would have suggested.

Finances

The previous television deal, signed in 1992, had been worth about £3m per club per season. The new deal, signed in 1997, was worth a total of £670m for four seasons. This equated to £167.5m per season, or just over £8m per club per season – almost three times the original deal. The teams were clearly spending a lot of this money on transfers. Attendances were up by almost 2%, in part due to Derby's move to Pride Park.

Other

The gulf in quality between Premier League football and the First Division was starting to become abundantly clear. For the first time, all three promoted teams were immediately relegated. This was particularly galling for Crystal Palace, having spent a small fortune on new players; although Barnsley, with the lowest £XI by some distance, must have feared the worst from day one.

As if to confirm this gap, the three relegated teams from the previous season finished in the top three in the First Division, although third-placed Sunderland failed to gain promotion after losing in the play-offs.

1998/99

Average transfer value (actual): £1,614,904   **+37.8% compared with 1997/98**

Highest Sq£:	£210,471,784	Newcastle
Highest £XI:	£106,197,289	Manchester United
Average £XI:	£49,767,648	
Highest gross spend (CTPP):	£92,532,939	Blackburn
Highest net spend (CTPP):	£58,851,194	Manchester United

This was Manchester United's "annus mirabilis" with three trophies: the Premier League, FA Cup and Champions League. They achieved this with the highest £XI (in the process becoming only the second team to break the £100m barrier, after Newcastle) and the highest net spend of anyone to date. (Though only the 3rd-highest Sq£.) This was Alex Ferguson's response to losing the title to Arsenal the previous season, and what dividends he reaped. Even so, United were still fielding on average 4.3 home-grown players per match.

The average fee paid across the division rocketed by almost 40%, setting a new record mark; 7.3% higher than the previous high in 1995/96. Not surprisingly, this also led to an increase in £XI, which finished a shade under £50m per club. This was clearly a result of the new television deals signed in the previous season, with the clubs now seeing the benefit of the extra cash.

The average variance to the expected club position based on £XI dropped to 4.7 places, still significantly higher than would be the norm a decade later. However, equality was about to end; from now on, the average would fall almost continuously, as even greater amounts of cash were thrown at the game.

Based on £XI, Newcastle should have been 2nd in the league, and quite comfortably at that; however, a second season of poor form left the Geordies languishing in 13th place. Alan Shearer was the main scoring threat, although he was not as prolific as previously, and no other player managed to get anywhere near double figures.

The worst underachievement in the history of the Premier League occurred this season. Blackburn, champions only four seasons earlier, should have been in the UEFA Cup places based on their £XI; however, they dropped 14 places compared with expectation to finish next to bottom, some six points short of safety. With only 38 goals and nobody netting more than five, this was quite simply a disastrous campaign, with the tone set by just one win in the first 14 games, leading to Roy Hodgson's dismissal.

Everton also continued to struggle, finishing 14th – seven places below their utilisation ranking. However, considered in the light of previous seasons, this represented the first tentative step forward for the Toffees under Walter Smith.

Top of the pile for overachievement came Derby, who with the third-least expensive £XI, worked their way up to 8th, only five points short of a place in Europe, leaving much more fancied sides such as Newcastle and Spurs in their wake. Equally strong performances were achieved by Leeds and West Ham, who both finished eight places above their £XI ranking, thus qualifying for Europe the following season. Leeds were on the cusp of their spending spree, but West Ham's success was notable since Harry Redknapp had turned in a profit of £5.5m in player sales during the season, thanks in no small part to John Hartson's January move to Wimbledon.

Largely as a result of the promotion of Middlesbrough, the Premier League saw a utilisation increase of £11m from the promoted teams when compared with the relegated teams of the previous season. Again, two of these teams were relegated immediately, but Boro's relatively expensive squad (with 12th-highest £XI) finished comfortably in mid-table.

Major transfers

Season	Buying club	Player	Original fee	CTPP
1998/99	Man United	Yorke D	£12,600,000	£30,864,726
1998/99	Man United	Stam J	£10,500,000	£25,720,605
1998/99	Wimbledon	Hartson J	£7,500,000	£18,371,861
1998/99	Blackburn	Davies K	£7,250,000	£17,759,465
1998/99	Newcastle	Ferguson D (II)	£7,000,000	£17,147,070

Managers

Four clubs made managerial changes for the start of the season. Chelsea appointed Gianluca Vialli and Liverpool added former French national team boss Gérard Houllier to form a joint-manager team with Roy Evans. This did not work according to plan and by November Evans had resigned, leaving Houllier in sole charge. Both Chelsea (3rd) and Liverpool (7th) finished marginally higher than their £XI would have suggested, with

Houllier enjoying the peak of Liverpool's youth development system originally set up by Kenny Dalglish in 1986: up to an average of almost four home-grown players in the XI each week, with Steve McManaman, Jamie Carragher, Robbie Fowler, Michael Owen and Dominic Matteo now joined in the squad by David Thompson and Steven Gerrard.

Four further changes were made during the course of the season. With Spurs struggling under Christian Gross, they appointed former Arsenal manager George Graham, to great surprise. Leeds replaced Graham by promoting David O'Leary to first-team manager. The Yorkshire club benefited most, with O'Leary taking them to 4th, eight places higher than their £XI ranking, although Graham did save Spurs from the ignominy of relegation.

Blackburn's disastrous start – the season's fifth-most expensive £XI languishing in bottom place – saw Roy Hodgson replaced by Brian Kidd, who joined from Manchester United. Kidd's efforts proved fruitless, as Rovers were relegated in 19th place – the biggest negative discrepancy between the actual table and £XI ranking. Nottingham Forest replaced Dave Bassett with Ron Atkinson in the hope that he could repeat his miracles with Sheffield Wednesday from the previous season, but Forest went straight back to the First Division in bottom place.

Finances

Attendances increased by 4.8% across the Premier League. However, at this stage only Manchester United had taken full advantage of their stadium development, with an average of just over 55,000 packing Old Trafford before its subsequent expansion. Of the other clubs, only Liverpool surpassed 40,000 on average.

1999/2000

Average transfer value (actual): £1,685,725   +4.4% compared with 1998/99

Highest Sq£:	£201,433,953	Newcastle
Highest £XI:	£118,233,197	Newcastle
Average £XI:	£48,903,156	
Highest gross spend (CTPP):	£83,776,131	Liverpool
Highest net spend (CTPP):	£61,717,430	Liverpool

Manchester United comfortably retained their title, finishing a massive 18 points clear of second-placed Arsenal. United made only a couple of signings to freshen things up, but given their success the previous season this was probably to be expected.

The average difference between £XI ranking and actual league position dropped significantly to 3.9 places, as the gap between the bigger spenders and the smaller clubs became more pronounced. Previously every club, with one exception (Sunderland in 1996/97), had an £XI of at least 10% of the most expensive side. In this season, however, three teams – Southampton, Bradford and Watford – all fell below 10%, which by definition would make it difficult for them to survive. The first two finished just outside the relegation zone, but Watford, at only 3.8% of Newcastle's £XI, finished clear bottom.

The average £XI dropped, which was not particularly surprising given the teams replacing the relegated clubs the previous season. With big spenders Blackburn having gone, a total of £105m was lost from the utilisation and replaced with a meagre £39m in total.

The best performance was achieved by newly promoted Sunderland, who finished 7th with an £XI ranked 17th, and costing less than a quarter of that of neighbours Newcastle. They did not spend vast amounts and managed to keep a reasonably settled team; their form saw them miss out on European football on goal difference, as they ended level on points with Aston Villa.

Just one place below Sunderland were Leicester, who also overachieved by some considerable distance – eight places. Like Sunderland, Leicester kept a settled team and spent only £4.6m (£10.8m) on new signings. Unlike Sunderland, Leicester were rewarded with a UEFA Cup place, for their win in the League Cup.

There were two teams who stood out as underperforming this season. Newcastle, once again, could not find the right blend on the pitch, and despite fielding the most expensive £XI, could manage only 11th place. Alan Shearer chipped in with 23 goals, but the Toon Army were bedevilled with inconsistency – just six more points would have seen them qualify for Europe. Even worse than Newcastle were Sheffield Wednesday. With a squad that should have been on the fringe of the European places, the Owls ended up in 19th position and were relegated. Only one player, Gilles de Bilde (no relation to Bob), managed to get into double figures in the scoring charts, and this was the root of Wednesday's problems. One goal per league game was never going to be enough to ensure their survival.

Major transfers

Season	Buying club	Player	Original fee	CTPP
1999–2000	Liverpool	Heskey E	£11,000,000	£25,813,374
1999–2000	Arsenal	Henry T	£10,000,000	£23,466,703
1999–2000	Chelsea	Sutton C	£10,000,000	£23,466,703
1999–2000	Liverpool	Hamann D	£8,000,000	£18,773,363
1999–2000	Coventry	Keane R (II)	£6,000,000	£14,080,022
1999–2000	Newcastle	Dyer K	£6,000,000	£14,080,022

The total amount spent by all clubs was £232.6m (£545.9m), 12 % lower than the previous year. Given the identity of the promoted and relegated clubs, this was not entirely surprising.

Managers
The only managerial change before the season was at Wimbledon, who replaced Joe Kinnear with Egil Olsen following Kinnear's heart problems. Olsen's tenure was disappointing and the Dons were relegated, perhaps unsurprisingly given the lack of major investment in the squad.

Only three managers were replaced during the season. Given the dreadful start made by Newcastle and their history of managerial changes, it was no surprise to see Ruud Gullit sacked at the end of September; Bobby Robson replacing him. The division's other worst-performing team, Sheffield Wednesday, also changed their manager. Danny Wilson's reign was terminated in March with Wednesday in deep relegation trouble. Peter Shreeves arrived in his place, but to no effect as the Owls were relegated.

The other change was an enforced one. Personal allegations against Dave Jones meant that Southampton put him on gardening leave during investigations, with Glenn Hoddle arriving in his place in January. Hoddle steered the club away from relegation, ending the season 11 points ahead of the danger zone in 15th place.

Finances
BSkyB, in addition to their television deal, acquired a 9.1% stake in Leeds for £13.8m. This was one of a number of deals by television companies, who were no doubt hoping that dedicated club TV channels would allow them to generate more sustainable and predictable cash flows.

There was a negligible increase in attendances (0.4%) from the previous season.

Other
The main external factor this season was the proposed expansion of the Champions League. With 32 teams now competing in the group stage from 2000/01, three teams from England became eligible for participation – a result of the performance of its clubs in Europe over the previous five years. Two teams went directly to the group stage and a further team had to negotiate the third qualifying round.

This had the effect of widening the gap between the haves and the have-nots, since clubs could expect to make millions from a successful run in the competition. More clubs were therefore gambling on their domestic performances in order to achieve this wealth through Europe. Leeds were the first to overstretch themselves to the point of disastrous consequences.

2000/01

Average transfer value (actual): £2,222,537   +31.8% compared with 1999/00

Highest Sq£	£189,391,588	Arsenal
Highest £XI:	£99,650,688	Arsenal
Average £XI:	£48,176,931	
Highest gross spend (CTPP):	£69,593,134	Chelsea
Highest net spend (CTPP):	£44,585,882	Leeds

Manchester United won the title for a third consecutive year, becoming the first club in almost 20 years to do so, and only the fourth ever. Their Sq£ was exactly the same as in the previous season, but their £XI fell to fifth overall. At the end of the season they were 10 points clear of Arsenal, although this could have been more; United lost three of the final five fixtures, with the title already secured. One of the more remarkable facts about the United story was that an average of 5.3 players, or almost half the team, were home grown, as compared with a divisional average of 1.9.

Arsenal had the highest £XI and Sq£, as Arsène Wenger built his team on expensive overseas purchases. With four major signings, Arsenal were starting to build for the success that would come in a couple of years' time.

The average difference between the actual finishing positions and the £XI ranking was 4.4, slightly higher than the previous year, due mainly to the performance of just five clubs.

The biggest success was Ipswich in their first season after promotion. With an £XI of just £21.9m, the Tractor Boys could easily have been expected to finish closer to the relegation zone, but under the guidance of George Burley they reached 5th place, which earned them the right to participate in the UEFA Cup the following season. One of the other promoted teams, Charlton, also proved successful: finishing 9th with an £XI ranked 18th. This was matched by Southampton, who finished 10th. The third promoted team, Manchester City, were relegated immediately, but this was with an £XI of just £24.8m.

Two teams underperformed quite badly. Coventry, who had been in the top flight since 1967, could not maintain their position. With a mid-ranking £XI of £34.9m, the Sky Blues fell well short of safety. However, Coventry were not the worst underachievers; this distinction fell to Newcastle once again. The Toon Army finished nine places below their £XI ranking, with goals drying up when Alan Shearer missed most of the second half of the season.

One of the most interesting features of utilisation this season was the development of two tiers in the rankings; the upper echelon featured clubs with an £XI of at least £66m, whereas the 9th-placed team could manage only £36m, so a chasm of some £30m had developed.

Major transfers

Season	Buying club	Player	Original fee	CTPP
2000/01	Leeds	Ferdinand R	£18,000,000	£32,037,760
2000/01	Chelsea	Hasselbaink J	£15,000,000	£26,698,133
2000/01	Arsenal	Wiltord S	£13,000,000	£23,138,382
2000/01	Spurs	Rebrov S	£11,000,000	£19,578,631
2000/01	Aston Villa	Angel JP	£9,500,000	£16,908,818

Managers

The first managerial change before the season began was at Leicester, where Peter Taylor replaced Martin O'Neill, who had left for Celtic. Leicester started well, even occupying top spot in October. However, a dreadful run after Christmas saw them slip to 13th, marginally lower than their £XI suggested.

The only other change at this stage was at Bradford; Paul Jewell accepted the job at Sheffield Wednesday and the Tykes appointed Chris Hutchings. The start made by Bradford was so bad that Hutchings was replaced by Jim Jefferies in November. However, Jefferies performed little better and Bradford, with the lowest Sq£ in the division, had their relegation confirmed in late April. By the end of the season, they were 16 points from safety.

Clubs who changed manager during the season had significantly different fortunes. Chelsea's poor start saw Gianluca Vialli replaced by Claudio Ranieri, who steadied the ship and guided the Blues to 6th place and a spot in the UEFA Cup, even though this was three places lower than they would have expected.

Glenn Hoddle was doing a fine job at Southampton, keeping them safely away from relegation, even with the second-lowest £XI in the division. It was therefore no shock when he was courted by Spurs, his former club. This came about when George Graham was dismissed at White Hart Lane for breach of contract. Spurs finished below Southampton and four places lower than their Sq£ suggested.

Finances

Attendances rose by 6.9% compared with the previous season. This was fuelled by two major redevelopments: Manchester United continued to expand Old Trafford, which now had a capacity of 68,000, and Newcastle took the capacity at St James' Park to 52,000. Both clubs were generating massive match-day revenue with their grounds effectively sold out for every match.

Qualification for the Champions League - the pot of gold at the end of the Premier League rainbow - proved to be a double-edged sword for Leeds. They did brilliantly to reach the semi-final, before losing to Valencia. However, this came at a price: the club slipped to 4th in the league, thereby missing out on the Champions League the following season.

2001/02

Average transfer value (actual): £3,018,200   **+35.8% compared with 2000/01**

Highest Sq£:	£225,870,100	Manchester United
Highest £XI:	£104,115,888	Arsenal
Average £XI:	£51,633,908	
Highest gross spend (CTPP):	£74,838,799	Manchester United
Highest net spend (CTPP):	£58,029,559	Fulham

This was a season when the link between £XI and position became clearer than ever before. The top six teams in utilisation all finished in the top six, and only one team in the entire division, Leicester, finished more than five places away from where they could have expected to be, based on their £XI.

So perhaps it should be no surprise that the team with the costliest £XI were champions, as Arsène Wenger's spending spree over the previous years finally came to fruition. Arsenal took the title with seven points to spare over second-placed Liverpool.

It was also a season when the gap between the values of the teams became more pronounced, with a major cut-off point coming after the top five and a further division coming at 9th. This compartmentalisation is shown in the average difference to the £XI ranking, which fell to a record low of just 2.7 places.

With the 15th-most expensive £XI, Leicester were always going to be in a battle for survival, especially since the team that had finished 13th the previous season had the third-lowest gross spend. The only teams with a lower spend were Derby, who were also relegated, and new boys Bolton, who survived, but only just.

The biggest gainers were Southampton, whose £XI indicated that they should finish in next-to-last place, but the Saints ended comfortably in 11th, some nine points above the relegation zone. Their £XI was just £14m, less than one seventh of champions Arsenal. Two other main gainers were newly promoted Bolton and second-placed Liverpool, who were still regularly utilising home-grown talents Owen, Gerrard and Carragher, although Robbie Fowler was sold to Leeds early in the campaign; providing money for Houllier to invest in the team the following summer.

Bolton had the least expensive £XI at just over 10% of Arsenal's, but Sam Allardyce showed his worth as manager for the first time in the Premier League, as he steered Wanderers to 16th and safety.

Major transfers

Season	Buying club	Player	Original fee	CTPP
2001/02	Man United	Verón J	£28,100,000	£36,829,602
2001/02	Man United	van Nistelrooy R	£19,000,000	£24,902,578
2001/02	Fulham	Marlet S	£13,500,000	£17,693,937
2001/02	Leeds	Keane R (II)	£12,000,000	£15,727,944
2001/02	Chelsea	Lampard F	£11,000,000	£14,417,282
2001/02	Leeds	Fowler R	£11,000,000	£14,417,282

In total the 20 clubs spent £377.3m, which equates to £494.5m in current terms; 15% lower than in 2000/01. However, because there were fewer transfers in total, the average transfer fee rose once again.

Managers

Two managers were changed at the start of the season. At West Ham, Glenn Roeder took over the reins from the departing Harry Redknapp. Roeder made a couple of shrewd signings, Don Hutchison and Tomáš Repka, for a combined fee of £10.5m (£13.8m), and steered the Hammers to 7th place, three places above their £XI ranking but some way short of Chelsea in 6th.

At Middlesbrough, Steve McLaren replaced the departing Terry Venables and, after a slow start, he steadied the ship. McLaren's real success would come in future years. Aston Villa were in mid-table when John Gregory resigned in January. After a brief spell in charge by joint caretakers John Deehan and Stuart Gray, Graham Taylor took over, but he could manage only 8th place, exactly where Villa would have expected to be on the basis of £XI.

In a desperate attempt to maintain their top-flight status, Leicester changed their manager twice during the season. Peter Taylor suffered a terrible start and was replaced by joint managers Dave Bassett and Micky Adams in September. Things improved slightly, but another bad run saw the Foxes relegated in early April, by which time Bassett had moved upstairs to leave Adams in sole charge. Another Midlands club, Derby, also changed their manager twice, with much the same effect as at Leicester. Jim Smith started the season but was replaced by Colin Todd in October, who in turn was replaced by John Gregory after a short spell by caretaker Billy McEwan. All of this managerial shuffling was to no avail as Derby, with the 18th-most expensive £XI, finished in 19th place.

Two other teams changed their manager this season: Everton, who replaced Walter Smith with David Moyes, and Southampton. With the Saints deep in relegation trouble in their new St Mary's home, it was no surprise to see Stuart Gray removed and replaced by Gordon Strachan. The Scotsman performed wonders; managing to get the second-lowest £XI up to 11th in the final table.

Finances

Sky renewed their contract, giving the Premier League a further three years of TV coverage on the satellite channel. The sums involved were now rocketing, with £1.02bn paid, equivalent to £17.1m per club per season. Not surprisingly, most of this was passed straight on in the form of increased transfer activity, as outlined above.

Southampton's move into their new home at St Mary's after 103 years at The Dell doubled their average attendance in one fell swoop. Other grounds continued their development and, in total, attendances increased by 4.6%.

Other
English clubs' progress in the Champions League earned them yet another qualifying place from this season onwards. The scramble for the coveted and lucrative top four places was about to become even more hectic, and concerns grew that this was creating a breakaway mini-league within the division.

At the end of the season, ITV Sport closed down. This channel had been broadcasting Football League matches, and although it did not affect the Premier League directly, it certainly caused a lot of concern, with the fear of a ripple effect, and a reduction in revenues and sponsorship spreading to the top tier. The collapse almost sent a number of Football League clubs to the wall, as their budgets for the following seasons included the significant revenues that the broadcaster would have provided.

2002/03

Average transfer value (actual): £2,451,510   −18.8% compared with 2001/02

Highest Sq£:	£196,837,878	**Arsenal**
Highest £XI:	£113,757,434	**Manchester United**
Average £XI:	£48,427,497	
Highest gross spend (CTPP):	£50,829,464	**Manchester United**
Highest net spend (CTPP):	£47,602,196	**Manchester United**

Having been stung by the loss of their crown in the previous season, Manchester United went about recovering it by smashing the transfer record to take Rio Ferdinand from Leeds – the second time he had enjoyed the status of being the most expensive player in the country. This immediately had the desired effect, as United wrested the title back from previous champions Arsenal. Indeed, Ferdinand was the only major signing of the season for United, as Ferguson atoned for the lack of a replacement for Jaap Stam in the previous campaign. United's finances allowed for the expensive purchase of Ferdinand since they still had an average of five home-grown players in the squad.

The overall difference between actual finishing position and £XI remained low, with the average variance being just 3.1 places. Indeed, but for Southampton's 10-place overachievement, the difference would have reached a new record low. Having secured survival when all looked lost in the previous season, Gordon Strachan steered the Saints to 8th place and an FA Cup Final which, thanks to Arsenal's qualification for the Champions League, handed a UEFA Cup place to Saints for the following season. Blackburn, with only the 12th-highest £XI, did even better in the league, attaining their UEFA Cup berth in 6th place.

The top five clubs – United, Arsenal, Newcastle, Chelsea and Liverpool – all finished in exactly the same order as their £XI would have forecast. The top four were all within 20% of United's £XI, with Liverpool dropping some way short at 65.8%. However, after this there was a huge gap to 6th-placed Middlesbrough on 43.6%. This sub-division of the top flight would continue for most of the remaining decade. Chelsea gained 4th position and the final Champions League qualifying place at Liverpool's expense; this would have major repercussions on the Premier League from the summer of 2003 onwards.

The biggest losers were Fulham, who, having spent big in the previous campaign, could not reproduce their form and finished seven places lower than expected, in 14th position. Other major disappointments were Leeds, who continued their downward slide, West Ham and Sunderland. The latter two clubs were both relegated, finishing five and six places respectively below expectation.

Major transfers
The fall in average transfer price was also reflected in the drop of more expensive signings. Whereas 29 transfers were conducted for in excess of £5m in 2001/02, the number had dropped to just 14 in 2002/03.

2002/03	Man United	Ferdinand R	£30,000,000	£48,409,013
2002/03	Man City	Anelka N	£13,000,000	£20,977,239
2002/03	Liverpool	Diouf E	£10,000,000	£16,136,338
2002/03	Newcastle	Woodgate J	£9,000,000	£14,522,704
2002/03	Newcastle	Viana H	£8,500,000	£13,715,887

Managers
After the underachievement of the previous season, Leeds replaced David O'Leary with the experienced former England coach Terry Venables. As Leeds' slide continued, Venables was sacked and replaced by Peter Reid. This was not to provide any respite though, as the Elland Road club fell to 15th.

Three other clubs changed manager, all in the bottom half of the table. Fulham sacked Jean Tigana and replaced him with Chris Coleman; West Ham put Trevor Brooking in temporary charge of affairs when Glenn Roeder left; and Sunderland replaced the departing Peter Reid with Howard Wilkinson and then Mick McCarthy.

The one common factor with all four of these changes was that the team did not benefit; all four teams finished between five and seven places lower than the £XI rankings would have suggested.

Finances
Attendances continued to creep up, increasing by 3% this season, largely as a result of promoted Birmingham and West Bromwich Albion. Only three teams were averaging over 40,000 per game: Liverpool (43,243), Newcastle (51,920) and Manchester United (67,630).

Other
The final day proved to be pivotal in the history of the Premier League. With all other European issues resolved, the only position still open was the final Champions League place which, as luck would have it, would be settled in favour of the victor of the match at Stamford Bridge between Chelsea and Liverpool. Chelsea won the match, gaining that final place in the Champions League, and shortly afterwards they would change hands in a deal that would forever alter the face of English football.

This season also saw the introduction of the transfer window, meaning that clubs could sign players only before the end of August or for a one-month period during January each season, although extensions were allowed in exceptional circumstances.

2003/04

Average transfer value (actual): £1,957,464   −20.2% compared with 2002/03

Highest Sq£:	£337,922,626	Chelsea
Highest £XI:	£153,144,833	Chelsea
Average £XI:	£48,862,303	
Highest gross spend (CTPP):	£228,361,725	Chelsea
Highest net spend (CTPP):	£227,351,274	Chelsea

Roman Abramovich. Two words, one name that would change the face of English football. Following Chelsea's qualification for the Champions League, the Russian oligarch decided to buy the club for £140m, then went on a spending spree the likes of which had never been seen before. All records were smashed: highest net spend (previously £61.7m), highest gross spend (£92.5m), highest average cost of £XI (£118.2m), highest Sq£ (£225.9m); all blown out of the water. How different things might have looked without the last-day win over Liverpool the previous season.

The intention was clear: conquer England and then rule in Europe. In some ways, the latter looked easier to achieve than the former. Chelsea reached the semi-finals of the Champions League, but were knocked out by Monaco. Having spent such vast amounts of money, Chelsea were expected to put in a strong push for their domestic league as well, a tournament they had not won since 1955.

Unfortunately for the Blues, their challenge coincided with possibly the strongest Arsenal side of all time. With just two signings since the previous year, the Gunners developed into a literally unbeatable team in the Premier League. For only the second time in top-flight football, and third time in English football history at any professional level, a team went the whole season without suffering a single defeat. This left Arsenal 11 points clear of Chelsea and 15 ahead of the defending champions, third-placed Manchester United.

The average variance between a team's expected position based on £XI and its actual finishing position increased to 4.6, but this was almost exclusively as a result of two teams, without whom the variance would have been just 3.5 places.

Bolton, who had only just survived in the previous year, flourished this season under Sam Allardyce's leadership. If they had been frugal in 2002/03, spending only £0.5m, they were positively Scrooge-like in 2003/04 as they spent not a penny on transfers. Nevertheless, they still managed to bring in eight players on free transfers and two more on loan deals. By the end of the season, they were in 8th place, only three points away from European qualification, with an £XI just £4.4m (or 2.9% of Chelsea's squad) – the least expensive to have ever appeared in the Premier League. (Bolton were one of the early examples of a team that diverted its entire transfer spend into wages and signing-on bonuses, taking advantage of the Bosman ruling.)

Going in the opposite direction were Manchester City, who should have been in the European places but finished 16th; still well clear of the drop zone, however. City had a reasonably expensive £XI, but failed to build significantly on that during 2003/04, spending only £7.5m in total.

It had never been more apparent that money was ruling the league than in this season, as the sub-divisions became even wider. The top five, not surprisingly, all had the highest £XI and therefore most expensive Sq£. Liverpool, in fifth place in £XI, had an average match-day squad cost of £87.5m (or only 60% of Chelsea's value) in current terms, whereas sixth-ranked Manchester City were at £45.5m (31.8% of Chelsea).

Major transfers
The total amount spent by the clubs in 2003/04 amounted to £274m (£553.8m) compared with £235.4m (£379.8m) in 2002/03, an increase of 45.8% in real terms. However, as this was spread over 140 sales as opposed to 96 in the previous season, the average transfer fee paid had fallen by 20.2%, with the difference being made up exclusively by Chelsea.

2003/04	Chelsea	Duff D	£17,000,000	£34,355,304
2003/04	Chelsea	Crespo H	£16,800,000	£33,951,124
2003/04	Chelsea	Mutu A	£15,800,000	£31,930,223
2003/04	Chelsea	Makélélé C	£13,900,000	£28,090,513

Managers

Aston Villa appointed David O'Leary as manager before the season started as replacement for Graham Taylor, and, after a poor start to the season, he drove them steadily up the table with an impressive run. A final-day defeat cost them 5th place and European qualification on goal difference from Newcastle.

Three other changes occurred during the season. Gordon Strachan quit his role as manager of Southampton; he was replaced by Paul Sturrock, after a brief caretaker spell by Steve Wigley. Sturrock successfully steered the Saints to mid-table safety.

The other two changes were less successful, with both teams finishing six places below their £XI ranking. Spurs, in 14th, dismissed Glenn Hoddle in September, and David Pleat was put in charge until the end of the season. At Leeds, Peter Reid was sacked and his replacement, Eddie Gray, was unable to stop their plummet towards Championship football. Indeed by this stage, Leeds were so short of money that their only transfers were either for free or on loan.

Finances

At the same time as Roman Abramovich was acquiring the ownership of Chelsea, Malcolm Glazer was taking his first steps in the long-term acquisition of Manchester United. The ownership was slowly increased until, in September, he had attained 3%, which required him to discuss his intentions with management. This was still a long way from outright ownership, which would occur at the end of the following season.

Attendances fell slightly (1.3%), mostly due to the fact that the promoted teams attracted lower attendances than the teams relegated in the previous season. Chelsea and Manchester City joined the +40,000 club, with City now occupying their new home at the City of Manchester Stadium, which had originally been built to host the 2002 Commonwealth Games.

Other

With the Sky deal up for renewal at the end of the season, the European Union threw a potential spanner in the works by insisting that a package of games had to be shown free-to-air on terrestrial television. The authorities would insist that the rights be sold in packages in future, allowing other broadcasters such as Setanta and ESPN to show football on their channels on a subscription basis. Far from reducing the amount of cash available to the Premier League, this would lead to a bidding war, pushing the cost of the deals up even further.

2004/05

Average transfer value (actual): £2,174,455   +11.1% compared with 2003/04

Highest Sq£:	£391,093,809	Chelsea
Highest £XI:	£195,163,149	Chelsea
Average £XI:	£47,012,872	
Highest gross spend (CTPP):	£182,560,004	Chelsea
Highest net spend (CTPP):	£167,096,525	Chelsea

Not content with their spend in the previous season, Chelsea, under new manager José Mourinho, went on another spree that only marginally fell short of the one from 12 months earlier. They did not even offload players to any great extent to fund these purchases, but simply loaned them out if it suited. The result was a squad worth almost double that of second-placed Arsenal and, after a 50-year gap and during the club's centenary season, a first Premier League title with a staggering 12 points to spare. Their points total was also a new record.

The average difference between the £XI ranking and actual table fell to just 3.2 places. As with last season, there were just two major variations, without which the total would have been just 2.1 places.

The best performance was by Bolton, who overachieved by 14 places, the highest since the Premier League's inaugural season. For the second season in a row, Sam Allardyce led his team to a fantastic finishing position with the least expensive £XI; with a value of £4.7m, it was only marginally higher than the previous season, but by contrast fell to just 2.4% of Chelsea's worth. At least this term, Bolton's achievement was rewarded with a place in the UEFA Cup, having finished behind Champions League winners Liverpool on goal difference.

Everton were also significant overachievers this season, finishing in 4th place just ahead of their Merseyside rivals and seven places higher than anticipated by the £XI ranking. David Moyes' team were therefore entered into the qualifying rounds of the Champions League; unfortunately for the Toffees, they met a Villarreal team heading to the semi-final. Everton's achievement is put in perspective by the value of their £XI - £27.3m compared with fourth-ranked Liverpool's £75.2m.

The biggest underachievers were once again Newcastle, as the Toon Army finished in 14th, nine places lower than forecast. With an £XI of £70.3m, they were streets ahead of the next-placed £XI, Tottenham, but with an ageing Alan Shearer failing to provide the expected goals (just seven in 26 starts), the Geordies found it difficult to record the necessary victories.

Bottom of the division were Southampton, six places below their £XI ranking. Without this failure by the Saints, the three newly promoted clubs would have gone straight back down, with only West Brom surviving, and that by a single point from Crystal Palace and Norwich. All three of these teams were in the bottom five in terms of £XI.

Major transfers

2004/05	Man United	Rooney W	£27,000,000	£49,119,283
2004/05	Chelsea	Drogba D	£24,000,000	£43,661,585
2004/05	Chelsea	Carvalho R	£19,850,000	£36,111,770
2004/05	Liverpool	Cissé D	£14,200,000	£25,833,105
2004/05	Chelsea	Ferreira P	£13,200,000	£24,013,872

Managers

Four clubs changed manager before the season started. Porto's Champions League-winning coach José Mourinho arrived at Chelsea, and Liverpool selected Valencia's UEFA Cup/double La Liga-winning coach Rafael Benítez.

Spurs also went for an overseas coach in Jacques Santini, but in November he left for personal reasons, to be replaced by his assistant, Martin Jol. After a brief spell in charge by John Carver, Graeme Souness took the reins at Newcastle, having left Blackburn (where he was replaced by Mark Hughes). Neither club fared well, with Newcastle and Rovers finishing nine and seven places respectively below their £XI ranking.

Harry Redknapp also took the helm at two clubs, starting the season at Portsmouth before moving onto Southampton, where, following the departure of previous manager Paul Sturrock, he failed to save the Saints from relegation. Back at Portsmouth, Velimir Zajec took over, but by March he too was gone, with Alain Perrin the new boss. With the fourth-least expensive £XI, it was a minor miracle that Portsmouth survived these managerial changes.

Two other teams changed manager with rather less dramatic effect, both finishing just one place lower than anticipated. Kevin Keegan left Manchester City in March, to be replaced by Stuart Pearce; and at West Brom, a combination of Gary Megson, and then Bryan Robson, managed to keep the Baggies in the Premier League by just two points.

Finances

With the Sky TV deal negotiated in 2001 repeated in 2004, clubs were receiving £17m per season from this source alone. Attendances were down by 3.2%, at least in part attributable to the relegated clubs having higher average attendances than those that replaced them in the Premier League.

During the course of the campaign, Malcolm Glazer further increased his stake in Manchester United. Shortly after the season finished, his stake stood at almost 60%, requiring him to make a formal bid for the entire company. When he reached 75% shortly afterwards, he delisted the company as a PLC and eventually bought out the remaining minority. There was some discontent amongst United's fans, and this would grow as the financial implications for the club became apparent over the coming seasons.

Other

English dominance in Europe was about to begin, not least because of the vast amounts of money being injected by wealthy owners, who saw their rewards both in financial terms through the lucrative Champions League format and the prestige that went with it. All four clubs made it through the group stage; two fell at the round of 16, and Chelsea and Liverpool met in the semi-final, producing a drama–filled night in the second leg at Anfield. The home team prevailed, despite a gulf in finances that meant the Reds had a Sqf value an astonishing £220m lower than that of their opponents (who were pushing towards the £400m barrier).

The final was one of the most remarkable in history, with Milan leading 3-0 at half time, thanks in no small part to former Chelsea player Hernán Crespo and future Chelsea player Andriy Shevchenko, before the Reds responded with three goals in six second–half minutes, ultimately securing victory in a penalty shoot–out.

For the next five years, England would have at least one representative in the final and two or three in the semi-finals, giving UEFA headaches over a number of factors: ticketing arrangements, travel and club finances arising from the way in which this success was being funded.

2005/06

Average transfer value (actual): £2,167,877   **−0.3% compared with 2004/05**

Highest Sqf:	£415,553,023	Chelsea
Highest £XI:	£229,619,425	Chelsea
Average £XI:	£51,112,423	
Highest gross spend (CTPP):	£105,470,736	Chelsea
Highest net spend (CTPP):	£56,019,924	Chelsea

Chelsea were once again record breakers; for the first time, their total squad cost had broken through the £400m (CTPP) barrier, and their £XI had pushed beyond £200m. Not surprisingly in the circumstances, they went on to claim their second consecutive title.

The disparity in £XIs was becoming increasingly pronounced; back in the first Premier League season in 1992/93, Norwich, with a utilisation ranking of 18th, were valued at 20.8% of that season's champions, Manchester United. In 2005/06, Spurs had a very similar £XI rating to Norwich's (relative to the champions) – worth just 20.7% of Chelsea's – yet Spurs were ranked sixth in £XI.

In all previous Premier League seasons, the average £XI across the whole division had hovered between 40% and 50% of the highest value. In 2003/04, it had dropped below 40% for the first time. In 2004/05, it stood at 24.4%, and in 2005/06 it fell again, to just 22.7% – this trend would bottom out in 2006/07 at just 20.9%. Clearly the Premier League was becoming anything but a level playing field. Competing with Chelsea was virtually impossible.

Manchester United, for so long the nation's richest club, were now trailing in Chelsea's wake, both in £XI and in the actual table. Still fielding on average over four home-grown players per match (compared with Chelsea's 1.2), they now stood at 74.4% of Chelsea's £XI, and finished eight points behind their London rivals.

The average difference between £XI ranking and the position in the actual table rose slightly to 3.6 places this season, with all the top five teams in the actual table within one place of their expected position based on utilisation. The finishing positions were starting to become more predictable.

For the third season in a row, Bolton were the best-performing team, once again finishing a massive 12 places above where expected. They relied heavily on the players from the previous campaign, supplementing this with only a couple of signings, including El-Hadji Diouf. Sam Allardyce was certainly getting the most from what was once again the least expensive £XI in the Premier League: a mere 3.7% of Chelsea's.

Two promoted teams – West Ham (seven places) and Wigan (eight places) – did better than expected, both achieving comfortable mid-table finishes and both having about 60% of their £XI contributed by players signed after their promotion had been confirmed. The other promoted club, Sunderland, also signed players, but spent nowhere near as much cash. With the second-lowest £XI, it was no surprise to see them cut adrift at the bottom of the table, some 23 points short of safety.

The two worst-performing teams were Middlesbrough and Aston Villa, who each finished seven places lower than expected. Boro relied mainly on their existing squad, although they did add Yakubu, whose goals proved crucial. Villa also suffered from a lack of goals, with new signing Milan Baroš finishing joint top scorer on just eight. Nevertheless, they were safe from any relegation concerns, being eight points ahead of city rivals Birmingham.

Major transfers

2005/06	Chelsea	Essien M	£26,000,000	£47,443,584
2005/06	Chelsea	Wright-Phillips S	£21,000,000	£38,319,818
2005/06	Newcastle	Owen M	£17,000,000	£31,020,805
2006/07	Arsenal	Walcott T	£12,000,000	£21,897,039
2005/06	Arsenal	Hleb A	£11,200,000	£20,437,236

Managers

There were no changes before the season started, but three clubs did replace managers in mid-season. None of the changes made any significant difference to the clubs' standings.

At Newcastle, the perennial underachievers, Graeme Souness was replaced by Glenn Roeder. Newcastle had hoped to be challenging for the Champions League places, but trailed some way behind in 7th, squeezing into the Intertoto Cup. At Portsmouth, Alain Perrin was struggling to keep Pompey's heads above water in the fight against relegation. He was replaced by Harry Redknapp, who put them on an even keel, finishing exactly where their utilisation predicted in 17th position, one place above the drop zone. Sunderland, effectively doomed from day one, replaced Mick McCarthy with Kevin Ball, but the gap was too big to bridge. The Black Cats managed just 26 goals all season, which left them without a hope of survival.

Finances

A report issued by the Football League highlighted the outflow of funds from unforeseen sources. In total, £7.9m was paid in agents' fees in respect of players' transfers. This figure would have been immeasurably higher for the Premier League, given the quantum jump in transfer values between the two divisions.

Attendances remained static overall, with a massive increase for Wigan and decent rises for West Ham and Sunderland. This was offset by the absence of Southampton, Norwich and Crystal Palace, who had higher attendances than the clubs that replaced them.

Other

Three of England's four representatives in the Champions League had a poor time in Europe. Manchester United were knocked out in the group stage, and Liverpool and Chelsea followed in the round of 16, leaving only Arsenal to fly the flag. This they did all the way to the final, before losing to Barcelona after goalkeeper Jens Lehmann received an early red card.

2006/07

Average transfer value (actual): £2,276,322   **+5.0% compared with 2005/06**

Highest Sq£:	£438,985,943	Chelsea
Highest £XI:	£255,266,748	Chelsea
Average £XI:	£53,485,842	
Highest gross spend (CTPP):	£119,562,079	Chelsea
Highest net spend (CTPP):	£79,939,762	Chelsea

For the third consecutive season, Chelsea recorded the highest £XI, Sq£ and both net and gross expenditure on transfers. Despite this, they were unable to retain their title and slipped to second place; the crown returning to Old Trafford. Chelsea's new record signing Andriy Shevchenko failed to make an impact on his arrival from AC Milan and was hugely disappointing: scoring only four goals and being loaned out for future seasons.

Although Chelsea, Manchester United, Arsenal and Liverpool were already being referred to as the 'big four', in reality Chelsea were so far ahead of everyone else financially that they were a category apart. Liverpool, for example, had an £XI only 32.5% of Chelsea's, despite ranking third in the utilisation table. Manchester United had more than double Liverpool's £XI, at £171.7m (69.2% of Chelsea's), in a season which saw the division's overall £XI at £53.5m.

The average difference between the expected position based on £XI ranking and the actual league placing fell to just 2.9 places. The top six teams in the actual table were all within one place of their anticipated position.

The star performers were Reading, who finished in 8th place despite having the lowest-valued £XI. This was all the more surprising as Reading had only just been promoted, and their £XI percentage (2.3%) in comparison with the costliest (Chelsea's) was the lowest of any team in the history of the Premier League Also mentioned in despatches are Bolton and Portsmouth, both of whom finished six places higher than expected. At Bolton, Sam Allardyce shelled out on transfer fees (rather than just wages) and raised his £XI from £8.9m in 2005/06 to £25.4m in 2006/07; ranking 13th. In the actual table, they finished as high as 7th, again qualifying for the UEFA Cup – a wonderful performance by a relatively small club.

Another Lancashire club, Wigan, proved to be amongst the biggest failures this season. They were unable to repeat their achievements of the previous campaign and Paul Jewell's charges fell to 17th, level on points with relegated Sheffield United. Nevertheless, given the dominance of rugby league and the lack of football tradition at the top level in the town, survival for Wigan was still a respectable achievement.

Worst performers of all, once again, were Newcastle. With Alan Shearer having retired, and Michael Owen almost permanently injured, manager Glenn Roeder could not get the team scoring enough goals. With only Obafemi Martins (11) scoring more than five, Newcastle slipped to 13th – when on £XI they could reasonably have expected a place in the top six.

Major transfers

2006/07	Chelsea	Shevchenko A	£30,800,000	£53,524,884
2006/07	Man United	Carrick M	£18,600,000	£32,323,469
2006/07	Chelsea	Cole A	£16,000,000	£27,805,135
2006/07	Chelsea	Mikel J	£12,000,000	£20,853,851
2006/07	Spurs	Berbatov D	£10,890,000	£18,924,870

In total, the clubs spent £652.7m in current terms, a new record high and 13% more than the previous season.

Managers

At the start of the season, Aston Villa replaced David O'Leary with Martin O'Neill. The first season proved to be a difficult one, with Villa finishing only 11th, despite having the eighth-most expensive £XI; although it was an improvement on the year before.

Also on the move was Iain Dowie at Charlton, replacing Alan Curbishley. Charlton performed poorly and Dowie himself was replaced by Les Reed and then Alan Pardew, but the managerial merry-go-round failed to save the Addicks from the drop. They finished five places lower than their £XI ranking.

Pardew had joined Charlton after leaving West Ham earlier in the season, following the takeover of the Upton Park club by Eggert Magnusson. At West Ham, the game of musical chairs was completed when Alan Curbishley accepted the role of manager.

There were two more managerial casualties towards the end of the season. First, Chris Coleman was fired at Fulham and replaced by Lawrie Sanchez, who had just enough time to save the Cottagers from the drop. At Bolton, Sam Allardyce's successful tenure came to an end when he resigned, to be replaced by assistant Sammy Lee. Allardyce was to join Newcastle after the season finished, but neither he nor Lee would enjoy success in their new roles.

Finances

Three clubs changed hands during the course of the season. In August, American businessman Randy Lerner purchased Aston Villa from Doug Ellis for £64m. In November, West Ham were sold to Icelandic businessman Eggert Magnusson. With the world economic crisis just around the corner, and Iceland particularly hard hit, West Ham and Magnusson were about to enter major turbulence. The final and largest of the three club sales was that of Liverpool to American tycoons George Gillett and Thomas Hicks. The pair paid David Moores £219m for the club, and immediately promised the development of a new stadium to replace the ageing Anfield, and give the Reds the same commercial opportunities afforded to Arsenal and Manchester United.

By now Arsenal had moved into a new stadium, after vacating their Highbury home at the end of the previous season. The Emirates Stadium cost £390m to build and has a capacity of over 60,000 all seated. This generates some £3m in revenue per match. The club also sold the naming rights to the Emirates airline for 15 years at a cost of £100m, which was used to pay down part of the funding debt.

With well-supported teams such as Sunderland and Birmingham being replaced by Reading and Watford, the average attendance rose only marginally; these decreases offset the massive increase enjoyed by Arsenal at their new home.

Other

Three English clubs reached the semi-finals of the Champions League, and one the final of the UEFA Cup, as England's dominance grew. Arsenal had bowed out at the round of 16 stage and Manchester United were eliminated by AC Milan in the semi-final. The other semi-final saw a repeat of two years earlier as Liverpool put out Chelsea, this time on penalties, to produce a repeat of the Istanbul final of 2005. This time, however, AC Milan got their revenge, despite this time being outplayed.

The UEFA Cup finalists were Middlesbrough, and even though they were comprehensively beaten by Sevilla in the final, this cemented manager Steve McLaren's reputation. He was subsequently offered the role of England national team manager.

2007/08

Average transfer value (actual): £3,504,886   +54.0% compared with 2006/07

Highest Sq£:	£432,360,309	Chelsea
Highest £XI:	£201,709,707	Chelsea
Average £XI:	£56,705,763	
Highest gross spend (CTPP):	£78,272,867	Liverpool
Highest net spend (CTPP):	£48,893,736	Manchester City

In a close-run battle, Manchester United retained their title, pushed all the way by Chelsea and Arsenal. The gap narrowed to two points to the Blues and four points to the Gunners, and even Liverpool in 4th had shown considerable improvement by reaching 76 points.

Chelsea again invested heavily, but this time everybody else did the same, hence the narrowing in the gap of the overall utilisation. Where the average had been just 20.9% of the highest value in 2006/07, it had now increased to 28.1%. This was partly due to a lowering of Chelsea's £XI from £255.3m to £201.7m, but also an increase in the £XI of the remaining teams in the division.

The average difference between expected position from £XI and the actual position fell to a new low of just 2.4 places. Fifteen of the clubs finished within just two places of their £XI ranking.

The best performers were Blackburn, who finished six places higher than expected in 7th place. Mark Hughes had his team playing at a level of roughly twice the £XI available. Their only major signing was Roque Santa Cruz, who cost a paltry £3.5m (£4.0m) and scored 19 goals in 36 starts. The main underachievers were Spurs, Newcastle and Birmingham. Spurs had a poor start and Martin Jol was sacked during a UEFA Cup tie, being replaced shortly afterwards by Juande Ramos. Ramos guided Spurs to 11th, which was still a disappointing return for the team ranked fourth in the £XI table, some £20m higher than rivals Arsenal.

Newcastle, who had replaced Glenn Roeder with new manager Sam Allardyce at the start of the season, were really struggling when his contract was terminated in January, the low point being a 3–0 home defeat by Liverpool. Kevin Keegan was welcomed with open arms as the new manager, but it quickly became clear that he too was having problems, especially after an extended absence from the game. Ultimately, Newcastle finished in 12th, one place behind Spurs and six lower than their £XI ranking.

Birmingham were relegated in 19th place, five places lower than their utilisation would have suggested. This was disappointing as the team, with an £XI of £30m, finished below Reading, who had an £XI of only £5.6m. Matters were not helped when Steve Bruce was tempted away from St Andrew's by the lure of a more secure job at Wigan, leaving Alex McLeish with a battle against relegation from the moment he arrived in November.

Major transfers

2007/08	Liverpool	Torres F	£20,000,000	£22,573,285
2007/08	Liverpool	Mascherano J	£18,600,000	£20,993,155
2007/08	Man United	Anderson	£18,000,000	£20,315,957
2007/08	Man United	Hargreaves O	£17,000,000	£19,187,293
2007/08	Man United	Nani	£17,000,000	£19,187,293

Managers

Aside from Sam Allardyce at Newcastle, the only new manager at the start of the season was Sven-Göran Eriksson, who had replaced Stuart Pearce. Eriksson had City playing well at the start of the season, and a Champions League place was looking a distinct possibility at Christmas. However, a poor second half to the season saw City slump to 9th, still one place above their £XI ranking.

The biggest shock of the season was the departure of José Mourinho at the end of September, who was immediately replaced by Avram Grant. Sam Allardyce's replacement at Bolton, Sammy Lee, lasted only until October due to the Trotters' poor performances and was replaced by Gary Megson. The 'Ginger Mourinho' rallied the troops and Bolton finished in 16th, two places above their £XI ranking and, crucially, saving themselves from relegation. At Fulham, Roy Hodgson caused a similar fightback, with the Cottagers 18th at Christmas when Lawrie Sanchez was removed. By the end of the season, Hodgson had done well to get them to 17th, one place lower than their £XI ranking.

The other change in the season had little overall impact, with Derby being relegated despite swapping Billy Davies for Paul Jewell in November.

Finances
Sky renewed their television contract this season, with their three-year deal worth a total of £1.7bn, equivalent to £28m per club per season. With other sponsorship deals for naming rights, overseas broadcasting and radio, the amounts available to the clubs were much higher than this figure. Not surprisingly, much of this money went straight on transfers.

Attendances were up 5% compared with the previous year, and now eight teams were averaging over 40,000: Manchester United (76,000), Arsenal (60,000), Newcastle (51,000), Liverpool (44,000), Sunderland (43,000), Manchester City (42,000), Chelsea (41,000) and Aston Villa (40,000).

At two north-west clubs, there were the first stirrings of discontent against the owners. At Manchester United, the level of debt was becoming an issue, with huge amounts of interest being paid to service the loans and therefore not available for players and salaries. At Liverpool, there were similar issues, however this was only worsened by the lack of stadium development that had been promised when the Americans took over a year earlier. With steel prices rising and European development grants potentially being withdrawn due to the inertia, it was looking increasingly unlikely that 'New Anfield' would be built, at least in the near future.

Other
In the Champions League, both finalists were from the Premier League for the first time. All four representatives reached the quarter-finals, with Chelsea edging out Liverpool in one of the semi-finals and going on to lose to Manchester United on penalties in the final in Moscow. This would represent the high watermark for English teams in Europe.

2008/09

Average transfer value (actual): £5,059,310   +44.4% compared with 2007/08

Highest Sq£:	£376,624,798	Chelsea
Highest £XI:	£168,193,359	Chelsea
Average £XI:	£54,585,228	
Highest gross spend (CTPP):	£101,255,160	Manchester City
Highest net spend (CTPP):	£86,008,244	Manchester City

Note: as the average transfer price dropped in the season after 2008/09, and all Current Transfer Purchase Prices are obviously stated at 2009/10 rates, the actual figures for 2008/09 are higher than the current values.

For a third consecutive season, Manchester United won the title despite not having the highest £XI. For a second consecutive season, Chelsea's utilisation fell, although it remained the highest in the division – 'just' £10m ahead of United. Indeed, the whole league had become more compacted in this respect, with the average £XI growing to 32.8%, compared with the low of 20.9% a couple of seasons previously.

This, however, had little impact on the field of play, with the 'big four' finishing once again in the Champions League positions. The average difference between £XI ranking and actual finishing position had increased to 3.7 places, largely as a result of the increase in the average utilisation mentioned above. This season, only eight of the 20 teams finished within two places of their ranking, although only one club differed by as much as 10 places.

The best performance was by Stoke, who in their first season back in the top flight finished in 12th place, despite having the second-least expensive £XI. At just £10.0m, they should have been cut adrift, but instead were on the edge of the European qualification placings for much of the early part of the season, before falling away after Christmas.

Not far behind Stoke in overachieving were Fulham and Wigan, both of whom had flirted with relegation the previous season. Wigan were comfortably in mid-table, whereas Fulham, thanks to the cup wins by members of the big four, qualified for the re-branded Europa League, in which they would enjoy an extended run.

Although Arsenal claimed 4th place and could boast the second-largest stadium, their £XI, in ninth place in the ranking, was just £55.5m, almost £40m behind fifth-placed Spurs. Their on-field success was built largely on the ability of Arsène Wenger to identify young, primarily overseas talent, buy at an inexpensive price and develop them into first-team players. It was enabling them to remain within the top four, but as yet, not challenge for the title right up until May.

The biggest underachievers, yet again, were Newcastle, but this time they paid the ultimate price of relegation. With an £XI of £63.5m – the sixth-highest in the division – the Geordies finished in 18th place, below Hull, whose utilisation was only £7.3m – the lowest in the division.

Major transfers
£733.6m (£573.6m) was spent in total, with Manchester City and Spurs both exceeding £100m.

2008/09	Man City	Robinho	£32,500,000	£25,411,527
2008/09	Man United	Berbatov D	£30,500,000	£23,847,740
2008/09	Liverpool	Keane R (II)	£19,000,000	£14,855,969
2008/09	Man City	Jo	£19,000,000	£14,855,969
2008/09	Man City	de Jong N	£17,000,000	£13,292,183
2008/09	Spurs	Bentley D	£17,000,000	£13,292,183

Managers
The main change pre-season was the replacement of Avram Grant with Luiz Felipe Scolari at Chelsea. Grant paid a high price for his failure to wrest the title back from Manchester United, although he was one post width away from being a European Champion. With Chelsea down the pecking order, Scolari himself was sacked in February and Guus Hiddink brought in, but he could not get the Blues to higher than third.

Two managers were replaced within 24 hours during September. First, Alan Curbishley left West Ham after disagreements with the board over transfer policy, to be replaced by Gianfranco Zola. Shortly after, Kevin Keegan resigned at Newcastle to be replaced by Joe Kinnear. Kinnear suffered a heart attack in February and was relieved of his duties by Chris Hughton and then Alan Shearer, who struggled in vain to keep the Magpies above the relegation zone.

Juande Ramos was sacked at Spurs, with Harry Redknapp taking over after he left Portsmouth, where Tony Adams would replace him. However, Adams was sacked in February to make way for Paul Hart. Redknapp's task at Spurs looked difficult when he took over, with the club bottom of the league after eight games. However, things quickly turned following a victory over previously unbeaten Liverpool and Spurs went on a wonderful run which saw them rise to 8th, just two points short of Fulham in the European places. At Sunderland, Roy Keane resigned just before Christmas and was replaced by Ricky Sbragia, although in league terms this had little overall effect on the Black Cats' position.

The final managerial change took place at Blackburn, where new manager Paul Ince, who had only joined the club in the summer, was sacked in December after a dreadful start, with Rovers sitting in 19th place. In came Sam Allardyce, who steadied the ship before gradually dragging Rovers to 15th in the league, one place above their £XI rank.

Finances

Club owners were coming under ever more intense spotlights, thanks to the way they had financed their acquisitions. At Newcastle, there were regular protests against Mike Ashley, who had spent a small fortune on players without success. He had put the club up for sale, but nobody had come forward with a firm bid.

Liverpool and Manchester United fans had become familiar with the term "leveraged buy-out", since this was the vehicle that had been used to purchase both clubs. This had the effect of putting the debt onto the club itself rather than the owner, meaning that the club not only had to pay off the capital but also the interest.

Manchester City were the big story financially, with the club purchased by the Abu Dhabi United Group, who immediately set about buying up available talent at often inflated prices in an attempt to gain entry to the Champions League. It bore striking comparisons with the early spending frenzy of Roman Abramovich's Chelsea four years earlier. However, this put manager Mark Hughes in the awkward position of seeing a procession of players arriving whom he had never previously considered and did not necessarily want. With City's £XI jumping to fifth, the blend of players on the pitch failed to keep pace with the utilisation as they eventually slumped to 10th in the actual table.

Other

English dominance in Europe began to wane a little this season, although the Premier League still provided three of the Champions League semi-finalists. Having knocked out Liverpool in an almighty quarter-final tussle, Chelsea then succumbed to Barcelona in the semis. In the other semi-final, Manchester United comfortably defeated Arsenal, but Barcelona were simply too good for United in the final in Rome.

2009/10

Average transfer value (actual): £3,955,840   −21.8% compared with 2008/09

Highest Sq£:	£401,297,570	**Chelsea**
Highest £XI:	£187,436,345	**Chelsea**
Average £XI:	£54,145,573	
Highest gross spend (CTPP):	£125,000,000	**Manchester City**
Highest net spend (CTPP):	£99,500,000	**Manchester City**

Note: In 2009/10, all values are the same under actual spend and CTPP.

Chelsea regained their title, with mostly the same squad as they had in the previous season. As the credit crunch tightened its grip on financial markets, football was not immune from its effects. The average fee fell by 21.8% to below £4m, and the highest ever number of loan deals were undertaken.

Nevertheless, in terms of utilisation, the table had never been closer to the rankings. **The average difference between the two measures fell to just 2.3 places. Thirteen teams finished within two places of their £XI ranking.** The biggest difference was just seven places, while the top two finished in the correct order and the bottom three had the three lowest £XI.

Two teams finished as many as five places above expectation – Blackburn and Stoke City. After the disaster at Newcastle, Sam Allardyce was looking more comfortable back in Lancashire, and at Rovers he had the team safely in mid-table with a large part of the season to spare. Tony Pulis at Stoke continued the good work from the previous season, and the Potters' strong home record made sure that they would be safe for another season of Premier League football.

Only one team dropped by more than five places below their £XI ranking – West Ham, who would have been expected to come 10th but finished one place above relegation in 17th. The season was incredibly difficult for the Hammers, with constant uncertainty about their ability to survive following the collapse of the Icelandic banking system, the sector in which West Ham's owners had made their money. This meant that West Ham were initially unable to make any transfer purchases.

With Chelsea able to field a slightly more expensive £XI than in the previous season, the gap between the teams became slightly wider. The average £XI across the division dropped to below 30% of Chelsea's value again, with five teams below 10% and half the division below 20%. The biggest leap was made by Manchester City, who were probably the most disappointed team at the end of the season when they failed to achieve their ambition of Champions League football. Liverpool also fell short of expectations.

Another facet of this season was the drop in the number of home-grown players. Although Manchester United, with an average of 3.8 home-grown players per match, tried to keep the average up, the division total fell to just 0.9 per match. In other words, less than one player in each team had been brought through their own youth development system. Three teams failed to have a single home-grown player start a game during the whole season – Birmingham, Wigan and Burnley.

Major transfers

2009/10	Man City	Tévez C	£25,500,000	£25,500,000
2009/10	Man City	Adebayor M	£25,000,000	£25,000,000
2009/10	Man City	Lescott J	£22,000,000	£22,000,000
2009/10	Liverpool	Aquilani A	£20,000,000	£20,000,000
2009/10	Chelsea	Zhirkov Y	£18,000,000	£18,000,000
2009/10	Liverpool	Johnson G (I)	£18,000,000	£18,000,000

Managers

This was a remarkably stable season for managers. Before the season started, Carlo Ancelotti was appointed as the new Chelsea boss in place of the departing Guus Hiddink.

The first casualty of the season was Paul Hart at Portsmouth, but this was hardly a surprise given Pompey's dreadful start to the season, which by Christmas looked as though relegation was as good as guaranteed. In his place came Avram Grant, who despite his best efforts, was unable to save Portsmouth. He did at least get Pompey to their second FA Cup Final in three seasons.

Manchester City were in a disappointing 6th place shortly before Christmas and Mark Hughes paid the price for a series of drawn matches. Hughes was replaced by Roberto Mancini, but despite a honeymoon period which saw City push on towards the top four, defeat against Spurs in the penultimate game of the season condemned them to 5th.

With Bolton occupying the last of the relegation places in December, Gary Megson was dismissed and replaced by Burnley's Owen Coyle. Coyle oversaw a great recovery by the Trotters, who finished 14th – nine points clear of relegation. At Burnley, Coyle was replaced by Brian Laws. However, the departure of the Scot led to the Clarets falling from 14th to 18th. This was broadly in line with the projected forecast, as the newly promoted club was widely expected to struggle, especially as they had the least expensive £XI.

Hull had managed to pull themselves as high as 14th in February. However, a run of four consecutive defeats saw them plummet to 19th and Phil Brown was replaced with Iain Dowie. This managerial change would be of little consequence as Hull finished in the same position at the end of the season, one place lower than their utilisation would have forecast.

Finances

A number of clubs changed ownership during the season, and for the first time, a Premier League club (Portsmouth) went into administration. Sunderland were acquired by Ellis Short in May 2009, but this was a relatively low-key affair. West Ham changed hands again following the Icelandic banking crisis in June 2009; this time to David Sullivan and David Gold, who bought the club in January. In October, the two Davids had sold their previous club Birmingham to Grandtop, a Hong Kong-based consortium.

Porstmouth, with four different owners, were in severe financial straits throughout the entire season. With the creditors circling, the club was banned from buying players and then placed into administration. This carried an automatic nine-point penalty, which was duly enforced. As Portsmouth were already in relegation trouble, the points deduction sealed their fate well before the end of the season.

At Liverpool and Manchester United, the publication of the clubs' accounts was met with horror. Liverpool, with more than £400m of debt, were paying £40m of interest a year to service that deficit. This was more than the sale value of Xabi Alonso, and all without having even started work on the stadium development project. At United, the official debt was an eye-watering £700m, which carried interest payments of £70m, and might well explain why more of the Cristiano Ronaldo transfer fee was not invested in the team. Disturbingly, a BBC investigation revealed that things were even worse, as the owners had opened a number of club shops in the United States with mortgages on the properties. However, following the collapse of property values, these stores now had negative equity and the club was responsible for covering the debts, potentially adding another £300m–500m to the debt.

Other

In the Champions League, the English clubs' demise continued. Liverpool were eliminated at the group stage, although they did reach the semi-final of the Europa League, where they lost to eventual winners Atlético Madrid, who prevailed over Fulham in the final. Chelsea were knocked out by Internazionale in the round of 16, while Arsenal and Manchester United went out in the quarter-finals to Barcelona and Bayern Munich respectively. In short, England had its worst European performance in five seasons.

Part Four
The Main Managers

Spending Overview

As judges, we always tend to apportion credit or blame for the success or failure of a transfer solely to the manager, but it's more complicated than that; he is often at the mercy of his scouting department, and those above him who have to agree to spend the money and then successfully negotiate a deal. Are they really *his* signings? (And this is before even getting onto the role of a Director of Football.) Even if the manager has watched the player in person on a number of occasions, he may find something different when he finally gets to work with him; for example, can the new arrival adapt to different ideas? Then there are myriad factors that go into making a signing look the part: settling into a new club (and possibly a brand new country); fitting into a new system; and the luck-permitting gifts of health and fitness.

The starting position of his club is also a key factor in an incoming manager's subsequent outlay: inherit a strong squad and not much investment is needed; inherit an ageing, unbalanced or just plain sub-standard collection of players, and it's a different challenge. And a manager who has had the time and money to assemble a squad according to his desires will be at a distinct advantage over a more recently appointed boss, who will be mixing and matching his own purchases with the best of what he has inherited.

To assess the following managers fairly, one problem had to be overcome: namely, that all of the 'top five' bosses had players still active at the clubs they originally brought them to – but some had far more than others, depending on whether or not the managers concerned are still the incumbents at their respective clubs, and if not, how much time has passed since they left. Thus the lowest active total is two: Claudio Ranieri's purchases of Frank Lampard and Petr Čech for Chelsea. However, by contrast, both Arsène Wenger and Alex Ferguson had entire squads of their own signings at their disposal. Therefore, all as-yet unsold players needed a monetary value.

To attain one, the list of players was sent to several trusted sources, and an average of their estimates taken as the current value. Now of course, many things affect a transfer value: form at the time; injury problems; contract length; age; the health of the market as a whole; the financial strength/weakness of the club; and so on. These were all taken into account, but equally, all can rapidly change. On the whole, the values decided upon should be good guesstimates, but that doesn't mean everyone will agree with them. (Out of interest, since the list was compiled, some players have indeed been transferred; and while the actual value was used in these cases, they did closely match the hypothesised figures).

The experts who gave their time were Ben Smith, football writer for *The Times*; Tor-Kristian Karlsen, a London-based Norwegian football analyst and former scout for Bayer Leverkusen and other German clubs; Chris Mann, author of the *The Equaliser* blog; Kevin Coleman, Editor of the *Back Page Football* website; and Graeme Riley, ruler of the TPI database.

Reminder: these figures do not include the assortment of teenage talent bought initially for youth and reserve teams, unless they made the breakthrough or cost more than a minimal fee. No signings beyond January 2010 are included, although if a player was sold in the summer of 2010, that was taken into account. While listing the actual fees, this section is largely about assessing genuine profits and losses, and the ratios between the two.

The Big Task

This section focuses on the managers of the big-hitting and high-spending clubs, looking at the top five ranking bosses in terms of average points per season (minimum of three campaigns) in the 18 Premier League seasons to date. These are some of the game's major names: José Mourinho, Alex Ferguson, Arsène Wenger, Rafael Benítez and Claudio Ranieri. In addition to these, some information on the next five in the list – Gianluca Vialli, Kenny Dalglish, Gérard Houllier, Roy Evans and Bobby Robson – is provided, with 11th-placed Kevin Keegan thrown in for good measure.

A manager's net spend is often used to show how frugal or profligate he has been. While it's far better than focusing on gross spend (outgoings only), it still has its limitations; not least, how much of the original squad he inherited could be sold in order to raise funds for his own purchases, and what prices those players might fetch.

For the purposes of this book, it is not the Ins and Outs during a manager's time in charge that we will focus on, but all of *his* signings and all of *their* eventual sale fees (or values), whether moved on under his own stewardship or by his successor/s.

Recouping Money From Purchases

While the primary aim when buying players is almost always to improve the team and the squad, the need to generate money from sales is something most clubs have to take into account; resale value is important in order to regenerate the team at a later date. The ideal scenario is to buy when young and cheap, just before the player is on everyone's radar. He then blossoms, gives several years of service and, just before he starts to decline, he is sold for a hefty fee (usually to someone who wants to make a marquee signing, and has more money than sense; often based somewhere in Madrid). The legendary Liverpool boss Bob Paisley was a master at this. "Let your players lose their legs on someone else's pitch" was how he described his approach. Arsène Wenger has also become known for this strategy. It's true that both of these managers kept a world-class, deep-lying forward well into his 30s (Dalglish and Bergkamp) – and therefore, until his value had run low; but with it eked out, in high quality instalments, on *their* pitches. However, they sold other stars – usually those for whom athleticism was crucial – before the rest of the watching world had realised that their best days were behind them.

In the Arsenal manager's case, he did this most notably with Patrick Vieira and Thierry Henry, two of the greatest players in the club's history. Neither was allowed to run the clock down into his 30s; sentiment was not part of the equation. Henry had cost £10.5m (£24.6m) and was sold for £16.1m (£28m) – a genuine profit of £3.4m, after an astonishing career. Vieira was even more profitable: £3.5m (£11.8m) when purchased in 1996; £13.7m (£25m) when sold in 2005, on the brink of his 30s. All those games, all those trophies, and genuine mark-ups at the end. It's hard to find many better examples than these.

For Arsenal to keep competitive and thrive, such transfer work has been essential. At Chelsea it's been a very different case; they were paying large fees to achieve success, only later turning their minds to how the club could be run as a viable business. Bad signings were no more than collateral damage.

Genuine Profit

One thing that becomes clear with Current Transfer Purchase Price is how infrequently genuine profits are made when a purchased player is later sold on. If a signing stays for a couple of seasons and then is moved on for a larger fee, the interim inflation has to be taken into account; he is being sold in a new market, one in which prices have altered. Given that inflation will generally push prices up, and that the ageing process will often see a player's value depreciate, genuine profits are few and far between. There's also the fact that at some clubs, successful signings – despite often being coveted by other clubs – don't *have* to be sold, unless finances force the issue.

In 18 years, Alex Ferguson has only made a genuine profit on six occasions; and four of those were marginal. Of course, the astonishing £55.3m mark-up on Cristiano Ronaldo (his original purchase price of £12.4m equates to £24.7m in today's money – with the £80m sale fee unaffected by inflation), allied to his performances and the trophies they led to, arguably makes Ronaldo the best purchase in Premier League history. Other signings contributed similar quality – not least Eric Cantona and Thierry Henry – but neither left his club £55m richer. A further nine members of the current United squad are valued more highly now than when they were brought to Old Trafford.

By contrast, Ferguson has genuinely lost money on 33 occasions, including an excess of £10m on 10 of those deals. Given the ages of Dimitar Berbatov and Rio Ferdinand, they will certainly join that list, as will Owen Hargreaves, now 29, even if he recovers from his injury hell.

Of those 33, more than a third were flops on the pitch as well as off it, with Juan Sebastián Verón and Jesper Blomqvist (£36.9m and £10.7m CTPP respectively) appearing particularly costly. (While £25.2m CTPP was recouped on the Argentine midfielder, £11.7m was the final loss in current terms). Taking inflation into account, £6.1m for Massimo Taibi looks worse than the £4.5m paid at the time for possibly the worst first-team keeper in United's history. By the starkest of contrasts, Eric Cantona's premature retirement robbed United of a sell-on fee, let alone more years of service, but even when the £1.2m becomes £8m CTPP, he remains one of football's all-time bargains.

However, to mitigate Ferguson's many losses, we have to note both his unprecedented time in the job and also the fact that – like any manager – in most cases he bought players to provide years of service; recouping money becomes an issue only if expensive players flop. Stars like Dwight Yorke and Roy Keane left for little or no money, having cost £27.6m and £22.4m respectively in current terms. But you cannot argue that United didn't get value for money out of the pair. Louis Saha, for whom United lost almost all £19.7m of his 'cost' when he left to join Everton, also played a role in success at Old Trafford, although that does seem a steep price for what he offered. However, the £5m paid for Henning Berg in 1997 – at the time a British record for a defender – does not seem so healthy at £16.8m. Andy Cole, Teddy Sheringham and Carlos Tévez all left for in excess of £10m less than was paid for them (CTPP), but none was a bad deal.

(On the subject of Tévez, he is included because his £9m loan fee (£10.2m) was to be used as part-payment on a final £25m deal after two years on 'loan' at United; before Alex Ferguson had a change of heart. The same applies to Javier Mascherano – whose £18.6m fee (£20.9m) includes £1.5m for an initial 18-month loan at Liverpool; in that case, the player did complete a full transfer. Both deals were very modern, and involved a third party – and no little confusion as to who actually owned their registrations.)

The second-longest-serving Premier League manager is Arsène Wenger. To date he has made a CTPP profit on nine players, with five of those netting vastly superior sums to those originally paid. However, his biggest financial return came against his will; Nicolas Anelka forcing his and Arsenal's hand in 1999. Having been picked up for a mere £500,000 (£1.3m) as a 17-year-old, he was sold just a couple of years later to Real Madrid for £23m. In current terms that equates to £54m, an incredible £52.7m profit. Although Arsenal didn't get years of service from the striker, he contributed heavily to a league and cup double. Given that he would have been on low wages for much of his short time at Highbury, it was win-win-win for the Gunners. Completing Wenger's genuine eight-figure mark-ups are Marc Overmars, £20.9m; Kolo Touré, £15.8m; Patrick Vieira, £13.2m; and Emmanuel Adebayor, £12.2m.

By contrast, Rafa Benítez often suffered heavy criticism over his transfer policies. A lot tended to be made of his gross spend, whilst his sales to raise that cash were often ignored. While there can be no denying that he had a high turnover of players between 2004 and 2010 – making for a large gross figure – many of these deals involved trading up. Spanish right-back Josemi, his very first buy, was replaced by Jan Kromkamp, in a swap deal; the Dutchman wasn't much better than the Spaniard, but Álvaro Arbeloa, whose fee was generated by selling Kromkamp to PSV Eindhoven, certainly was. In all of these deals, money was coming in at roughly the same rate it was going out. Arbeloa was sold to Real Madrid for £3.5m in 2009, meaning that even with inflation, everything more or less equalled out (a £35,317 profit on all these transactions). While Josemi and Kromkamp didn't offer a lot, Arbeloa was a bargain, and his sale price was relatively low only because he was in the final year of his contract.

Xabi Alonso remains Benítez's one genuine big-profit sale: bought for £10.5m (£19.1m) and sold for £30m, making a mark-up of almost £11m in 'real' terms. Five others – Jan Kromkamp, Scott Carson, Andriy Voronin, Yossi Benayoun and Antonio Núñez – raised some genuine profit.

Appointed Chelsea manager in 2000, Claudio Ranieri only made a profit of any real note on Arjen Robben, whose £13m (£23.7m) fee was turned into £24m (£27.1m) by the approach of Real Madrid: £3.4m higher in genuine terms. However, six years after his dismissal, Frank Lampard and Petr Čech remain as central figures at Stamford Bridge; at 32, Lampard has limited sell-on value, but what an inspired buy he has proved to be in West London.

José Mourinho, who succeeded Ranieri in 2004 and managed Chelsea until 2007, can still claim 11 signings in the Chelsea first-team squad. However, of his purchases to have been sold since his departure, only four sales have resulted in genuine profits, and none of them massively so. Tal Ben-Haim, brought in on a free from Bolton, was sold for what now equates to £4.7m. With fellow free transfer Steve Sidwell – out of his depth at the Bridge – earning the club £4.3m in genuine profit, the pair highlights how picking up players on Bosman deals can offer some reward, even if they don't make the first XI. While they bolstered the squad, neither Ben-Haim nor Sidwell – or indeed a third Bosman, Peruvian Claudio Pizzaro – impressed during their short stay, at a time when the money – and the titles – dried up. Given the wages involved, it's debatable as to whether or not these signings were quite as cost effective as first appears, but they were at least good enough to provide some cover.

Then there's Michael Ballack – another 'free' transfer; but one who just happened to cost £121,000 a week. However, at least the renowned German, after a shaky start, was a regular in the team; not least when winning the most recent league title, in 2010.

Preceding both of the aforementioned big spenders at Chelsea was player-turned-manager, Gianluca Vialli. Six of his signings during two years as boss led to genuine profits, the greatest of which was the £7.5m profit garnered when Eiður Guðjohnsen was sold to Barcelona after a number of years of effective service in West London. On the whole Vialli bought fairly well – with Jimmy Floyd Hasselbaink and Marcel Desailly particularly impressive – although his record shows an overall loss of £94.5m on his 23 signings. (More than a quarter of this loss came when Hasselbaink left on a free transfer in 2004, at the age of 32; the original genuine fee of £26.7m having run down to nothing in just four years. It suggests that while the striker himself was top-class, his age at the time of purchase made him a 'limited time only' investment, and that Chelsea overpaid.)

Appointed as boss of Newcastle during Vialli's tenure at the Bridge, Bobby Robson's signings during his five-year spell at his hometown club led to genuine profit on seven occasions. Two of these were fairly healthy: the transfers of Jermaine Jenas to Spurs for a £6.2m genuine mark-up, and Jonathan Woodgate (also currently of Spurs) to Real Madrid in 2004 for £9.9m more in real terms than the St James' Park club paid just a year earlier. Strangely, for one of those guilty of the club's aforementioned exorbitant cost per point, Robson's investments weren't too bad on the whole.

Indeed, this is a bit of a Newcastle dichotomy: both Kevin Keegan and Kenny Dalglish also have better records in the transfer market than they did in winning points at a reasonable rate while at St James'. Maybe this is what fuelled the turnover of expensive players – quite a few signings over the years left for genuine profits. These include: Woodgate and Jenas, as previously mentioned, but also James Milner, Craig Bellamy, Les Ferdinand, David Ginola, David Batty, Darren

Huckerby, Shay Given and Dietmar Hamann. While no-one could get Newcastle to punch their financial weight after 1994, just about enough money was coming back into the club to perpetuate the spending cycle. This is perhaps clearest with Andy Cole, who was signed in 1993, while the club were in the second tier of English football (and as such, his signing isn't included in Keegan's figures). When Cole moved to Manchester United two years later, the fee, in today's terms, equates to £25.6m. This allowed Newcastle to go out and buy Alan Shearer for a British record £15m – or £39.7m CTPP.

Keegan's signings for Newcastle (1992-1997 and 2008) and Manchester City (2001-2005) led to a genuine profit on 11 occasions, but none topped the £5m mark; Les Ferdinand coming closest, at £4.5m. His major 'loss' came with Alan Shearer's retirement; the entire £39.7m written off. However, most Newcastle fans would suggest that it was money well spent, even if no trophies were won.

However, Kenny Dalglish, who succeeded Keegan as both Liverpool's no.7 and Newcastle's manager, registered a genuine profit on no fewer than 14 occasions; and this from just four seasons of top-flight purchasing during the Premier League era. (As with Keegan and Ferguson, excluded are pre-1992 transfers, and those players purchased when his club was in a lower division.) Three of these profits are only moderately healthy – between £3m and £6m: Chris Sutton, Didi Hamann and Ian Pearce – but a further three are big enough to exceed £12m: Graeme Le Saux, Henning Berg and Alan Shearer (who netted a genuine profit of £17.7m, along with the goals that lifted the 1995 championship for Blackburn).

The manager with the fewest sell-on successes is Gérard Houllier. Despite each and every one of his signings between 1998 and 2004 now having left Liverpool, only two made a genuine profit; the £7.4m racked up on Milan Baroš wasn't bad business at all, especially as the player was fairly hit-and-miss. Baroš, like the other success, Djimi Traoré, played a part in the incredible 2005 Champions League victory; as such, they are part of Anfield folklore, if not exactly legends in their own right. (Houllier did make a small profit on free transfer Alou Diarra, but the French midfielder spent his entire three years at the club out on loan, and therefore, as with profits returned in similar circumstances by Ferguson, Wenger and Benítez, does not qualify.)

The following table refers to the genuine profits and losses of the 11 managers, represented as ratios; 1:1 means that for every CTPP pound lost, the same was recouped *after* inflation, whereas 1:9 signifies a loss nine times greater than the amount that was recovered.

On the whole, it arguably highlights those who possessed a better eye in the transfer market, but equally, it could be a reflection on the spending policy of the club that employed them (such as the need to sell before buying). With the exception of Kenny Dalglish and Kevin Keegan, these managers were employed by only one Premier League club between 1992 and 2010; Dalglish and Keegan managed two: both had stints at Newcastle, as well as Blackburn and Manchester City respectively.

Manager	Profit/Genuine Increase in Value	Loss/Genuine Decrease in Value	Ratio
Wenger	£208,922,365	£194,105,347	1:1
Benítez	£65,081,076	£68,895,851	1:1
Dalglish	£64,342,062	£129,207,722	1:2
Robson	£22,810,452	£58,462,493	1:3
Ferguson	£83,924,300	£367,913,518	1:4
Vialli	£23,714,079	£118,168,946	1:5
Keegan	£15,234,061	£99,399,774	1:7
Mourinho	£20,736,577	£261,207,169	1:13
Evans	£3,811,990	£64360599	1:18
Houllier	£9,533,017	£195,064,557	1:22
Ranieri	£4,199,955	£249,457,937	1:64

So, on the whole, Alex Ferguson has a Loss/Decrease value four times as high as his Profit/Increase value. While he has largely spent wisely, this statistic shows clear backing in the transfer market; backing resulting in trophies more often than not, but where genuine losses on players have often been made. The club's financial strength over the years, much of it on the back of success on the pitch, has made for a self-perpetuating cycle.

To put this into context, José Mourinho's ratio is 1:13 – 13 times as much money lost or wiped from values, in genuine terms, as has been 'gained' to date. But neither of these can hold a candle to Claudio Ranieri in terms of diminishing returns: 62 times as much money was 'lost' as was recouped. On the flip side, both Rafa Benítez and Arsène Wenger possess ratios that are virtually 1:1; for every penny spent, the same amount has been generated in genuine terms. (Wenger has a small profit, Benítez a fractional loss). This clearly shows the different financial realities of all the clubs involved.

Top Five Managers

José Mourinho, Alex Ferguson, Arsène Wenger, Rafael Benítez and Claudio Ranieri are the top points scorers, based on seasonal averages, in the Premier League's 18-year history.

Their spending records make for an interesting comparison. Mourinho and Ranieri spent big and recouped little from their transfers; Ferguson also spent big, but in a more sporadic fashion, as befits someone in charge of his club for every one of the Premier League years; Benítez was limited more to the mid-range of the market; and Wenger's desire to splash the cash has clearly diminished over the course of his career. Each signed a number of world-class players, for a variety of fees. Each also signed his fair share of duds.

As such, it's worth taking a look at their spending policies, and how it affected their ability to succeed.

José Mourinho 88.5 pts

Total Spend (Original Fee)	Total Spend (CTPP)	Total Sales (Original Fee)	Total Sales (CTPP)
£224,150,000	£390,616,119	£153,150,000	£191,082,873

Players	23
Profit/Genuine Increase in Value	£20,736,577
Loss/Genuine Decrease in Value	£261,207,169
Average Profit on a Player	£3,967,072
Average Loss on a Player	£16,325,448
Overall Loss	**£240,470,592**

Excluding those brought in for the youth set-up, José Mourinho signed 23 players for a total of £218.2m. In today's money, those transfers equate to an expenditure of £380.2m. In total, of all those transfers, just £9.7m genuine profit has been recouped, with estimates of a further £11m available if Alex and Hilário were cashed in on immediately. However, eight players have been sold for a combined CTPP loss of £143.6m (more than half of that taken up by *just two* players: Andriy Shevchenko and Shaun Wright-Phillips), and a further seven players, if sold today, would lose £102.9m. That means that the overall debit is £240.5m in 2010 prices.

But does that make it bad business? Of course not, given the success that has followed, and that having an immediately self-sustaining business was never the original aim of Roman Abramovich. (There were also rumours that Shevchenko *wasn't even Mourinho's signing*, but that of the owner.) Players like Ricardo Carvalho,

Michael Essien, Ashley Cole, Florent Malouda and Didier Drogba were part of the title-winning team of 2010, and any reduction in their value has been down to age (in the cases of Drogba, Cole, Malouda and Carvalho, with the latter recently bought by Mourinho for Real Madrid), or simply the fact that they were purchased at a time when prices were generally higher (Essien).

It's fair to say that Mourinho was only meeting the task presented to him, and meeting it successfully. However, it was an approach that gave him a distinct advantage over some of his rivals.

Player	Original Fee	CTPP	Sale Fee	Sales CTPP	CTPP 'Genuine' Profit/Loss
Genuine Profit					
Ben–Haim T	£0	£0	£6,000,000	£4,691,359	£4,691,359
Sidwell S	£0	£0	£5,500,000	£4,300,412	£4,300,412
Kežman M	£5,000,000	£9,096,164	£5,300,000	£9,641,933	£545,769
Jarošik J	£3,000,000	£5,457,698	£3,100,000	£5,656,735	£199,037
TOTAL	£8,000,000	£14,553,862	£19,900,000	£24,290,439	£9,736,577
AVERAGE	£2,000,000	£3,638,466	£4,975,000	£6,072,610	£2,434,144
Break Even					
Ballack	£0	£0	£0	£0	£0
Pizarro C	£0	£0	£0	£0	£0
Genuine Loss					
Di Santo F	£3,000,000	£3,385,993	£2,000,000	£2,000,000	£1,385,993
Diarra L (I)	£2,800,000	£5,109,309	£2,000,000	£2,257,329	£2,851,980
Del Horno A	£8,000,000	£14,598,026	£4,800,000	£8,341,540	£6,256,486
Tiago	£10,000,000	£18,192,327	£6,500,000	£11,860,896	£6,331,431
Boulahrouz K	£7,000,000	£12,164,746	£0	£0	£12,164,746
Carvalho R	£19,850,000	£36,111,770	£6,700,000	£6,700,000	£29,411,770
Wright–Phillips S	£21,000,000	£38,319,818	£8,500,000	£6,646,092	£31,673,726
Shevchenko A	£30,800,000	£53,524,884	£0	£0	£53,524,884
TOTAL	£102,450,000	£181,406,873	£30,500,000	£37,805,857	£143,601,016
AVERAGE	£12,806,250	£22,675,859	£3,812,500	£4,725,732	£17,950,127

Player	Original Fee	CTPP	Sale Fee	Sales CTPP	CTPP 'Genuine' Profit/Loss
Current Squad					
Value Increased					
Alex	£0	£0	£10,000,000	£10,000,000	£10,000,000
Hilário	£0	£0	£1,000,000	£1,000,000	£1,000,000
TOTAL	£0	£5,213,463	£17,666,667	£17,666,667	£12,453,204
AVERAGE	£0	£1,737,821	£5,500,000	£5,500,000	£5,500,000
Value Decreased					
Kalou S	£9,000,000	£15,640,389	£9,000,000	£9,000,000	£6,640,389
Cole A	£16,000,000	£27,805,135	£20,750,000	£20,750,000	£7,055,135
Malouda F	£13,500,000	£15,236,968	£8,000,000	£8,000,000	£7,236,968
Mikel J	£12,000,000	£20,853,851	£11,000,000	£11,000,000	£9,853,851
Ferreira P	£13,200,000	£24,013,872	£4,250,000	£4,250,000	£19,763,872
Essien M	£26,000,000	£47,443,584	£25,000,000	£25,000,000	£22,443,584
Drogba D	£24,000,000	£43,661,585	£13,750,000	£13,750,000	£29,911,585
	£113,700,000	£194,655,384	£91,750,000	£91,750,000	£102,905,384
TOTAL	£104,700,000	£179,014,995	£82,750,000	£82,750,000	£96,264,995
AVERAGE	£16,242,857	£27,807,912	£13,107,143	£13,107,143	£14,700,769

Alex Ferguson (83) 81.6 pts pro rata

Total Spend (Original Fee)	Total Spend (CTPP)	Total Sales (Original Fee)	Total Sales (CTPP)
£428,760,000	£717,458,146	£382,908,334	£433,468,928

Players	64
Profit/Genuine Increase in Value	£83,924,300
Loss/Genuine Decrease in Value	£367,913,518
Average Loss on a Player	£8,912,240
Average Profit on a Player	£7,128,379
Overall Loss	**£283,989,218**

To date, excluding signings from the summer of 2010 and a whole host of kids for the youth and reserve setups, Alex Ferguson has made 64 forays into the transfer market since the Premier League was formed, seeing his investment blossom (in genuine financial terms) in fewer than 25% of those cases. Of the 43 players who have subsequently been sold, five broke even, five went for a profit and 33 represented a loss. And of the five sold for profit, only Cristiano Ronaldo's figure is above £1.5m; of course, a £55m genuine profit just happens to be a piffling 37 times that amount. That leaves 10 of the current squad whose values have genuinely risen, and 11 whose values have fallen.

Of the players still at the clubs the 'top five' managers signed them for, Wayne Rooney was valued highest by the *Pay As You Play* panel, at £51m. What's interesting is that his 2004 transfer, in today's prices – £49m – is almost identical to what the panel believed he is currently worth on the open market. That suggests that his value has risen in line with inflation, but remains similar, in real terms, to what it was six years ago. What Rooney has lost from his career in terms of potential years ahead of him – he's now 24, not 18 – he has gained by solidifying his reputation as one of the top three Premier League strikers. He no longer has 12-14 years ahead of him in the top flight, having already spent six at Old Trafford, but anyone wishing to buy him would get a more experienced, reliable player. As such, on top of the trophies he's helped United win, he has proven to be a shrewd *investment*.

How many truly great signings has Ferguson made since 1992? With at least one missing the cut-off as he was signed before that point (Peter Schmeichel), it's fair to list the following as part of a mythical Premier League 'elite squad': Eric Cantona, Roy Keane, Ruud van Nistelrooy, Jaap Stam, Rio Ferdinand, Wayne Rooney and Cristiano Ronaldo. At £8m CTPP, Cantona is Ferguson's one *absolute bargain*; the only one who cost less than £22m in today's money – with Rooney and Ferdinand up around the £50m-mark, and the rest between £22m and £25m. But if you're going to spend hefty fees and not risk bankrupting your club, they are the kind of players to sign. (Even though it seemed to make sense at the time, the £36m spent on Juan Sebastián Verón proved less astute.) Next comes a list of some of the more successful players from the past 18 years, albeit perhaps not quite good enough to get into that elite squad: Andy Cole, Ole Gunnar Solskjær, Dwight Yorke and Edwin van der Sar, with Nemanja Vidić, and possibly Patrice Evra in need of a fraction more time (to prove their longevity) to be considered worthy of promotion.

One way that Ferguson kept his transfer spending down was by having the luxury of being able to select a large number of home-grown players. While he's yet to bring too many through in recent times (a fairly common trend across the entire league), that one first group of graduates – between 1991 and 1995 – continues to keep proving its worth. Even now, nearly two decades on, Paul Scholes and Ryan Giggs look irreplaceable. It was Ferguson's foresight in overhauling the United youth set-up in the '80s that allowed for this success; however, had he been sacked in 1990, when his days looked numbered, he may never have been given the credit for it.

Player	Original Fee	CTPP	Sale Fee	Sales CTPP	CTPP 'Genuine' Profit/Loss
Genuine Profit					
Ronaldo C	£12,240,000	£24,735,819	£80,000,000	£80,000,000	£55,264,181
Manucho	£890,000	£1,004,511	£2,500,000	£2,500,000	£1,495,489
Dublin D	£1,000,000	£6,656,206	£1,950,000	£7,387,762	£731,556
Nevland E	£0	£0	£250,000	£586,668	£586,668
Howard T	£2,300,000	£4,648,070	£3,000,000	£5,213,463	£565,393
TOTAL	**£16,430,000**	**£37,044,606**	**£87,700,000**	**£95,687,893**	**£58,643,287**
AVERAGE	**£3,286,000**	**£7,408,921**	**£17,540,000**	**£19,137,579**	**£11,728,657**
Break Even					
Van der Gouw R	£0	£0	£0	£0	£0
Djordjic B	£0	£0	£0	£0	£0
Bosnich M	£0	£0	£0	£0	£0
Miller L	£0	£0	£0	£0	£0
Blanc L	£0	£0	£0	£0	£0
Prunier W	loan	£0	£0	£0	£0
Goram A	loan	£0	£0	£0	£0
Larsson H	loan	£0	£0	£0	£0
Genuine Loss					
Heinze G	£6,900,000	£12,552,706	£10,600,000	£11,963,841	£588,865
Culkin N	£250,000	£657,380	£0	£0	£657,380
Greening J	£1,000,000	£3,376,079	£2,000,000	£2,621,324	£754,755
Dong	£500,000	£1,010,450	£0	£0	£1,010,450
Ricardo	£1,500,000	£2,420,451	£0	£0	£2,420,451
Poborský K	£3,500,000	£9,259,377	£2,000,000	£6,752,158	£2,507,219
Cruyff J	£800,000	£2,700,863	£0	£0	£2,700,863
Carroll R	£2,500,000	£3,276,655	£0	£0	£3,276,655
Fortune Q	£1,500,000	£3,520,006	£0	£0	£3,520,006
Bellion D	£2,000,000	£4,041,777	£0	£0	£4,041,777

Player	Original Fee	CTPP	Sale Fee	Sales CTPP	CTPP 'Genuine' Profit/Loss
Johnsen R	£1,200,000	£4,051,295	£0	£0	£4,051,295
Tošić Z	£16,300,000	£12,744,858	£8,000,000	£8,000,000	£4,744,858
Stam J	£10,500,000	£25,720,605	£16,500,000	£21,625,923	£4,094,682
Djemba–Djemba E	£3,500,000	£7,073,151	£1,350,000	£2,455,964	£4,617,187
Forlán D	£7,500,000	£9,829,965	£2,800,000	£5,093,852	£4,736,113
Solskjær O	£1,500,000	£5,064,118	£0	£0	£5,064,118
May D	£1,400,000	£5,304,034	£0	£0	£5,304,034
van Nistelrooy R	£19,000,000	£24,902,578	£11,000,000	£19,116,030	£5,786,548
Smith A (II)	£7,050,000	£12,825,591	£6,000,000	£6,771,986	£6,053,605
Taibi M	£4,500,000	£10,560,017	£2,500,000	£4,449,689	£6,110,328
Kléberson	£5,930,000	£11,983,938	£2,500,000	£4,561,883	£7,422,055
Cantona E	£1,200,000	£7,987,447	£0	£0	£7,987,447
Silvestre M	£4,000,000	£9,386,681	£750,000	£586,420	£8,800,261
Tévez C*	£9,000,000	£10,158,002	£0	£0	£10,158,002
Blomqvist J	£4,400,000	£10,778,158	£0	£0	£10,778,158
Verón J	£28,100,000	£36,829,602	£12,500,000	£25,261,253	£11,568,349
Sheringham T	£3,500,000	£11,816,276	£0	£0	£11,816,276
Barthez F	£7,800,000	£13,883,029	£0	£0	£13,883,029
Cole AA	£7,000,000	£26,520,170	£7,500,000	£9,829,965	£16,690,205
Berg H	£5,000,000	£16,880,394	£0	£0	£16,880,394
Saha L	£12,850,000	£25,968,568	£8,000,000	£6,255,145	£19,713,423
Keane R (I)	£3,750,000	£22,390,103	£0	£0	£22,390,103
Yorke D	£12,600,000	£30,864,726	£2,000,000	£3,227,268	£27,637,458
TOTAL	**£198,030,000**	**£396,339,050**	**£96,000,000**	**£138,572,701**	**£257,766,349**
AVERAGE	**£6,000,909**	**£12,010,274**	**£2,909,091**	**£4,199,173**	**£7,811,101**

Current Squad

Player	Original Fee	CTPP	Sale Fee	Sales CTPP	CTPP 'Genuine' Profit/Loss
Value Increased					
Rafael da Silva	£2,600,000	£2,032,922	£6,750,000	£6,750,000	£4,717,078
Foster B	£1,000,000	£1,824,753	£6,000,000	£6,000,000	£4,175,247
Evra P	£5,500,000	£10,036,143	£13,500,000	£13,500,000	£3,463,857
Fabio da Silva	£2,600,000	£2,032,922	£5,000,000	£5,000,000	£2,967,078
Vidić N	£7,000,000	£12,773,273	£15,500,000	£15,500,000	£2,726,727
Obertan G	£3,000,000	£3,000,000	£5,625,000	£5,625,000	£2,625,000
Rooney W	£27,000,000	£49,119,283	£51,666,667	£51,666,667	£2,547,384
Owen M	£0	£0	£2,000,000	£2,000,000	£2,000,000
De Laet R	£3,000,000	£2,345,679	£2,375,000	£2,375,000	£29,321
Possebon R	£3,000,000	£2,345,679	£2,375,000	£2,375,000	£29,321
TOTAL	**£54,700,000**	**£85,510,654**	**£110,791,667**	**£110,791,667**	**£25,281,013**
AVERAGE	**£5,470,000**	**£8,551,065**	**£11,079,167**	**£11,079,167**	**£2,528,101**
Value Decreased					
Park J-S	£4,000,000	£7,299,013	£7,000,000	£7,000,000	£299,013
Biram Diouf M	£4,000,000	£4,000,000	£3,666,667	£3,666,667	£333,333
Kuszczak T	£2,500,000	£4,344,552	£4,000,000	£4,000,000	£344,552
Valencia L	£16,000,000	£16,000,000	£14,750,000	£14,750,000	£1,250,000
Van der Sar E	£2,000,000	£3,649,506	£875,000	£875,000	£2,774,506
Nani	£17,000,000	£19,187,293	£13,250,000	£13,250,000	£5,937,293
Carrick M	£18,600,000	£32,323,469	£9,333,333	£9,333,333	£22,990,136
Anderson	£18,000,000	£20,315,957	£8,500,000	£8,500,000	£11,815,957
Hargreaves O	£17,000,000	£19,187,293	£2,875,000	£2,875,000	£16,312,293
Berbatov D	£30,500,000	£23,847,740	£13,000,000	£13,000,000	£10,847,740
Ferdinand R	£30,000,000	£48,409,013	£11,166,667	£11,166,667	£37,242,346
				£110,147,169	
TOTAL	**£159,600,000**	**£198,563,836**	**£88,416,667**	**£88,416,667**	**£110,147,169**
AVERAGE	**£14,509,091**	**£18,051,258**	**£8,037,879**	**£8,037,879**	**£10,013,379**

Arsène Wenger 76.4 pts

Total Spend (Original Fee)	Total Spend (CTPP)	Total Sales (Original Fee)	Total Sales (CTPP)
£251,640,000	£437,915,454	£361,519,167	£452,732,473

Players	67
Profit/Genuine Increase in Value	£208,922,365
Loss/Genuine Decrease in Value	£194,105,347
Average Loss on a Player	£4,468,881
Average Profit on a Player	£10,086,995
Overall Profit	**£14,817,019**

Although not quite the most successful manager in the Premier League, Arsène Wenger does have the honour of being the most noted game-changer. If Ferguson is the epitome of evergreen consistency, and Mourinho blitzed the league with a bombastic blast, Wenger altered thinking. Although he was not alone in dragging English football out of the dark ages, his continental approach upon arriving in 1996 helped revolutionise the game in this country. Tony Adams was swiftly turned from an alcoholic, striker-kicking, Row Z-finding 'donkey' into a confident libero who wrote poetry, read philosophy and played the piano. That in itself could stand as the French manager's epitaph.

However, it's also clear that Wenger's fortunes have faded since the arrival of serious money into the hands of some of his rivals. Up until 2005, Arsenal finished either 1st or 2nd; since then, 3rd has been the best, and 4th the worst. And but for an infamous case of food poisoning, they might even have finished 5th, below their toilet-bound rivals, Spurs.

Regarded as something of a master in the transfer market, these figures suggest that Wenger's reputation is perfectly justified: the only one of the 11 main managers in credit on his dealings. At times Wenger spent big, but often later recouped that money and more. And he's seen the values of cheap young players like Nicolas Anelka and Cesc Fàbregas rise incredibly; Anelka left for £53m in today's money, and Fàbregas is valued at £41m by the panel.

One expensive flop was José Antonio Reyes, although he wasn't without his moments. (That said, his fee, which was heavily reliant on certain targets being met, did not reach the £17.6m widely reported.) Sylvain Wiltord was a reasonable success on the pitch, though the running down of his contract meant an original CTPP fee of £24.3m dwindled to zero. In terms of wasting more than a few million on a player who offered nothing, Francis Jeffers is the one really obvious blot on his copybook.

Contrary to popular opinion, Wenger's success at Highbury in his first eight years was tied to big spending (although not all of it his). While Mourinho spent vastly bigger sums and didn't produce football that the neutrals loved (not that he cared), Wenger got brilliant results – in terms of trophies and style – from fairly expensive sides. It's only since their spending has dropped – and Chelsea's has risen – that the Gunners have fallen away as a title force and perennial threat to Manchester United. But at least they do remain annual Champions League participants.

When Arsenal won the league for the first time under the guise of the Premier League, it was with the second-most expensive side in the competition. On average, only Newcastle fielded a more expensive £XI, and even then by only a minimal amount. Players like Ian Wright, David Seaman, Martin Keown, David Platt and Dennis Bergkamp were all costly purchases for the Gunners, but the passing of time makes those fees seem less significant. (TPI shows otherwise.)

The next season, Arsenal's £XI dropped to fourth in the rankings; they dropped to 2nd in the table. They rose to third in the rankings a year later, but remained 2nd in the table. They topped the rankings a year later, again when finishing 2nd. But this was now the construction of a powerful, fast-improving side. They ranked top in 2001/02, and also won the title, with 87 points. They dropped to third in the rankings a year later, when Manchester United moved to the top of both the chart and the league, but Arsenal returned to the summit a year later – with Wenger's best Premier League season to date. Due to Chelsea's fairly shrewd investment, and Newcastle's continued scattergun spending, Arsenal ranked down in fourth in 2003/04, but went unbeaten the whole season in racking up 90 points, Wenger's best tally to date.

By then, Chelsea were a year into the process of building an übersquad, but it took a little time to gel; by the time it did, a year later, Arsenal found themselves squeezed from the top two (and to date, never to return). When Arsenal finished 2nd in 2003, their side cost 94% of that of the champions, United. When they finished 3rd in 2005, it cost only 50% of Chelsea's title-triumphing XI; another year later, it was down to 42%. One further year on, in 2006/07, it was a mere 26% of Mourinho's XI. Over the next three seasons, the Gunners never rose above 34% of the most expensive Premier League £XI.

The last time Arsenal ranked in the top three for spending was 2005/06; 'only' 67 league points, but the same team ran Barcelona close in the Champions League Final. By 2008/09, they ranked ninth in the Premier League in terms of £XI.

Part of the frustration of Arsenal fans in recent years has been how Wenger has often refused to spend money; a situation almost unique in football. The board said the money was there, but the manager chose to put his faith in the younger players at his disposal. In some ways this approach has indeed led to success – continued entry into the Champions League, and some exciting football along the way; in others, it's been viewed as a failure – no trophy since 2005, and inexperience at times telling. However, to remain competitive while the club was both building and paying off the loan for a new stadium (which will earn it fortunes in time) has to be viewed as a job well done.

Player	Original Fee	CTPP	Year	Sale Fee	Sales CTPP	CTPP 'Genuine' Profit/Loss
Genuine Profit						
Anelka N	£500,000	£1,322,768	1996/97	£23,000,000	£53,973,418	£52,650,650
Overmars M	£7,000,000	£23,632,552	1997/98	£25,000,000	£44,496,889	£20,864,337
Adebayor M	£3,000,000	£5,474,260	2005/06	£25,000,000	£25,000,000	£19,525,740
Touré K	£150,000	£196,599	2001/02	£16,000,000	£16,000,000	£15,803,401
Vieira P	£3,500,000	£11,816,276	1997/98	£13,700,000	£24,999,119	£13,182,843
Diarra L (II)	£2,000,000	£2,257,329	2007/08	£5,500,000	£6,207,653	£3,950,324
Henry T	£10,500,000	£24,640,038	1999/00	£16,100,000	£27,978,917	£3,338,879
Pennant J	£1,500,000	£3,674,372	1998/99	£3,000,000	£5,457,698	£1,783,326
Diawara K	£2,500,000	£6,123,954	1998/99	£3,000,000	£7,348,744	£1,224,790
TOTAL	**£30,650,000**	**£79,138,147**		**£130,300,000**	**£211,462,438**	**£132,324,291**
AVERAGE	**£3,405,556**	**£8,793,127**	**0**	**£14,477,778**	**£23,495,826**	**£14,702,699**
Break Even						
Šuker D	£0	£0	1999/00	£0	£0	£0
Campbell S (I)	£0	£0	2001/02	£0	£0	£0
Flamini M	£0	£0	2004/05	£0	£0	£0
Poom M	£0	£0	2005/06	£0	£0	£0
Garde R	£0	£0	1996/97	£0	£0	£0
Bischoff A	£0	£0	2008/09	£0	£0	£0
Genuine Loss						
Wiltord S	£13,000,000	£23,138,382	2000/01	£0	£0	£23,138,382
Lauren	£7,000,000	£12,459,129	2000/01	£500,000	£868,910	£11,590,219
Van Bronckhorst G	£8,500,000	£11,140,627	2001/02	£0	£0	£11,140,627
Kanu N	£4,500,000	£11,023,117	1998/99	£0	£0	£11,023,117
Edu	£6,000,000	£10,679,253	2000/01	£0	£0	£10,679,253
Pires R	£6,000,000	£10,679,253	2000/01	£0	£0	£10,679,253
Reyes J	£10,500,000	£21,219,452	2003/04	£10,000,000	£11,286,643	£9,932,809
Hleb A	£11,200,000	£20,437,236	2005/06	£15,000,000	£11,728,397	£8,708,839
Gallas W	£5,000,000	£8,689,105	2006/07	£0	£0	£8,689,105
Jeffers F	£10,000,000	£13,106,620	2001/02	£2,600,000	£4,730,005	£8,376,615
Silva G	£4,500,000	£7,261,352	2002/03	£1,000,000	£781,893	£6,479,459
Cygan P	£5,500,000	£8,874,986	2002/03	£2,000,000	£3,475,642	£5,399,344
Grimandi G	£1,500,000	£5,064,118	1997/98	£0	£0	£5,064,118
Senderos P	£2,500,000	£5,052,251	2003/04	£0	£0	£5,052,251
Silvinho	£4,000,000	£9,386,681	1999/00	£3,500,000	£4,587,317	£4,799,364
Boa Morte L	£1,750,000	£5,908,138	1997/98	£500,000	£1,173,335	£4,734,803
Luzhny O	£1,800,000	£4,224,007	1999/00	£0	£0	£4,224,007
Ljungberg F	£3,000,000	£7,348,744	1998/99	£3,000,000	£3,385,993	£3,962,751
Vivas N	£1,600,000	£3,919,330	1998/99	£0	£0	£3,919,330

Player	Original Fee	CTPP	Year	Sale Fee	Sales CTPP	CTPP 'Genuine' Profit/Loss
Lehmann J	£1,250,000	£2,526,125	2003/04	£0	£0	£2,526,125
Eduardo	£7,500,000	£8,464,982	2007/08	£6,000,000	£6,000,000	£2,464,982
Wright R	£6,000,000	£7,863,972	2001/02	£3,500,000	£5,647,718	£2,216,254
Petit E	£3,500,000	£11,816,276	1997/98	£7,500,000	£9,829,965	£1,986,311
Manninger A	£1,000,000	£3,376,079	1997/98	£960,000	£1,549,088	£1,826,991
Danilevičius T	£1,000,000	£1,779,876	2000/01	£0	£0	£1,779,876
Stepanovs I	£1,000,000	£1,779,876	2000/01	£0	£0	£1,779,876
Upson M	£1,000,000	£3,376,079	1997/98	£1,000,000	£1,613,634	£1,762,445
Grondin D	£500,000	£1,224,791	1998/99	£0	£0	£1,224,791
Wreh C	£300,000	£1,012,824	1997/98	£0	£0	£1,012,824
Mendez A	£250,000	£844,020	1997/98	£0	£0	£844,020
Shaaban R	£500,000	£806,817	2002/03	£0	£0	£806,817
Tavlaridis E	£600,000	£786,397	2001/02	£0	£0	£786,397
Malz S	£650,000	£1,525,336	1999/00	£580,000	£1,032,328	£493,008
Lupoli A	£200,000	£363,847	2004/05	£0	£0	£363,847
TOTAL	**£133,100,000**	**£247,159,078**		**£187,940,000**	**£279,153,306**	**£179,468,210**
AVERAGE	**£3,914,706**	**£7,269,385**		**£1,695,294**	**£1,990,908**	**£5,278,477**

Current Squad

Player	Original Fee	CTPP	Year	Sale Fee	Sales CTPP	CTPP 'Genuine' Profit/Loss
Value Increased						
Fàbregas F	£2,250,000	£4,547,025	2003/04	£41,000,000	£41,000,000	£36,452,975
van Persie R	£3,000,000	£6,062,701	2003/04	£18,750,000	£18,750,000	£12,687,299
Song A	£1,000,000	£1,737,821	2006/07	£6,666,667	£6,666,667	£4,928,846
Ramsey A	£5,000,000	£3,909,466	2008/09	£7,875,000	£7,875,000	£3,965,534
Vermaelen T	£10,000,000	£10,000,000	2009/10	£13,750,000	£13,750,000	£3,750,000
Diaby V	£3,500,000	£6,386,636	2005/06	£10,000,000	£10,000,000	£3,613,364
Nasri S	£12,800,000	£10,008,232	2008/09	£13,250,000	£13,250,000	£3,241,768
Sagna B	£6,000,000	£6,771,986	2007/08	£9,750,000	£9,750,000	£2,978,014
Arshavin A	£15,000,000	£11,728,397	2008/09	£13,250,000	£13,250,000	£1,521,603
Vela C	£2,000,000	£3,649,506	2005/06	£5,000,000	£5,000,000	£1,350,494
Eboué E	£1,540,000	£2,801,618	2004/05	£3,500,000	£3,500,000	£698,382
Almunia M	£500,000	£909,616	2004/05	£1,600,000	£1,600,000	£690,384
Mannone V	£350,000	£638,664	2005/06	£1,266,667	£1,266,667	£628,003
Denílson	£3,400,000	£5,908,591	2006/07	£6,000,000	£6,000,000	£91,409
TOTAL	**£66,340,000**	**£75,060,259**		**£151,658,334**	**£151,658,334**	**£76,598,075**
AVERAGE	**£4,738,571**	**£5,361,447**		**£10,832,738**	**£10,832,738**	**£5,471,291**

Value Decreased

Player	Original Fee	CTPP	Year	Sale Fee	Sales CTPP	CTPP 'Genuine' Profit/Loss
Fabiański L	£2,000,000	£2,257,329	2007/08	£2,000,000	£2,000,000	£257,329
Silvestre M	£750,000	£586,420	2008/09	£87,500	£87,500	£498,920
Rosický T	£6,800,000	£11,817,182	2006/07	£6,500,000	£6,500,000	£5,317,182
Walcott T	£12,000,000	£21,897,039	2005/06	£13,333,333	£13,333,333	£8,563,706
TOTAL	**£21,550,000**	**£36,557,970**		**£21,920,833**	**£21,920,833**	**£14,637,137**
AVERAGE	**£5,387,500**	**£9,139,493**		**£5,480,208**	**£5,480,208**	**£3,659,284**

Rafael Benítez 72.1 pts

Total Spend (Original Fee)	Total Spend (CTPP)	Total Sales (Original Fee)	Total Sales (CTPP)
£225,700,000	£291,099,801	£280,008,372	£287,285,026

Players	40
Profit/Genuine Increase in Value	£65,081,076
Loss/Genuine Decrease in Value	£68,895,851
Average Loss on a Player	£3,510,044
Average Profit on a Player	£4,087,311
Overall Loss	**£3,814,775**

It may come as a surprise to some to see Rafa Benítez more or less match Arsène Wenger in terms of recouping money on his signings or seeing their values increase. Those who followed his work more closely, however, will appreciate the pattern.

Benítez inherited a patchy squad in 2004; some great players, such as Steven Gerrard, Jamie Carragher, Sami Hyypiä and Dietmar Hamann, but Michael Owen was already intent on a move away, and – crucially – many of the better players signed by his predecessor were either in their mid-to-late 20s or prone to injury. There was the improbable 2005 Champions League success, but it was achieved by eking out the most from what he had – tactical acumen rather than 11 supremely talented footballers – and with the added new dimension provided by Xabi Alonso and Luis García. Tellingly, the Reds registered only 58 points in the league in 2005; a similar number to Gérard Houllier in his final season. This was not a strong squad.

All told, the Spaniard's time on Merseyside was one long battle to get what he wanted and needed; only briefly, in 2007, did he really get his way, with the purchase of Fernando Torres, Yossi Benayoun, Javier Mascherano, Lucas Leiva and Ryan Babel. In the first half of his tenure, with chairman David Moores struggling to finance the club and the lack of a proposed new stadium, Benítez was often denied the funds for reasonably-priced purchases. Simão Sabrosa was due to sign for £10m in 2005, but the fee was jacked up to £13m at the last moment. Daniel Alves, Alexandre Pato and Theo Walcott were all approached, and were all keen to sign, but the manager's desires were not backed by the board or the owners; soon after, these players left their original clubs for more than Liverpool had been quoted.

The difference from Gérard Houllier was that Benítez's younger signings were his best: Alonso, Torres, Pepe Reina, Daniel Agger and Mascherano were all aged 21 or 22 when signed. This made perfect business sense for Liverpool, and each added a hitherto unseen quality to the side.

However, Benítez's signings from 2008 onwards were generally not successful enough. Robbie Keane was a major disappointment, although he was shipped out quickly before his value dipped too low (especially as he was 28). Albert Riera started brilliantly, then faded to obscurity; Andrea Dossena only made a couple of memorable contributions. And Alberto Aquilani, though gifted, only really got going in the last two months of his (to date, only) season due to a prolonged injury problem upon arrival; with Benítez sacked, the Italian was shipped out on loan to Juventus. True, Glen Johnson, from right-back, did add a new dimension to the Reds' attacking play, and David N'Gog, though clearly a rough diamond, is developing nicely. But on the whole, not a lot was gained from these deals in terms of football.

Part of the problem towards the end of Benítez's reign was that when a signing went wrong – such as Keane – the funds from any sale were not forthcoming; the manager wanted to invest the money in Stevan Jovetić, but was denied. The club was in heavy debt following the leveraged buyout by Tom Hicks and George Gillett, and interest repayments needed servicing. Although Benítez still bought a couple of expensive players in both 2008 and 2009, others were having to be sold first; the value of the squad was diminishing, at a time when he was expected to challenge for the title (simply because Liverpool *always used to*). And replacing Xabi Alonso, who was sold for £30m – after the midfielder had helped inspire the Reds to an 86-point finish that would have been enough to win the league in many seasons – proved harder than ever could have been imagined. Alonso had fallen out with the manager in 2008 after two indifferent seasons, but this fall-out inspired the midfielder to his best campaign yet; it could have been win-win, with the player moving on a year later for £30m and the club getting a genuine stab at the title in 2009, but finding a player who could control the tempo of a game like the Spaniard was nigh-on impossible.

Having parted company with Liverpool in June 2010, Benítez left with a record that showed that, on average, his signings increased their genuine value by more than they lowered it; an achievement that only Wenger can match. However, the slightly higher number of 'losses' – 20 to 16 (with five break-evens) put Benítez ever so slightly into debit overall. As with all managers whose signings remain at the same club, the values of players will continue to rise and fall in the coming years. On the pitch, Liverpool regained their reputation as one of Europe's finest sides, and the money earned from extended Champions League runs between 2005 and 2009 accounted for a lot of the manager's spending. And while the league title was ultimately a step too far, no other team has ever failed to be crowned champions when accruing as many as 86 points; achieved with Torres missing roughly half of the season. Sometimes you can be great, but get forgotten if someone else is *a little bit better*.

Player	Original Fee	CTPP	Year	Sale Fee	Sales CTPP	CTPP 'Genuine' Profit/Loss
Alonso X	£10,500,000	£19,101,944	2004/05	£30,000,000	£30,000,000	£10,898,056
Kromkamp J	£2,000,000	£3,475,624	2005/06	£2,700,000	£4,692,116	£1,216,492
Carson S	£750,000	£1,364,425	2004/05	£3,600,000	£4,063,191	£2,698,766
Voronin A	£0	£0	2007/08	£1,800,000	£1,800,000	£1,800,000
Benayoun Y	£5,000,000	£5,643,321	2007/08	£6,000,000	£6,000,000	£356,679
Núñez A	£2,000,000	£3,638,465	2004/05	£2,000,000	£3,649,506	£11,041
TOTAL	£20,250,000	£33,223,779		£46,100,000	£50,204,813	£16,981,034
AVERAGE	£3,375,000	£5,537,297		£7,683,333	£8,367,469	£2,830,172

Break Even

Player	Original Fee	CTPP	Year	Sale Fee	Sales CTPP	CTPP 'Genuine' Profit/Loss
Fowler R	£0	£0	2005/06	£0	£0	£0
Zenden B	£0	£0	2005/06	£0	£0	£0
Pellegrino M	£0	£0	2004/05	£0	£0	£0
Paletta G	£2,000,000	£3,475,642	2006/07	£2,000,000	£3,475,642	£0

Genuine Loss

Player	Original Fee	CTPP	Year	Sale Fee	Sales CTPP	CTPP 'Genuine' Profit/Loss
Mascherano J	£18,200,000	£20,993,155	2006/07	£20,000,000	£20,000,000	£993,155
Josemi	£2,000,000	£3,638,465	2004/05	£2,000,000	£3,475,624	£162,841
Hobbs J	£750,000	£1,368,565	2005/06	£500,000	£500,000	£868,565
Sissoko M	£5,600,000	£10,218,618	2005/06	£8,200,000	£9,255,047	£963,571
Dossena A	£7,000,000	£5,473,252	2008/09	£4,500,000	£4,500,000	£973,252
Arbeloa A	£2,600,000	£4,518,334	2006/07	£3,500,000	£3,500,000	£1,018,334
Bellamy C	£6,000,000	£10,426,926	2006/07	£7,500,000	£8,464,982	£1,961,944
Riera A	£8,000,000	£6,255,145	2008/09	£4,200,000	£4,200,000	£2,055,145
González M	£4,500,000	£8,211,389	2005/06	£4,200,000	£4,740,390	£3,470,999
Crouch P	£7,000,000	£12,773,273	2005/06	£11,000,000	£8,600,824	£4,172,449
Keane R (II)	£19,000,000	£14,855,969	2008/09	£12,000,000	£9,382,718	£5,473,251
Morientes F	£6,300,000	£11,461,166	2004/05	£3,000,000	£5,213,463	£6,247,703
García L	£6,000,000	£10,915,396	2004/05	£3,600,000	£4,063,191	£6,852,205
Pennant J	£6,700,000	£11,643,400	2006/07	£0	£0	£11,643,400
TOTAL	£121,900,000	£169,452,474		£132,300,000	£139,576,694	£46,856,814
AVERAGE	£7,117,857	£9,482,361		£6,014,286	£6,135,446	£3,346,915

Current Squad

Value Increased

Player	Original Fee	CTPP	Year	Sale Fee	Sales CTPP	CTPP 'Genuine' Profit/Loss
Torres F	£20,000,000	£22,573,285	2007/08	£48,750,000	£48,750,000	£26,176,715
N'Gog D	£1,500,000	£1,172,840	2008/09	£6,750,000	£6,750,000	£5,577,160
Maxi Rodríguez	£0	£0	2009/10	£4,500,000	£4,500,000	£4,500,000
Reina J	£6,000,000	£10,948,519	2005/06	£14,333,333	£14,333,333	£3,384,814
Insúa E	£1,000,000	£1,128,664	2006/07	£4,500,000	£4,500,000	£3,371,336
Aurélio F	£0	£0	2006/07	£2,625,000	£2,625,000	£2,625,000
Agger D	£5,000,000	£9,123,766	2005/06	£10,833,333	£10,833,333	£1,709,567
El Zhar N	£200,000	£347,564	2006/07	£2,000,000	£2,000,000	£1,652,436
Degen P	£0	£0	2008/09	£1,000,000	£1,000,000	£1,000,000
Lucas L	£6,000,000	£6,771,986	2007/08	£7,500,000	£7,500,000	£728,014
TOTAL	£39,700,000	£52,066,624		£102,791,666	£102,791,666	£50,725,042
AVERAGE	£3,970,000	£5,206,662		£10,279,167	£10,279,167	-£5,072,504

Value Decreased

Player	Original Fee	CTPP	Year	Sale Fee	Sales CTPP	CTPP 'Genuine' Profit/Loss
Škrtel M	£6,500,000	£7,336,318	2007/08	£6,750,000	£6,750,000	£586,318
Kyrgiakos S	£2,000,000	£2,000,000	2009/10	£1,125,000	£1,125,000	£875,000
Kuyt D	£9,000,000	£12,164,746	2006/07	£8,833,333	£8,833,333	£3,331,413
Johnson G (I)	£18,000,000	£18,000,000	2009/10	£13,000,000	£13,000,000	£5,000,000
Babel R	£11,500,000	£12,979,639	2007/08	£7,833,333	£7,833,333	£5,146,306
Aquilani A	£17,100,000	£17,100,000	2009/10	£10,000,000	£10,000,000	£7,100,000
TOTAL	£64,100,000	£69,580,703		£47,541,666	£47,541,666	£22,039,037
AVERAGE	£10,683,333	£11,596,784		£7,923,611	£7,923,611	£3,673,173

Claudio Ranieri 67.8 pts

Total Spend (Original Fee)	Total Spend (CTPP)	Total Sales (Original Fee)	Total Sales (CTPP)
£183,500,000	£342,093,984	£83,633,333	£101,716,803

Players	23
Profit/Genuine Increase in Value	£4,000,918
Loss/Genuine Decrease in Value	£249,457,937
Average Loss on a Player	£9,346,739
Average Profit on a Player	£1,399,985
Overall Loss	£245,257,982

Unfairly ridiculed as the 'tinkerman', Ranieri was an early proponent of rotation; a method that all recent league-winning managers have relied on. So in some ways he was ahead of his time. The Italian bought a lot of good players to Chelsea, and two – Frank Lampard and Petr Čech – remain cornerstones of the team. But his record in the market is damaged by that first year of Roman Abramovich's reign, when signings were made at an almost chaotic rate. To make matters worse, he was sacked within a year – despite taking the Blues to 2nd place, with 79 points, and all the way to a Champions League semi-final (something Mourinho never bettered).

As is the norm, Mourinho wanted different types of players, and so many of Ranieri's signings were either sidelined or sold off at a loss. However, successes such as Claude Makélélé, Damien Duff, Arjen Robben, Petr Čech, Frank Lampard and Joe Cole were integral to the successful 2004-2006 period. By contrast, Adrian Mutu, Hernán Crespo, Glen Johnson, Wayne Bridge and Scott Parker did not live up to their billing. Since then, Johnson, Bridge and Parker have re-established their reputations, but none settled at Chelsea.

Not content with sullying the transfer copybook of just Alex Ferguson, Juan Sebastián Verón led to a genuine loss of £25.2m for Chelsea, too. All in all, Ranieri laid plenty of the foundations that Mourinho benefited from, but it required the Portuguese's signings – such as Drogba and Carvalho – and his own brand of mind-altering management to take the Blues to the title.

Player	Original Fee	CTPP	Year	Sale Fee	Sales CTPP	CTPP 'Genuine' Profit/Loss
Genuine Profit						
Robben A	£13,000,000	£23,650,025	2004/05	£24,000,000	£27,087,942	£3,437,917
Gallas W	£6,200,000	£8,126,104	2001/02	£5,000,000	£8,689,105	£563,001
AVERAGE	£19,200,000	£31,776,129		£29,000,000	£35,777,047	-£4,000,918
AVERAGE	£7,400,000	£12,411,276		£10,700,000	£13,811,261	-£1,399,985

Break Even

De Lucas E	£0	£0	2002/03	£0	£0	£0
Ambrosio M	£0	£0	2003/04	£0	£0	£0

Genuine Loss

Oliveira F	£500,000	£655,331	2001/02	£0	£0	£655,331
Sullivan N	£500,000	£1,010,450	2003/04	£0	£0	£1,010,450
Jokanović S	£1,700,000	£3,025,788	2000/01	£0	£0	£3,025,788
Bridge W	£7,000,000	£14,146,302	2003/04	£12,000,000	£9,382,718	£4,763,584
Johnson G (I)	£6,000,000	£12,125,401	2003/04	£4,000,000	£4,514,657	£7,610,744
Smertin A	£3,800,000	£7,679,421	2003/04	£0	£0	£7,679,421
Parker S	£10,000,000	£20,209,002	2003/04	£6,500,000	£11,860,896	£8,348,106
Zenden B	£7,500,000	£9,829,965	2001/02	£0	£0	£9,829,965
Petit E	£7,500,000	£9,829,965	2001/02	£0	£0	£9,829,965
Grønkjær J	£7,800,000	£13,883,029	2000/01	£2,200,000	£4,002,312	£9,880,717
Cole J	£6,600,000	£13,337,941	2003/04	£0	£0	£13,337,941
Geremi	£6,900,000	£13,944,211	2003/04	£0	£0	£13,944,211
Verón J	£12,500,000	£25,261,253	2003/04	£0	£0	£25,261,253
Duff D	£17,000,000	£34,355,304	2003/04	£5,000,000	£8,689,105	£25,666,199
Makélélé C	£13,900,000	£28,090,513	2003/04	£0	£0	£28,090,513
Mutu A	£15,800,000	£31,930,223	2003/04	£0	£0	£31,930,223
Crespo H	£16,800,000	£33,951,124	2003/04	£0	£0	£33,951,124
TOTAL	**£141,800,000**	**£273,265,223**		**£93,900,000**	**£121,317,252**	**£234,815,535**
AVERAGE	**£8,341,176**	**£16,074,425**	**0**	**£1,747,059**	**£2,261,746**	**£13,812,679**

Current Squad

Value Decreased

Lampard F	£11,000,000	£14,417,282	2001/02	£11,333,333	£11,333,333	£3,083,949
Čech P	£8,500,000	£17,177,652	2003/04	£10,500,000	£10,500,000	£6,677,652
TOTAL	**£19,500,000**	**£31,594,934**		**£21,833,333**	**£21,833,333**	**£9,761,601**
AVERAGE	**£9,750,000**	**£15,797,467**	**0**	**£10,916,667**	**£10,916,667**	**£4,880,801**

Conclusions

2010/11 - Inflation Projections

With the winter transfer window still on the horizon, the 2010/11 figures remain incomplete. To date, 98 transfers have taken place this season; clubs are on course to match the 125 of the previous year.

The average fee for those 98 deals is £3,763,010, a drop of 4.87% from £3,955,840 in 2009/10. Should this inflation figure remain at -4.87%, it will mean that all of the 'values' of players listed in this project will be slightly lower when updated in the summer of 2011.

Listed below are the current squad costs, first in actual terms, then in inflated terms. The CTPP does not take into account 2010/11 inflation, because that figure has not yet been finalised.

Squad Cost

Rank	Team	Actual fee	Rank	Team	CTPP
1	Manchester City	£322,580,000	1	Chelsea	£309,066,978
2	Manchester United	£227,700,000	2	Manchester City	£306,287,489
3	Chelsea	£215,156,000	3	Manchester United	£297,947,338
4	Spurs	£191,250,000	4	Spurs	£185,609,879
5	Aston Villa	£108,800,000	5	Liverpool	£128,251,686
6	Liverpool	£108,660,000	6	Aston Villa	£122,844,244
7	Arsenal	£96,240,000	7	Arsenal	£117,990,804
8	Sunderland	£87,160,000	8	Everton	£86,461,016
9	Everton	£80,060,000	9	Sunderland	£85,291,530
10	Newcastle	£68,440,000	10	West Ham	£76,625,474
12	Fulham	£58,045,000	12	Fulham	£59,725,285
11	West Ham	£61,065,000	11	Newcastle	£62,090,351
14	Birmingham	£44,900,000	13	Birmingham	£50,938,372
13	Stoke	£47,250,000	14	Stoke	£45,695,170
15	Bolton	£42,600,000	15	Bolton	£42,380,361
16	Wolves	£38,550,000	16	Wolves	£40,364,741
17	Wigan	£37,330,000	17	Blackburn	£37,437,964
18	West Brom	£34,425,000	18	Wigan	£36,643,462
19	Blackburn	£32,150,000	19	West Brom	£32,142,628
20	Blackpool	£6,280,000	20	Blackpool	£6,211,443

This table shows that although Manchester City have the most expensive squad in conventional terms – some £107m more than Chelsea's – the Londoners still retain the top spot when inflation is taken into account. Even though City have spent circa £25m on several different players – just like Chelsea – the difference is that when Drogba, Essien et al were being purchased, it was a lot more money in that particular market. In 2004/05, the average fee was £2,174,455; in 2010, it had risen to £3,955,840, almost twice as much.

What's fascinating is how closely matched the top three are in terms of CTPP squad cost. This is a trio of "£300m" squads, some £110m more than Spurs in 4th place, and almost £200m more than Liverpool in 5th.

Summer Transfer Window

Manchester City were clearly the biggest spenders in the summer of 2010, with a net outlay of almost £100m, more than five times that of Chelsea, the next club on the list.

The biggest sellers were Liverpool, who made a profit over the course of the window; they came in just behind Aston Villa (who benefited from the sale of James Milner) in terms of making money on their transactions.

Summer Transfer Window

Rank	Team	Bought	Sold	+/-	BUY	Ranking SELL
1	Manchester City	£121,900,000	£28,500,000	-£93,400,000	1	2
2	Chelsea	£31,600,000	£14,150,000	-£17,450,000	2	6
3	Birmingham	£16,400,000	£-	-£16,400,000	7	17
4	Spurs	£15,000,000	£600,000	-£14,400,000	10	14
5	Stoke	£15,750,000	£1,900,000	-£13,850,000	9	12
6	Wolves	£15,850,000	£2,250,000	-£13,600,000	8	10
7	West Brom	£11,750,000	£-	-£11,750,000	11	17
8	Arsenal	£17,900,000	£7,200,000	£10,700,000	5	8
9	Wigan	£11,500,000	£2,000,000	-£9,500,000	12	11
10	Manchester United	£22,400,000	£14,350,000	-£8,050,000	4	5
11	West Ham	£8,350,000	£2,800,000	-£5,550,000	14	9
12	Newcastle	£5,000,000	£-	-£5,000,000	16	17
13	Blackpool	£4,500,000	£550,000	-£3,950,000	17	15
14	Bolton	£2,400,000	£500,000	-£1,900,000	18	16
15	Everton	£1,500,000	£1,000,000	-£500,000	19	13
16	Blackburn	£-	£-	£-	20	17
17	Sunderland	£17,500,000	£18,150,000	£650,000	6	4
19	Fulham	£8,600,000	£11,000,000	£2,400,000	13	7
18	Liverpool	£25,000,000	£34,800,000	£9,800,000	3	1
20	Aston Villa	£8,000,000	£19,500,000	£11,500,000	15	3

So what does all this tell us about the season ahead? Can City really land the Premier League crown? (Although, in their case, securing a place in the Champions League is surely their first priority.)

Based on the first six league games, Chelsea were making more of their Sq£, fielding 72% of it in their £XI. By contrast, City's £XI was around £50m cheaper, with 58% of their squad utilised in those early matches. Somewhat bizarrely, Manchester United had fielded only 35% of their overall squad cost; partly down to expensive new signings not yet featuring, and also down to absentees like Ferdinand, Anderson and Hargreaves.

All of this seems to suggest that Chelsea have the strongest XI, not least because it's largely well established. As reigning champions, they also know what it takes to lift the title, and most of the players from their most recent title-winning team remain in place. By contrast, City seem to be scrambling around for the right formula, mixing expensive elements without quite getting it right, and having some expensive duds in reserve; this is, after all, still very much a work in progress. However, they do seem to be improving, with enough of the summer's major signings – particularly James Milner and Yaya Touré – likely to make a lasting impact and thus make a top-four finish highly likely. Precedent tells us that to actually win the league – as 'first timers' – they need an £XI at least 98% of the most expensive side. To date, it has been only 79%, suggesting that Chelsea's investments currently hold the edge. But precedents, just like records, are there to be overturned.

Conclusions

Even with all the data presented in this book, it's impossible to say for certain that a particular league title was 'bought' or that a specific relegation was down to bad management. Luck, positive and negative momentum, and a whole host of vagaries all play roles in determining what happens during the course of a football season. But if a single match can be totally unpredictable (on the day that I write this, West Brom were at one point leading 3-0 at Arsenal), then a larger sample size – 38 matches – reduces the impact of fortune, both good and bad.

Contrary to popular wisdom, things don't even out exactly – after all, no higher power exists to bring immaculate balance (and if there are football gods, one assumes that they exist purely to mock us, not provide parity on refereeing decisions) – but a whole campaign is a better barometer for the quality of a football team or a manager than one or two games.

If this is true, then looking at things over the course of a number of seasons further limits the influence of luck and *force majeure* (not to be confused with the Ultravox lead singer on a particularly aggressive day). Any manager can have a bad season if he's shorn of his best players or forced to manage amid internal squabbles that make the Gaza Strip look like a Butlins holiday camp; the problem comes when he makes a habit of it, or when such extenuating circumstances do not exist. Weighting the figures of managers against realistic levels of achievement helps us to focus more accurately on their qualities and deficiencies, but there will always be exceptions to the rule, where sense cannot be made of what the figures suggest.

We feel that we have successfully highlighted the increasing importance of money in achieving success in the Premier League era, and how the trends are heading towards a real lack of competitive balance; since 2007, the league has been an oligopoly on a number of occasions, including 2010/11. But there will always be seasons when someone bucks the trend. Perhaps it is these last vestiges of unpredictability – as well as the skill on display in what is a far more technically adroit division than it was 20 years ago – that keep the sport so dear to our hearts; along with the fact that some teams still resort to the kind of direct football rarely seen beyond these shores, a kind which, though severely upsetting the purists, adds 'flavour' to the league, and allows one or two minnows to ambush their richer rivals. (Seeing people brought down a peg or two is a very British pleasure.) England's top division may not be as faultless as Sky Sports would have us believe, but despite the financial imbalance caused largely as a result of their broadcasting rights, there is still plenty to celebrate, and talking points aplenty. The 'product', as it's now referred to, remains largely good.

However, there's no escaping the need to lessen the gap between rich and poor. In the case of clubs like Manchester United, Arsenal and Liverpool, wealth was in the most part accrued due to success on the field, through the piecemeal construction of their histories over a century or more; winning trophies meant the ability to attract better players and bigger crowds, and virtuous circles were in place to help them grow and prosper.

This contrasts with the 'super benefactor' scenarios of Chelsea and Manchester City – although this is not to say that those clubs were by any means small or lacking in history to begin with. And ultimately, as the current rules stand, it doesn't matter how a club gains its wealth, the money is theirs to spend as they please; you can't criticise them for making the most of what's at their disposal. (Although it is unsettling to witness the rather random nature of billionaires from Russia, Abu Dhabi and America selecting clubs with which they had no previous connection, and then bestowing – or draining – money at their leisure.) Equally, plenty have tried to buy success and failed; those who succeeded had more than just cash. It's just easier to respect achievements that were more against the odds.

A more equitable league would help stop more of football's core support from growing disillusioned; plenty have been turned off by the way the sport is headed. The Premier League needs its wealth to attract the best players and managers from around the world, but a more even distribution of those resources would enable the quality of football to remain high (or even improve, with fewer paupers needing to revert to crude tactics), and add more interest to the outcome each May. The impending Financial Fair Play Rules by UEFA may be one of the last hopes in helping to restore some kind of balance to the situation, although no matter what happens, there will always be some clubs who are richer than others.

Context

Hopefully we now have a better idea of how certain managers have performed, based not on what their clubs may have achieved in the past, but on the reality of the situations they faced. It's clear, given the way the financial situation has developed in the last decade, that the almost-automatic expectation for clubs like Arsenal and Liverpool to challenge for the league is no longer appropriate, just as it's not realistic to expect certain other teams to qualify for the Champions League or escape relegation. New laws of achievement seem to apply.

Perhaps forgotten men like Jim Smith, Mike Walker and Alan Pardew will get some long-overdue kudos, and their more famous but oft-maligned colleagues, such as Sam Allardyce and Rafael Benítez, will be shown some belated appreciation (even if they almost certainly won't be affording it to each other). We feel that the data shows that it wasn't purely money behind Alex Ferguson's success at Manchester United, but that in some seasons – particularly the first few years, and at times when rivals posed a greater threat – it played a more pronounced role; and that Blackburn's title under Kenny Dalglish was not down to cash alone – but that without it, they would have struggled to put up a challenge. Our findings also make a strong case for Arsenal having paid more for their success than people perhaps realised, but all the while making clear the excellent work of Arsène Wenger, in two distinct stages to his career in England. We also feel we've proven the case for Chelsea being virtually impossible to compete with during those few seasons when their astronomical spending was allied to a new manager as strong as José Mourinho.

Ultimately, managers will come and go for a variety of reasons, and many will feel that they were robbed of the chance to conclude what they had started. (Although perhaps, in some cases, this might be akin to an infant crying at having his baked bean wall art wiped away before its finishing touches are smeared on.) Others will have known that they'd taken things as far as they could, having spent time and/or money only to end up further back than where they started from.

Perhaps this book comes down hardest on those who barely got a chance to get going. But that's part of the problem with how we judge new managers in relation to what they are actually trying to achieve at the outset; it's fair to say that most start by trying to become hard to beat, by laying down a solid defensive platform from which to build. However, this doesn't beguile us. After all, it's difficult to be seduced by someone who makes themself intentionally ugly. In real life, we get to experience things the other way around: beautifully thickened eye-lashes, carefully applied make-up, gravity-defying push-up bra; it's only later that the baggy t-shirts and ghostly-grey underwear are presented to us in all their underwhelming glory.

Definitive

So, is Allardyce a better manager than Mourinho? Is Coppell a better manager than Ferguson? Despite the data, the instinctive answer remains 'no'. However, maybe it's also true that each couldn't do the other's job quite as well. No-one would say that Martin Keown was a better player than Thierry Henry at Arsenal, but most defenders knew which one they'd rather have running at them at full tilt, and most strikers knew which one they'd rather be marked by (and in the case of Keown, *marked* tended to mean six stud-shaped abrasions).

And no two managers have had the exact same circumstances to work under; even those in the same era have faced different challenges, and even those who managed the same club did so at different times (unless they job-shared for a while). They experienced their own specific fortune, good and bad, and made their own idiosyncratic decisions, successful or not. They all made disastrous signings at one point or another, and most will have had their fair share of inspired dealings, too. Some inherited world-beaters; others, panel-beaters (and sadly, and problematically for managers who see performances affected by the personal lives of their charges, one or two wife-beaters, too). No two managers have ever been dealt the same hand.

It's easy to label managers idiots for buying an expensive flop. But using logic, nothing easily explains why Andriy Shevchenko, at 29, and costing over £50m in today's money, looked hapless, while at the same age, the hitherto hopeless Bobby Zamora began to look like a 20-goal-a-season target man. Teams of statisticians could be put on around-the-clock duty, and still not explain that one. So we must be careful of making definitive statements.

Final Word

If this book helps in some small way to show the dangerous road down which the Premier League has been headed, then that will be ample reward for the effort put into the project. With any luck, it will alter perceptions of some of the more criticised managers, and highlight the ones who punched above their weight in financial terms. Perhaps it will enable clubs to think more clearly about the suitability of managers to certain jobs, by helping to put their achievements into context, rather than just appointing the flavour of the month.

And maybe *Pay As You Play* will help a few fans settle some arguments. But of course, endless debating is one of the most enjoyable things about being a football fan in the first place; so hopefully, more than anything else, it will also help to create a myriad new talking points.

That Harry Redknapp, he's ...

Appendix

Notes, Season Charts,
Graphs & Miscellany

£XI Rank	1992-3	% of most expensive £XI	£XI	Cost Per Point	Manager	£XI / League Table Side-by-Side Comparison	Actual League Table	Lge Pos	Actual Points
1	Manchester United	100.00%	£73,379,127	£873,561	Alex Ferguson	Manchester United	Manchester United	1	84
2	Liverpool	86.40%	£63,386,101	£1,074,341	Graeme Souness	Liverpool	Aston Villa	2	74
3	Aston Villa	76.10%	£55,828,533	£754,440	Ron Atkinson	Aston Villa	Norwich City	3	72
4	Manchester City	74.90%	£54,951,737	£964,066	Peter Reid	Manchester City	Blackburn Rovers	4	71
5	Everton	67.00%	£49,154,498	£927,443	Howard Kendall	Everton	QPR	5	63
6	Tottenham Hotspur	65.30%	£47,929,439	£812,363	Doug Livermore	Tottenham Hotspur	Liverpool	6	59
7	Arsenal	61.80%	£45,350,952	£809,838	George Graham	Arsenal	Sheffield Weds	7	59
8	Blackburn Rovers	61.10%	£44,840,643	£631,558	Kenny Dalglish	Blackburn Rovers	Tottenham Hotspur	8	59
9	Leeds United	59.40%	£43,562,492	£854,167	Howard Wilkinson	Leeds United	Manchester City	9	57
10	Chelsea	47.50%	£34,847,617	£622,279	Porterfield/Webb	Chelsea	Arsenal	10	56
11	Sheffield Weds	45.30%	£33,232,694	£563,266	Trevor Francis	Sheffield Weds	Chelsea	11	56
12	Crystal Palace	37.00%	£27,163,661	£554,360	Steve Coppell	Crystal Palace	Wimbledon	12	54
13	Middlesbrough	29.30%	£21,527,280	£489,256	Lenny Lawrence	Middlesbrough	Everton	13	53
14	Oldham Athletic	27.00%	£19,817,269	£404,434	Joe Royle	Oldham Athletic	Sheffield United	14	52
15	Nottingham Forest	25.00%	£18,308,529	£457,713	Brian Clough	Nottingham Forest	Coventry City	15	52
16	Wimbledon	22.30%	£16,389,323	£303,506	Joe Kinnear	Wimbledon	Ipswich Town	16	52
17	Southampton	21.40%	£15,707,854	£314,157	Ian Branfoot	Southampton	Leeds United	17	51
18	Norwich City	20.80%	£15,263,156	£211,988	Mike Walker	Norwich City	Southampton	18	50
19	Coventry City	20.10%	£14,717,664	£283,032	Bobby Gould	Coventry City	Oldham Athletic	19	49
20	QPR	19.70%	£14,485,173	£229,923	Gerry Francis	QPR	Crystal Palace	20	49
21	Sheffield United	16.70%	£12,254,551	£235,664	Dave Bassett	Sheffield United	Middlesbrough	21	44
22	Ipswich Town	10.90%	£8,007,258	£153,986	John Lyall	Ipswich Town	Nottingham Forest	22	40
		Average	Average	£569,334				Av	
		45.20%	£33.2m						57

£XI Rank	1993-4	% of most expensive £XI	£XI	Cost Per Point	Manager	£XI / League Table Side-by-Side Comparison	Actual League Table	Lge Pos	Actual Points
1	Manchester Utd	100.00%	£82,208,197	£1,002,271	Alex Ferguson	Manchester Utd	Manchester United	1	92
2	Liverpool	82.20%	£75,596,708	£1,259,945	Souness/Evans	Liverpool	Blackburn Rovers	2	84
3	Blackburn Rovers	79.60%	£72,657,419	£865,088	Kenny Dalglish	Blackburn Rovers	Newcastle United	3	77
4	Aston Villa	65.00%	£59,937,492	£1,051,535	Ron Atkinson	Aston Villa	Arsenal	4	71
5	Manchester City	62.00%	£57,091,337	£1,268,596	Brian Horton	Manchester City	Leeds United	5	70
6	Leeds	59.30%	£54,585,789	£779,797	Howard Wilkinson	Leeds	Wimbledon	6	65
7	Arsenal	56.60%	£52,243,495	£735,824	George Graham	Arsenal	Sheffield Weds	7	64
8	Everton	45.80%	£50,609,592	£1,150,218	Kendall/Mike Walker	Everton	Liverpool	8	60
9	Sheff Wed	53.60%	£49,203,605	£768,806	Trevor Francis	Sheff Wed	QPR	9	60
10	Tottenham Hotspur	49.00%	£45,121,429	£1,002,698	Ossie Ardiles	Tottenham Hotspur	Aston Villa	10	57
11	Newcastle	48.60%	£44,674,648	£580,190	Kevin Keegan	Newcastle	Coventry City	11	56
12	Chelsea	35.00%	£32,175,544	£630,893	Glenn Hoddle	Chelsea	Norwich City	12	53
13	QPR	22.10%	£20,247,595	£337,460	Gerry Francis	QPR	West Ham United	13	52
14	West Ham	22.00%	£20,240,743	£389,245	Billy Bonds	West Ham	Chelsea	14	51
15	Oldham	20.80%	£19,155,372	£478,884	Joe Royle	Oldham	Tottenham Hotspur	15	45
16	Wimbledon	20.70%	£19,131,042	£294,324	Joe Kinnear	Wimbledon	Manchester City	16	45
17	Southampton	18.30%	£16,828,329	£391,356	Ian Branfoot/Alan Ball	Southampton	Everton	17	44
18	Ipswich	15.50%	£14,245,674	£331,295	John Lyall	Ipswich	Southampton	18	43
19	Coventry	15.30%	£14,068,024	£251,215	Bobby Gould/Phil Neal	Coventry	Ipswich Town	19	43
20	Sheff Utd	14.70%	£13,500,963	£321,452	Dave Bassett	Sheff Utd	Sheffield United	20	42
21	Norwich	13.00%	£12,026,451	£226,914	Walker/Deehan	Norwich	Oldham Athletic	21	40
22	Swindon	10.60%	£9,710,377	£323,679	John Gorman	Swindon	Swindon Town	22	30
		Average	Average	£656,445					Av
		45.20%	£33.2m						56.5

£XI Rank	1994-5	% of most expensive £XI	£XI	Cost Per Point	Manager	£XI / League Table Side-by-Side Comparison	Actual League Table	Lge Pos	Actual Points
1	Blackburn Rovers	100.00%	£87,541,696	£983,615	Kenny Dalglish	Blackburn Rovers	Blackburn Rovers	1	89
2	Manchester United	92.70%	£81,691,903	£928,317	Alex Ferguson	Manchester United	Manchester United	2	88
3	Liverpool	90.60%	£79,006,929	£1,067,661	Roy Evans	Liverpool	Nottingham Forest	3	77
4	Newcastle United	72.70%	£63,595,172	£883,266	Kevin Keegan	Newcastle United	Liverpool	4	74
5	Leeds United	70.30%	£61,410,086	£841,234	Howard Wilkinson	Leeds United	Leeds United	5	73
6	Aston Villa	63.10%	£55,740,913	£1,161,269	Ron Atkinson/Brian Little	Aston Villa	Newcastle United	6	72
7	Arsenal	62.20%	£54,681,810	£1,072,192	Graham/Houston	Arsenal	Tottenham Hotspur	7	62
8	Tottenham Hotspur	61.90%	£54,021,591	£871,316	Brian Horton	Tottenham Hotspur	QPR	8	60
9	Manchester City	60.90%	£53,964,209	£1,101,310	Ardiles/Francis	Manchester City	Wimbledon	9	56
10	Sheffield Weds	59.30%	£51,525,412	£1,010,302	Trevor Francis	Sheffield Weds	Southampton	10	54
11	Everton	57.40%	£49,725,461	£994,509	Mike Walker/Joe Royle	Everton	Chelsea	11	54
12	Nottingham Forest	44.40%	£38,686,634	£502,424	Frank Clark	Nottingham Forest	Arsenal	12	51
13	Chelsea	43.90%	£38,273,858	£708,775	Glenn Hoddle	Chelsea	Sheffield Weds	13	51
14	West Ham United	30.90%	£26,479,505	£529,590	Harry Redknapp	West Ham United	West Ham United	14	50
15	Crystal Palace	23.30%	£20,719,726	£460,438	Alan Smith	Crystal Palace	Everton	15	50
16	Coventry City	21.20%	£18,332,749	£366,655	Joe Kinnear	Coventry City	Coventry City	16	50
17	Wimbledon	21.10%	£17,990,750	£321,263	Phil Neal/Ron Atkinson	Wimbledon	Manchester City	17	49
18	Norwich City	20.00%	£17,191,422	£399,801	John Deehan	Norwich City	Aston Villa	18	48
19	Ipswich Town	18.80%	£16,337,887	£605,107	Alan Ball	Ipswich Town	Crystal Palace	19	45
20	Southampton	18.70%	£16,312,836	£302,090	Lyall/Burley	Southampton	Norwich City	20	43
21	Leicester City	18.00%	£15,477,234	£533,698	Little/MacDonald/McGhee	Leicester City	Leicester City	21	29
22	QPR	17.30%	£15,373,795	£256,230	Francis/Wilkins	QPR	Ipswich Town	22	27
	Average	Average	£722,776						Av
	43.17%	£42.45m							56.9

£XI Rank	1995-6	% of most expensive £XI	£XI	Cost Per Point	Manager	£XI / League Table Side-by-Side Comparison	Actual League Table	Lge Pos	Actual Points
1	Liverpool	100%	£89,313,515	£1,257,937	Roy Evans	Liverpool	Manchester United	1	82
2	Blackburn	99%	£88,456,548	£1,450,107	Ray Harford	Blackburn	Newcastle United	2	78
3	Newcastle Utd	91%	£80,903,917	£1,037,230	Kevin Keegan	Newcastle Utd	Liverpool	3	71
4	Arsenal	89%	£79,580,015	£1,263,175	Bruce Rioch	Arsenal	Aston Villa	4	63
5	Man Utd	79%	£70,776,892	£863,133	Alex Ferguson	Man Utd	Arsenal	5	63
6	Everton	66%	£59,093,309	£968,743	Joe Royle	Everton	Everton	6	61
7	Leeds Utd	64%	£57,179,904	£1,329,765	Howard Wilkinson	Leeds Utd	Blackburn Rovers	7	61
8	Tottenham	60%	£53,312,942	£873,983	Gerry Francis	Tottenham	Tottenham Hotspur	8	61
9	Aston Villa	56%	£50,321,269	£798,750	Brian Little	Aston Villa	Nottingham Forest	9	58
10	Sheffield Weds	52%	£45,960,362	£1,149,009	David Pleat	Sheffield Weds	West Ham United	10	51
11	Man City	49%	£43,779,635	£1,152,096	Alan Ball	Man City	Chelsea	11	50
12	Middlesbrough	45%	£40,458,312	£940,891	Bryan Robson	Middlesbrough	Middlesbrough	12	43
13	Notts Forest	37%	£33,301,087	£574,157	Frank Clark	Notts Forest	Leeds United	13	43
14	Chelsea	37%	£32,901,859	£658,037	Glenn Hoddle	Chelsea	Wimbledon	14	41
15	West Ham Utd	29%	£25,466,868	£499,350	Harry Redknapp	West Ham Utd	Sheffield Weds	15	40
16	Coventry City	27%	£24,095,651	£634,096	Ron Atkinson	Coventry City	Coventry City	16	38
17	Wimbledon	24%	£21,416,399	£522,351	Joe Kinnear	Wimbledon	Southampton	17	38
18	Southampton	22%	£19,737,670	£519,412	Dave Merrington	Southampton	Manchester City	18	38
19	QPR	18%	£16,373,975	£496,181	Ray Wilkins	QPR	QPR	19	33
20	Bolton	16%	£13,903,192	£479,420	McFarland/Todd	Bolton	Bolton Wanderers	20	29
		Average 52.98%	Average £47.31	£873,391					Av 52.1

£XI Rank	1996-7	% of most expensive £XI	£XI	Cost Per Point	Manager	£XI / League Table Side-by-Side Comparison	Actual League Table	Lge Pos	Actual Points
1	Newcastle	100.00%	£107,815,548	£1,585,523	Keegan/Dalglish	Newcastle	Manchester United	1	75
2	Liverpool	70.20%	£81,099,634	£1,192,642	Roy Evans	Liverpool	Newcastle United	2	68
3	Arsenal	64.70%	£75,225,361	£1,106,255	Houston/Rice/Wenger	Arsenal	Arsenal	3	68
4	Blackburn Rovers	61.80%	£70,796,265	£1,685,625	Ray Harford/Tony Parkes	Blackburn Rovers	Liverpool	4	68
5	Everton	60.40%	£64,983,811	£1,547,234	Joe Royle/Dave Watson	Everton	Aston Villa	5	61
6	Manchester United	51.40%	£59,611,462	£794,819	Alex Ferguson	Manchester United	Chelsea	6	59
7	Middlesbrough	48.90%	£54,361,357	£1,181,769	Bryan Robson	Middlesbrough	Sheffield Weds	7	57
8	Leeds United	47.50%	£52,342,499	£1,137,880	Wilkinson/Graham	Leeds United	Wimbledon	8	56
9	Aston Villa	47.30%	£52,180,765	£855,422	Brian Little	Aston Villa	Leicester City	9	47
10	Tottenham Hotspur	44.20%	£50,013,727	£1,087,255	Gerry Francis	Tottenham Hotspur	Tottenham Hotspur	10	46
11	Sheffield Weds	42.50%	£47,423,694	£831,995	David Pleat	Sheffield Weds	Leeds United	11	46
12	Chelsea	42.40%	£44,558,534	£755,229	Ruud Gullit	Chelsea	Derby County	12	46
13	Coventry City	34.00%	£37,508,379	£914,839	Atkinson/Strachan	Coventry City	Blackburn Rovers	13	42
14	West Ham United	29.00%	£31,555,340	£751,318	Harry Redknapp	West Ham United	West Ham United	14	42
15	Nottingham Forest	27.60%	£30,751,938	£904,469	Clark/Pearce	Nottingham Forest	Everton	15	42
16	Wimbledon	16.80%	£18,710,301	£334,113	Joe Kinnear	Wimbledon	Southampton	16	41
17	Leicester City	16.30%	£17,489,007	£372,107	Martin O'Neill	Leicester City	Coventry City	17	41
18	Southampton	16.00%	£17,363,053	£423,489	Graeme Souness	Southampton	Sunderland	18	40
19	Derby County	15.90%	£16,918,782	£367,800	Jim Smith	Derby County	Middlesbrough	19	39
20	Sunderland	9.50%	£10,410,540	£260,264	Peter Reid	Sunderland	Nottingham Forest	20	34
		Average	Average	£904,502				Av	50.9
		42.50%	£47.00m						

£XI Rank	1997-98	% of most expensive £XI	£XI	Cost Per Point	Manager	£XI / League Table Side-by-Side Comparison	Actual League Table	Lge Pos	Actual Points
1	Newcastle United	100.00%	£86,288,655	£1,961,106	Kenny Dalglish	Newcastle United	Arsenal	1	78
2	Arsenal	93.90%	£85,245,901	£1,092,896	Arsène Wenger	Arsenal	Manchester United	2	77
3	Blackburn Rovers	87.90%	£78,122,446	£1,346,939	Roy Hodgson	Blackburn Rovers	Liverpool	3	65
4	Manchester United	79.10%	£70,995,161	£922,015	Alex Ferguson	Manchester United	Chelsea	4	63
5	Sheffield Weds	72.60%	£64,675,132	£1,469,889	Pleat/Shreeves/Atkinson	Sheffield Weds	Leeds United	5	59
6	Everton	70.80%	£59,995,559	£1,499,889	Howard Kendall	Everton	Blackburn Rovers	6	58
7	Chelsea	70.30%	£59,061,096	£937,478	Gullit/Vialli	Chelsea	Aston Villa	7	57
8	Aston Villa	62.10%	£54,385,867	£954,138	Little/Gregory	Aston Villa	West Ham United	8	56
9	Tottenham Hotspur	61.40%	£53,184,324	£1,208,735	Francis/Gross	Tottenham Hotspur	Derby County	9	55
10	Liverpool	57.60%	£52,311,762	£804,796	Roy Evans	Liverpool	Leicester City	10	53
11	Leeds United	47.00%	£40,524,693	£686,859	George Graham	Leeds United	Coventry City	11	52
12	West Ham United	43.10%	£36,624,199	£654,004	Harry Redknapp	West Ham United	Southampton	12	48
13	Coventry City	39.60%	£33,389,906	£642,114	Gordon Strachan	Coventry City	Newcastle United	13	44
14	Bolton Wanderers	33.40%	£28,825,972	£720,649	Colin Todd	Bolton Wanderers	Tottenham Hotspur	14	44
15	Crystal Palace	30.10%	£27,301,685	£827,324	Coppell & 4 Others	Crystal Palace	Wimbledon	15	44
16	Leicester City	26.80%	£21,380,985	£403,415	Martin O'Neill	Leicester City	Sheffield Weds	16	44
17	Southampton	23.50%	£21,105,564	£439,699	Dave Jones	Southampton	Everton	17	40
18	Wimbledon	21.60%	£18,985,433	£431,487	Joe Kinnear	Wimbledon	Bolton Wanderers	18	40
19	Derby County	20.60%	£17,134,462	£311,536	Jim Smith	Derby County	Barnsley	19	35
20	Barnsley	12.70%	£11,674,175	£333,548	Danny Wilson	Barnsley	Crystal Palace	20	33
	Average	52.70%	Average £46.1m	£882,426				Av	52.2

£XI Rank	1998-9	% of most expensive £XI	£XI	Cost Per Point	Manager	£XI / League Table Side-by-Side Comparison	Actual League Table	Lge Pos	Actual Points
1	Manchester United	100.00%	£106,197,289	£1,344,269	Alex Ferguson	Manchester United	Manchester United	1	79
2	Newcastle United	95.20%	£94,802,568	£2,060,925	Ruud Gullit	Newcastle United	Arsenal	2	78
3	Arsenal	79.90%	£81,681,147	£1,047,194	Arsène Wenger	Arsenal	Chelsea	3	75
4	Chelsea	77.20%	£79,770,946	£1,063,613	Gianluca Vialli	Chelsea	Leeds United	4	67
5	Blackburn Rovers	64.50%	£68,190,692	£1,948,305	Roy Hodgson/Brian Kidd	Blackburn Rovers	West Ham United	5	57
6	Tottenham Hotspur	62.10%	£63,994,422	£1,361,583	Gross/Graham	Tottenham Hotspur	Aston Villa	6	55
7	Everton	55.50%	£57,306,124	£1,332,701	Walter Smith	Everton	Liverpool	7	54
8	Sheffield Weds	54.10%	£56,196,808	£1,221,670	Danny Wilson	Sheffield Weds	Derby County	8	52
9	Aston Villa	52.80%	£55,399,823	£1,007,270	John Gregory	Aston Villa	Middlesbrough	9	51
10	Liverpool	50.50%	£53,575,564	£992,140	Evans/Houllier	Liverpool	Leicester City	10	49
11	Middlesbrough	41.20%	£41,633,291	£816,339	Bryan Robson	Middlesbrough	Tottenham Hotspur	11	47
12	Leeds United	40.40%	£40,975,998	£611,582	Graham/O'Leary	Leeds United	Sheffield Weds	12	46
13	West Ham	36.20%	£36,590,883	£641,945	Harry Redknapp	West Ham	Newcastle United	13	46
14	Coventry City	33.90%	£33,704,955	£802,499	Gordon Strachan	Coventry City	Everton	14	43
15	Wimbledon	27.00%	£27,899,843	£664,282	Joe Kinnear	Wimbledon	Coventry City	15	42
16	Nottingham Forest	25.50%	£26,128,582	£870,953	Bassett/Adams/Atkinson	Nottingham Forest	Wimbledon	16	42
17	Leicester City	25.50%	£24,523,983	£500,489	Martin O'Neill	Leicester City	Southampton	17	41
18	Derby County	19.80%	£20,336,645	£391,089	Jim Smith	Derby County	Charlton Athletic	18	36
19	Southampton	14.60%	£15,231,079	£371,490	Dave Jones	Southampton	Blackburn Rovers	19	35
20	Charlton Athletic	10.50%	£11,212,325	£311,453	Alan Curbishley	Charlton Athletic	Nottingham Forest	20	30
		Average	Average	£968,090					Av
		48.32%	£49.7m						51.2

£XI Rank	1999-0	% of most expensive £XI	£XI	Cost Per Point	Manager	£XI / League Table Side-by-Side Comparison	Actual League Table	Lge Pos	Actual Points
1	Newcastle United	100.00%	£118,233,197	£2,273,715	Ruud Gullit/Robson	Newcastle United	Manchester United	1	91
2	Manchester United	82.00%	£104,323,670	£1,146,414	Alex Ferguson	Manchester United	Arsenal	2	73
3	Arsenal	77.10%	£96,609,330	£1,323,415	Arsène Wenger	Arsenal	Leeds United	3	69
4	Chelsea	66.20%	£78,961,634	£1,214,754	Gianluca Vialli	Chelsea	Liverpool	4	67
5	Liverpool	55.90%	£66,752,063	£996,299	Gérard Houllier	Liverpool	Chelsea	5	65
6	Tottenham Hotspur	49.30%	£61,512,490	£1,160,613	George Graham	Tottenham Hotspur	Aston Villa	6	58
7	Sheffield Weds	42.50%	£52,526,867	£1,694,415	Wilson/Shreeves	Sheffield Weds	Sunderland	7	58
8	Coventry City	41.40%	£51,054,060	£1,160,320	John Gregory	Coventry City	Leicester City	8	55
9	Aston Villa	41.00%	£48,981,184	£844,503	Gordon Strachan	Aston Villa	West Ham United	9	55
10	Leeds United	39.20%	£45,206,309	£655,164	David O'Leary	Leeds United	Tottenham Hotspur	10	53
11	Everton	35.70%	£42,036,440	£840,729	Walter Smith	Everton	Newcastle United	11	52
12	Middlesbrough	33.50%	£40,401,814	£776,958	Bryan Robson	Middlesbrough	Middlesbrough	12	52
13	West Ham United	29.20%	£35,937,087	£653,402	Harry Redknapp	West Ham United	Everton	13	50
14	Wimbledon	26.70%	£32,588,009	£987,515	Egil Olsen	Wimbledon	Coventry City	14	44
15	Derby County	23.30%	£28,058,404	£738,379	Jim Smith	Derby County	Southampton	15	44
16	Leicester City	21.10%	£24,961,687	£453,849	Martin O'Neill	Leicester City	Derby County	16	38
17	Sunderland	20.20%	£23,968,182	£413,245	Peter Reid	Sunderland	Bradford City	17	36
18	Southampton	8.80%	£11,137,623	£253,128	Jones/Hoddle	Southampton	Wimbledon	18	33
19	Bradford City	8.30%	£10,243,172	£284,533	Paul Jewell	Bradford City	Sheffield Weds	19	31
20	Watford	3.80%	£4,569,906	£190,413	Graham Taylor	Watford	Watford	20	24
		Average	Average	£903,090				Av	
		40.26%	£48.9m						52.4

£XI Rank	2000-1	% of most expensive £XI	£XI	Cost Per Point	Manager	£XI / League Table Side-by-Side Comparison	Actual League Table	Lge Pos	Actual Points
1	Arsenal	100.00%	£99,650,688	£1,423,581	Arsène Wenger	Arsenal	Manchester United	1	80
2	Newcastle United	92.70%	£90,123,779	£1,767,133	Bobby Robson	Newcastle United	Arsenal	2	70
3	Chelsea	89.20%	£87,051,048	£1,427,066	Vialli/Ranieri	Chelsea	Liverpool	3	69
4	Liverpool	81.80%	£80,534,293	£1,167,164	Alex Ferguson	Liverpool	Leeds United	4	68
5	Manchester United	78.60%	£78,358,412	£979,480	Gérard Houllier	Manchester United	Ipswich Town	5	66
6	Leeds United	78.50%	£75,705,900	£1,113,322	John Gregory	Leeds United	Chelsea	6	61
7	Aston Villa	74.70%	£73,885,223	£1,368,245	David O'Leary	Aston Villa	Sunderland	7	57
8	Tottenham Hotspur	66.10%	£66,144,462	£1,349,887	Graham/Hoddle	Tottenham Hotspur	Aston Villa	8	54
9	Leicester City	37.00%	£35,699,250	£743,734	Robson/Venables	Leicester City	Charlton Athletic	9	52
10	Middlesbrough	36.90%	£35,242,875	£839,116	Peter Taylor	Middlesbrough	Southampton	10	52
11	Coventry City	35.40%	£34,928,070	£1,027,296	Gordon Strachan	Coventry City	Newcastle United	11	51
12	Sunderland	33.40%	£32,130,818	£563,699	Walter Smith	Sunderland	Tottenham Hotspur	12	49
13	Everton	32.90%	£31,875,119	£758,931	Peter Reid	Everton	Leicester City	13	48
14	Derby County	28.50%	£27,972,160	£666,004	Jim Smith	Derby County	Middlesbrough	14	42
15	West Ham United	26.00%	£25,539,885	£608,093	Harry Redknapp	West Ham United	West Ham United	15	42
16	Manchester City	26.00%	£24,776,768	£728,728	Joe Royle	Manchester City	Everton	16	42
17	Ipswich Town	22.30%	£21,868,403	£331,339	George Burley	Ipswich Town	Derby County	17	42
18	Charlton Athletic	21.50%	£20,926,167	£402,426	Alan Curbishley	Charlton Athletic	Manchester City	18	34
19	Southampton	11.10%	£11,295,243	£217,216	Hoddle/Gray	Southampton	Coventry City	19	34
20	Bradford City	10.00%	£9,830,047	£378,079	Hutchings/McCall/Jefferie	Bradford City	Bradford City	20	26
		Average	Average	£893,027				Av	
		49.13%	£48.17m						51.9

£XI Rank	2001-2	% of most expensive £XI	£XI	Cost Per Point	Manager	£XI / League Table Side-by-Side Comparison	Actual League Table	Lge Pos	Actual Points
1	Arsenal	100.00%	£104,115,888	£1,196,734	Arsène Wenger	Arsenal	Arsenal	1	87
2	Newcastle Utd	97.70%	£101,678,125	£1,432,036	Bobby Robson	Newcastle Utd	Liverpool	2	80
3	Chelsea	93.80%	£97,619,495	£1,525,305	Claudio Raniero	Chelsea	Manchester United	3	77
4	Leeds Utd	91.50%	£95,297,942	£1,443,908	David O'Leary	Leeds Utd	Newcastle United	4	71
5	Man Utd	91.40%	£95,175,852	£1,236,050	Alex Ferguson	Man Utd	Leeds United	5	66
6	Liverpool	69.60%	£72,439,177	£905,490	Gérard Houllier	Liverpool	Chelsea	6	64
7	Tottenham Hotspur	61.70%	£64,290,271	£1,285,805	Glenn Hoddle	Tottenham Hotspur	West Ham United	7	53
8	Aston Villa	50.30%	£52,384,939	£1,047,699	Gregory/Taylor	Aston Villa	Aston Villa	8	50
9	Fulham	46.40%	£48,360,708	£1,099,107	Jean Tigana	Fulham	Tottenham Hotspur	9	50
10	West Ham Utd	38.30%	£39,917,617	£753,163	Glenn Foeder	West Ham Utd	Blackburn Rovers	10	46
11	Everton	38.20%	£39,813,096	£925,886	Smith/Moyes	Everton	Southampton	11	45
12	Blackburn	37.40%	£38,909,807	£845,865	Graeme Souness	Blackburn	Middlesbrough	12	45
13	Middlesbrough	32.20%	£33,535,044	£745,223	Steve McClaren	Middlesbrough	Fulham	13	44
14	Ipswich Town	27.40%	£28,521,423	£792,262	George Burley	Ipswich Town	Charlton Athletic	14	44
15	Leicester	27.00%	£28,145,447	£1,005,195	Taylor/Bassett/Adams	Leicester	Everton	15	43
16	Sunderland	25.20%	£26,216,892	£655,422	Peter Reid	Sunderland	Bolton Wanderers	16	40
17	Charlton	22.30%	£23,245,224	£528,301	Alan Curbishley	Charlton	Sunderland	17	40
18	Derby County	16.60%	£17,296,489	£576,550	Smith/Todd/Gregory	Derby County	Ipswich Town	18	36
19	Southampton	13.50%	£14,025,241	£311,672	Gray/Strachan	Southampton	Derby County	19	30
20	Bolton	11.20%	£11,689,493	£292,237	Sam Allardyce	Bolton	Leicester City	20	28
		Average	Average						Av
		49.59%	£51.63m	£930,198					51.9

£XI Rank	2002-3	% of most expensive £XI	£XI	Cost Per Point	Manager	£XI / League Table Side-by-Side Comparison	Actual League Table	Lge Pos	Actual Points
1	Manchester United	100.00%	£113,757,434	£1,370,571	Alex Ferguson	Manchester United	Manchester United	1	83
2	Newcastle United	94.40%	£109,175,613	£1,582,255	Arsène Wenger	Newcastle United	Arsenal	2	78
3	Arsenal	93.90%	£107,202,951	£1,374,397	Bobby Robson	Arsenal	Newcastle United	3	69
4	Chelsea	83.70%	£98,277,155	£1,466,823	Claudio Ranieri	Chelsea	Chelsea	4	67
5	Liverpool	65.80%	£75,690,207	£1,182,659	Gérard Houllier	Liverpool	Liverpool	5	64
6	Middlesbrough	43.60%	£48,280,186	£985,310	Steve McClaren	Middlesbrough	Blackburn Rovers	6	60
7	Manchester City	40.80%	£44,196,262	£866,593	Tigana/Coleman	Manchester City	Everton	7	59
8	Fulham	38.40%	£43,635,853	£909,080	Kevin Keegan	Fulham	Southampton	8	52
9	Tottenham Hotspur	36.30%	£42,584,548	£851,691	Glenn Hoddle	Tottenham Hotspur	Manchester City	9	51
10	Leeds United	33.20%	£39,064,624	£831,162	Venables/Reid	Leeds United	Tottenham Hotspur	10	50
11	Everton	32.70%	£38,591,103	£654,086	David Moyes	Everton	Middlesbrough	11	49
12	Blackburn Rovers	29.70%	£34,295,509	£571,592	Graeme Souness	Blackburn Rovers	Charlton Athletic	12	49
13	West Ham United	27.90%	£33,210,297	£790,721	Roeder/Brooking	West Ham United	Birmingham City	13	48
14	Sunderland	23.70%	£26,718,540	£1,406,239	Reid/Wilkinson/McCarthy	Sunderland	Fulham	14	48
15	Aston Villa	21.00%	£24,995,357	£555,452	Graham Taylor	Aston Villa	Leeds United	15	47
16	Charlton Athletic	20.40%	£23,594,460	£481,520	Alan Curbishley	Charlton Athletic	Aston Villa	16	45
17	Birmingham City	18.90%	£20,869,206	£434,775	Steve Bruce	Birmingham City	Bolton Wanderers	17	44
18	Southampton	16.50%	£19,030,480	£365,971	Gordon Strachan	Southampton	West Ham United	18	42
19	West Brom	14.40%	£16,110,691	£619,642	Gary Megson	West Brom	West Brom	19	26
20	Bolton Wanderers	7.50%	£9,269,455	£210,669	Sam Allardyce	Bolton Wanderers	Sunderland	20	19
		Average	Average	£875,561					Av
		42.12%	£48.42m						52.5

£XI Rank	2003-4	% of most expensive £XI	£XI	Cost Per Point	Manager	£XI / League Table Side-by-Side Comparison	Actual League Table	Lge Pos	Actual Points
1	Chelsea	100.00%	£153,144,833	£1,938,542	Claudio Ranieri	Chelsea	Arsenal	1	90
2	Newcastle United	77.20%	£108,983,681	£1,946,137	Bobby Robson	Newcastle United	Chelsea	2	79
3	Manchester United	67.80%	£99,223,823	£1,322,984	Alex Ferguson	Manchester United	Manchester United	3	75
4	Arsenal	63.70%	£95,692,961	£1,063,255	Arsène Wenger	Arsenal	Liverpool	4	60
5	Liverpool	60.00%	£87,479,159	£1,457,986	Gérard Houllier	Liverpool	Newcastle United	5	56
6	Manchester City	31.80%	£45,510,620	£1,110,015	Kevin Keegan	Manchester City	Aston Villa	6	56
7	Middlesbrough	31.50%	£43,439,831	£904,996	Steve McClaren	Middlesbrough	Charlton Athletic	7	53
8	Tottenham Hotspur	29.10%	£43,315,868	£962,575	Hoddle/Pleat	Tottenham Hotspur	Bolton Wanderers	8	53
9	Blackburn Rovers	27.20%	£40,603,272	£922,802	Graeme Souness	Blackburn Rovers	Fulham	9	52
10	Everton	25.90%	£37,835,043	£970,129	David Moyes	Everton	Birmingham City	10	50
11	Aston Villa	24.90%	£37,067,183	£661,914	David O'Leary	Aston Villa	Middlesbrough	11	48
12	Fulham	24.10%	£34,781,860	£668,882	Chris Coleman	Fulham	Southampton	12	47
13	Birmingham City	17.50%	£31,674,835	£633,497	Peter Reid/Eddie Gray	Birmingham City	Portsmouth	13	45
14	Leeds United	17.40%	£25,206,260	£763,826	Steve Bruce	Leeds United	Tottenham Hotspur	14	45
15	Southampton	17.20%	£24,903,708	£529,866	Strachan/Wigley/Sturrock	Southampton	Blackburn Rovers	15	44
16	Charlton Athletic	15.40%	£22,563,217	£425,721	Alan Curbishley	Charlton Athletic	Manchester City	16	41
17	Wolves	11.00%	£16,371,073	£496,093	Dave Jones	Wolves	Everton	17	39
18	Portsmouth	9.70%	£13,829,508	£307,322	Harry Redknapp	Portsmouth	Leicester City	18	33
19	Leicester City	8.40%	£12,268,172	£371,763	Micky Adams	Leicester City	Leeds United	19	33
20	Bolton Wanderers	2.90%	£4,359,571	£82,256	Sam Allardyce	Bolton Wanderers	Wolves	20	33
		Average	Average	£877,028					Av
		33.14%	£48.91m						51.6

£XI Rank	2004-5	% of most expensive £XI	£XI	Cost Per Point	Manager	£XI / League Table Side-by-Side Comparison	Actual League Table	Lge Pos	Actual Points
1	Chelsea	100.00%	£195,163,150	£2,054,349	Jose Mourinho	Chelsea	Chelsea	1	95
2	Manchester United	79.00%	£149,992,332	£1,947,952	Alex Ferguson	Manchester United	Arsenal	2	83
3	Arsenal	50.80%	£101,747,999	£1,225,880	Arsène Wenger	Arsenal	Manchester United	3	77
4	Liverpool	39.40%	£75,171,147	£1,296,054	Rafael Benitez	Liverpool	Everton	4	61
5	Newcastle United	38.30%	£70,322,499	£1,598,239	Graeme Souness	Newcastle United	Liverpool	5	58
6	Tottenham Hotspur	22.10%	£42,241,107	£812,329	Santini/Martin Jol	Tottenham Hotspur	Bolton Wanderers	6	58
7	Blackburn Rovers	17.20%	£34,427,471	£819,702	Keegan/Stuart Pearce	Blackburn Rovers	Middlesbrough	7	55
8	Manchester City	17.00%	£34,309,725	£659,802	Souness/Mark Hughes	Manchester City	Manchester City	8	52
9	Aston Villa	16.80%	£32,768,410	£697,200	David O'Leary	Aston Villa	Tottenham Hotspur	9	52
10	Middlesbrough	16.20%	£29,767,392	£541,225	Steve McClaren	Middlesbrough	Aston Villa	10	47
11	Everton	14.30%	£27,229,901	£446,392	David Moyes	Everton	Charlton Athletic	11	46
12	Fulham	13.90%	£26,422,741	£600,517	Chris Coleman	Fulham	Birmingham City	12	45
13	Birmingham City	13.20%	£24,809,786	£551,329	Steve Bruce	Birmingham City	Fulham	13	44
14	Southampton	12.30%	£23,285,695	£727,678	Sturrock/Wigley/Redknap	Southampton	Newcastle United	14	44
15	Charlton Athletic	11.60%	£21,926,495	£476,663	Alan Curbishley	Charlton Athletic	Blackburn Rovers	15	42
16	West Brom	8.60%	£16,188,399	£476,129	Megson/Burrows/Robson	West Brom	Portsmouth	16	39
17	Portsmouth	8.20%	£15,422,996	£395,461	Redknapp/Zajec/Perrin	Portsmouth	West Brom	17	34
18	Norwich City	4.60%	£9,007,504	£272,955	Nigel Worthington	Norwich City	Crystal Palace	18	33
19	Crystal Palace	2.90%	£5,313,507	£161,015	Iain Dowie	Crystal Palace	Norwich City	19	33
20	Bolton Wanderers	2.40%	£4,739,177	£81,710	Sam Allardyce	Bolton Wanderers	Southampton	20	32
		Average	Average	£792,129				Av	
		24.40%	£47.01m						51.5

£XI Rank	2005-6	% of most expensive £XI	£XI	Cost Per Point	Manager	£XI / League Table Side-by-Side Comparison	Actual League Table	Lge Pos	Actual Points
1	Chelsea	100.00%	£229,619,425	£2,523,290	Jose Mourinho	Chelsea	Chelsea	1	91
2	Manchester United	74.40%	£161,688,549	£1,948,055	Alex Ferguson	Manchester United	Manchester United	2	83
3	Arsenal	41.80%	£96,270,276	£1,436,870	Arsène Wenger	Arsenal	Liverpool	3	82
4	Liverpool	41.30%	£93,220,381	£1,136,834	Rafael Benitez	Liverpool	Arsenal	4	67
5	Newcastle United	34.10%	£74,364,866	£1,282,153	Souness/Roeder	Newcastle United	Tottenham Hotspur	5	65
6	Tottenham Hotspur	20.70%	£46,594,380	£716,837	Martin Jol	Tottenham Hotspur	Blackburn Rovers	6	63
7	Middlesbrough	19.00%	£41,802,628	£928,947	Steve McClaren	Middlesbrough	Newcastle United	7	58
8	Everton	17.80%	£39,988,801	£799,776	David Moyes	Everton	Bolton Wdrs	8	56
9	Aston Villa	14.10%	£33,026,043	£786,334	David O'Leary	Aston Villa	West Ham United	9	55
10	Manchester City	14.00%	£29,085,345	£676,403	Stuart Pearce	Manchester City	Wigan Athletic	10	51
11	Blackburn Rovers	11.80%	£26,697,110	£423,764	Mark Hughes	Blackburn Rovers	Everton	11	50
12	Birmingham City	10.70%	£23,759,497	£698,809	Steve Bruce	Birmingham City	Fulham	12	48
13	Charlton Athletic	8.80%	£20,020,387	£425,966	Alan Curbishley	Charlton Athletic	Charlton Athletic	13	47
14	Fulham	8.70%	£19,449,214	£405,192	Chris Coleman	Fulham	Middlesbrough	14	45
15	West Brom	8.40%	£19,337,852	£644,595	Bryan Robson	West Brom	Manchester City	15	43
16	West Ham United	7.80%	£18,390,112	£334,366	Alan Pardew	West Ham United	Aston Villa	16	42
17	Portsmouth	7.60%	£18,007,799	£473,889	Perrin/Jordan/Redknapp	Portsmouth	Portsmouth	17	38
18	Wigan Athletic	5.50%	£13,028,010	£255,451	Paul Jewell	Wigan Athletic	Birmingham City	18	34
19	Sunderland	3.90%	£9,014,820	£600,988	Sam Allardyce	Sunderland	West Brom	19	30
20	Bolton Wdrs	3.70%	£8,882,976	£158,625	McCarthy/Kevin Ball	Bolton Wdrs	Sunderland	20	15
		Average	Average	£832,857					Av
		22.70%	£51.12m						52.1

£XI Rank	2006-7	% of most expensive £XI	£XI	Cost Per Point	Manager	£XI / League Table Side-by-Side Comparison	Actual League Table	Lge Pos	Actual Points
1	Chelsea	100.00%	£255,266,748	£3,075,503	Jose Mourinho	Chelsea	Manchester United	1	89
2	Manchester United	69.20%	£171,702,282	£1,929,239	Alex Ferguson	Manchester United	Chelsea	2	83
3	Liverpool	32.50%	£84,110,888	£1,236,925	Rafael Benitez	Liverpool	Liverpool	3	68
4	Tottenham Hotspur	29.10%	£75,417,340	£1,256,956	Martin Jol	Tottenham Hotspur	Arsenal	4	68
5	Arsenal	26.80%	£71,372,631	£1,049,598	Arsène Wenger	Arsenal	Tottenham Hotspur	5	60
6	Newcastle United	24.40%	£62,673,539	£1,457,524	Glenn Roeder	Newcastle United	Everton	6	58
7	Everton	22.00%	£56,242,198	£969,693	David Moyes	Everton	Bolton Wanderers	7	56
8	Aston Villa	17.50%	£45,328,516	£906,570	Martin O'Neill	Aston Villa	Reading	8	55
9	Middlesbrough	15.50%	£38,931,084	£846,328	Gareth Southgate	Middlesbrough	Portsmouth	9	54
10	Blackburn Rovers	11.10%	£28,380,195	£545,773	Mark Hughes	Blackburn Rovers	Blackburn Rovers	10	52
11	Wigan	11.10%	£28,280,551	£673,346	Paul Jewell	Wigan	Aston Villa	11	50
12	Man City	10.70%	£26,589,063	£699,712	Stuart Pearce	Man City	Middlesbrough	12	46
13	Bolton	9.60%	£25,386,672	£453,333	Allardyce/Sammy Lee	Bolton	Newcastle United	13	43
14	Charlton Athletic	9.60%	£24,611,116	£723,856	Dowie/Reed/Pardew	Charlton Athletic	Manchester City	14	42
15	Portsmouth	7.90%	£21,246,017	£393,445	Harry Redknapp	Portsmouth	West Ham United	15	41
16	West Ham United	7.00%	£18,590,693	£453,432	Pardew/Curbishley	West Ham United	Fulham	16	39
17	Fulham	6.40%	£16,643,952	£426,768	Coleman/Sanchez	Fulham	Wigan Athletic	17	38
18	Sheffield United	2.90%	£7,482,720	£196,914	Neil Warnock	Sheffield United	Sheffield United	18	38
19	Watford	2.50%	£6,665,000	£238,036	Adrian Boothroyd	Watford	Charlton Athletic	19	34
20	Reading	2.30%	£6,140,190	£111,640	Steve Coppell	Reading	Watford	20	28
		Average	Average						Av
		20.91%	£53.53m	£882,230					52.1

£XI Rank	2007-8	% of most expensive £XI	£XI	Cost Per Point	Manager	£XI / League Table Side-by-Side Comparison	Actual League Table	Lge Pos	Actual Points
1	Chelsea	100.00%	£201,709,707	£2,373,055	Mourinho/Grant	Chelsea	Manchester United	1	87
2	Manchester United	88.50%	£171,806,255	£1,974,785	Alex Ferguson	Manchester United	Chelsea	2	85
3	Liverpool	49.00%	£96,562,289	£1,270,556	Rafael Benítez	Liverpool	Arsenal	3	83
4	Tottenham Hotspur	43.50%	£86,504,982	£1,880,543	Jol/Juande Ramos	Tottenham Hotspur	Liverpool	4	76
5	Arsenal	32.90%	£68,063,312	£820,040	Arsène Wenger	Arsenal	Everton	5	65
6	Newcastle United	30.50%	£61,362,190	£1,427,028	Allardyce//Keegan	Newcastle United	Aston Villa	6	60
7	Everton	28.60%	£56,726,407	£872,714	David Moyes	Everton	Blackburn Rovers	7	58
8	Aston Villa	26.50%	£52,872,104	£881,202	Martin O'Neill	Aston Villa	Portsmouth	8	57
9	West Ham United	19.40%	£39,481,513	£805,745	Alan Curbishley	West Ham United	Manchester City	9	55
10	Manchester City	19.00%	£36,546,872	£664,489	Sven Göran Eriksson	Manchester City	West Ham United	10	49
11	Middlesbrough	18.90%	£36,524,437	£869,629	Gareth Southgate	Middlesbrough	Tottenham Hotspur	11	46
12	Portsmouth	18.20%	£36,082,368	£633,024	Harry Redknapp	Portsmouth	Newcastle United	12	43
13	Blackburn Rovers	15.80%	£31,893,640	£549,890	Mark Hughes	Blackburn Rovers	Middlesbrough	13	42
14	Birmingham	15.80%	£31,530,984	£900,885	Bruce/Black/McLeish	Birmingham	Wigan Athletic	14	40
15	Sunderland	15.30%	£29,163,759	£747,789	Roy Keane	Sunderland	Sunderland	15	39
16	Wigan Athletic	14.20%	£28,353,106	£708,828	Hutchings/Barlow/Bruce	Wigan Athletic	Bolton Wanderers	16	37
17	Fulham	14.10%	£27,910,126	£775,281	Sanchez/Hodgson	Fulham	Fulham	17	36
18	Bolton Wanderers	11.10%	£22,568,094	£609,943	Sammy Lee/Megson	Bolton Wanderers	Reading	18	36
19	Derby County	6.30%	£12,363,429	£1,123,948	Billy Davies/Paul Jewell	Derby County	Birmingham City	19	35
20	Reading	3.00%	£6,089,682	£169,153	Steve Coppell	Reading	Derby County	20	11
		Average	Average	£1,002,927				Av	52
		28.53%	£56,705,762.80						

£XI Rank	2008-9	% of most expensive £XI	£XI	Cost Per Point	Manager	£XI / League Table Side-by-Side Comparison	Actual League Table	Lge Pos	Actual Points
1	Chelsea	100.00%	£168,193,359	£2,026,426	Scolari/Hiddink	Chelsea	Manchester United	1	90
2	Manchester United	95.50%	£158,436,770	£1,760,409	Alex Ferguson	Manchester United	Liverpool	2	86
3	Liverpool	57.90%	£96,049,949	£1,116,860	Rafael Benitez	Liverpool	Chelsea	3	83
4	Tottenham Hotspur	56.80%	£93,623,149	£1,835,748	Ramos/Redknapp	Tottenham Hotspur	Arsenal	4	72
5	Manchester City	40.70%	£65,296,040	£1,305,921	Mark Hughes	Manchester City	Everton	5	63
6	Newcastle United	37.30%	£63,534,985	£1,868,676	Keegan/Kinnear + 2 more	Newcastle United	Aston Villa	6	62
7	Aston Villa	37.00%	£61,519,261	£992,246	Martin O'Neill	Aston Villa	Fulham	7	53
8	Everton	33.40%	£57,423,207	£911,479	Arsène Wenger	Everton	Tottenham Hotspur	8	51
9	Arsenal	33.30%	£55,517,927	£771,082	David Moyes	Arsenal	West Ham United	9	51
10	West Ham United	25.20%	£43,121,938	£845,528	Curbishley/Zola	West Ham United	Manchester City	10	50
11	Portsmouth	20.50%	£33,826,136	£825,028	Redknapp/Adams/Hart	Portsmouth	Wigan Athletic	11	45
12	Sunderland	19.30%	£30,979,607	£860,545	Keane/Sbragia	Sunderland	Stoke City	12	45
13	Fulham	17.50%	£28,856,017	£544,453	Roy Hodgson	Fulham	Bolton Wdrs	13	41
14	Middlesbrough	17.20%	£28,496,787	£890,525	Gareth Southgate	Middlesbrough	Portsmouth	14	41
15	Bolton Wdrs	15.80%	£25,557,065	£623,343	Gary Megson	Bolton Wdrs	Blackburn Rovers	15	41
16	Blackburn Rovers	14.00%	£23,643,950	£576,682	Paul Ince/Sam Allardyce	Blackburn Rovers	Sunderland	16	36
17	Wigan Athletic	13.80%	£23,306,044	£517,912	Steve Bruce	Wigan Athletic	Hull City	17	35
18	West Brom	10.60%	£16,929,210	£529,038	Tony Mowbray	West Brom	Newcastle United	18	34
19	Stoke City	6.20%	£10,047,765	£223,284	Tony Pulis	Stoke City	Middlesbrough	19	32
20	Hull City	4.50%	£7,345,398	£209,869	Phil Brown	Hull City	West Brom	20	32
	Average	Average						Av	
	32.80%	£54.58m		£961,753					52.1

£XI Rank	2009-10	% of most expensive £XI	£XI	Cost Per Point	Manager	£XI / League Table Side-by-Side Comparison	Actual League Table	Lge Pos	Actual Points
1	Chelsea	100.00%	£187,436,346.00	£2,179,492	Carlo Ancelotti	Chelsea	Chelsea	1	86
2	Manchester United	76.30%	£141,384,155.00	£1,663,343	Alex Ferguson	Manchester United	Manchester United	2	85
3	Manchester City	66.80%	£121,147,357.00	£1,808,170	Hughes/Mancini	Manchester City	Arsenal	3	75
4	Liverpool	48.50%	£90,993,156.00	£1,444,336	Rafael Benitez	Liverpool	Tottenham Hotspur	4	70
5	Tottenham Hotspur	42.70%	£78,370,565.00	£1,119,580	Harry Redknapp	Tottenham Hotspur	Manchester City	5	67
6	Aston Villa	38.80%	£72,569,119.00	£1,133,892	Martin O'Neill	Aston Villa	Aston Villa	6	64
7	Arsenal	34.00%	£64,865,090.00	£864,868	Arsène Wenger	Arsenal	Liverpool	7	63
8	Everton	28.60%	£52,788,697.00	£865,388	David Moyes	Everton	Everton	8	61
9	Sunderland	28.50%	£51,778,219.00	£1,176,778	Steve Bruce	Sunderland	Birmingham City	9	50
10	West Ham United	20.00%	£37,948,146.00	£1,084,233	Gianfranco Zola	West Ham United	Blackburn Rovers	10	50
11	Birmingham City	15.40%	£28,467,758.00	£569,355	Alex McLeish	Birmingham City	Stoke City	11	47
12	Bolton Wdrs	14.10%	£25,703,674.00	£659,069	Megson-Coyle	Bolton Wdrs	Fulham	12	46
13	Wigan Athletic	12.80%	£23,779,041.00	£660,529	Roberto Martinez	Wigan Athletic	Sunderland	13	44
14	Fulham	12.20%	£22,465,156.00	£488,373	Roy Hodgson	Fulham	Bolton Wdrs	14	39
15	Blackburn Rovers	11.10%	£20,724,566.00	£414,491	Sam Allardyce	Blackburn Rovers	Wolves	15	38
16	Stoke City	9.60%	£17,420,065.00	£370,640	Tony Pulis	Stoke City	Wigan Athletic	16	36
17	Wolves	8.10%	£15,042,447.00	£395,854	Mick McCarthy	Wolves	West Ham United	17	35
18	Hull City	6.10%	£11,031,204.00	£367,707	Phil Brown/Iain Dowie	Hull City	Burnley	18	30
19	Portsmouth	5.90%	£10,823,811.00	£569,674	Paul Hart/Avram Grant	Portsmouth	Hull City	19	30
20	Burnley	4.50%	£8,172,883.00	£272,429	Owen Coyle/Brian Laws	Burnley	Portsmouth*	20	19
		Average	Average	£905,410					Av
		29.20%	£54.15m						51.7

Top-Ranking Transfers (CTPP) Players who played in the Premier League 1992-2010

#	Club	Player	CTPP	Original fee	Year transferred
1	Chelsea	Shevchenko A	£53,524,884	£30,800,000	2006/07
2	Man Utd	Rooney W	£49,119,283	£27,000,000	2004/05
3	Man Utd	Ferdinand R	£48,409,013	£30,000,000	2002/03
4	Chelsea	Essien M	£47,443,584	£26,000,000	2005/06
5	Chelsea	Drogba D	£43,661,585	£24,000,000	2004/05
6	Newcastle	Shearer A	£39,683,045	£15,000,000	1996/97
7	Chelsea	Wright-Phillips S	£38,319,818	£21,000,000	2005/06
8	Man Utd	Verón J	£36,829,602	£28,100,000	2001/02
9	Chelsea	Carvalho R	£36,111,770	£19,850,000	2004/05
10	Chelsea	Duff D	£34,355,304	£17,000,000	2003/04
11	Chelsea	Crespo H	£33,951,124	£16,800,000	2003/04
12	Man Utd	Carrick M	£32,323,469	£18,600,000	2006/07
13	Leeds	Ferdinand R	£32,037,760	£18,000,000	2000/01
14	Chelsea	Mutu A	£31,930,223	£15,800,000	2003/04
15	Newcastle	Owen M	£31,020,805	£17,000,000	2005/06
16	Man Utd	Yorke D	£30,864,726	£12,600,000	1998/99
17	Chelsea	Makélélé C	£28,090,513	£13,900,000	2003/04
18	Chelsea	Cole A	£27,805,135	£16,000,000	2006/07
19	Chelsea	Hasselbaink J	£26,698,133	£15,000,000	2000/01
20	Man Utd	Cole AA	£26,520,170	£7,000,000	1994/95
21	Man Utd	Saha L	£25,968,568	£12,850,000	2003/04
22	Liverpool	Cissé D	£25,833,105	£14,200,000	2004/05
23	Liverpool	Heskey E	£25,813,374	£11,000,000	1999/00
24	Man Utd	Stam J	£25,720,605	£10,500,000	1998/99
25	Man City	Tévez C	£25,500,000	£25,500,000	2009/10
26	Man City	Robinho	£25,411,527	£32,500,000	2008/09
27	Chelsea	Verón J	£25,261,253	£12,500,000	2003/04
28	Man City	Adebayor M	£25,000,000	£25,000,000	2009/10
29	Man Utd	van Nistelrooy R	£24,902,578	£19,000,000	2001/02
30	Man Utd	Ronaldo C	£24,735,819	£12,240,000	2003/04
31	Arsenal	Henry T	£24,640,038	£10,500,000	1999/00
32	Chelsea	Ferreira P	£24,013,872	£13,200,000	2004/05
33	Man Utd	Berbatov D	£23,847,740	£30,500,000	2008/09
34	Chelsea	Robben A	£23,650,025	£13,000,000	2004/05
35	Middlesbro	Ravanelli F	£23,632,552	£7,000,000	1997/98
36	Aston Villa	Collymore S	£23,632,552	£7,000,000	1997/98
37	Arsenal	Overmars M	£23,632,552	£7,000,000	1997/98
38	Chelsea	Sutton C	£23,466,703	£10,000,000	1999/00
39	Arsenal	Wiltord S	£23,138,382	£13,000,000	2000/01
40	Liverpool	Torres F	£22,573,285	£20,000,000	2007/08
41	Man Utd	Keane R (I)	£22,390,103	£3,750,000	1993/94
42	Liverpool	Collymore S	£22,350,904	£8,500,000	1995/96
43	Man City	Lescott J	£22,000,000	£22,000,000	2009/10
44	Blackburn	Shearer A	£21,965,480	£3,300,000	1992/93
45	Arsenal	Walcott T	£21,897,039	£12,000,000	2005/06
46	Arsenal	Reyes J	£21,219,452	£10,500,000	2003/04
47	Liverpool	Mascherano J	£20,993,155	£18,200,000	2006/07
48	Man City	Anelka N	£20,977,239	£13,000,000	2002/03
49	Chelsea	Mikel J	£20,853,851	£12,000,000	2006/07
50	Arsenal	Hleb A	£20,437,236	£11,200,000	2005/06
51	Man Utd	Anderson	£20,315,957	£18,000,000	2007/08
52	Spurs	Ferdinand L	£20,256,473	£6,000,000	1997/98
53	Chelsea	Parker S	£20,209,002	£10,000,000	2003/04
54	Liverpool	Aquilani A	£20,000,000	£20,000,000	2009/10
55	Newcastle	Asprilla H	£19,721,386	£7,500,000	1995/96
56	Arsenal	Bergkamp D	£19,721,386	£7,500,000	1995/96
57	Spurs	Rebrov S	£19,578,631	£11,000,000	2000/01
58	Liverpool	Saunders D	£19,302,998	D2900000	1992/93
59	Man Utd	Hargreaves O	£19,187,293	£17,000,000	2007/08
60	Man Utd	Nani	£19,187,293	£17,000,000	2007/08
61	Liverpool	Alonso X	£19,101,944	£10,500,000	2004/05
62	Blackburn	Sutton C	£18,942,978	£5,000,000	1994/95
63	Spurs	Berbatov D	£18,924,870	£10,890,000	2006/07
64	Liverpool	Hamann D	£18,773,363	£8,000,000	1999/00
65	Liverpool	Rush I	£18,637,377	D2800000	1992/93

#	Club	Player	CTPP	Original fee	Year transferred
66	Newcastle	Speed G	£18,568,434	£5,500,000	1997/98
67	Wimbledon	Hartson J	£18,371,861	£7,500,000	1998/99
68	Chelsea	Bosingwa J	£18,284,361	£16,200,000	2007/08
69	Chelsea	Tiago	£18,192,327	£10,000,000	2004/05
70	Liverpool	Johnson G (I)	£18,000,000	£18,000,000	2009/10
71	Chelsea	Zhirkov Y	£18,000,000	£18,000,000	2009/10
72	Blackburn	Davies K	£17,759,465	£7,250,000	1998/99
73	Fulham	Marlet S	£17,693,937	£13,500,000	2001/02
74	Newcastle	Luque A	£17,517,631	£9,600,000	2005/06
75	Man City	Santa Cruz R	£17,500,000	£17,500,000	2009/10
76	Spurs	Bent D	£17,494,296	£15,500,000	2007/08
77	Newcastle	Martins O	£17,378,209	£10,000,000	2006/07
78	Chelsea	Čech P	£17,177,652	£8,500,000	2003/04
79	Newcastle	Ferguson D (II)	£17,147,070	£7,000,000	1998/99
80	Chelsea	Anelka N	£16,929,964	£15,000,000	2007/08
81	Aston Villa	Angel JP	£16,908,818	£9,500,000	2000/01
82	Man Utd	Berg H	£16,880,394	£5,000,000	1997/98
83	Aston Villa	Young A	£16,769,972	£9,650,000	2006/07
84	Man City	Curle K	£16,640,516	D2500000	1992/93
85	Man City	Phelan T	£16,640,516	£2,500,000	1992/93
86	Arsenal	Wright I	£16,640,516	D2500000	1992/93
87	Aston Villa	Merson P	£16,534,675	£6,750,000	1998/99
88	Sheff Wed	Sinton A	£16,419,409	£2,750,000	1993/94
89	Liverpool	Diouf E	£16,136,338	£10,000,000	2002/03
90	Sheff Wed	Walker D	£16,120,874	£2,700,000	1993/94
91	Newcastle	Peacock D	£16,120,874	£2,700,000	1993/94
92	Leeds	Deane B	£16,120,874	£2,700,000	1993/94
93	Blackburn	Batty D	£16,120,874	£2,700,000	1993/94
94	Man Utd	Valencia L	£16,000,000	£16,000,000	2009/10
95	Man City	Touré K	£16,000,000	£16,000,000	2009/10
96	Blackburn	Warhurst P	£15,822,339	£2,650,000	1993/94
97	Newcastle	Ferdinand L	£15,777,109	£6,000,000	1995/96
98	Man Utd	Pallister G	£15,309,274	D2300000	1992/93
99	Liverpool	Stewart P	£15,309,274	£2,300,000	1992/93
100	Aston Villa	Saunders D	£15,309,274	£2,300,000	1992/93
101	Chelsea	Malouda F	£15,236,968	£13,500,000	2007/08
102	Everton	Barmby N	£15,211,834	£5,750,000	1996/97
103	Sheff Wed	Di Canio P	£15,192,355	£4,500,000	1997/98
104	Newcastle	Pistone A	£15,192,355	£4,500,000	1997/98
105	Middlesbro	Merson P	£15,192,355	d4500000	1997/98
106	Blackburn	Ferguson B	£15,156,752	£7,500,000	2003/04
107	Everton	Ferguson D (II)	£15,154,383	£4,000,000	1994/95
108	Everton	Johnson A (I)	£14,945,260	£8,600,000	2006/07
109	Liverpool	Ruddock N	£14,926,735	£2,500,000	1993/94
110	Newcastle	Boumsong J-A	£14,917,710	£8,200,000	2005/06
111	Man City	Jo	£14,855,969	£19,000,000	2008/09
112	Liverpool	Keane R (II)	£14,855,969	£19,000,000	2008/09
113	Spurs	Durie G	£14,643,654	D2200000	1992/93
114	Liverpool	Wright M	£14,643,654	D2200000	1992/93
115	Everton	Cottee T	£14,643,654	D2200000	1992/93
116	Chelsea	Del Horno A	£14,598,026	£8,000,000	2005/06
117	Newcastle	Woodgate J	£14,522,704	£9,000,000	2002/03
118	Everton	Kanchelskis A	£14,462,350	£5,500,000	1995/96
119	Leeds	Fowler R	£14,417,282	£11,000,000	2001/02
120	Chelsea	Lampard F	£14,417,282	£11,000,000	2001/02
121	Everton	Bilić S	£14,348,335	£4,250,000	1997/98
122	Blackburn	Flowers T	£14,329,666	£2,400,000	1993/94
123	Spurs	Zokora D	£14,250,132	£8,200,000	2006/07
124	Liverpool	Ince P	£14,179,531	£4,200,000	1997/98
125	Spurs	Defoe J	£14,146,302	£7,000,000	2003/04
126	Chelsea	Bridge W	£14,146,302	£7,000,000	2003/04
127	Newcastle	Dyer K	£14,080,022	£6,000,000	1999/00
128	Coventry	Keane R (II)	£14,080,022	£6,000,000	1999/00
129	Spurs	Sheringham T	£13,978,033	£2,100,000	1992/93
130	Chelsea	Fleck R	£13,978,033	£2,100,000	1992/93
131	Chelsea	Geremi	£13,944,211	£6,900,000	2003/04
132	Bolton	Anelka N	£13,902,567	£8,000,000	2006/07
133	Man Utd	Barthez F	£13,883,029	£7,800,000	2000/01
134	Chelsea	Grønkjær J	£13,883,029	£7,800,000	2000/01

#	Club	Player	CTPP	Original fee	Year transferred
135	Middlesbro	Barmby N	£13,804,970	£5,250,000	1995/96
136	Newcastle	Robert L	£13,761,951	£10,500,000	2001/02
137	Newcastle	Viana H	£13,715,887	£8,500,000	2002/03
138	Middlesbro	Yakubu	£13,685,649	£7,500,000	2005/06
139	Liverpool	Babb P	£13,638,944	£3,600,000	1994/95
140	Newcastle	Marcelino E	£13,610,688	£5,800,000	1999/00
141	Liverpool	Clough N	£13,583,329	£2,275,000	1993/94
142	Middlesbro	Alves A	£13,543,971	£12,000,000	2007/08
143	Aston Villa	Stone S	£13,472,698	£5,500,000	1998/99
144	Newcastle	Fox R	£13,434,062	£2,250,000	1993/94
145	Chelsea	Cole J	£13,337,941	£6,600,000	2003/04
146	Spurs	Anderton D	£13,312,412	D2000000	1992/93
147	Nottm Forest	Sheringham T	£13,312,412	D2000000	1992/93
148	Man Utd	Parker P	£13,312,412	D2000000	1992/93
149	Leeds	Rocastle D	£13,312,412	£2,000,000	1992/93
150	Arsenal	Keown M	£13,312,412	£2,000,000	1992/93
151	Spurs	Bentley D	£13,292,183	£17,000,000	2008/09
152	Man City	de Jong N	£13,292,183	£17,000,000	2008/09
153	Liverpool	Scales J	£13,260,085	£3,500,000	1994/95
154	Chelsea	Casiraghi P	£13,227,740	£5,400,000	1998/99
155	Spurs	Modrić L	£13,135,805	£16,800,000	2008/09
156	Arsenal	Jeffers F	£13,106,620	£10,000,000	2001/02
157	West Ham	Upson M	£13,033,657	£7,500,000	2006/07
158	Blackburn	Dailly C	£12,982,782	£5,300,000	1998/99
159	Liverpool	Babel R	£12,979,639	£11,500,000	2007/08
160	Chelsea	Di Matteo R	£12,963,128	£4,900,000	1996/97
161	Sunderland	Flo T	£12,909,070	£8,000,000	2002/03
162	Leeds	Yeboah A	£12,881,225	£3,400,000	1994/95
163	Newcastle	Hamann D	£12,860,303	£5,250,000	1998/99
164	Man Utd	Smith A (II)	£12,825,591	£7,050,000	2004/05
165	Leeds	Dacourt O	£12,815,104	£7,200,000	2000/01
166	West Ham	Ashton D	£12,773,273	£7,000,000	2005/06
167	Spurs	Jenas J	£12,773,273	£7,000,000	2005/06
168	Man Utd	Vidić N	£12,773,273	£7,000,000	2005/06
169	Liverpool	Crouch P	£12,773,273	£7,000,000	2005/06
170	Arsenal	Adebayor M	£12,773,273	£7,000,000	2005/06
171	Man Utd	Tošić Z	£12,744,858	£16,300,000	2008/09
172	Everton	Yakubu	£12,697,473	£11,250,000	2007/08
173	Spurs	Postiga H	£12,630,626	£6,250,000	2003/04
174	Man Utd	Heinze G	£12,552,706	£6,900,000	2004/05
175	Middlesbro	Juninho Paulista	£12,490,211	£4,750,000	1995/96
176	Arsenal	Platt D	£12,490,211	£4,750,000	1995/96
177	Newcastle	Cort C	£12,459,129	£7,000,000	2000/01
178	Arsenal	Lauren	£12,459,129	£7,000,000	2000/01
179	Aston Villa	Dublin D	£12,247,907	£5,000,000	1998/99
180	Liverpool	Kuyt D	£12,164,746	£7,000,000	2006/07
181	Chelsea	Boulahrouz K	£12,164,746	£7,000,000	2006/07
182	Newcastle	Andersson A (II)	£12,153,884	£3,600,000	1997/98
183	Chelsea	Johnson G (I)	£12,125,401	£6,000,000	2003/04
184	Man Utd	Ince P	£12,081,014	D1815000	1992/93
185	Man City	Barry G	£12,000,000	£12,000,000	2009/10
186	Aston Villa	Downing S	£12,000,000	£12,000,000	2009/10
187	Man Utd	Kléberson	£11,983,938	£5,930,000	2003/04
188	Nottm Forest	Collymore S	£11,941,388	d2000000	1993/94
189	Man City	Rocastle D	£11,941,388	£2,000,000	1993/94
190	Liverpool	Dicks J	£11,941,388	£2,000,000	1993/94
191	Leeds	White D (I)	£11,941,388	£2,000,000	1993/94
192	Aston Villa	Townsend A	£11,941,388	£2,000,000	1993/94
193	Leeds	Sharpe L	£11,904,914	£4,500,000	1996/97
194	Chelsea	Zola G	£11,904,914	£4,500,000	1996/97
195	Newcastle	Parker S	£11,860,896	£6,500,000	2005/06
196	Aston Villa	Baroš M	£11,860,896	£6,500,000	2005/06
197	Spurs	Armstrong C (I)	£11,832,831	£4,500,000	1995/96
198	Liverpool	McAteer J	£11,832,831	£4,500,000	1995/96
199	Leeds	Brolin T	£11,832,831	£4,500,000	1995/96
200	Arsenal	Rosický T	£11,817,182	£6,800,000	2006/07

Players who were transferred before the Premier League was formed have the first Premier League season listed as their transfer date.

Additional Managerial Statistics by Club

(Permanent managers only)

Arsenal

George Graham (two full seasons):

- Average points % of champs: 71.92%
- Average £XI rank: 7
- Average final position: 7
- Average Sq£: £81.1m
- Average age of team: 26.93

George Graham/Stewart Houston (Houston replaced Graham in February 1995 but both are credited with season data 1994/95):

- Average points % of champs: 57.30%
- Average £XI rank: 7
- Average final position: 12
- Average Sq£: £107.6m
- Average age of team: 27.77

Bruce Rioch:

- Average points % of champs: 76.83%
- Average £XI rank: 4
- Average final position: 5
- Average Sq£: £117.4m
- Average utilisation of max: 89.10%
- Average age of team: 28.79

Stewart Houston/Arsene Wenger
(Wenger replaced Houston in September 1996 but both are credited with season data 1996/97):

- Average points % of champs: 90.67%
- Average £XI rank: 3
- Average final position: 3
- Average Sq£: £117.9m
- Average age of team: 29.28

Arsene Wenger:

- Average points % of champs: 89.26%
- Average £XI rank: 3.62
- Average final position: 2.38
- Average Sq£: £163.8m
- Average age of team: 26.66

Aston Villa

Ron Atkinson (two full seasons):

- Average points % of champs: 75.03%
- Average £XI rank: 3.5
- Average final position: 6
- Average Sq£: £77.4m
- Average utilisation of max: 70.54%
- Average age of team: 27.16

Ron Atkinson/Brian Little
(Little replaced Atkinson in November 1994 but both are credited with season data 1994/95):

- Average points % of champs: 53.93%
- Average £XI rank: 6
- Average final position: 18
- Average Sq£: £107m
- Average utilisation of max: 63.67%
- Average age of team: 27.52

Brian Little (two full seasons):

- Average points % of champs: 79.08%
- Average £XI rank: 9
- Average final position: 4.5
- Average Sq£: £74.9m
- Average utilisation of max: 52.37%
- Average age of team: 25.41

Brian Little/John Gregory
(Gregory replaced Little in February 1998 but both are credited with season 1997/98 data):

- Average points % of champs: 73.08%
- Average £XI rank: 8
- Average final position: 7
- Average Sq£: £103.9m
- Average utilisation of max: 63.03%
- Average age of team: 25.87

John Gregory (three full seasons):

- Average points % of champs: 66.95%
- Average £XI rank: 7.67
- Average final position: 6.67
- Average Sq£: £106.8m
- Average utilisation of max: 57.11%
- Average age of team: 26.82

John Gregory/Graham Taylor
(Taylor replaced Gregory in February 2002 but both are credited with season 2001/02 data):

- Average points % of champs: 57.47%
- Average £XI rank: 8
- Average final position: 8
- Average Sq£: £116m
- Average utilisation of max: 50.31%
- Average age of team: 27.01

Graham Taylor (one full season):

- Average points % of champs: 54.22%
- Average £XI rank: 15
- Average final position: 16
- Average Sq£: £71.5m
- Average utilisation of max: 21.97%
- Average age of team: 25.90

David O'Leary:

- Average points % of champs: 52.62%
- Average £XI rank: 9.67
- Average final position: 10.67
- Average Sq£: £66.1m
- Average utilisation of max: 18.46%
- Average age of team: 25.45

Martin O'Neill:

- Average points % of champs: 67.11%
- Average £XI rank: 7.25
- Average final position: 7.25
- Average Sq£: £92.3m
- Average utilisation of max: 29.82%
- Average age of team: 26.47

Barnsley

Danny Wilson:

- Average points % of champs: 44.87%
- Average £XI rank: 20
- Average final position: 19
- Average Sq£: £24m
- Average utilisation of max: 13.53%
- Average age of team: 26.17

Birmingham

Steve Bruce (stats based on four full seasons)

- Average points % of champs: 49.53%
- Average £XI rank: 14
- Average final position: 13.25

- Average Sq£: £55.5m
- Average utilisation of max: 14.47%
- Average age of team: 27.76

Steve Bruce/Alex McLeish
(McLeish replaced Bruce in November 2007 but both are credited with season 2007/08 data):

- Average points % of champs: 40.23%
- Average £XI rank: 14
- Average final position: 19
- Average Sq£: £58m
- Average utilisation of max: 15.63%
- Average age of team: 25.26

Alex McLeish (one full season):

- Average points % of champs: 58.14%
- Average £XI rank: 11
- Average final position: 9
- Average Sq£: £52.9m
- Average utilisation of max: 15.19%
- Average age of team: 27.54

Blackburn

Kenny Dalglish:

- Average points % of champs: 91.94%
- Average £XI rank: 4
- Average final position: 2.3
- Average Sq£: £119.5m
- Average utilisation of max: 79.97%
- Average age of team: 25.7

Ray Harford (one full season):

- Average points % of champs: 74.39%
- Average £XI rank: 2
- Average final position: 7
- Average Sq£: £171.2m
- Average utilisation of max: 99.04%
- Average age of team: 26.66

Ray Harford/Tony Parkes
(Parkes replaced Harford in October 1996 but both are credited with season 1996/97 data):

- Average points % of champs: 56%
- Average £XI rank: 4
- Average final position: 13
- Average Sq£: £132.3m
- Average utilisation of max: 65.66%
- Average age of team: 27.02

Roy Hodgson (one full season):

- Average points % of champs: 74.36%
- Average £XI rank: 3
- Average final position: 6
- Average Sq£: £118.8m
- Average utilisation of max: 90.54%
- Average age of team: 26.88

Roy Hodgson/Brian Kidd
(Kidd replaced Hodgson in December 1998 but both are credited with season 1998/99 data):

- Average points % of champs: 44.30%
- Average £XI rank: 5
- Average final position: 19
- Average Sq£: £191m
- Average utilisation of max: 64.21%
- Average age of team: 25.55

Graeme Souness:

- Average points % of champs: 58.02%
- Average £XI rank: 11
- Average final position: 10.33
- Average Sqf: £87.9m
- Average utilisation of max: 31.34%
- Average age of team: 27.67

Graeme Souness/Mark Hughes
(Hughes replaced Souness in September 2004 but both are credited with 2004/05 data):

- Average points % of champs: 44.21%
- Average £XI rank: 8
- Average final position: 15
- Average Sqf: £80.5m
- Average utilisation of max: 17.58%
- Average age of team: 27.90

Mark Hughes:

- Average points % of champs: 64.77%
- Average £XI rank: 11.33
- Average final position: 7.67
- Average Sqf: £54.4m
- Average utilisation of max: 12.85%
- Average age of team: 28.12

Paul Ince/Sam Allardyce
(Allardyce replaced Ince in December 2008 but both are credited with season 2008/09 data):

- Average points % of champs: 45.56%
- Average £XI rank: 16
- Average final position: 15
- Average Sqf: £48.1m
- Average utilisation of max: 14.06%
- Average age of team: 28.28

Sam Allardyce (one full season):

- Average points % of champs: 58.14%
- Average £XI rank: 15
- Average final position: 10
- Average Sqf: £47.3m
- Average utilisation of max: 11.06%
- Average age of team: 27.43

Bolton

Roy McFarland & Colin Todd
(joint managers until McFarland was sacked in January 1996 leaving Todd in sole charge for the remainder of the season):

- Average points % of champs: 35.37%
- Average £XI rank: 20
- Average final position: 20
- Average Sqf: £33.1m
- Average utilisation of max: 15.57%
- Average age of team: 27.10

Colin Todd:

- Average points % of champs: 51.28%
- Average £XI rank: 14
- Average final position: 18
- Average Sqf: £64.7m
- Average utilisation of max: 33.41%
- Average age of team: 27.93

Sam Allardyce (five full seasons):

- Average points % of champs: 56.09%
- Average £XI rank: 20
- Average final position: 11
- Average Sqf: £16.8m
- Average utilisation of max: 5.70%
- Average age of team: 28.55

Sam Allardyce/Sammy Lee
(Lee replaced Allardyce in April 2007 but both are credited with season 2006/07 data):

- Average points % of champs: 62.92%
- Average £XI rank: 13
- Average final position: 7
- Average Sqf: £32.1m
- Average utilisation of max: 9.95%
- Average age of team: 28.22

Sammy Lee/Gary Megson
(Megson replaced Lee in October 2007 but both are credited with season data 2007/08):

- Average points % of champs: 42.53%
- Average £XI rank: 18
- Average final position: 16
- Average Sqf: £49.5m
- Average utilisation of max: 11.19%
- Average age of team: 27.37

Gary Megson (one full season):

- Average points % of champs: 45.56%
- Average £XI rank: 15
- Average final position: 13
- Average Sqf: £35.5m
- Average utilisation of max: 15.20%
- Average age of team: 27.24

Gary Megson/Owen Coyle
(Coyle replaced Megson in January 2010 but both are credited with season data 2009/10):

- Average points % of champs: 45.35%
- Average £XI rank: 12
- Average final position: 14
- Average Sqf: £40m
- Average utilisation of max: 13.71%
- Average age of team: 27.39

Bradford

Paul Jewell:

- Average points % of champs: 39.56%
- Average £XI rank: 19
- Average final position: 17
- Average Sqf: £20.2m
- Average utilisation of max: 8.66%
- Average age of team: 29.87

Chris Hutchings/Jim Jefferies
(Jefferies replaced Hutchings in November 2000 but both are credited with season season data 2000/01):

- Average points % of champs: 32.50%
- Average £XI rank: 20
- Average final position: 20
- Average Sqf: £26.5m
- Average utilisation of max: 9.86%
- Average age of team: 30.09

Burnley

Owen Coyle/Brian Laws
(Laws replaced Coyle in January 2010 but both are credited with season data 2009/10):

- Average points % of champs: 34.88%
- Average £XI rank: 20
- Average final position: 18
- Average Sqf: £13.8m
- Average utilisation of max: 4.36
- Average age of team: 28.19

Charlton

Alan Curbishley:

- Average points % of champs: 54.16%
- Average £XI rank: 16.43
- Average final position: 12
- Average Sqf: £37.1m
- Average utilisation of max: 15.62%
- Average age of team: 27.41

Iain Dowie/Les Reed/Alan Pardew
(Reed replaced Dowie in November 2006, before Pardew replaced Reed in December 2006; all three are credited with season data 2006/07):

- Average points % of champs: 38.20%
- Average £XI rank: 14
- Average final position: 19
- Average Sqf: £47.2m
- Average utilisation of max: 9.64%
- Average age of team: 26.84

Chelsea

Ian Porterfield/Dave Webb
(Webb replaced Porterfield in Feb 1993 but both are credited with season data 1992/93):

- Average points % of champs: 66.67%
- Average £XI rank: 10
- Average final position: 11
- Average Sqf: £76.3m
- Average utilisation of max: 47.49%
- Average age of team: 26.32

Glenn Hoddle:

- Average points % of champs: 59.03%
- Average £XI rank: 13
- Average final position: 12
- Average Sqf: £67m
- Average utilisation of max: 38.48%
- Average age of team: 26.43

Ruud Gullit (one full season):

- Average points % of champs: 78.67%
- Average £XI rank: 12
- Average final position: 6
- Average Sqf: £69.1m
- Average utilisation of max: 41.33%
- Average age of team: 28.04

Ruud Gullit/Gianluca Vialli
(Vialli replaced Gullit in February 1998 but both are credited with season data 1997/98):

- Average points % of champs: 80.77%
- Average £XI rank: 7
- Average final position: 4
- Average Sqf: £95.1m
- Average utilisation of max: 68.45%
- Average age of team: 27.87

Gianluca Vialli (two full seasons):

- Average points % of champs: 83.18%
- Average £XI rank: 4
- Average final position: 4
- Average Sqf: £134.9m
- Average utilisation of max: 70.95%
- Average age of team: 28.76

Gianluca Vialli/Claudio Ranieri
(Ranieri replaced Vialli in September 2000 but both are credited with season data 2000/01):

- Average points % of champs: 76.25%
- Average £XI rank: 3
- Average final position: 6
- Average Sqf: £172.9m

- Average utilisation of max: 87.36%
- Average age of team: 28.08

Claudio Ranieri (three full seasons):

- Average points % of champs: 80.69%
- Average £XI rank: 2.67
- Average final position: 4
- Average Sqf: £220.9m
- Average utilisation of max: 93.38%
- Average age of team: 26.85

José Mourinho (three full seasons):

- Average points % of champs: 97.75%
- Average £XI rank: 1
- Average final position: 1.33
- Average Sqf: £415.3m
- Average utilisation of max: 100%
- Average age of team: 25.92

José Mourinho/Avram Grant
(Grant replaced Mourinho in September 2007 but both are credited with season data 2007/08:

- Average points % of champs: 97.70%
- Average £XI rank: 1
- Average final position: 2
- Average Sqf: £432.4m
- Average utilisation of max: 100%
- Average age of team: 27

Luiz Felipe Scolari/Guus Hiddink
(Hiddink replaced Scolari in Feb 2009 but both are credited with season data 2008/09):

- Average points % of champs: 92.22%
- Average £XI rank: 1
- Average final position: 3
- Average utilisation of max: 100%
- Average age of team: 27.35

Carlo Ancelotti:

- Average points % of champs: 100%
- Average £XI rank: 1
- Average final position: 1
- Average Sqf: £401.3m
- Average utilisation of max: 100%
- Average age of team: 28.73

Coventry

Bobby Gould (one full season):

- Average points % of champs: 61.90%
- Average £XI rank: 19
- Average final position: 15
- Average Sqf: £31.9m
- Average utilisation of max: 20.06%
- Average age of team: 26.36

Bobby Gould/Phil Neal
(Neal replaced Gould in October 1993 but both are credited with season data 1993/94):

- Average points % of champs: 60.87%
- Average £XI rank: 19
- Average final position: 11
- Average Sqf: £26.4m
- Average utilisation of max: 15.26%
- Average age of team: 26.05

Phil Neal/Ron Atkinson
(Atkinson replaced Neal in Feb 1995 but both are credited with season data 1994/95):

- Average points % of champs: 56.18%
- Average £XI rank: 17
- Average final position: 16
- Average Sqf: £43.6m

- Average utilisation of max: 20.55%
- Average age of team: 27.47

Ron Atkinson (one full season):

- Average points % of champs: 46.34%
- Average £XI rank: 16
- Average final position: 16
- Average Sqf: £43.1m
- Average utilisation of max: 26.98%
- Average age of team: 27.09

Ron Atkinson/Gordon Strachan
(Strachan replaced Atkinson in November 1996 but both are credited with season data 1996/97):

- Average points % of champs: 54.67%
- Average £XI rank: 13
- Average final position: 17
- Average Sqf: £62.9m
- Average utilisation of max: 34.79%
- Average age of team: 27.93

Gordon Strachan (four full seasons):

- Average points % of champs: 52.67%
- Average £XI rank: 11.75
- Average final position: 14.75
- Average Sqf: £67.3m
- Average utilisation of max: 36.73%
- Average age of team: 26.81

Crystal Palace

Steve Coppell:

- Average points % of champs: 58.33%
- Average £XI rank: 12
- Average final position: 20
- Average Sqf: £36.8m
- Average utilisation of max: 37.02%
- Average age of team: 25.16

Alan Smith:

- Average points % of champs: 50.56%
- Average £XI rank: 15
- Average final position: 19
- Average Sqf: £38.5m
- Average utilisation of max: 23.67%
- Average age of team: 25.48

Iain Dowie:

- Average points % of champs: 34.74%
- Average £XI rank: 19
- Average final position: 18
- Average Sqf: £15.3m
- Average utilisation of max: 2.72%
- Average age of team: 25.69

Steve Coppell/Attilio Lombardo & Tomas Brolin
(Coppell became Director of Football midway through 1997/98 with Lombardo & Brolin appointed as temporary player managers; all three are credited with season data 1997/98):

- Average points % of champs: 42.31%
- Average £XI rank: 15
- Average final position: 20
- Average Sqf: £69m
- Average utilisation of max: 31.64%
- Average age of team: 25.58

Derby County

Jim Smith (five full seasons):

- Average points % of champs: 58.39%
- Average £XI rank: 17
- Average final position: 12.40
- Average Sqf: £48.9m

- Average utilisation of max: 21.30%
- Average age of team: 25.93

Jim Smith/Colin Todd/John Gregory
(Todd replaced Smith in Oct 2001 before Gregory replaced Todd in January 2002 but all three managers are credited with season data 2001/02):

- Average points % of champs: 34.48%
- Average £XI rank: 18
- Average final position: 19
- Average Sqf: £55.2m
- Average utilisation of max: 16.61%
- Average age of team: 25.84

Billy Davies/Paul Jewell:
(Jewell replaced Davies in November 2007 but both managers are credited with season data 2007/08)

- Average points % of champs: 12.64%
- Average £XI rank: 19
- Average final position: 20
- Average Sqf: £31m
- Average utilisation of max: 6.13%
- Average age of team: 28.66

Everton

Howard Kendall (two full seasons):

- Average points % of champs: 57.19%
- Average £XI rank: 5.50
- Average final position: 15
- Average Sqf: £102.8m
- Average utilisation of max: 68.26%
- Average age of team: 26.96

Howard Kendall/Mike Walker
(Walker replaced Kendall in January 1994 but both are credited with season data 1993/94):

- Average points % of champs: 47.83%
- Average £XI rank: 8
- Average final position: 17
- Average Sqf: £84.4m
- Average utilisation of max: 54.89%
- Average age of team: 27.58

Mike Walker/Joe Royle
(Royle replaced Walker in November 1994 but both are credited with season data 1994/95):

- Average points % of champs: 56.18%
- Average £XI rank: 11
- Average final position: 15
- Average Sqf: £112.8m
- Average utilisation of max: 56.80%
- Average age of team: 26.99

Joe Royle
(Dave Watson replaced Royle in April 1997. Royle has been credited with the full data from season 1996/97 as Watson was caretaker manager for just one month):

- Average points % of champs: 65.20%
- Average £XI rank: 5.50
- Average final position: 10.50
- Average Sqf: £110.2m
- Average utilisation of max: 63.22%
- Average age of team: 27.43

Walter Smith (three full seasons):

- Average points % of champs: 53.96%
- Average £XI rank: 10
- Average final position: 14.33
- Average Sqf: £93.3m
- Average utilisation of max: 40.59%
- Average age of team: 26.54

Walter Smith/David Moyes
(Moyes replaced Smith in March 2002 but both are credited with season data 2001/02):

- Average points % of champs: 49.43%
- Average £XI rank: 11
- Average final position: 15
- Average Sqf: £73.5m
- Average utilisation of max: 38.24%
- Average age of team: 27.80

David Moyes (eight full seasons):

- Average points % of champs: 64.30%
- Average £XI rank: 8.88
- Average final position: 7.88
- Average Sqf: £86.5m
- Average utilisation of max: 25.17%
- Average age of team: 27.28

Fulham

Jean Tigana (one full seasons):

- Average points % of champs: 50.57%
- Average £XI rank: 9
- Average final position: 13
- Average Sqf: £86.9m
- Average utilisation of max: 46.45%
- Average age of team: 27.63

Jean Tigana/Chris Coleman
(Coleman replaced Tigana in April 2003 but both are credited with season data 2002/03):

- Average points % of champs: 57.83%
- Average £XI rank: 7
- Average final position: 14
- Average Sqf: £86.9m
- Average utilisation of max: 38.85%
- Average age of team: 27.25

Chris Coleman (three full seasons):

- Average points % of champs: 52.28%
- Average £XI rank: 12.67
- Average final position: 11.33
- Average Sqf: £56m
- Average utilisation of max: 14.91%
- Average age of team: 27.40

Chris Coleman/Lawrie Sanchez
(Sanchez replaced Coleman in April 2007 but both are credited with season data 2006/07):

- Average points % of champs: 43.82%
- Average £XI rank: 17
- Average final position: 16
- Average Sqf: £38m
- Average utilisation of max: 6.52%
- Average age of team: 28.28

Lawrie Sanchez/Roy Hodgson
(Hodgson replaced Sanchez in December 2007 but both are credited with season data 2007/08):

- Average points % of champs: 41.38%
- Average £XI rank: 17
- Average final position: 17
- Average Sqf: £60.5m
- Average utilisation of max: 13.84%
- Average age of team: 27.92

Roy Hodgson (two full seasons):

- Average points % of champs: 56.19%
- Average £XI rank: 13.50
- Average final position: 9.50
- Average Sqf: £52.9m
- Average utilisation of max: 14.57%

- Average age of team: 28.94

Hull City

Phil Brown (credited with two full seasons)

- Average points % of champs: 36.89%
- Average £XI rank: 19
- Average final position: 18
- Average Sqf: £24.4m
- Average utilisation of max: 5.13%
- Average age of team: 27.89

Ipswich

John Lyall (two full seasons):

- Average points % of champs: 54.32%
- Average £XI rank: 20
- Average final position: 17.50
- Average Sqf: £17.8m
- Average utilisation of max: 13.18%
- Average age of team: 27.60

John Lyall/George Burley
(Burley replaced Lyall in December 1994 but both are credited with season data 1994/95):

- Average points % of champs: 30.34%
- Average £XI rank: 20
- Average final position: 22
- Average Sqf: £33.3m
- Average utilisation of max: 18.63%
- Average age of team: 27.98

George Burley (two full seasons):

- Average points % of champs: 61.94%
- Average £XI rank: 15.50
- Average final position: 11.50
- Average Sqf: £39.6m
- Average utilisation of max: 24.67%
- Average age of team: 26.75

Leeds Utd

Howard Wilkinson (four full seasons):

- Average points % of champs: 67.82%
- Average £XI rank: 6.75
- Average final position: 10
- Average Sqf: £97.4m
- Average utilisation of max: 63.18%
- Average age of team: 26.74

Howard Wilkinson/George Graham
(Graham replaced Wilkinson in September1996 but both are credited with season data 1996/97):

- Average points % of champs: 61.33%
- Average £XI rank: 8
- Average final position: 11
- Average Sqf: £96.5m
- Average utilisation of max: 48.55%
- Average age of team: 26.88

George Graham (one full season):

- Average points % of champs: 75.64%
- Average £XI rank: 11
- Average final position: 5
- Average Sqf: £64m
- Average utilisation of max: 46.96%
- Average age of team: 25.70

George Graham/David O'Leary
(O'Leary replaced Graham in October 1998 but both are credited with season data 1998/99):

- Average points % of champs: 84.81%
- Average £XI rank: 12
- Average final position: 4
- Average Sqf: £79.7m
- Average utilisation of max: 38.58%
- Average age of team: 24.77

David O'Leary (three full seasons):

- Average points % of champs: 78.9%
- Average £XI rank: 7
- Average final position: 4
- Average Sqf: £132.1m
- Average utilisation of max: 67.97%
- Average age of team: 24.79

Terry Venables/Peter Reid
(Reid replaced Venables in March 2003 but both are credited with season data 2002/03):

- Average points % of champs: 56.63%
- Average £XI rank: 10
- Average final position: 15
- Average Sqf: £135.7m
- Average utilisation of max: 34.34%
- Average age of team: 25.87

Peter Reid/Eddie Gray
(Gray replaced Reid in November 2003 until the end of the season but both are credited with season data 2003/04):

- Average points % of champs: 36.67%
- Average £XI rank: 13
- Average final position: 19
- Average Sqf: £85.4m
- Average utilisation of max: 20.68%
- Average age of team: 25.12

Leicester

Brian Little/Mark McGhee
(McGhee replaced Little in December 1994 but both are credited with season data 1994/95):

- Average points % of champs: 32.58%
- Average £XI rank: 21
- Average final position: 21
- Average Sqf: £30m
- Average utilisation of max: 17.68%
- Average age of team: 26.12

Martin O'Neill:

- Average points % of champs: 63.27%
- Average £XI rank: 16.50
- Average final position: 9.25
- Average Sqf: £40.1m
- Average utilisation of max: 21.30%
- Average age of team: 27.01

Peter Taylor (one full season):

- Average points % of champs: 60%
- Average £XI rank: 10
- Average final position: 13
- Average Sqf: £66.6m
- Average utilisation of max: 35.37%
- Average age of team: 27.32

Peter Taylor/Dave Bassett & Micky Adams
(Bassett & Adams replaced Taylor in October 2001 but all three are credited with season data 2001/02):

- Average points % of champs: 32.18%
- Average £XI rank: 15
- Average final position: 20
- Average Sqf: £60.4m
- Average utilisation of max: 27.03%

- Average age of team: 27.16

Micky Adams (one full season):

- Average points % of champs: 36.67%
- Average £XI rank: 19
- Average final position: 18
- Average Sqf: £28.8m
- Average utilisation of max: 8.01%
- Average age of team: 29.30

Liverpool

Graeme Souness (one full season):

- Average points % of champs: 70.24%
- Average £XI rank: 2
- Average final position: 6
- Average Sqf: £131.4m
- Average utilisation of max: 86.38%
- Average age of team: 25.67

Graeme Souness/Roy Evans
(Evans replaced Souness in January 1994 but both are credited with season data 1993/94):

- Average points % of champs: 65.22%
- Average £XI rank: 2
- Average final position: 8
- Average Sqf: £150.2m
- Average utilisation of max: 81.98%
- Average age of team: 26.38

Roy Evans (four full seasons):

- Average points % of champs: 85.93%
- Average £XI rank: 4
- Average final position: 3.5
- Average Sqf: £146.8m
- Average utilisation of max: 81.52%
- Average age of team: 25.64

Roy Evans/Gerard Houllier
(Evans were initially appointed as joint managers but Houllier took full charge after Evans resigned in November 1998. Both are credited with season data 1998/99):

- Average points % of champs: 68.35%
- Average £XI rank: 10
- Average final position: 7
- Average Sqf: £113m
- Average utilisation of max: 50.45%
- Average age of team: 25.55

Gerard Houllier (five full seasons):

- Average points % of champs: 79.12%
- Average £XI rank: 5.20
- Average final position: 3.60
- Average Sqf: £147.2m
- Average utilisation of max: 65.66%
- Average age of team: 25.14

Rafa Benítez:

- Average points % of champs: 80.62%
- Average £XI rank: 3.5
- Average final position: 4
- Average Sqf: £177m
- Average utilisation of max: 44.26%
- Average age of team: 26.22

Manchester City

Peter Reid:

- Average points % of champs: 67.86%
- Average £XI rank: 4
- Average final position: 9
- Average Sqf: £69.5m
- Average utilisation of max: 74.89%

- Average age of team: 26.21

Brian Horton:

- Average points % of champs: 51.98%
- Average £XI rank: 6.50
- Average final position: 16.50
- Average Sqf: £102.7m
- Average utilisation of max: 61.81%
- Average age of team: 26.35

Alan Ball:

- Average points % of champs: 46.34%
- Average £XI rank: 11
- Average final position: 18
- Average Sqf: £92.4m
- Average utilisation of max: 49.02%
- Average age of team: 26.04

Joe Royle:

- Average points % of champs: 42.50%
- Average £XI rank: 16
- Average final position: 18
- Average Sqf: £45.1m
- Average utilisation of max: 24.86%
- Average age of team: 25.99

Kevin Keegan (two full seasons):

- Average points % of champs: 53.50%
- Average £XI rank: 7
- Average final position: 12.50
- Average Sqf: £75.2m
- Average utilisation of max: 34.04%
- Average age of team: 27.83

Kevin Keegan/Stuart Pearce
(Pearce replaced Keegan in March 2005 but both are credited with season data 2004/05):

- Average points % of champs: 54.74%
- Average £XI rank: 7
- Average final position: 8
- Average Sqf: £69.3m
- Average utilisation of max: 17.64%
- Average age of team: 27.30

Stuart Pearce (two full seasons):

- Average points % of champs: 47.22%
- Average £XI rank: 11
- Average final position: 14.50
- Average Sqf: £52.6m
- Average utilisation of max: 11.54%
- Average age of team: 26.80

Sven Goran Eriksson:

- Average points % of champs: 63.22%
- Average £XI rank: 10
- Average final position: 9
- Average Sqf: £84.3m
- Average utilisation of max: 18.12%
- Average age of team: 24.45

Mark Hughes (one full season):

- Average points % of champs: 55.56%
- Average £XI rank: 5
- Average final position: 10
- Average Sqf: £158.6m
- Average utilisation of max: 38.82%
- Average age of team: 24.46

Mark Hughes/Roberto Mancini
(Mancini replaced Hughes in December 2009 but both are credited with season data 2009/10):

- Average points % of champs: 77.91%
- Average £XI rank: 3
- Average final position: 5
- Average Sqf: £223.5m

- Average utilisation of max: 64.63%
- Average age of team: 27.70

Manchester Utd

Alex Ferguson:

- Average points % of champs: 96.70%
- Average £XI rank: 2.61
- Average final position: 1.56
- Average Sqf: £198.1m
- Average utilisation of max: 83.60%
- Average age of team: 26.59

Middlesbrough

Lenny Lawrence:

- Average points % of champs: 52.38%
- Average £XI rank: 13
- Average final position: 21
- Average Sqf: £32.6m
- Average utilisation of max: 29.34%
- Average age of team: 26.40

Bryan Robson (four full seasons):

- Average points % of champs: 56.53%
- Average £XI rank: 10.50
- Average final position: 13
- Average Sqf: £82m
- Average utilisation of max: 42.27%
- Average age of team: 27.28

Bryan Robson/Terry Venables
(Venables was appointed co-manager in December 2000 but both are credited with season data 2000/01):

- Average points % of champs: 52.50%
- Average £XI rank: 9
- Average final position: 14
- Average Sqf: £75m
- Average utilisation of max: 35.82%
- Average age of team: 29.34

Steve McLaren:

- Average points % of champs: 54.29%
- Average £XI rank: 8.60
- Average final position: 11
- Average Sqf: £80.4m
- Average utilisation of max: 27.29%
- Average age of team: 27.39

Gareth Southgate:

- Average points % of champs: 45.17%
- Average £XI rank: 11.33
- Average final position: 14.67
- Average Sqf: £74.3m
- Average utilisation of max: 16.77%
- Average age of team: 25.18

Newcastle Utd

Kevin Keegan (three full seasons):

- Average points % of champs: 86.57%
- Average £XI rank: 6
- Average final position: 3.67
- Average Sqf: £110.3m
- Average utilisation of max: 70.56%
- Average age of team: 26.42

Kevin Keegan/Kenny Dalglish
(Dalglish replaced Keegan in January 1997 but both are credited with season data 1996/97):

- Average points % of champs: 90.67%
- Average £XI rank: 1
- Average final position: 2

- Average Sq£: £165.3m
- Average utilisation of max: 100%
- Average age of team: 27.31

Kenny Dalglish (one full season):

- Average points % of champs: 56.41%
- Average £XI rank: 1
- Average final position: 13
- Average Sq£: £200.4m
- Average utilisation of max: 100%
- Average age of team: 27.09

Kenny Dalglish/Ruud Gullit
(Gullit replaced Dalglish in August 1998 but both are credited with season data 1998/99):

- Average points % of champs: 58.23%
- Average £XI rank: 2
- Average final position: 13
- Average Sq£: £210.5m
- Average utilisation of max: 89.27%
- Average age of team: 25.48

Ruud Gullit/Bobby Robson
(Robson replaced Gullit in September 1999 but both are credited with season data 1999/00):

- Average points % of champs: 57.14%
- Average £XI rank: 1
- Average final position: 11
- Average Sq£: £201.5m
- Average utilisation of max: 100%
- Average age of team: 26.83

Bobby Robson (four full seasons):

- Average points % of champs: 72.68%
- Average £XI rank: 2.25
- Average final position: 5.75
- Average Sq£: £174.2m
- Average utilisation of max: 88.38%
- Average age of team: 25.64

Bobby Robson/Graeme Souness:
(Souness replaced Robson in September 2004 but both are credited with season data 2004/05):

- Average points % of champs: 46.32%
- Average £XI rank: 5
- Average final position: 14
- Average Sq£: £122.3m
- Average utilisation of max: 36.03%
- Average age of team: 25.94

Graeme Souness/Glenn Roeder
(Roeder replaced Souness in February 2006 but both are credited with season data 2005/06):

- Average points % of champs: 63.74%
- Average £XI rank: 5
- Average final position: 7
- Average Sq£: £161m
- Average utilisation of max: 32.39%
- Average age of team: 26.60

Glenn Roeder (one full season):

- Average points % of champs: 48.31%
- Average £XI rank: 6
- Average final position: 13
- Average Sq£: £145.7m
- Average utilisation of max: 24.55%
- Average age of team: 26.11

Sam Allardyce/Kevin Keegan
(Keegan replaced Allardyce in January 2008 but both are credited with season data 2007/08):

- Average points % of champs: 49.43%
- Average £XI rank: 6

- Average final position: 12
- Average Sq£: £114.8m
- Average utilisation of max: 30.42%
- Average age of team: 27.03

Kevin Keegan/Joe Kinnear/Alan Shearer
(Kinnear replaced Keegan in September 2008 then Shearer replaced Kinnear in April 2009; all three are credited with season data 2008/09):

- Average points % of champs: 37.78%
- Average £XI rank: 6
- Average final position: 18
- Average Sq£: £128.4m
- Average utilisation of max: 37.77%
- Average age of team: 26.78

Norwich City

Mike Walker (one full season):

- Average points % of champs: 85.71%
- Average £XI rank: 18
- Average final position: 3
- Average Sq£: £30.8m
- Average utilisation of max: 20.80%
- Average age of team: 26.36

Mike Walker/John Deehan
(Deehan replaced Walker in January 1994 but both are credited with season data 1993/94):

- Average points % of champs: 57.61%
- Average £XI rank: 21
- Average final position: 12
- Average Sq£: £24.5m
- Average utilisation of max: 13.04%
- Average age of team: 27.12

John Deehan (one full season):

- Average points % of champs: 48.31%
- Average £XI rank: 18
- Average final position: 20
- Average Sq£: £34.6m
- Average utilisation of max: 19.64%
- Average age of team: 25.73

Nigel Worthington:

- Average points % of champs: 34.74%
- Average £XI rank: 18
- Average final position: 19
- Average Sq£: £15.8m
- Average utilisation of max: 4.62%
- Average age of team: 27.61

Nottingham Forest

Brian Clough:

- Average points % of champs: 47.62%
- Average £XI rank: 15
- Average final position: 22
- Average Sq£: £50m
- Average utilisation of max: 24.95%
- Average age of team: 25.54

Frank Clark:

- Average points % of champs: 78.62%
- Average £XI rank: 12.5
- Average final position: 6
- Average Sq£: £64.7m
- Average utilisation of max: 40.74%
- Average age of team: 26.52

Frank Clark/Stuart Pearce
(Pearce replaced Clark in December 1996 but both are credited with season data 1996/97):

- Average points % of champs: 45.33%
- Average £XI rank: 15
- Average final position: 20
- Average Sq£: £69.8m
- Average utilisation of max: 28.52%
- Average age of team: 28.49

Dave Bassett/Ron Atkinson
(Atkinson replaced Bassett in January 1999 but both are credited with season data 1998/99):

- Average points % of champs: 37.97%
- Average £XI rank: 16
- Average final position: 20
- Average Sq£: £52.6m
- Average utilisation of max: 24.60%
- Average age of team: 27.49

Oldham

Joe Royle:

- Average points % of champs: 50.91%
- Average £XI rank: 14.5
- Average final position: 20
- Average Sq£: £36.8m
- Average utilisation of max: 23.89%
- Average age of team: 25.73

Portsmouth

Harry Redknapp (three full seasons):

- Average points % of champs: 58.73%
- Average £XI rank: 15
- Average final position: 10
- Average Sq£: £46.3m
- Average utilisation of max: 11.75%
- Average age of team: 28.35

Harry Redknapp/ Velimir Zajec/Alain Perrin
(Zajec replaced Redknapp in November 2004 before Zajec was replaced by Alain Perrin in April 2005. All three are credited with season data 2004/05):

- Average points % of champs: 41.05%
- Average £XI rank: 17
- Average final position: 16
- Average Sq£: £27.9m
- Average utilisation of max: 7.90%
- Average age of team: 27.61

Alain Perrin/Harry Redknapp
(Redknapp replaced Perrin in December 2005 but both are credited with season data 2005/06):

- Average points % of champs: 41.76%
- Average £XI rank: 17
- Average final position: 17
- Average Sq£: £45.7m
- Average utilisation of max: 7.84%
- Average age of team: 26.73

Harry Redknapp/Tony Adams/Paul Hart
(Adams replaced Redknapp in October 2008 before Adams was replaced by Hart in February 2009; all three are credited with season data 2008/09):

- Average points % of champs: 45.56%
- Average £XI rank: 11
- Average final position: 14
- Average Sq£: £68.3m
- Average utilisation of max: 20.11%

- Average age of team: 28.54

Paul Hart/Avram Grant
(Grant replaced Hart in November 2009 but both are credited with season data 2009/10):

- Average points % of champs: 22.09%
- Average £XI rank: 19
- Average final position: 20
- Average Sq£: £36.1m
- Average utilisation of max: 5.77%
- Average age of team: 28.80

Queens Park Rangers

Gerry Francis (two full seasons):

- Average points % of champs: 70.11%
- Average £XI rank: 16.50
- Average final position: 7
- Average Sq£: £29.8m
- Average utilisation of max: 20.85%
- Average age of team: 26.96

Gerry Francis/Ray Wilkins
(Wilkins replaced Francis in November 1994 but both are credited with season data 1994/95):

- Average points % of champs: 67.42%
- Average £XI rank: 22
- Average final position: 8
- Average Sq£: £26.6m
- Average utilisation of max: 17.56%
- Average age of team: 26.80

Ray Wilkins (one full season):

- Average points % of champs: 40.24%
- Average £XI rank: 19
- Average final position: 19
- Average Sq£: £31.2m
- Average utilisation of max: 18.33%
- Average age of team: 26.18

Reading

Steve Coppell:

- Average points % of champs: 51.59%
- Average £XI rank: 20
- Average final position: 13
- Average Sq£: £18m
- Average utilisation of max: 2.71%
- Average age of team: 27.27

Sheffield Utd

Dave Bassett:

- Average points % of champs: 53.78%
- Average £XI rank: 20.50
- Average final position: 17
- Average Sq£: £26.2m
- Average utilisation of max: 15.67%
- Average age of team: 25.94

Neil Warnock:

- Average points % of champs: 42.70%
- Average £XI rank: 18
- Average final position: 18
- Average Sq£: £25.3m
- Average utilisation of max: 2.93%
- Average age of team: 26.08

Sheffield Wednesday

Trevor Francis:

- Average points % of champs: 65.70%

- Average £XI rank: 10
- Average final position: 9
- Average Sq£: £78.8m
- Average utilisation of max: 52.50%
- Average age of team: 27.17

David Pleat (two full seasons):

- Average points % of champs: 62.39%
- Average £XI rank: 10.50
- Average final position: 11
- Average Sq£: £87.3m
- Average utilisation of max: 47.72%
- Average age of team: 27.22

David Pleat/Ron Atkinson
(Atkinson replaced Pleat in November 1997 but both are credited with season data 1997/98):

- Average points % of champs: 56.41%
- Average £XI rank: 5
- Average final position: 16
- Average Sq£: £104m
- Average utilisation of max: 74.95%
- Average age of team: 27.57

Danny Wilson
(although Wilson was sacked in March 2000 he is credited with two full seasons data – 1998/99, 1999/00):

- Average points % of champs: 46.15%
- Average £XI rank: 7.50
- Average final position: 15.50
- Average Sq£: £89.7m
- Average utilisation of max: 48.67%
- Average age of team: 28.06

Southampton

Ian Branfoot (one full season):

- Average points % of champs: 59.52%
- Average £XI rank: 17
- Average final position: 18
- Average Sq£: £33.8m
- Average utilisation of max: 21.41%
- Average age of team: 26.38

Ian Branfoot/Alan Ball
(Ball replaced Branfoot in January 1994 but both are credited with season data 1993/94):

- Average points % of champs: 46.74%
- Average £XI rank: 17
- Average final position: 18
- Average Sq£: £34.7m
- Average utilisation of max: 18.25%
- Average age of team: 27.11

Alan Ball (one full season):

- Average points % of champs: 60.67%
- Average £XI rank: 19
- Average final position: 10
- Average Sq£: £32.8m
- Average utilisation of max: 18.66%
- Average age of team: 25.76

Dave Merrington:

- Average points % of champs: 46.34%
- Average £XI rank: 18
- Average final position: 17
- Average Sq£: £29.8m
- Average utilisation of max: 22.10%
- Average age of team: 26.25

Graeme Souness:

- Average points % of champs: 54.67%
- Average £XI rank: 18
- Average final position: 16

- Average Sq£: £42.4m
- Average utilisation of max: 16.10%
- Average age of team: 25.91

Dave Jones (two full seasons):

- Average points % of champs: 56.72%
- Average £XI rank: 18
- Average final position: 14.50
- Average Sq£: £43.5m
- Average utilisation of max: 19.40%
- Average age of team: 27.78

Dave Jones/Glenn Hoddle (Hoddle replaced Jones in January 2000 but both are credited with season data 1999/00):

- Average points % of champs: 48.35%
- Average £XI rank: 18
- Average final position: 15
- Average Sq£: £29.3m
- Average utilisation of max: 9.42%
- Average age of team: 27.26

Glenn Hoddle/Stuart Gray
(Gray replaced Hoddle in March 2001 but both are credited with season data 2000/01):

- Average points % of champs: 65%
- Average £XI rank: 19
- Average final position: 10
- Average Sq£: £22.5m
- Average utilisation of max: 11.33%
- Average age of team: 26.92

Stuart Gray/Gordon Strachan
(Strachan replaced Gray in October 2001 but both are credited with season data 2001/02):

- Average points % of champs: 51.72%
- Average £XI rank: 19
- Average final position: 11
- Average Sq£: £35.8m
- Average utilisation of max: 13.47%
- Average age of team: 27.44

Gordon Strachan (one full season):

- Average points % of champs: 62.65%
- Average £XI rank: 18
- Average final position: 8
- Average Sq£: £40m
- Average utilisation of max: 16.73%
- Average age of team: 27.72

Gordon Strachan/Paul Sturrock
(Sturrock replaced Strachan in March 2004 but both are credited with season data 2003/04):

- Average points % of champs: 52.22%
- Average £XI rank: 15
- Average final position: 12
- Average Sq£: £52m
- Average utilisation of max: 16.26%
- Average age of team: 28.41

Steve Wigley/Harry Redknapp
(Redknapp replaced Wigley in December 2004 but both are credited with season data 2004/05):

- Average points % of champs: 33.68%
- Average £XI rank: 14
- Average final position: 20
- Average Sq£: £50.3m
- Average utilisation of max: 11.93%
- Average age of team: 28.60

Stoke City

Tony Pulis:

- Average points % of champs: 52.33%
- Average £XI rank: 17.50
- Average final position: 11.50
- Average Sq£: £29.7m
- Average utilisation of max: 7.63%
- Average age of team: 28.51

Sunderland

Peter Reid (four full seasons):

- Average points % of champs: 58.57%
- Average £XI rank: 16.50
- Average final position: 12.25
- Average Sq£: £45.8m
- Average utilisation of max: 21.77%
- Average age of team: 27.07

Peter Reid/Howard Wilkinson/Mick McCarthy
(Wilkinson replaced Reid in October 2002 but Wilkinson was then replaced by McCarthy in March 2003. All three are credited with season data 2002/03):

- Average points % of champs: 22.89%
- Average £XI rank: 14
- Average final position: 20
- Average Sq£: £73.1m
- Average utilisation of max: 23.49%
- Average age of team: 26.08

Mick McCarthy
(although McCarthy was sacked in March 2006 only he is credited with season 2005/06 data as Kevin Ball was only appointed as caretaker manager for two months):

- Average points % of champs: 16.48%
- Average £XI rank: 19
- Average final position: 20
- Average Sq£: £20m
- Average utilisation of max: 3.93%
- Average age of team: 24.93

Roy Keane (one full season):

- Average points % of champs: 44.83%
- Average £XI rank: 15
- Average final position: 15
- Average Sq£: £60.4m
- Average utilisation of max: 14.46%
- Average age of team: 24.92

Roy Keane/Ricky Sbragia
(Sbragia replaced Keane in December 2008 but both are credited with season data 2008/09):

- Average points % of champs: 40%
- Average £XI rank: 12
- Average final position: 16
- Average Sq£: £70.5m
- Average utilisation of max: 18.42%
- Average age of team: 26.10

Steve Bruce:

- Average points % of champs: 51.16%
- Average £XI rank: 9
- Average final position: 13
- Average Sq£: £80m
- Average utilisation of max: 27.62%
- Average age of team: 25.30

Swindon Town

John Gorman:

- Average points % of champs: 32.61%
- Average £XI rank: 22
- Average final position: 22
- Average Sq£: £15.4m
- Average utilisation of max: 10.53%
- Average age of team: 27.19

Tottenham

Doug Livermore:

- Average points % of champs: 70.24%
- Average £XI rank: 6
- Average final position: 8
- Average Sq£: £82.7m
- Average utilisation of max: 65.32%
- Average age of team: 24.76

Ossie Ardiles (one full season):

- Average points % of champs: 48.91%
- Average £XI rank: 10
- Average final position: 15
- Average Sq£: £87.6m
- Average utilisation of max: 48.93%
- Average age of team: 25.11

Ossie Ardiles/Gerry Francis
(Francis replaced Ardiles in November 1994 but both are credited with season data 1993/94):

- Average points % of champs: 69.66%
- Average £XI rank: 9
- Average final position: 7
- Average Sq£: £90.7m
- Average utilisation of max: 61.64%
- Average age of team: 25.89

Gerry Francis (two full seasons):

- Average points % of champs: 67.86%
- Average £XI rank: 9
- Average final position: 9
- Average Sq£: £105m
- Average utilisation of max: 53.04%
- Average age of team: 27

Gerry Francis/Christian Gross
(Gross replaced Francis in November 1997 but both are credited with season data 1997/98):

- Average points % of champs: 56.41%
- Average £XI rank: 9
- Average final position: 14
- Average Sq£: £121.8m
- Average utilisation of max: 61.64%
- Average age of team: 27.38

Christian Gross/George Graham
(Graham replaced Gross in October 1998 but both are credited with season data 1998/99):

- Average points % of champs: 59.49%
- Average £XI rank: 6
- Average final position: 11
- Average Sq£: £139.2m
- Average utilisation of max: 60.26%
- Average age of team: 26.65

George Graham (one full season):

- Average points % of champs: 58.24%
- Average £XI rank: 6
- Average final position: 10
- Average Sq£: £142.4m
- Average utilisation of max: 52.03%
- Average age of team: 26.72

George Graham/Glenn Hoddle
(Hoddle replaced Graham in March 2001 but both are credited with season data 2000/01):

- Average points % of champs: 61.25%
- Average £XI rank: 8
- Average final position: 12
- Average Sq£: £141.5m
- Average utilisation of max: 66.38%
- Average age of team: 26.34

Glenn Hoddle (two full seasons):

- Average points % of champs: 58.86%
- Average £XI rank: 8
- Average final position: 9.50
- Average Sq£: £119.9m
- Average utilisation of max: 49.59%
- Average age of team: 28.42

Glenn Hoddle/David Pleat
(Pleat replaced Hoddle in September 2003 but both are credited with season data 2003/04):

- Average points % of champs: 50%
- Average £XI rank: 8
- Average final position: 14
- Average Sq£: £98.4m
- Average utilisation of max: 28.28%
- Average age of team: 26.23

Jaques Santini/Martin Jol
(Jol replaced Santini in November 2004 but both are credited with season data 2004/05):

- Average points % of champs: 54.74%
- Average £XI rank: 6
- Average final position: 9
- Average Sq£: £88.4m
- Average utilisation of max: 21.64%
- Average age of team: 24.80

Martin Jol (two full seasons):

- Average points % of champs: 69.42%
- Average £XI rank: 5
- Average final position: 5
- Average Sq£: £119m
- Average utilisation of max: 24.92%
- Average age of team: 24.95

Martin Jol/Juande Ramos
(Ramos replaced Jol in October 2007 but both are credited with season data 2007/08):

- Average points % of champs: 52.87%
- Average £XI rank: 4
- Average final position: 11
- Average Sq£: £185.3m
- Average utilisation of max: 42.89%
- Average age of team: 25.49

Juande Ramos/Harry Redknapp
(Redknapp replaced Jol in October 2008 but both are credited with season data 2008/09):

- Average points % of champs: 56.67%
- Average £XI rank: 4
- Average final position: 8
- Average Sq£: £215.5m
- Average utilisation of max: 55.66%
- Average age of team: 24.90

Harry Redknapp:

- Average points % of champs: 81.40%
- Average £XI rank: 5
- Average final position: 4
- Average Sq£: £179m
- Average utilisation of max: 41.81%
- Average age of team: 25.31

Watford

Graham Taylor:

- Average points % of champs: 26.37%
- Average £XI rank: 20
- Average final position: 20
- Average Sqf: £11.2m
- Average utilisation of max: 3.87%
- Average age of team: 26.14

Adrian Boothroyd:

- Average points % of champs: 31.46%
- Average £XI rank: 19
- Average final position: 20
- Average Sqf: £15.7m
- Average utilisation of max: 2.61%
- Average age of team: 25.14

West Bromwich Albion

Gary Megson (one full season):

- Average points % of champs: 31.33%
- Average £XI rank: 19
- Average final position: 19
- Average Sqf: £25.2m
- Average utilisation of max: 14.16%
- Average age of team: 27.20

Gary Megson/Bryan Robson
(Robson replaced Megson in November 2004 but both are credited with season data 2004/05):

- Average points % of champs: 35.79%
- Average £XI rank: 16
- Average final position: 17
- Average Sqf: £35.5m
- Average utilisation of max: 8.29%
- Average age of team: 27.12

Bryan Robson (one full season):

- Average points % of champs: 32.97%
- Average £XI rank: 15
- Average final position: 19
- Average Sqf: £47.1m
- Average utilisation of max: 8.42%
- Average age of team: 26.42

Tony Mowbray:

- Average points % of champs: 35.56%
- Average £XI rank: 18
- Average final position: 20
- Average Sqf: £33.2m
- Average utilisation of max: 10.07%
- Average age of team: 25.03

West Ham Utd

Billy Bonds:

- Average points % of champs: 56.52%
- Average £XI rank: 14
- Average final position: 13
- Average Sqf: £45.4m
- Average utilisation of max: 21.95%
- Average age of team: 28.06

Harry Redknapp:

- Average points % of champs: 61.61%
- Average £XI rank: 13.71
- Average final position: 10.71
- Average Sqf: £67.6m
- Average utilisation of max: 31.56%
- Average age of team: 27.12

Glenn Roeder:

- Average points % of champs: 55.76%

- Average £XI rank: 11.5
- Average final position: 12.5
- Average Sqf: £71.6m
- Average utilisation of max: 33.77%
- Average age of team: 27.33

Alan Pardew (one full season):

- Average points % of champs: 60.44%
- Average £XI rank: 16
- Average final position: 9
- Average Sqf: £42.4m
- Average utilisation of max: 8.01%
- Average age of team: 25.80

Alan Pardew/Alan Curbishley
(Curbishley replaced Pardew in December 2006 but both are credited with season data 2006/07):

- Average points % of champs: 46.07%
- Average £XI rank: 16
- Average final position: 15
- Average Sqf: £65m
- Average utilisation of max: 7.28%
- Average age of team: 25.22

Alan Curbishley (one full season):

- Average points % of champs: 56.32%
- Average £XI rank: 9
- Average final position: 10
- Average Sqf: £87.8m
- Average utilisation of max: 19.57%
- Average age of team: 26.57

Alan Curbishley/Gianfranco Zola
(Zola replaced Curbishley in September 2008 but both are credited with season data 2008/09):

- Average points % of champs: 56.67%
- Average £XI rank: 10
- Average final position: 9
- Average Sqf: £98.9m
- Average utilisation of max: 25.64%
- Average age of team: 26.56

Gianfranco Zola (one full season):

- Average points % of champs: 40.70%
- Average £XI rank: 10
- Average final position: 17
- Average Sqf: £71.3m
- Average utilisation of max: 20.25%
- Average age of team: 25.72

Wigan

Paul Jewell:

- Average points % of champs: 49.37%
- Average £XI rank: 14.5
- Average final position: 13.5
- Average Sqf: £41.5m
- Average utilisation of max: 8.38%
- Average age of team: 28.01

Chris Hutchings/Steve Bruce
(Bruce replaced Hutchings in November 2007 but both are credited with season data 2007/08):

- Average points % of champs: 45.98%
- Average £XI rank: 16
- Average final position: 14
- Average Sqf: £58.1m
- Average utilisation of max: 14.06%
- Average age of team: 27.65

Steve Bruce (one full season):

- Average points % of champs: 50%
- Average £XI rank: 17

- Average final position: 11
- Average Sqf: £56.8m
- Average utilisation of max: 13.86%
- Average age of team: 26.43

Roberto Martinez:

- Average points % of champs: 41.86%
- Average £XI rank: 13
- Average final position: 16
- Average Sqf: £52.7m
- Average utilisation of max: 12.69%
- Average age of team: 26.29

Wimbledon

Joe Kinnear:

- Average points % of champs: 61.73%
- Average £XI rank: 16.29
- Average final position: 11.43
- Average Sqf: £38m
- Average utilisation of max: 21.95%
- Average age of team: 26.57

Egil Olsen:

- Average points % of champs: 36.26%
- Average £XI rank: 14
- Average final position: 18
- Average Sqf: £74.1m
- Average utilisation of max: 27.56%
- Average age of team: 26.72

Wolves

Dave Jones:

- Average points % of champs: 36.67%
- Average £XI rank: 17
- Average final position: 20
- Average Sqf: £30.8m
- Average utilisation of max: 10.69%
- Average age of team: 29.50

Mick McCarthy:

- Average points % of champs: 44.19%
- Average £XI rank: 17
- Average final position: 15
- Average Sqf: £28.1m
- Average utilisation of max: 8.03%
- Average age of team: 25.71